KATHARINE HEPBURN

the untold story

Advocate
LIFE STORIES

KATHARINE HEPBURN
the untold story

James Robert Parish

Advocate
BOOKS

NEW YORK

© 2005 by James Robert Parish. All rights reserved.

Manufactured in the United States of America.

This hardcover original is published by Advocate Books, an imprint of Alyson Books.
P.O. Box 1253, Old Chelsea Station, New York, New York 10113-1251.
Distribution in the United Kingdom by Turnaround Publisher Services Ltd.,
Unit 3, Olympia Trading Estate, Coburg Road, Wood Green,
London N22 6TZ England.

First edition: October 2005

05 06 07 08 09 ✳ 10 9 8 7 6 5 4 3 2 1

ISBN 1-55583-891-X
ISBN-13 978-1-55583-891-1

Library of Congress Cataloging-in-Publication Data
    Parish, James Robert.
        Katharine Hepburn: the untold story / Parish, James Robert.—1st ed.
        ISBN 1-55583-891-X; ISBN-13 978-1-55583-891-1 (pbk.)
        Includes bibliographical references and index.
        1. Hepburn, Katharine, 1907-2003. 2. Motion picture actors and actresses—United
    States—Biography.
    PN2287.H45 P37 2005
    791.4302'8'092—DC22   2005048206
    [B]

Credits
Jacket photography from Everett Collection.
Jacket design by Matt Sams.

In memory of DeWitt Bodeen (1908–1988),
a fine friend, mentor, and screenwriter

CONTENTS

Acknowledgments

I wish to thank the following for their kind cooperation on this project:
Patrick Agan, Valerie Allen, the late Jimmy Bangley, Jean Barbour, Bayonet and Cross Farms Advisory Committee (Samuel Shramko), Cari Beauchamp, Sheila Benson, Billy Rose Theater Collection of the New York Public Library at Lincoln Center, Bison Archives (Marc Wanamaker), Ralph Bowers, Ronald L. Bowers, Steve Campbell, Jeffrey L. Carrier, Robert Cashill, Charles Casillo, David Chierichetti, John Cocchi, Stephen Cole, Ron Collier, John Connolly, Manuel Cordova, Bobby Cramer, Daniel Cubias, Ernest Cunningham, Michael Danahy, David Manners Web site (John Norris and Peter Thorpe), Derek Davidson, Bernard F. Dick, Michael Doherty, Douglas Fairbanks Center for Motion Picture Study (Jenny Romero), Echo Book Shop, David Ehrenstein, Ed Epstein, Filming Today Press (G. D. Hamann), Prof. James Fisher, Germantown Historical Society (Marion Rosenbaum), Alex Gildzen, Kristan Ginther, Bill Givens, Bruce Gold, Eve Golden, Beverly Gray, Larry Grobel, Pierre Guinle, L. Harkins, Harry Haun, Robert Hofler, Lee Israel, Laurie Jacobson, JC Archives, Richard B. Jewell, Lynn Kear, Matthew Kennedy, Kent State University—Special Collections and Archives (Jeanne Somers and Cara Gilgenbach), Anna Labbate, Richard Lamparski, Cloris Leachman, Russell Leven, Bill Levy, Emanuel Levy, Carlton L. Maddox, Alvin H. Marill, Mart Martin, Lee Mattson, Rick McKay, Mrs. Earl Meisinger, Jim Meyer, Eric Monder, Michael Morris, Museum of Television and Radio—New York (Jane Klain and Kimberly O'Quinn), New Canaan [Connecticut] Library (Phebe Kirkham), Stephen O'Brien, Jay Ogletree, Old Saybrook Historical Society, Photofest (Howard Mandelbaum and Tom Toth), Claudia Roth Pierpont, Michael R. Pitts, Seth Poppel, Robert Priebe, Buddy Radisch, Barry Rivadue, Jerry Roberts, David Rode, Jonathan Rosenthal, John Rossman, Sharon Roye, Robert A. Schanke, Brad Schreiber, Margie Schultz, Arleen Schwartz, Joan Seaton, Nat Segaloff, Sam Sherman, Anthony Slide, André Soares, Sophia Smith Collection—Smith College (Margaret Jessup), James Spada, Sam Staggs, David Stenn, Steve Taravella, Allan Taylor (editori-

al consultant, copy editor, and indexer), Vincent Terrace, Michael Tunison, Turtle Bay Association, UCLA Special Collections (Julie Graham), USC Cinema-Television Library (Ned Comstock), Lou Valentino, Jerry Vermilye, Tom Waldman, Jane Ellen Wayne, Selden West, Don Wigal, Yale University Library, Robert Young Jr., and Joseph Yranski.

The following graciously provided interviews/information in person, by e-mail, by letter, or by telephone:

Rene Auberjonois, Betsy Blair, Jack Bradford, Kevin Brownlow, Jack Dabdoub, Dick DeNeut, Sandford Dody, Michael Druxman, Jean Porter Dmytryk, Anne Edwards, Tucker Fleming, Joan Fontaine, Joel Freeman, Boze Hadleigh, Peter Handford, Travis Michael Holder, Earl Holliman, Val Holley, Marsha Hunt, Milton Ingerman, MD, Richard B. Jewell, Terry Kingsley-Smith, Karen Sharpe Kramer, Kat Kramer, Miles Kreuger, Marion Kubichan, Arthur Laurents, David Lewin, Miller Lide, Matthew Lombardo, Axel Madsen, Pamela Mann, the late Lon McCallister, Patrick McGilligan, Jane Merrow, Kate Mulgrew, Lois Nettleton, Irwin Nissen, Patrick Pacheco, James Prideaux, Lawrence J. Quirk, James-Daniel Radiches, Rex Reed, Jay Robinson, George Schonbrunn, Stephen M. Silverman, Norman Spencer, Kevin Thomas, Steven Whitney, Stone "Bud" Whitney, Jane Wyatt, and those additional sources who requested to remain anonymous.

Special thanks to my literary agent, Stuart Bernstein, and to my editor, Angela Brown.

AUTHOR'S NOTE

"Whatever Hepburn's relationship was or wasn't with Spencer Tracy, to whom she was devoted but never married, the romantic ideal built around the fantasy and possibilities of that duo gave Hepburn even more currency among women as she aged. She was perceived as both keeper of the flame and someone who would not let anything (certainly not age and infirmity) get in the way of tending her garden and living just the way she wanted. Without a Tracy in her past to represent the great love of her life, which even feminists usually require as a lucky charm, this might have seemed sad, even tragic."

—*journalist Jami Bernard, 2003*

I grew up watching Katharine Hepburn's films in theaters and on TV. Later I had the treat of seeing her perform on the Broadway stage. I first wrote about this charismatic, driven Hollywood star in an extensive chapter in *The RKO Gals* (1974), published at a time when I and the world were a lot more innocent and circumspect.

It was not until after the death of veteran movie star Spencer Tracy (1900–1967) that the world first learned what many in the film colony had been aware of for a long time: Kate and the married Spencer, who costarred in nine movies, had enjoyed a tremendously close offcamera relationship for twenty-six years. In such books as Garson Kanin's *Tracy and Hepburn* (1971) it was suggested that this intimate, complex, enduring friendship was indeed one of the great romantic passions of the twentieth century. In reviewing Kanin's anecdotal account Charles Champlin (*Los Angeles Times* film critic) clarified why Tinseltown and the media supposedly had kept quiet about the lengthy affair: "The simple explanation is that Tracy and Miss Hepburn sustained their...professional and personal association with such impeccable taste that no wisp of scandal stirred that was certainly true... But the larger explanation, I like to believe, is that the writers [i.e., journalists] understood that they were in the presence of an association at once so beautiful and genuine and so shaded with a sadness that a kind of conspiracy of compassionate silence was the only conceivable response."

Later, in 1997, when Christopher Andersen wrote of the celebrated screen couple and their "remarkable love story," he titled his tome *An Affair to Remember*. And after Katharine's death in June 2003, Angela Lansbury, an MGM studio alumnus who had worked with Hepburn and Tracy in *State of the Union* (1948), observed of Kate and Spencer's personal involvement: "We all knew but nobody ever said anything. In those days it wasn't discussed. They were totally hand in glove, totally comfortable and unself-conscious about their relationship. She wasn't the sort of woman that many men would be attracted to—the snuggly, cuddly woman in the movies at that time. And yet because of her enormous affection and love for Spencer, she had the ability to subjugate this almost manly quality she had at times and became this wonderfully warm, irresistible woman."

Meanwhile, in the last decades of Hepburn's lengthy life—especially after the death of Tracy's widow, Louise, in the 1980s—Kate herself constantly extolled Spencer as her great affair of the heart. ("I loved Spencer Tracy. I would have done anything for him.") Since independent-minded Hepburn, a salty New Englander, long had the reputation of being honest to a fault (sometimes to the point of rudeness), the public felt it had further confirmation that the offscreen union of these two icons was definitely a full-bodied love affair in the conventional heterosexual fashion.

Over recent decades many people have accepted this idealistic legend of the Hepburn-Tracy partnership as a majestic, albeit adulterous, alliance. However, more sophisticated souls in Hollywood and elsewhere were not so easily convinced. They still wondered about all those long-recurring rumors that Katharine's close bonds in life to several women extended far beyond traditional platonic attachments. Further, they speculated, this multi-Oscar winner had used her one and only marriage (1928-1934) as a union of convenience and cover-up (much like studly movie star Rock Hudson, a closeted homosexual, did with his marriage to his agent's secretary in the 1950s). These doubters of Hepburn's heterosexuality also questioned her alliances to other key men in her life (e.g., talent agent Leland Hayward, film director

John Ford, billionaire Howard Hughes, and Tracy). They reasoned that these associations were generally far more platonic than the surface facts suggested or that Hepburn's own statements constantly intimated.

In short, it was gossiped that Kate was a closeted lesbian (or, at least, bisexual) whose mannish attitudes, attire, and manners were far more indicative of her sexual nature than a reflection of her role as a pioneering feminist. It was argued that Hepburn hid the actual details of her real emotional liaisons to 1) preserve her fantasies of a capacity to have heterosexual love; and 2) protect her acting career from the taint of scandalous revelations about her true lifestyle.

✳ ✳ ✳

In *Katharine Hepburn: The Untold Story* my main objective is to dig beneath the many layers of myths regarding this unique icon—some created by film studio publicity departments and the media, others by the rumor mill at large, and many fabricated by the crafty Miss Hepburn herself. My chief focus is to provide a fresh perspective on the star's seemingly straightforward but actually extremely ambiguous private life. This investigation includes Katharine's close bonds to such women as socialite Laura Harding, film industry worker Jane Loring, and veteran performer–acting coach Constance Collier; Hepburn's extremely tight professional and personal ties to Hollywood film director George Cukor, a well-known gay man; her much-touted intimacy with (actually) alcoholic and frequently sadistic Spencer Tracy; as well as Hepburn's cryptic association with Howard Hughes et al, connections that have over the years confused the public on the issue of this leading lady's genuine sexual orientation.

With someone as richly complex and private as Miss Hepburn—who grew up in the reserved, conservative traditions of the early twentieth century—one must burrow deeply beneath the public image to reach the core of the true person. Because this celebrity was so tremendously influenced by childhood traumas and a resultant fierce need to protect herself from acknowledging her deepest emotions (even to herself), it is far from easy to uncover the carefully controlled person beneath the seeming exceptionally candid public celebrity. Adding to the difficulty of unveiling the real woman is the fact that by the late 1960s, when Hepburn made herself far more accessible to the media, she was then on a great mission. Her task was to preserve her carefully crafted public persona as an iconoclastic movie and stage star…at all costs.

As tenacious Hepburn concocted her own mystique, she reinterpreted her life to perpetuate best her legend as she envisioned it. In that respect she was as artful as Marlene Dietrich or Joan Crawford in manipulating her image for the masses. In Hepburn's case, however, most of her public naively assumed that, because she seemed so forthright and down-to-earth about herself and the important people in her fascinating life, her words and deeds always could be accepted at face value.

In later years staunch Kate worked as hard at this elaborate fabrication as she had years before on building and maintaining her impressive show business career. With interviewers the elder Hepburn remained her usual gruff, abrupt self (which in the past had alienated the press). However, now the media and the public saw the enduring show business veteran as adorable and accordingly venerated her as a wondrous national treasure. In this exalted mode she pontificated on many subjects that further endeared her as a pathfinding nonconformist and feminist to her beguiled fans—all the while distorting the reality of her convoluted past.

In this mode—full of apparent honesty—the veteran performer made tantalizing statements that seemed to say one thing but could have far deeper, much more intriguing meanings. For example, she boasted, "I have lived with perfect freedom. I've lived like a man. I've got my own house. I live alone. I always have. So I haven't lived like a woman at all. I can mend anything, do all the tough work in the house, in the garden…I wouldn't change anything I have done." She further distracted the public from examining the real Kate by now insisting of her beloved craft, which had brought her so much fame and fortune: "I've always been more interested in what painters have to say—because painting interests me more than acting. You do it by yourself, you don't say somebody's else's lines." What does this chameleon truly mean by such statements, which jolt the foundations of what we thought we knew of the legendary superstar?

Welcome then to the perplexing, often contradictory, and always intriguing world of Katharine Hepburn, a master of illusion both on and off the screen.

Chapter One
ESCAPING TO FRANCE

"I had many women friends who were very close to me and if you had that, then people thought you were a lesbian. It didn't affect me at all, because it wasn't true. If it were and they'd have found [out] about it somehow, it would have. It's nobody business. Nowadays, I'm forced to be interested in a lot of people's sex lives, which I find exhausting."
—*Katharine Hepburn, 1992*

In March 1934, U.S. president Franklin D. Roosevelt had been in the White House for a year and was continuing to spearhead liberal legislation to combat the cumulative effects of the Great Depression. In Indiana that month notorious gangster John Dillinger broke out of jail and was still eluding law enforcers. Also during that March, Detroit-based automaker Henry Ford restored the $5 per day wage for workers at his assembly line plant. In Europe, Germany's Adolf Hitler was further consolidating the power of his aggressive Third Reich.

Meanwhile, in New York City, on March 18, twenty-five-year-old Katharine Hepburn was about to embark on a transatlantic voyage to Paris. Recently the movie star had suffered a crushing career blow when she returned to Broadway in *The Lake*. Her starring vehicle had opened the previous December to largely negative reviews, and the drama would fold after only 55 performances.

Two days before Hepburn's scheduled departure to France she had won a Best Actress Academy Award for her starring performance in the film *Morning Glory* (1933). Still reeling from her recent theater debacle, she had not bothered to return to Los Angeles to attend the movie industry ceremonies. Although *Morning Glory* had done extremely well at the box office, as had her next, *Little Women* (1933), her subsequent big-screen vehicle, *Spitfire* (1934), interrupted her winning box-office record. When released in March the RKO Pictures stinker had generated few positive critical responses. Relatively few moviegoers were bothering to see this sluggish showcase for a badly miscast Kate.

* * *

Only the less informed onlooker would have assumed that Hepburn's husband, Ogden Ludlow (a.k.a. Ludlow Ogden Smith), would be Kate's traveling companion aboard the ocean liner *Paris*. Those in the know appreciated that for much of the time since Hepburn's 1928 marriage to Luddy the couple had been sharing a Manhattan residence in name only. This was especially true after ambitious Hepburn embarked on a Hollywood career in mid 1932. Since then her constant cohort and housemate on the West Coast had been socialite Laura Harding. It seemed wherever Hepburn went in Los Angeles—on or off the RKO studio lot—Harding was at her side. The inseparable duo had made the film colony wonder about the exact nature of their extremely close relationship.

More urbane members of the film community assumed Kate was a lesbian or bisexual like Tinseltown's Marlene Dietrich, Greta Garbo, Claudette Colbert, Tallulah Bankhead, Kay Francis, Miriam Hopkins, and Lilyan Tashman. This sexual orientation, so industry observers reasoned, explained in large part why Kate so rarely participated in industry social events, preferring to remain at home most evenings with Laura. To further substantiate their assessment of Hepburn's sexuality, the film colony crowd cited Kate's partiality to regularly wearing men's slacks about town or sometimes dressing in overalls as she drove around Los Angeles in her unfeminine station wagon. (More knowing members of the press also speculated among themselves as to the full extent of the Kate-Laura association. However, these media folk knew better than to defy the establishment's code of "What goes on in Hollywood, stays in Hollywood." Thus they avoided calling overt attention to such a risqué situation to the unsophisticated general public.)

When Kate fled the rigors of filmmaking to star in *The Lake*, Laura Harding had also retreated back to Manhattan. As on the West Coast, the two women remained inseparable pals and confidants in New York. Luddy Smith rarely entered the picture. (By now Hepburn was thinking seriously of divorcing this pawn on her pathway to success.)

* * *

During the troubled rehearsals for *The Lake,* Hepburn quickly came to realize that the show's producer-director, Jed Harris, was not her ally but her dedicated enemy. She had fancied that working with the great showman would not only bring her great stage glory but help the theater veteran restore his sagging fortunes (and make her a noble helper in the process). Instead, her grand plan went afoul. Harris sadistically taunted his leading lady during preproduction, robbing her of any confidence in front of the footlights. As her self-belief sank, she reacted by becoming snobbish and overly self-defensive with fellow cast members. The more Hepburn masochistically tried to please the ogre Harris, the more he psychologically stomped on and embarrassed his leading lady during rehearsals. By the time the imported British play opened on Broadway in December 1933, Kate was an emotional zombie onstage.

After the critics lambasted Hepburn for her ineffective emoting in *The Lake,* she had two major responses. One was to vow to herself to somehow improve her inept acting during whatever remaining performances the show had. (Because of Kate's movie fame, there was still a sufficiently large number of theatergoers willing to attend this unfortunate showcase.) The star's other reaction was a determination to regain, somehow, her self-confidence—if not in actuality, then at least in a good facsimile. It was Kate's goal to convince the world as quickly as possible that she did not care a bit that her Broadway return had been a fiasco and that she had no fear about her career falling to pieces.

At these critical professional and personal junctures Kate found comfort from her past acting coach, the matronly Frances Robinson-Duff. More importantly, Hepburn latched onto a fresh ally—a new woman in her life, Suzanne Steele.

Who was this mysterious lady who has left such a faint imprint in the annals of show business? Various people described Miss Steele as fat, svelte, or alternately attractively proportioned. Some sources insisted this American had been once an opera singer, a fact never substantiated. What is known of this smart, personable individual is that she had been educated in France. On the New York stage in 1933 she had performed all the roles in her translated version of Molière's *The School for Wives*. In April of that same year she had arranged a trio of Sunday night programs at Manhattan's Little Theater titled "Literature Across the Footlights."

One night after watching a Broadway performance of *The Lake*, Suzanne Steele went backstage to introduce herself to the star. (If this be the truth of how the two actually first met, it was rather amazing in itself. At the time Hepburn had jangled nerves and was even more reclusive than usual. It seemed unlikely that she would admit a stranger to her dressing room after the rigors of the evening's performance.) As the account goes, Suzanne and Kate had an immediate rapport, and in short order Steele volunteered to coach Kate on weekends in her challenging stage role. Hepburn, obviously at an extremely vulnerable point in her life and intrigued by the magnetic Suzanne, surprisingly agreed to this offer out of the blue.

As the weeks passed and Hepburn's nerves calmed, the benefit of the assorted coaching by Robinson-Duff and Steele gave Kate the direction and confidence to improve her stage interpretation in *The Lake* (even though the critics never came back to reevaluate her performance). During this transition period in which Hepburn's self-assurance reemerged she found little time for the loyal Laura, who was now forced onto the sidelines.

As support staff during this trying time, Kate relied not only on her theater maid and her hairdresser (borrowed from RKO), but also her chauffeur-bodyguard, Charles Newhill. The former boxer had already become a trusted retainer and would remain with Hepburn for twenty years till sickness forced his retirement. During her Broadway run one of Newhill's chief duties was to escort his employer nightly out of the theater. If the crowd of fans gathered by the stage door had not thinned out sufficiently by the time she was ready to go home, Charles would lead his employer through the darkened theater and out the front entrance.

More complicated was Hepburn's romantic life in this hectic period. Laura Harding had traveled east to share in her friend's Broadway triumph and willingly remained on hand to console her pal when the situation turned sour. Now the aristocratic socialite felt rebuffed as the interloper, Suzanne Steele, became the significant new focus in Kate's life. The new friendship—at Laura's expense—continued after *The Lake* closed on February 10, 1934. That Steele was now emotionally (and, likely, romantically) important to Hepburn was underlined when Kate chose Suzanne (not Laura, nor Hepburn's passive, doting husband Luddy, nor the star's Hollywood agent–reputed boyfriend, Leland Hayward) to accompany the Oscar winner on her transatlantic voyage.

✻   ✻   ✻

On, March 18, 1934, Kate and officious Suzanne embarked on the *Paris* bound from New York to Le Havre, France. At dockside Hepburn refused to stop to pose for photographers. She strode furiously aboard the luxury vessel using a third-class gangway to avoid most of the newsmen. She and Steele rushed to the stateroom they would share on the six-day voyage across the Atlantic. When the press, eager to file stories about the celebrities on the passenger liner, discovered the whereabouts of the movie star's stateroom, they rushed there and kept banging on the door to the Hepburn-Steele suite. Eventually, Suzanne opened the door and stepped forth—alone. Obviously pleased at this occasion to grab the limelight and full of self-importance, Suzanne informed the newsmen that she and her "old friend" Kate planned to spend "four or five weeks, visiting Paris and the Riviera."

By the time the two women reached France on March 24, they were scarcely talking to one another. The crossing had been difficult due to unpleasant weather, leaving Kate feeling poorly and in a bad mood. Then too, Hepburn had been put off by her friend's fondness for drinking and bossiness. On her part, Suzanne had been sorely disappointed that her famous companion insisted they keep away as much as possible from the other passengers. Always eating in their stateroom and taking early-morning (or late-evening) strolls in order to avoid scrutiny was not Steele's vision of how to travel with a celebrity. Disembarking from the *Paris*, the trouser-clad Kate sullenly pushed past the press to a waiting car. Meanwhile, enterprising Suzanne again took the opportunity to be front and center. She told the assembled reporters that, contrary to rumor, Kate was not in France to obtain a divorce from Luddy.

After four days ashore, Hepburn boarded the *Paris* for its return voyage to New York. Steele was not aboard. However, other, more noteworthy passengers were exotic screen siren Marlene Dietrich and her young daughter, Maria, and writer Ernest Hemingway. The latter arranged to meet Kate, who proved to be amused by this famous, virile married man. When the *Paris* docked back in New York, Hepburn was in a far more amiable mood, even agreeing—at Hemingway's prompting—to meet with the waiting newsmen. She explained, "The only reason I didn't see you when I went away was that I had nothing to say. I talk so little for publication because I'm so indiscreet." When pressed about the nature of her aborted trip to gay Paree, she responded, "I just needed a vacation and took it—that's good enough reason, isn't it? And I came back because I got homesick." She insisted the journey had been undertaken on "impulse," saying, "I don't know from one minute to another what I'm going to do." No mention was made of Hepburn's recent traveling companion.

As for Suzanne Steele, she quickly disappeared from the public scene. Having so abruptly entered into the inner circle of Hepburn's life, she just as quickly vanished. Each had had a professional and personal agenda during their brief, little-documented alliance. However, Suzanne had quickly worn on Kate's patience. As the latter regained her professional confidence, she was no longer susceptible to the aggressive newcomer's demanding friendship.

Once Kate was back in New York, it was not long before she and Laura Harding made up. Their special chumminess began anew, with Hepburn's temporary defection forgiven, if not forgotten.

Chapter Two
THE HOUSE OF HEPBURNS

"I admired my parents, and they admired me. It was beautiful. They were fun and kind. They had imagination, and they were interesting."
— *Katharine Hepburn, 1993*

Throughout his life, Katharine Hepburn's father, Dr. Thomas Norval Hepburn (1879–1962), frequently cautioned his eldest daughter, "Don't get stuck in the past, not if you want to keep moving forward, anyway." This transplanted Virginian was a great believer in focusing on the present—the immediate. Like his wife, Katharine Martha Houghton (1878–1951), he experienced a quite difficult upbringing and suffered several family tragedies, which, in the self-reliant traditions of his adopted New England, he decided were best never discussed—not even with his own family. Such reasoning allowed him to wipe the slate clean, relatively, of unpleasant memories and permitted the emotionally constricted, highly opinionated, and hot-tempered man to function effectively in his self-focused world. His bright, intelligent spouse, Katharine, while so progressive in her political and social thoughts and actions, went along with the dictates of her strong-willed husband. Because she so adored him, she gave him her most precious gift: domestic subservience.

The Hepburns' history very much shaped the future of Katharine Houghton Hepburn.

* * *

Norval Thomas Hepburn (at Johns Hopkins University he would switch his first and middle names) was born on December 18, 1879, the fifth and last-born child of Reverend Sewell Stavely Hepbron (later changed to Hepburn) and Selina Lloyd Powell. The father, of Scottish descent, came from an impoverished family in Missouri and had relocated to Hanover County in Virginia shortly before the outbreak of the Civil War. Soon thereafter he wed "Nina," who came from an important Richmond family who had fallen on reduced circumstances (her father operated a girls' boarding school). While Sewell certainly could not match Nina's strong social pedigree, he gave his new household respectability when he accepted the post of rector at St. Paul's Episcopal parish.

Following the devastating War Between the States, the Hepburns, like their rural neighbors, struggled to survive. To bolster his small income, practical-minded Mrs. Hepburn converted their rectory into a rooming house and was forced to cater to a succession of boarders over the years. Parson Hepburn, described as a "simple man with a very simple philosophy of life," had his share of eccentricities. One of his economical quirks was to utilize the same bar of soap and washcloth for both bathing and washing his teeth. It became a family custom carried on for some years by his granddaughter Kate.

When the local doctor in Hanover County died in the late 1880s, the reverend took over his chores. These included making monthly rounds of the impoverished territory, providing medical and dental assistance to his flock. In 1893, while the Hepburns and members of the congregation were decorating their church for the Christmas holiday, a candle tipped over, and a blaze soon consumed the structure. In such financially difficult times, it was two years before the community could raise the needed funds to build a new church. Meanwhile, the resolute parson held services at the local courthouse and did his best to buoy his parishioners' spirits. Such determination had a lifelong effect on Tom, the clergyman's youngest child.

While the reverend hoped the boy would follow in his professional footsteps, independent-minded Tom was far more interested in his father's medical activities than his religious duties. The young man decided to become a physician. By now, in strong reaction to the constant hardships of his childhood, Tom had formed his core values, which revolved around his rebellion against most established institutions (e.g., formalized religion, the Republican political party, and big business). Young Hepburn, a bright, industrious worker, was accepted at Randolph-Macon College in close-by

Ashland. At this Methodist university he shone in academics and proved to be an all-around athlete. The latter was the result of his self-imposed regimen of physical fitness and self-discipline, which included such routines as commencing each day with an icy-cold shower. (It was a habit his daughter, the future screen star, would adopt for her entire life.)

Believing that he had a firm grasp of life's key principles, and having a large ego, Tom used his managerial position at the *Randolph-Macon Monthly* to editorialize to his readers. His published dictates to his campus mates, including such topics as using self-restraint against too much frivolity during the holidays or encouraging his peers to be open-minded about sexual equality should they attend graduate school and find women among their number. No matter the subject matter, Hepburn's spirited essays were consistently earnest, confident, and considered by many at the time to be highly radical.

Tom graduated from Randolph-Macon in 1900. After receiving his master's degree (in pre-med studies) from the same institution, he entered Johns Hopkins School of Medicine in Baltimore, Maryland. To pay his expenses, he taught fencing and tumbling. Then, in 1901, at a fencing match held at the apartment of his classmate, Edith Houghton, he encountered her eldest sister, Katharine ("Kit"). He was impressed by this free-spoken, appealing young woman with impressive broad shoulders. On her part, Kit was immediately attracted by this muscular, blue-eyed future doctor with his striking bright red flock of hair. She announced to Edith, "That's the one!" When Edith cautioned her impetuous sister that Tom had no financial stability and was thus not good marriage material, strong-willed Kit rejoined, "Never mind my future! My present is all that matters. I'd marry him even if I knew it meant I'd die in a year, and—and—and go to hell!"

* * *

Katharine Martha Houghton (pronounced HOE-ton) was born on February 2, 1878, the first of three daughters of Alfred Augustus Houghton and his second wife, Caroline Garlinghouse. (Alfred's previous marriage had ended with his spouse's death in 1873. They had one child, Mary.)

The Houghtons proudly traced their lineage—and the family's dynasty—back to Amory Houghton Sr. (1813–1882). This forebear was one of thirteen children born on the family's meager farm in Bolton, Massachusetts. A determined self-starter, Amory was only in his mid teens when he relocated to Cambridge, Massachusetts, where he became an apprentice carpenter. Quick to grasp his trade, he soon gathered together enough money to buy out his trainee contract. By age twenty the enterprising Houghton had borrowed $300 to open his own firm as a contractor and builder.

In 1836, already married to a store owner's daughter and having started a family, Amory expanded his business by selling such useful commodities as cement, coal, and hay. As the business prospered, he moved into the import-export business. Growing restless in his established trade, Houghton became involved in the manufacture of glass. His firm, the Union Glass Co., thrived during the Civil War. Thereafter, seeking yet new challenges, Amory sold that operation and moved the family to Brooklyn, New York, where he planned to convert the failing Brooklyn Flint Glass Co. into a thriving enterprise. Hardly had he begun the challenge when, in late 1867, the new venture took a disastrous turn. The factory burned down.

At this critical juncture, Amory was fortuitously petitioned by the inventor of a glass Venetian blind to relocate to upstate New York, to Corning, to help establish a glass factory in that city. By the fall of 1868 the Corning Flint Glass Works was in operation. A few years later, the promising new endeavor suffered a financial downturn. It led to Amory Sr. retiring to a Westchester County farm, while his son Amory Jr., now thirty-three, was asked by the plant's new owner to supervise the faltering business. As Amory Jr. struggled to turn the company into a flourishing operation, his younger brother, Alfred, never having a true knack for business, was undergoing his own financial peril. Rather than work for his older sibling at Corning, he chose to open the Buffalo Scale Company and to set up a residence in nearby West Hamburg. About this time Alfred, a widower with a one-year-old girl, wed Caroline Garlinghouse. In the next years Caroline gave birth to three daughters: Kit (1878), Edith (1879), and Marion (1884). Meanwhile, under the dynamic leadership of the rigid, ambitious Amory Jr., the Corning Glass Works expanded tremendously and the now very wealthy Houghton family became a mainstay of the city's social set.

In fall 1892, Caroline's health began deteriorating. Unknown to the children but preying on husband Alfred's mind, she had been diagnosed with cancer. The strain of a second wife going through a deadly illness contributed immensely to Alfred Houghton's emotional decline. Following the family mode he kept his feelings bottled up inside, unable and unwilling to share his mounting distress and escalating depression with others. It led to his suffering a severe case of nervous exhaustion. To alleviate the burden on his already hard-pressed household, Alfred went against his best interest and agreed to recuperate in Corning at the mansion of his dictatorial brother and his strait-laced family.

After two weeks in his new atmosphere, the deeply depressed Alfred "seemed" to be recuperating. In fact, he felt so fit that on the evening of October 28, 1892, he insisted to his sibling that he planned to take a carriage ride on his own. When he did not return later that night, search parties were organized. The next morning Alfred's body was found in the lumberyard near the Glass Works. He had fatally shot himself with a revolver.

Amory telegraphed his sister-in-law of her husband's apparent suicide. (According to the conservative customs of the time, such shocking matters as suicides were *never* mentioned in polite society as such but were referred to as unfortunate passings and so forth.) The news struck fourteen-year-old Kit especially hard, particularly now that she had become aware of her mother's terminal illness. Scarcely had her father been buried than Kit found herself keeping vigil at her dying mother's bedside. At one point the fast-fading woman whispered to her grieving daughter, "I want you to go Bryn Mawr [College], and then I want you to make sure that Edith and Marion go there too. You must all get an education." The progressive thinking parent desperately wanted her offspring to gain the armor of higher learning, which would give them options in life that society and circumstances had denied to her because she was a woman. Kit promised Mrs. Hepburn that she would follow through on this pledge—no matter what.

❊   ❊   ❊

Now orphaned, Kit and her two younger sisters became the wards of Amory Houghton Jr. and were forced to live under his stately roof and obey his far-reaching, suffocating dictates. As a self-made entrepreneur, he ruled both his business and his household with an iron fist. He was unused to being challenged or contradicted by workers, family, or neighbors, let alone by a member of the "weaker" sex. But in her way, headstrong teenage Kit was already a rock of self-determination, strengthened by the family tragedies and shame (over her father's suicide) she and her siblings had endured. When she informed her stern uncle of her mother's unusual final wish, the capitalist scoffed at the idea of his nieces attending Bryn Mawr—let alone any college. (At the time, relatively few women, no matter what their social or financial means, attended universities.) At best, he announced, they might be allowed to attend a finishing school—one of his own selection. Thereafter, he ordained, they must dutifully do what any sensible woman should: marry well. Meanwhile, the disciplinarian continued to monitor their every last expense, keeping a minutely detailed ledger of all disbursements he made on their behalf—intending that he be fully compensated for such cash outlays.

A constricted life controlled by her uncle was unacceptable to feisty Kit, and she articulately voiced her opposition. Unmoved by her arguments on the subject, the patriarch finally shipped the trio of girls to a relative's home in Canadaigua, New York. He hoped that in this out-of-the-way resort town they might forget their ridiculous notions about wanting to attend Bryn Mawr. (Meanwhile, Amory planned to settle on which finishing school to send these rebellious children.)

However, overbearing Amory had not counted on Kit's tremendous willpower to fulfill her deathbed promise. Scarcely had the sisters arrived at their relatives' country home than Kit conspired with her siblings to make such grand nuisances of themselves that their frustrated hosts would pack the visitors back to Corning. Thus on a nightly basis the trio made a racket in their bedroom, which was directly over the family's parlor. It was not too many days before the three guests were returned to their uncle.

Once they were back in Corning, Amory dealt sternly with his insubordinate charges, determined to make them toe the mark he deemed proper for well-bred young ladies of the day. Houghton felt confident that as their guardian he had final say in all matters. However, a stipulation in their father's will set forth that Amory was only to be appointed temporary guardian should the girls be orphaned. As Kit soon discovered, the document contained a clause saying she, as the eldest surviving offspring, could choose their permanent guardian. Stern, self-important Mr. Houghton had full confidence

that when the matter reached the courts for approval that Kit would naturally select him.

On the appointed day in the hall of justice, smug Amory was astounded
when Kit brashly told the judge that she wanted an attorney acquaintance of
her cousin (Amory's oldest son, Alanson) to be made their guardian. The
lawyer in question, a great believer in women's education, "happened" to be
in court that fateful day and agreed to the guardianship. The court
announced that it would have no option but to ratify Kit's unusual choice. A
chagrined Amory then had a sudden change of heart—at least on the surface—and stated he would allow his three nieces to attend college in exchange
for his being appointed permanent guardian.

As it developed, crafty Uncle Amory was convinced that either he could
persuade his charges to abandon their bizarre educational notion or that,
somehow, they would fail to qualify for entrance to Bryn Mawr College. He
was wrong on all scores. Soon after her sixteenth birthday, Kit, accompanied
by her uncle, embarked by train to Philadelphia, where they would stay while
she underwent two days of entrance exams. (Reportedly, Houghton did his
best to distract his charge from studying for the crucial tests, even keeping
her up late on the nights before the tests. However, despite everything she
passed and was enrolled at the suburban Philadelphia college.)

Kit began her studies at Bryn Mawr in the fall of 1895. She was high-spir-
ited by nature, and this trait became more pronounced once she was on
campus, no longer under her harsh uncle's supervision. She preferred horseback riding to classroom studies and proved to be a general cutup, more
focused on undertaking dares and having fun than studying. Meanwhile,
while gaining popularity with her more subdued classmates, she came under
the scrutiny of the college's pioneering, progressive, and most unconventional president, Martha Carey Thomas. (Another aspect of the singular,
dynamic Miss Thomas was that she was a lesbian who had a succession of
lovers over the years.) Earnest President Thomas felt that this unrestrained
new student was disrupting order on campus (especially by violating the
school's no-smoking rule).

After President Thomas conferred with the delinquent Miss Houghton,
the latter saw the error of her ways in being so self-willful and disrespectful
of the opportunities being afforded her on campus. In the coming school

terms Kit's grades improved noticeably. Now she used her excess energy on the playing fields, where she proved to be an adept athlete (especially at basketball), and as part of her participation in student council affairs, she tested the waters as a public speaker. Nevertheless, when she graduated in 1899, the spunky, headstrong Kit listed this as her future goal: "To raise hell with established customs."

Not willing to immediately settle into the expected path of marriage and domesticity, Kit continued her education at Radcliffe College in Massachusetts, where she earned a master's degree in mid 1900. To celebrate the occasion, she and Mary Towne, her best friend from college, embarked on a celebratory trip to the Continent. As usual, Kit was short of money (still being on a strict allowance from Uncle Amory) but managed the trip anyway—including, on the way home, a detour to Monte Carlo, where she won at the gaming tables.

Back in the United States, Kit had mixed thoughts about her future. She had followed through on her mother's wish that she attend college and had ensured that both her sisters followed in her academic footsteps. Now at a crossroads, she hesitated about abandoning the traditional path for women of breeding: making a good marriage. Wavering in her thoughts about what to do next, she visited her sister Edith, who was now a first-year student at Johns Hopkins School of Medicine. Kit relocated to Baltimore, where she stayed with Edith and earned an income by tutoring. It was there in 1901 that she first met the dynamic Tom Hepburn. In a flash Kit knew what she truly wanted in life: to marry this handsome doctor-in-the-making and to raise a family with him.

The courtship between Tom and Kit veered from the traditional in that he internalized his positive feelings about her while she was openly aggressive in wanting to cement their growing relationship with marriage. As she informed her sister Edith—then keeping company with Donald Hooker, himself a future physician—Tom was "more of a sitter than a suitor." Just when go-getter Kit thought she had pushed the advantage and that Hepburn might actually propose, he announced suddenly that he was about to embark on a special surgery internship at the University of Heidelberg. Appreciating that this was an important opportunity, Kit masked her disappointment and wished her suitor well abroad. While Tom studied in Germany, he and Kit exchanged a volley of letters. However, as the many weeks passed, she felt there was still no positive change in their status that would lead toward marriage.

Frustrated by the stalemate, Kit took a bold step for those times. She wrote her beau a letter that became the subject of a much-repeated tale in years to come within the Hepburn and Houghton families. In her next correspondence to Tom, Kit did the closest thing to directly asking if Hepburn intended to wed her. She penned, "The best thing about our relationship is that whenever one of us marries, it won't hurt our relationship at all." Her message was loud and clear to Tom. Astonished by her provocative statement, he responded as she hoped. He informed Kit, "How can you say such a thing? I'll never marry anyone if I don't marry you!"

That November of 1904, Tom (having graduated from Johns Hopkins) and Kit wed despite the disapproval of Amory Houghton Jr. At the small service, they were joined in matrimony by his father, the Reverend Hepburn. The newlyweds then moved to Hartford, Connecticut, where Tom had arranged to intern at the Hartford Hospital under the tutelage of Dr. Oliver Cotton Smith, a noted surgeon who specialized in urology. The couple's future was set.

Chapter Three
SHAPING A LIFE

"The single most important thing anyone needs to know about me is that I am totally, completely, the product of two fascinating individuals who happened to be my parents. I've had a pretty remarkable life, but compared to my mother and father, I'm dull."

—Katharine Hepburn, 1986

In middle age and increasingly thereafter, Katharine Hepburn would persistently paint a picture of her childhood as idyllic, a blissful period in which emotional setbacks, physical losses, or unfortunate circumstances were largely, blithely, and conveniently tossed aside as irrelevant in shaping her personality and future life. As time went on, Kate became progressively more insistent that everyone regard her youth as a time of great contentment and wonderful nurturing. She wanted—badly needed—the world (and herself) to believe that her growing up had been a period in which she sensibly was able to shuck off most negative situations without acknowledging how deeply—even critically—they may have affected and shaped her life. In her philosophy—a carryover from her father's tenets—if one successfully ignored the existence or effects of bad events, then, of course, they never happened.

As Hepburn moved into her golden years she became a much cherished living legend—venerated because of her professional accomplishments in a remarkably long and generally distinguished show business career. Her positive regard was enhanced by the public's growing reverence for her once-pioneering stance as an independent woman and her determination to carry on as full a life as possible even in old age. Due to Hepburn's newfound posture as a beloved institution, most people (media and the public alike) accepted most everything she said as the gospel truth. Her credibility was greatly enhanced over the decades because this charmingly eccentric celebrity was revered by most as a no-nonsense Yankee who unhesitatingly and sometimes rudely spoke the unvarnished "truth." As such, her pronouncements—ranging from how best to slice a grape to why Spencer Tracy and Laurette Taylor were superior actors to her convenient reinterpretations of her past—were lumped together as fact.

But one has to ponder the deep-seated psychological need that caused Hepburn to color her past so much in interviews. Why was it necessary for her—long after the facts—to go to such extremes to pick out upbeat events in her childhood and find such exemplary family traits to support her assertion that she had been blessed with an idyllic upbringing surrounded by extraordinary parents, marvelous siblings, and a youth full of luck...luck...luck. Why did she have to go to such lengths to gloss over agonizing situations and painful feelings that occurred in her youth? Why were they not worth her (re)examining in the context of how she had chosen to live out the rest of her life?

Granted, the future movie star was raised in a period of far greater emotional and moral restraint than anything experienced today. Such self-control was a carryover from the Victorian era and, in the Hepburns' case, highly influenced by the traditional general reticence and stoicism so much a part of the makeup of many New Englanders. In this constrictive atmosphere of the early twentieth century, numerous subjects were never discussed in polite company. Equally so, many unconventional emotions and thoughts were held in very strict check, not to be shared even with close family members in the safety of the home.

Even with this then social norm in mind, the Hepburn household went to extremes. Both Dr. Hepburn and his wife, Kit, had experienced difficult childhoods, which, although highly contrasting, led them both to be far more circumspect than the average person of the day in dealing with their feelings. (In contrast, the couple, who had been brought together by their great physical attraction for one another, had little difficulty in being open about their continued lust for each other. This extended to their relaxed attitude about the human anatomy, with the doctor thinking nothing of parading around the family house in the nude, giving little regard to who else might be about. This "eccentricity" had little or nothing to do with the fact that Tom Hepburn was a physician.)

Perhaps the full tenor of the repressed emotional atmosphere at the Hepburns' was best suggested by the movie star herself when she was quoted in a 1952 *Time* magazine cover story as saying, "Discipline was drummed into me. The attitude of the time was reflected by my mother's guardian [Amory Houghton Jr.], who used to say, 'I hope that if my mother dropped dead at my feet, I wouldn't change my expression.' They really played it cool, didn't they?" (As usual, here Kate was glossing over rather than scrutinizing a rather astounding family trait: i.e., the excessive need of her family—and herself—to always keep one's emotions in full check.)

This family "virtue" of super restraint led Kate to ignore and/or block out unpleasant aspects of her childhood—and, indeed, of her adulthood. Occasionally, in later life, she referenced this self-censorship in conversations and interviews, but generally she made such remarks in such an offhanded way that few listeners ever bothered to consider what might lie behind the apparently casual statements. For example, when she told *Ladies' Home Journal* in 1975, "There are things in my life I would never discuss with anyone. I don't even discuss them with myself," it merely encouraged the awestruck interviewer to explain away this (characteristic) lack of introspection with, "She was brought up with certain codes and manners and there were certain things you just did not say or do." A few years later, Hepburn informed *Us* magazine of how she then spent her time, "I'm writing a lot now—just isolated stories, not the story of my life. That I'm never going to tell. And nobody else is either, because they don't know the real secrets." (Such "secrets" would, of course, include Kate's sexual orientation, her feelings regarding sexual intimacy, and her inability, or refusal, to be emotionally close to others in an unrestrained manner.)

Another of the star's camouflaging tactics over the years was to react strongly against any psychological school of thought that might set the responsibility for the results of a child's formative years with the youngster's family or childhood associates. Kate reasoned, "Now we are taught you must blame your father, your sisters, your brothers the school, the teacher; you can blame anyone, but never blame yourself. It's never your fault. But it's always your fault because if you wanted to change, you're the one who's got to change. It's as simple as that, isn't it?"

Further shunning the notion of analyzing the past, or even the present, to better understand oneself and how one interacts with others, Kate advised celebrity interviewer Rex Reed in 1979, "I'm sick and tired of a whole generation of kids who say 'I'm tired' or 'I'm nervous' or this and that. If you're tired, give yourself some gas and get to the top of that hill. Why you can't do something is of practically no interest at all to me, unless you say I'm trying to walk up a hill and I've got a size eight foot and I'm wearing a size five shoe and I can't take another step. To this I would say take off your shoes and hop on my back and I'll carry you the rest of the way. But it's a poor habit of life to blame anyone but yourself for anything."

(One of the few members of the press to openly question Hepburn's persistent avoidance of scrutinizing her actions and attitudes to better understand why she did what she did was Margaret Carlson in a mid-1992 *Time* magazine cover story. The journalist assessed, "Hepburn is no more introspective in person than she was in her off-the-top-of-her-head, sentence-fragment memoir [1991's *Me*]. Hepburn does not like people who 'make a fuss.'" A. Scott Berg, in 2003's *Kate Remembered*, includes several instances of his many conversations with Hepburn in her later years in which he hit a stone wall when it came to getting her to analyze her emotions or to explain how troublesome situations had truly affected the course of her life.)

❋　❋　❋

Hartford, Connecticut, located at the end of the navigable section of the Connecticut River, was established in 1623 as a Dutch trading post. Thirteen years later, English settlers led by the Reverend Thomas Hooker (an ancestor of Kit Hepburn's brother-in-law Donald Hooker) left Massachusetts and formed a colony there, naming it after Hertford, England. The Fundamental Orders adopted by this New England colony in 1639 was the first document in American history to establish a government by the consent of the people and led to the territory's nickname "The Constitution State."

From its start as an agricultural center, Hartford grew into a significant trading hub on the Connecticut River. Many ships set sail from the city with valuable cargos, and the hazards of the high seas led local merchants to be concerned about financial as well as personal losses. This led to their banding together to share the risks and in turn prompted the formation of the insurance industry (and to such firms as the Hartford Fire Insurance Group, founded in 1810). Soon, Hartford became America's insurance capital. Meanwhile, pioneering manufacturers such as Samuel Colt set up shop in the city. The *Hartford Courant,* established in 1764, is ranked the country's oldest continuously published newspaper, while the U.S.'s oldest public art museum, the Wadsworth Athenaeum, was founded in 1844. Adding to the area's cultural luster, authors including Mark Twain and Harriet Beecher Stowe located in Hartford because, as Twain explained, "Of all the beautiful towns it has been my fortune to see, this is the chief."

* * *

When Tom Hepburn agreed to intern at Hartford Hospital, he had many reasons to do so. As a young man he had seen his older brothers and father suffer from venereal disease (largely the result of their indiscretions with indiscriminate sexual partners). As a reaction the future doctor developed a strong interest in urology and sexual hygiene. He knew that working under the tutelage of Dr. Oliver Cotton Smith at Hartford Hospital would be excellent training in this relatively new specialty as well as the veteran physician's other area of expertise, surgery. Already autocratic in manner, Hepburn sensed that in Hartford, compared to a larger city, he would have far greater opportunity to shine and rise in his profession. Then too, he wished to separate Kit from the influence of Edith (by now having abandoned her medical studies) and her husband-to-be, Donald Hooker (who would establish a medical practice in Baltimore). Moreover, since both Tom and Kit enjoyed the outdoors and hoped to raise a large family, they felt that Connecticut's capital still retained sufficient rural aspects to give the Hepburns a true sense of country living.

Arriving in Hartford, the Hepburns found convenient living quarters across the street from the hospital in a dilapidated red-brick house, in which they rented half of the space. Because it was against the rules for interns to be married—let alone live away from the medical premises—avuncular Dr. Smith helped the couple skirt the regulations by living nearby and having Tom set up a bell system that ran to the interns' quarters. Thus, when Hepburn (soon known as "Hep") was summoned to handle a case, he could immediately scoot across the street without alerting his superiors to his actual lodgings.

On November 8, 1905, Kit gave birth to their first child, Thomas. As would become tradition with all the Hepburn children, Tom was given Kit's family name as his middle name. Meanwhile, once Hepburn completed his internship he opened his practice a few blocks away from their run-down home at 22 Hudson Street. Intent on standing out from the medical flock, he took the unorthodox step of specializing in surgery, disdaining to have a general practice.

As the young doctor struggled to gain a foothold in the fast-expanding community of Hartford, his family continued to grow. On Sunday, May 12, 1907, Katharine Houghton Hepburn was born at 3:47 P.M. Kathy (or Katy), as she was known to her family, had her father's red hair, ruddy complexion, and freckles.

Within a year, the Hepburn family required more living space, and as the doctor's practice was slowly developing, the household was able to relocate to 133 Hawthorn Street. The spacious three-story Victorian-style cottage with a red-brick facing boasted two acres of property dotted with shade trees. It was bordered on one side by railroad tracks and the adjacent remains of a tennis court. A brook ran along another side of the property, and nearby was a park with its own pond. It was an ideal setting in which to raise children, especially when the father intended that his offspring fully embrace his love of rugged outdoor athleticism.

If anything within the Hepburns' new home made a strong impression on young Kate, it was Dr. Hepburn's austere study. For there, left over from the house's prior owner (a literary figure), was a marble mantelpiece inscribed with the intriguing phrase, "Listen to the Song of Life." The future movie legend would recall years later, "I used to stare at it, and at first, I had no idea what it meant—so I asked Dad to explain it to me—he did and I still didn't understand—I asked mother, Tom—It got to be a joke—then, one day, I understood it all by myself and I knew it was good advice and I've been listening ever since."

In this era it was still customary for families of the upper classes to have servants to undertake basic household chores. The Hepburns had an African-American maid who came from the same part of Virginia as had Dr.

Hepburn. With her husband busy nearly seven days a week at his office or assisting with surgeries at the hospital, it fell to Kit Hepburn and her domestic help to care for her two young children.

At Hartford Hospital many fellow physicians regarded the egotistical, somewhat pompous Hepburn with suspicion, not only for his refusal to follow the customs of the profession but because he was gradually making a name for himself as a medical innovator with many newfangled notions (including the use of equipment such as the x-ray machine to diagnose patients' medical conditions). The more Tom went against the other, more conventional doctors, the more he became a self-satisfied iconoclast who thrived on irritating his more complacent colleagues. Buoyed by the ongoing conflicts, he became more and more self-centered and hot-tempered, demanding ever-increasing respect from the medical staff and workers as if such obeisance would compensate for his inner insecurity at navigating through uncharted professional waters.

In 1910, Dr. Hepburn became a staunch medical crusader. The catalyst occurred when a well-to-do female patient confessed to the doctor that she had contracted syphilis through her husband, who had gotten the disease at a whorehouse he visited during his bachelor party. Although the physician immediately treated the couple, the wife failed to respond and died painfully weeks later. Both Dr. Hepburn and Kit (who had come to know the woman) were distraught at her passing. Jumping into action, Tom banded together with other local physicians, intent on wiping out the large number of brothels thriving in Hartford. The men formed the Connecticut Social Hygiene Association.

To spread his message, Dr. Hepburn had to circumvent customs of the time, which made such topics as venereal disease forbidden in polite conversation. He found his answer in a preface that Irish playwright George Bernard Shaw had written for a translation of a French play (*Damaged Goods*), a drama dealing with syphilis. Hepburn wrote to Shaw for permission to reprint and distribute the preface. His request was granted. Thus embarked on his campaign, Hepburn soon convinced Charles Eliot, president emeritus of Harvard University, to be head of the newly formed American Social Hygiene Association. In turn, Eliot asked Hepburn to be the organization's executive secretary, which paid a good salary. However, the doctor refused to abandon his medical career. Years later, Kate interpreted this decision to mean, "Daddy always believed that if you stick to one thing—*one thing*—long enough, and work at it hard enough, you might even get it right." This thought became her guiding rule through her own professional life.

* * *

While Dr. Hepburn was vehemently promoting his social hygiene causes, Kit offered him her full moral support and became vocal with her peers on behalf of the sensitive cause. The reformer within her also took offense that workers at the nonunion plants down the street from the Hepburn home had no place to eat their lunches. (They had to squat on the sidewalk or lean against or straddle a fence.) This led her one day to invite the workers to make use of the Hepburns' grassy expanse for their lunch. Unused to being orderly, the careless factory workers made a mess of the Hepburns' yard. It was a disturbing lesson for the budding crusader. However, anxious for her own special place in the sun, Kit was determined to fill a growing void in her life (just as her sister Edith had already established a home for unwed mothers in Baltimore). While she loved her children, being a mother was not enough to satisfy Kit's desire to prove that her life had special meaning.

Kit's focus became solidified when Emmeline Pankhurst (1858–1928), the British-born suffragette, came to speak in Hartford as part of her American tour. Dr. Hepburn suggested that his wife might find the discussion of interest. Attending the local event, Mrs. Hepburn was exhilarated by Pankhurst's impassioned speech. That afternoon, at the family's traditional five o'clock tea, Kit recounted to her husband the day's exciting event. Swept up in the fervor of Pankhurst's crusade, Kit mentioned that she wanted to get involved in the cause. She insisted that she cared not how her activities might offend her stuffy, conservative neighbors. However, she feared the repercussions that her daring activities might have on her spouse's medical practice.

Tom's reply was, "Of course it will hurt, but do it anyway. If I can't succeed anyway, then I deserve to fail. Life isn't worth living unless you do what you believe in. Jump into the fray!"

Such a response on the doctor's part was a mixture of many things. On the positive side, it was noble regarding the cause involved and thoughtful of his wife's need to expand her sense of self-worth. On the other hand, it was arrogant and impractical of him to be so cocksure and reckless to believe that he could buck public opinion in the long run and continue to support his growing family. It was also, perhaps, a bit manipulative in wanting to bind his wife further to his own crusading activities by making her a more active participant as a fellow do-gooder.

Then there was the matter of the two Hepburn children—and those to come. Was either parent giving careful thought to how their extracurricular activities might affect their offspring? Certainly it would mean both parents would have far less time to focus on the children. In addition, if the Hepburns were unmindful of possible negative social consequences resulting from their championing then-unpopular (and/or daring) causes, what of the effect on their youngsters, who might be shunned by the more narrow-minded townsfolk?

Seemingly missing, ignoring, or covering over any thoughtful reaction to the cumulative effect of her parents' decision on her and her siblings, the adult Katharine Hepburn instead would choose to enthuse about this key family decision. "How Daddy dared to do what he did I just don't know. He didn't have that much money at the beginning, and he was really taking a gamble that Mother's involvement wouldn't cost him patients. But he never regretted Mother's decision to take up the fight. Never. He reveled in it."

Chapter Four
PUSHING ONWARD

"The world is so huge that if you haven't got your own little box to hold you, it gets scary. As a child, I was energetic, overactive and rather daring. But I was given a box: chores to do and clear boundaries of good behavior. I found confidence in the circle of home life I went whirling around in because of these boundaries. I felt safe and loved."
—*Katharine Hepburn, 1984*

Kit Hepburn's growing involvement in the women's suffrage movement—and her continued participation in the antiprostitution campaign—required a good deal of her energy, time, and focus. It necessitated that she perfect her skills at public speaking, learn to seize any opportunity—big or small—to proselytize for her causes, and be willing to do whatever it took (e.g., writing and distributing pamphlets, creating and carrying placards to be used for picketing the "enemy," convening recruitment meetings, writing editorials for local newspapers to gain new followers for the crusades). Buoyed by her ever-expanding, demanding, and exhausting activities, Kit was fortunate to have domestic help (such as Ida Gheezy, the African-American cook, and Fanny Ciarrier, the European-born nanny) to keep the household running on schedule and in the manner that Dr. Hepburn deemed proper for a man of his rising prominence. (The fact that Kit's children received increasingly less of the mother's personal attention may have been a subconscious decision on the parent's part. Mrs. Hepburn, like her spouse, was not a demonstrative person—especially when it came to displaying love. Like her husband, Kit found it quite difficult to be overtly affectionate with the children. This constant busyness on the parents' part may well have provided the salve to their consciences needed to excuse their inability to find ways to be openly warm with their young brood. This incapacity would affect all their children, one way or another, for the rest of their lives.)

As Kate grew from infant to toddler and beyond, a few particular memories would stick in her mind. "The first thing I remember is the bathroom in our house in Connecticut. It was huge compared to the ordinary bathroom; the tub was set in a wooden casing with a wide ledge. The largest fireplace in the house was in that room. My father insisted on the practice of cold baths for everyone in his family, no matter what the weather.... I remember standing by the fire until I was practically roasted, then leaping up on the ledge, sitting there, looking down with horror into the icy water, and finally saying, 'Well, here I go!' and plunging in. I still take cold baths—not showers, *baths* because then you get really cold—and find them refreshing."

In the coming years the Hepburns had four additional children: Richard (1911), Robert (1913), Marion (1918), and Margaret (1920). Kit's frequent pregnancies did not halt her impassioned efforts for what she believed was right. There was the time in the later 1910s that Mrs. Hepburn and her pro–equal rights cohorts rushed off to Washington, D.C., to picket the White House, then occupied by President and Mrs. Woodrow Wilson. Recalling her mother's daring escapade decades later, Kate detailed, "Most of them [i.e., the suffragist picketers] were arrested. But Mother was pregnant at the time and so she wasn't. The ladies who'd been taken off [by the police] had marvelous pins with jail bars on them and 'Votes for Women' across them. I can remember those pins and being furious that Mother didn't have one."

As the Hepburn household expanded to its final count of two parents, six children, and the staff of domestic help, the family, who had relocated temporarily to a nondescript home at 352 Laurel Street, moved a few miles away to a bigger house at 201 Bloomfield Avenue in West Hartford. The latest family home was located in a fashionable section of the city adjacent to a golf course where athletic Dr. Hepburn could indulge in his favorite sport and later teach the game to his offspring, especially his most willing and apt pupil: Kate. This Bloomfield Avenue address became the Hepburns' final Hartford home.

Meanwhile, as the Hepburns became more established in Hartford, the city's better social set debated whether the couple were earnest do-gooders who were championing worthy causes or were merely troublemakers bringing to the fore matters (e.g., closing whorehouses, social hygiene, women's suffrage, the tenets of socialism and Marxism) that were much better not discussed in polite society. The result was that a number of Hartford's socially (more) elite shunned the Hepburns as distasteful rebels who seemed to entertain an increasingly array of suspect types, such as suffragist Emmeline Pankhurst, anarchist Emma Goldman, birth control advocate Margaret Sanger, and many others.

The growing reputation of "those" strange and radical Hepburns also affected how the other physicians viewed Dr. Hepburn at the Hartford Hospital. Already regarded by some as a dangerous innovator and insistent self-promoter, Tom now came under the "taint" of his and his wife's battle against the conservative tide in the city by their controversial stance on—and untoward publicizing of—the existence of local bawdy houses and the bid for women's voting rights.

Not only were the senior Hepburns scorned by many of Hartford's "better" class, but their children (especially the elder ones, Tom and Kate) came in for a great deal of censure and rebuff. Many local parents set the example for their offspring to ignore, exclude, or taunt the Hepburn kids, who came from such a radical household. It didn't help matters that Mrs. Hepburn often recruited her older children to actively assist with her causes, having them distribute pamphlets and message-laden balloons to passersby.

While Dr. and Mrs. Hepburn may have been so self-sufficient and caught up in the whirlwind of their various campaigns that they could shake off as unimportant the discrimination from their peers, certainly this (semi)ostracism of both the parents (and, in turn, themselves) by many neighbors had its impact on the Hepburn children. For one thing, it made the youngsters far more willing than normal to make the family household their center of activity. Increasingly, the somewhat isolated children turned to one another to share free-time activities and to gain validation and perspective on life.

Years later, in 1990, Kate would say matter-of-factly, "I was very close to my family, so I didn't need to go outside for entertainment." As a result, she said, "I don't make friends easily to this day." Putting a good spin on this childhood exclusion, she would recollect in an upbeat manner, "My parents were funny, vigorous and right on top of all the new thinking, but I was mightily snubbed as a kid by many, many people, which put a good chip on my shoulder to get ahead and show that I was worth something." She also reacted—although she never thought of it as such—to the ongoing situation by cherishing and accentuating her uniqueness, which became a lifelong habit. Like her parents, she reasoned (or rationalized), "What other people thought didn't concern us much, anyway. Most people are raised to believe they are just as good as the next person. I was always told I was better."

＊　＊　＊

As of 1913 the Hepburns acquired a summer home. It was located at Fenwick, a borough within Old Saybrook. Connecticut's third oldest town, Old Saybrook was situated where the Connecticut River met Long Island Sound. It was about 45 miles southeast of Hartford, 101 miles northeast of New York City, and 105 miles southwest of Boston. Set off from most of Old Saybrook by a causeway and looking far more akin to Nantucket than Connecticut because of its cedar-shingled beach homes, Fenwick was a small but separate entity with its own government, the Board of Warden and Burgesses. (It was Morgan G. Bulkeley, a former state governor and president of Aetna Life Insurance Co., who had been a prime mover behind Fenwick's development.) Most of the locals were upper-class conservatives, much in contrast to the radical, offbeat (i.e., peculiar) Hepburn household.

The beach house, at 10 Mohegan Avenue, cost $2,400 to acquire. (Initially, to cover the costs, Edith Houghton Hooker, her husband, Donald, and their growing family shared the summer home, as did other members of the sizable Hepburn-Houghton clan.) It was a huge, weather-beaten, shingled Victorian "monstrosity" with three brick chimneys. The structure sat on three acres and had more than 600 feet of waterfront on Long Island Sound. It also has its own beach and pond. Two long jetties gave protection for boats and swimmers.

At Fenwick, as the Hepburns came to refer to their beloved beach retreat, casualness was the order of the day. As in Hartford, the home was often overflowing with overnight guests, day visitors, and individuals popping in and out briefly for this or that reason. The highly eclectic mix included relatives, fellow crusaders, social acquaintances, visiting notables from cultural and scientific fields, and various locals. Such a hectic ebb and flow of people coming and going must have been taxing for the household staffs, but Dr. and Mrs. Hepburn seemed to thrive on the frenzied schedule. It allowed them a social setting in which they were always the main focus, a forum to express their liberal views, and a venue in which to debate (or argue) with others or among themselves on any subject. No subject was excluded for fear of offending the innocent ears of their young children who might overhear the discussions.

It was custom for the Hepburn youngsters to sit at the dining table or in the parlor absorbing whatever topic—no matter its political, sexual, or cultural nature—their elders were thrashing out. They were permitted—and encouraged—to enter into the conversation *if* they felt they had something to contribute to the discussion. If not, they were expected to sit quietly and listen to the adults.

The Hepburns' favorite topic was politics. Occasionally such discussions might become so passionate that the debate would turn into a heated argument. On more than one occasion, Kit grew so agitated that she threw something (e.g., a coffeepot) at her dogmatic husband.

While Kate Hepburn would later enthuse about the educational virtues of such intellectual and cultural stimulation from these constant domestic debates, her younger sister Margaret ("Peg") would make an interesting observation in late 2003 for the *Hartford Magazine*. She acknowledged proudly to reporter Owen McNally, "I got my education at the dining room table." Then she added a most telling remark: "The conversation was never anything of a personal nature. There were no personal 'anythings' in our family. They were all political…"

Also out-of-bounds for dinner-table discussions was the state of one's health. Kate recalled, "If you weren't feeling well nobody wanted to hear about it. We all feel sick every now and then, let's face it. But we were brought up as kids to please, *please* go upstairs and keep it to yourself. Go to bed, go to sleep, or something—you were just supposed to stay out of sight until you felt better."

Another of the customs in the Hepburn household was to punish any misbehavior on the children's part—especially fighting among themselves— by Dr. Hepburn slapping or spanking the offending offspring. At least on the surface, it maintained a disciplined atmosphere among the youngsters while the freewheeling parents busily pursued their unorthodox causes and professional lives. (Kate soon learned not to cry when she was being disciplined. "I found that irritated Dad more than anything!")

❋   ❋   ❋

If social causes, culture, and individualism were highly regarded values in the Hepburn household, religion was not. According to Kate: "My father was the son of a minister of a church in Virginia and I think he was never [religious]—mother was absolutely anti-religious, so we never went to church. And…I found this terrifying at first in Fenwick and made them buy me a hat and I went to church and sat. And then I found that after a brief sort of summer span of six or eight weeks, I thought they were right." This concluded for the rest of Kate's life any direct involvement with organized religion.

> *In her elder years Hepburn would articulate that because the concept of God and heaven (and hell) involved the intangible, she could not fathom its actuality—let alone its relevance—and thus she gave it no further thought. For her, one's rewards (and punishments) occurred in the tangible, real world of the here and now. Late in life she often said, "I'm not afraid to die. I think I'll just go to sleep." On another occasion, she phrased it, "I rather look forward to dying. It's a tremendous relief, isn't it? The Big Sleep."*

❋   ❋   ❋

As a youngster, Kate's best (and often only real) friend was her year-and-one-half older brother, Tom, whom she so closely resembled in looks and who also boasted an overabundance of freckles. This adored boy was her great protector, as she, in turn, was the defender of her young siblings, especially her two sisters, who were several years her junior. One of Kate's favorite indoor activities was playacting and she began putting on play(lets) for and with her brothers and sisters as well as those neighborhood children who were allowed to mingle with the Hepburn brood. By participating in these fantasy exercises Kate felt less shy and temporarily forgot how tremendously self-conscious she was about her freckles, which covered not only her face but her body as well.

At their Hartford home and at Fenwick, these little dramas became the children's favorite pastimes, with the skits, costumes, and sets becoming increasingly more elaborate. Always a take-charge person, Kate often wrote, directed, and starred in these mini-vehicles, much like she would do in her screen role as Jo March in *Little Women* (1933). One of the future leading lady's "best" roles was in her production of *Beauty and the Beast,* in which she played the beast. One of the children's showcases earned sufficient money for them to send a contribution to a Navajo tribe out west so they could purchase a Victrola.

Occasionally, at school (West Middle School) young Kate participated in theatrical activity. Once she recited "The Wreck of the Hesperus" and made quite an impression on her audience. About a year later, she agreed to perform "The Battle of Blenheim." This time around, she developed stage fright. In the process, she lost her voice, forgot her lines, and left the presentation platform in deep humiliation.

* * *

A key ingredient of Kate's childhood (and later) was athletics. Dominating Dr. Hepburn encouraged his offspring to spend as much free time as possible out of doors, whether in Hartford or at Fenwick. In the city the family would take vigorous weekend walks into the countryside with competitions to see which child could pick the best bunch of wildflowers. Drawing on his own enthusiasm for athletics, the father relentlessly pushed his brood into ever more sophisticated gymnastic exercise. It might be wrestling one another, climbing a tree, or dangling—acrobat-style—from a trapeze created by stretching a rope between a tree limb and the main house. All the youngsters were expected to participate in these activities.

While Tom, the eldest, was agile in such varied workouts, his heart never seemed to be in the physical activities as much as Kate's. From the start, she was daddy's girl (he called her "Redtop"). Explaining her worship of this imperious man—which seemed to far exceed her feelings for her mother—Hepburn enthused, "There are men of action and men of thought, and if you ever get a combination of the two well, that's the top—you've got someone like Dad." (This adoration obviously set the standard for the type of man who would most emotionally appeal to Kate in adulthood.)

To constantly gain and reaffirm her undemonstrative father's admiration and fuller attention Kate did her best to excel in all sports. Overcoming fear or caution, she became bold in her efforts to triumph in these physical contests between family members and others. "My first interest as a child was pleasing my father. My aim in life was to have him look on me with approval. I used to do rash and terrifying things to draw his attention hoping to make him proud of me. I'd get into the most harrowing scrapes, and he'd have to get me out. Once, I remember, I climbed up into King Philip's cave…high on the side of a sheer mountain. I got stuck. Father had about all he could do to rescue me."

Whether it be scurrying up a high tree, hanging perilously from the tightrope in the family yard, riding her bicycle all about town, hitching a snow sled ride by attaching a rope to the rear bumper of Dr. Hepburn's car as he scurried around local streets, or diving, swimming, and sailing at Fenwick, Kate became addicted to the challenges set forth by her beloved but emotionally impassive dad. If Mrs. Hepburn had concerns about her eldest girl being in peril from such physical dares—or becoming too much of a confirmed tomboy—she trusted in Kate's nimbleness to keep her out of harm's way. Besides, in such matters, the mother knew she must defer to her husband's athletic dictates for their children. Having little interest in sports herself, she instead focused on training her children's minds.

※　※　※

Forced by circumstances to be largely isolated from children in other households, Kate had two idols close at hand: her dad and brother Tom. (There was also her passion for William S. Hart and other cowboy stars of silent movies she saw on excursions to local movie palaces with her dad. Mrs. Hepburn thought movies were foolish and would not attend.) Then an outsider cropped into the mix for young Kate. It was working-class William Ingham at the Old Saybrook beach community. Ingham's fish shed was just down the beach from Fenwick.

On one occasion, Ingham saved Tom and Kate's lives when he discovered them, one rough day, three miles down the channel, with their little boat being swept toward the ocean. Because her new hero was tall, skinny, and wore hip boots, Hepburn swore she'd never marry unless her husband was tall and skinny. What Kate especially loved about Ingham was that he chatted with her as an equal. Whenever the Hepburns were at the beach house, Kate spent every spare minute with her cherished mentor. It was he who taught her how to cut fillets of flounders, how to row a heavy boat, and so forth. (Her friendship with the fisherman inspired her with visions of one day pushing her boat through the waves to rescue a drowning crew.)

Years back, Ingham's father had purchased the fishing rights to the nearby waters at Fenwick. As time passed and the community became more upscale, the elitist summer colony united to revoke such rights. Loyal to her friend, Kate asked her dad to recommend one of the state's best lawyers to defend William. Although Ingham lost his case, he won a cash settlement and with the proceeds went into the ice business. As late as the 1930s, Kate never allowed an electric refrigerator to be installed at Fenwick, insisting out of great loyalty to her longtime friend that the family stick to utilizing an old-fashioned icebox.

＊　＊　＊

To accentuate her difference from her peers and to satisfy her strong tomboy nature (a masculine-like aspect of her personality than she retained throughout life), Kate Hepburn, from age nine to thirteen, shaved her head every summer. She insisted she did so to keep cool, but a Hepburn household servant observed, "She wore it short so the boys couldn't get handholds. She and Tom beat up on those kids that plagued them. Kathy beat up on the biggest bully of the lot—beat up on him plenty." Kate even had a special nickname for her alter ego. She called herself "Jimmy." (There was another possible contributing factor to Hepburn's desire to act like and be considered a boy—especially as she grew into adolescence. If she regarded herself more male than female, that might make her growing attraction to women seem all that more "normal.")

＊　＊　＊

By the time Kate was twelve she was attending Hartford's Oxford School, the sister private institution to Kingswood where Tom was already enrolled. There, besides academics (which included such odious, to Kate, subjects as Latin and physics, and time-consuming violin lessons), young Miss Hepburn took horseback riding. Acquiring equestrian skill was another way to demonstrate her athletic prowess to her emotionally unexpressive dad.

In this period, adolescent Kate went to her first dance wearing one of those old-fashioned dresses Mrs. Hepburn impetuously purchased for her at a charity sale. When brother Tom overheard one boy ask another, "Who's that goofy-looking girl standing against the wall?" Tom knocked the boy down and duly reported the remark to his mother. Thereafter, Kate's clothes were more carefully chosen. Later in life, when commenting on this telling childhood episode—which again demonstrated how unlike in look, background, and garb she was from her classmates—Hepburn observed, "I was never a member of the club. I never knew what other girls were talking about."

Another aspect of the maturing Kate during this time was the strong adolescent crush she developed on Cathy Watson, her gym teacher. Although others contemporaries of Hepburn would describe Watson as rather mannish in shape and stance, and a person full of gruff actions, Hepburn saw her physical education instruction through a far different light. She would describe the individual in loving, flattering detail, "She had a soft and gentle face, soft sandy hair—it was long as she did it in a knot and a velvet ribbon she wore around her head. I just remember that I thought about her and watched her and waited for her and brought her presents. I can't even remember what she sounded like—just love, it was. First crush."

Chapter Five
INTO THE ABYSS

"You cannot live with yesterday's tragedy. You must go onward, onward. It's like swimming in Long Island Sound—you just have to dive in and do it."
—*Katharine Hepburn, 1993*

In the summer of 1920, Katharine Hepburn was thirteen, still a child in many ways. Once again she was at her beloved Fenwick where she could run free and be the unbridled barefoot tomboy "Jimmy." She swam, sailed, and strolled along the beach exploring the beauty of the coastline. Her favorite companion remained her beloved older brother, the overly sensitive Tom. With him, their next two younger siblings (Dick and Bob), as well as an outside acquaintance, Robinson Smith, the children continued to put on their imaginative home dramatics. Among their presentations were *Blue Beard* with Kate in the meaty title role—albeit a man's part—and Smith costumed to portray the leading lady.

That May, Kit Hepburn had given birth to Margaret, her sixth and final offspring, and with the Hepburns' prior child, Marion, only two years old, the Fenwick household was even more than usual full of commotion and distractions. Kate, however, focused on reaffirming that she was still daddy's favorite girl, especially now that she had two far younger female rivals in the family. (One can only wonder what thoughts must have flitted through Hepburn's adolescent mind. Did she, for example, associate her mother with being responsible for bringing into the domestic sphere two competitors who would also be vying for their dad's approval?)

During this same summer, the forty-something Mrs. Hepburn, anxious to get back to vigorous physical activity following the sedentary last months of her recent pregnancy, decided to improve her skill at springboard diving. To practice, she used the new board mounted at the end of the pier at Fenwick. Kate observed these practice sessions and soon began mastering the dive herself. No one was going to outdo her in bidding for Dr. Hepburn's attention—especially not her mother.

One of Kate's vivid memories from this tranquil holiday was of running "along the beach, out to the lighthouse to see Mr. Knowles, the lighthouse keeper, shouting to myself as I ran how I was going to save the world. I think young girls have this powerful sense that, somehow, they're going to change the world."

✳   ✳   ✳

Come September, the family returned full-time to their Hartford life. With the Nineteenth Amendment to the U.S. Constitution having been passed in 1919, Mrs. Hepburn was seeking new arenas in which she could become a standard-bearer. Now forty-two and wanting no further children, Kit suggested to her spouse that she reactivate her dream of running for election to the U.S. Senate. Iron-willed Dr. Hepburn had set ideas of what a woman should or should not do, especially if it meant such activity would take his wife away for long periods from supervising the home front. Then too, being a politician would force her family into the limelight, and Dr. Hepburn had a lifelong detestation of personal publicity. As a result, when she mentioned her desire to campaign for national public office, he sardonically responded, "Well, fine, Kit. When do we get our divorce?" That was the end of any "discussion" on that matter. Instead, Mrs. Hepburn sublimated her frustration by campaigning on behalf of planned parenthood, the highly controversial cause being spearheaded by Margaret Sanger, a nurse. Over the coming years, Kit and Margaret would work together closely for their beliefs on local, state, and national levels.

Young Tom, already grown into a handsome young man, went back to the all-boys Kingswood School where he did well both in academics and on the football field, although he seemed to be far more fidgety and anxious than of late and still was very much an outsider among his classmates. (As a child Tom Jr. had developed a recurrent nervous facial tic and body twitches said to be the result of Saint Vitus' dance, a variation of rheumatic fever. For a

36

time the boy had a tutor to help him with his homework, and his father instituted a stiff regimen of physical activity, insistent that strong exercise would help his child return to normalcy. Eventually the youngster seemed to mostly grow out of his ailment.)

Meanwhile, Kate returned to the three-story building of the all-girls Oxford School. By now she had finally made a few pals there (including Lucy Goodwin and the Field girls). However, by and large she was still considered different by her peers and regarded with suspicion. As was Hepburn's custom, she reacted to her classmates' antipathy as a challenge. It led her to strive even harder to outdo her more conventional schoolmates. For example, the avowed tomboy disliked the "aesthetic dancing" classes that were part of the class's curriculum to help teach the girls to become refined, feminine young women. However, Kate forced herself to participate in such dance-related projects as a charity benefit program the Oxford School gave at the Hartford Club. Within the program Kate was one of the "Forget-Me-Nots" in "The Dances of the Flowers."

Since Kate had a natural bent for athletics, she pushed herself hard to win sports competitions at school, including those in figure skating, tennis, and, her best skill, golf. It bothered her very much when another student, lanky Oisey Taylor, beat her at the high jump. Losing such contests not only was a defeat known to all at Oxford, but it also made Kate feel that she was letting down her beloved father.

❊   ❊   ❊

March 1921 brought the annual Easter recess from school. As a treat for her two elder children, who had acquitted themselves better than expected in the classroom, Mrs. Hepburn arranged for a holiday train trip to New York City. It was not a new destination for the youngsters, who on previous family jaunts to Manhattan had visited such landmarks as the Statue of Liberty.

This time Mrs. Hepburn and the children were to be the houseguests of Mary R. Towle. The latter, one of Kit Hepburn's Bryn Mawr classmates, had become a good friend to the Hepburns and was known to the children as "Aunty." Mary was a single woman who practiced law on lower Broadway in offices that she shared with her very dear companion, the unmarried Bertha

Rembaugh (another Bryn Mawr graduate). Bertha had a house on Charlton Street (in Greenwich Village). Next door, at Number 21, was Mary's home, where Kit, Tom, and Kate were to be houseguests.

Joyfully exploring the city with their mother and Mary, Tom and Kate begged to remain with Aunty for a few additional days after Mrs. Hepburn's planned return to Hartford on Thursday. Kit and Mary quickly agreed to the revised plan. The youngsters happily explored Greenwich Village and the Fifth Avenue shops. They took in such cultural events as a performance of the great dancer Anna Pavlova. On Friday evening, April Fool's Day, 1921, the siblings went uptown with their maiden benefactor to attend a movie. It was playing at the Selwyn Theater on West Forty-second Street, which was in the heart of the sparkling, bustling Broadway district full of brightly lit theater marquees boasting the names of glittering stars in their latest stage vehicles. Kate was agog at her brush with the exciting world of Broadway.

The children saw a new film based on a novel by the distinguished one-time Hartford resident Mark Twain. The silent picture (*A Connecticut Yankee in King's Arthur Court*) had debuted a few weeks earlier, and there had been good word of mouth about its entertainment values. After the movie Tom confessed to a sympathetic Kate that a hanging scene within the movie had given him the "horrors."

The next day the Hepburn youngsters romped in Central Park, chaperoned by ebullient Uncle Lloyd Hepburn, a bachelor. That evening Aunty arranged for several other adolescents to be guests in her Charlton Street home for an evening of entertainment. During the party Tom was persuaded to play the banjo, at which he was most adept. He sang several (overly) romantic numbers, which caused the young guests—but certainly not Kate—to tease him about his repertoire of dreamy—and unmanly—love songs. Thereafter, Tom turned quiet and became a bit sullen for the rest of the evening.

At about ten P.M. the gathering ended. With the guests gone, Tom and Kate retired for the night. The next morning they were scheduled to return by train to Hartford. Kate's room was on the ground floor, while her brother's was upstairs in a sort of attic. Before going up that night, the boy took occasion to thank Mary Towle for "the most pleasant experience of my life."

Once in his room, Tom changed into his pajamas and then placed his trousers on the bureau. He carefully placed a suitcase on top of them to ensure that they would be wrinkle-free in the morning for the trek home. He then turned out the light and went to bed.

Morning came and Mary Towle's maid went off to church for an early Easter Sunday service. By eight A.M. Mary and Kate were at the breakfast table, but Tom had yet to make an appearance. After waiting additional minutes for her brother to appear, Kate decided he needed to be awakened or they might miss their train, which was to depart from Grand Central Station at 10:20 A.M.

At first she called to him from the base of the stairs. When there was no reply, she went upstairs. She knocked on the closed door to Tom's bedroom, but still there was no answer. A bit concerned, she slowly twisted the doorknob and walked into the darkened room. She saw his trousers on the dresser and noticed that his bed had been slept in. Nervously walking further in the room she saw a shadowy figure hanging near a corner of the room. Then in a horrific moment it all became clear. It was Tom's stiffened body dangling from a noose (made from a blue muslin curtain tie—some sources say assembled from torn strips of a bedsheet). The "rope" had been suspended from a ceiling rafter and anchored to a metal bedspring on the floor. The victim's knees were buckled slightly forward and his feet rested on the floor. Nearby was a tipped-over packing case.

Kate's terrible screams at about 9:15 A.M. brought Mary rushing upstairs. They tried unsuccessfully to untie the noose. While Miss Towle hastened to summon an ambulance, the dead boy's sister grasped his body and struggled to push it upward to reduce the rope's tautness. Seventeen minutes later, a physician from St. Vincent's Hospital arrived on the scene and pronounced the young man dead. He estimated that the boy had expired five or six hours earlier and that from the look of everything, it had been a suicide. By now two patrolmen from the Fourteenth Precinct were on hand to sort out the matter, interviewing Kate, Mary Towle, and Bertha Rembaugh (from next door). Uncle Lloyd was summoned to talk to the police about the boy's behavior during his final day.

A few hours later, at eleven A.M., Kit Hepburn, back in Hartford, received the tragic news of Tom's strange death. She relayed the awful information to Dr. Hepburn, who in turn contacted the Manhattan police and questioned their assumption that the boy had killed himself. The father suggested a theory that perhaps a burglar had broken into the house and murdered the boy. The law enforcers reviewed the facts to the disheartened man, who agreed eventually that his hypothesis did not make sense. Soon thereafter, Dr. and Mrs. Hepburn, accompanied by a family friend (Jo Bennett), took a train to New York City. Heading to the city, a distraught Kit wondered to herself if there were possible genetic ties between her father, Alfred, having committed suicide in 1892 and Tom's rash end to his life all these years later. (There were also other suicides on both sides of the family to consider: Alfred and Kit's brother Charles had ended his life in 1897, while one of Dr. Hepburn's brothers, Charles, had jumped—or fallen—to his death in 1915. Days after Tom's demise, another of Dr. Hepburn's siblings, Sewell Jr., also a doctor, would kill himself.)

When the distraught Hepburns arrived at Grand Central Station reporters were on hand to obtain a statement from the grieving parents. Over and over they shouted to Dr. Hepburn for an explanation for the calamity. At one point, he answered, "God only knows why. My son was normal in mind and body, and the taking of his own life can be accounted for only from a medical point, that he was suddenly afflicted with adolescent insanity…. He was an athlete, bronzed with health and exercise. He won his colors with the football team of his school last fall, and had expressed his ambition to finish studies at the preparatory school and enter Yale University, to study surgery, and, as he said, 'follow in father's footsteps.'"

By the next morning, Monday, Dr. Hepburn had return to Hartford, hoping to distract himself with his office appointments and hospital rounds. (Mrs. Hepburn and Kate stayed in Manhattan to be on hand to claim the boy's body from the medical examiner and to escort the corpse home for burial.) However, Hartford was already ablaze with the grim news of young Tom's death. That day's *Hartford Courant* carried a front-page story bannered: "DR. HEPBURN'S SON, 15, HANGS HIMSELF WHILE VISITING IN NEW YORK… Dead Boy, Swinging From Curtain, Found by Sister in Home of Aunt—Despondency Suspected."

The family reeled from the loss of its eldest child and the taint of scandal and shame that surrounded his sudden death. Stunned by the loss of Tom in such an unthinkable manner, traumatized Kate tried to rationalize her brother's aberrant behavior. She had a sudden thought. Her father used to entertain the children with accounts of his days at Randolph-Macon College. In particular, she remembered him telling the older children about the time that he and his campus pals played a trick on the visiting squad from a Northern college. They staged a mock lynching using a local African American who had the knack for contorting his neck muscles so that he would not be choked. Kate now recalled that the movie she and Tom had seen the Friday night before the tragedy had included a similar stunt. Perhaps that, the girl desperately suggested, had "inspired" her brother's fatal action.

(Tom's death also now reminded Kate of the repressed incident from the year before when Dr. Hepburn and Kate had come home one day to find Tom toying with a self-made noose. The youngster claimed he was only playacting a hanging, and the episode—serious as it would seem to most parents—was allowed to be passed over in this household where delicate emotional matters were uncharted waters for any discussion or action.)

Anxious to remove the stigma of suicide from the family, Dr. Hepburn immediately seized upon Kate's college anecdote theory and provided *The New York Times* with a fresh interpretation of the "facts" regarding Tom's hanging. He told the paper, "I am convinced that I have done the boy an injustice. In the first place his whole life and temperament does not coincide with the suicide theory. While subject as a small boy to a few facial habits, he had outgrown them and was in the best mental condition that I have ever seen him. That he had no intention of taking his life is borne out by the fact that he had purchased tickets and parlor car seats for his return to Hartford with his sister…. The bed showed that he had slept without restlessness…. He left no note or sign of mental distress… I am now convinced that the boy was the victim of an accident as the result of a foolish stunt."

When Dr. Gonzales, the assistant medical examiner for the city of New York, filed his report, Tom's death was listed as "Asphyxia by Hanging (suicide)." The remains were released to the family. Dr. and Mrs. Hepburn and Kate, accompanied by Jo Bennett, boarded a ferry to accompany the body to the crematorium across the Hudson River. On the dreadful boat trip no one talked. The parents stood apart from one another. In far happier times they had trouble communicating their feelings to each other. Now, in their extreme grief, they had no experience in breaking through the emotional barriers that each maintained so strongly.

Thirteen-year-old Kate, numb with pain and loss, intently observed her parents on the ferry journey. She waited for them, if not to comfort one another, to at least console her. The only sign of emotion she saw on that fateful trek was the unusual occurrence of Kit Hepburn openly crying. (It was the first and only time Kate would ever recall her mother doing so.) On the voyage, Kate remained at her father's side, while some distance away, Jo Bennett sought to soothe the distressed Mrs. Hepburn.

Some days later Dr. Hepburn, accompanied by his son Bob (who had recently turned eight years old) went to Springfield, Massachusetts, to collect Tom's remains from where the crematorium had shipped them. Because the parent was against "any fancy thing to control the ashes," the bereaved settled on transporting the boy's ashes in a used candy box.

The funeral was delayed several days because Dr. Hepburn's father had the task of driving from Virginia to Annapolis, Maryland, to say prayers at the burial of his forty-seven-year-old son, Sewell, who had recently ended his own life. Some days later the clergyman arrived in Hartford to accompany the Hepburns to Cedar Hill Cemetery, where the boy's ashes were buried in the family plot. A simple grave marker designated his burial site.

Thereafter, Dr. and Mrs. Hepburn studiously avoided any discussion regarding their late son. Essentially, they shut out all conscious memories of their first-born.

However, Kate, bereft at losing such a kindred spirit as Tom, could not stop thinking about the tragedy. At one point the devastated adolescent was convinced that the events following the discovery of her brother's body were not as they had actually happened. As a rationalization to convince herself that she had done something constructive, she created a dream memory. In this fantasy she was alone when she discovered Tom hanging from the ceiling beam and she cut him down. Next, she had, so she told herself, run across the street to a doctor's home. In her scenario she had knocked hysterically on the door and a maid had finally answered the banging. Kate had blurted out, "My brother—he's dead," to which the disinterested domestic had supposedly responded, "Then the doctor can't help him, can he?" "No," replied a shocked Kate. The servant slammed the door and Kate returned to Aunty's home knowing that it was too late to save Tom. So ended the details of Kate's fabricated, soothing reconstruction of the catastrophe.

Despite the passing decades, Kate could never forget that horrendous

Sunday when Tom was taken so abruptly from her. In repeatedly rehashing the situation, Hepburn brooded endlessly about what might have caused her darling brother to do something so irreversible. She replayed the events of that fateful weekend in Manhattan time after time. As the years went on, she wondered if she now imagined that before retiring that catastrophic night Tom had actually said to her, "You're my girl, aren't you? You're my favorite girl in the whole world."

Many years later, long after Katharine Hepburn had become a film star who maintained a brownstone on East Forty-ninth Street, she had her driver take her back to the scene of the tragedy. Mary Towle's fine house was long gone, but memories of that street and the horrible event that took place at Number 21 flooded back in vivid details. After a while, the trauma was too great for the show business luminary. Throughout the drive back to her midtown residence, Kate vomited uncontrollably.

Chapter Six
OUT OF THE ASHES

"Naturally my brother's death flattened me emotionally. It was a major tragedy. Did it push me further into make-believe? Who knows? I would think it must have. It must have..."

—*Katharine Hepburn, 1988*

Years after her darling brother's suicide, Kate Hepburn confided (if that word can be used for a woman who so carefully orchestrated the distribution of "facts" and "thoughts" about her past) to an interviewer, "Tom's death threw me even closer to Dad and Mother. When we would speak together, it was a very different conversation than they would have had with anyone else. Our relationship was very, very close because they *made* it close. So did I."

However, one subject not open for discussion between parents and daughter was Tom's tragic demise. This did not stop Kate from rerunning the details of the tragedy over and over in her mind and occasionally discussing it with others who had known Tom. In her autobiography, Hepburn wrote, "There seemed to be a sort of feeling at the time that he might have made a pass at his girl and maybe it didn't work out and maybe in despair he..." In A. Scott Berg's *Kate Remembered* he quotes Kate saying late in life about her beloved Tom: "He was never really charged up quite like the rest of us. I had heard that maybe a girl had rejected him—who knows maybe a boy. What it was, he simply could not cope."

(Kate's offhanded reference to a "boy" having rebuffed Tom ties in to a persistent rumor that her brother, purportedly a repressed homosexual, had become attracted to a handsome young man in Hartford in the months before his suicide. This young man, while amused by the attention and frequent gifts that Tom bestowed on him, was heterosexual. As the account goes, the Hepburn lad arranged to meet his love object after school one day in the nearby woods. Tom made a fumbling sexual pass at the older boy. However, at the crucial moment a few of Hepburn's classmates came upon the scene—whether by chance or prearrangement with the older boy is not clear. The scornful schoolmates not only pounced on the humiliated Tom and beat him up, but also threatened to spread the word at school after the coming Easter holidays about Hepburn's faggoty behavior. Supposedly, Tom, who shared all his innermost thoughts and secrets with Kate (as she did with him) had told her of the mortifying situation and the potential that soon he would be further humiliated by his classmates. This account of Tom's sexual orientation, similar to later anecdotes concerning brother Richard, provides a possible indicator that Kate's alternative lifestyle was not an anomaly in the Hepburn household.)

Over the years, as Hepburn became a worldwide celebrity, out of courtesy or from lack of research, most media articles on Kate would refer to Tom's death—*if* at all—as a "passing" with no indication of the scandalous aspects of the young man's death. Unofficially, there remains much speculation among show business chroniclers and devotees of Hepburn lore about the precipitating causes of Tom's suicide. Besides the aforementioned hypothesis of the young man's fear of being revealed as gay, there was a theory suggesting that his passing was caused by Dr. Hepburn's plan to send his eldest son away to boarding school. According to this rationale, the authoritarian father's dictate that his boy should now become fully prepared to enter college in a pre-med course set out a bleak career path that went strongly against the youth's artistic nature. The mounting pressure, it is surmised, was too much for sensitive Tom. Another premise was that the combination of Tom's recurrent rheumatic fever, tics, and untreated depressions had left him vulnerable in pursuing the demanding physical regimen that his unyielding father constantly demanded of him throughout the years. He had, it was proposed, finally snapped under the weight of living up to his dictatorial, volatile father's constant monitoring.

Others have conjectured that there might have been an even more traumatic catalyst for Tom having hanged himself. In this radical interpretation of the dynamics of Tom's unfortunate final deed, it is speculated that his especially strong relationship with sister Kate was surmounting the bounds of propriety among siblings—whether on both participants' part or from the (sub)conscious desires of Kate, the more aggressive of the two. According to this supposition, during the Easter vacation stay in Manhattan Kate and/or Tom had pushed the situation too far and the thin-skinned young man could not cope with the knowledge of his "unnatural" desire for his sister.

*　*　*

In spring 1921, following Tom's terrible death, grief-stricken Kate Hepburn suddenly found herself taking on new roles in the household. She determined to take Tom's place in her father's heart by following through on what her brother's passing had prevented—his becoming a doctor. (Eventually, it would be younger brother Robert who became a physician, thus carrying on the family's profession—even sharing medical offices with his dad.) Thus Kate became both son and daughter to her father. Meanwhile, as her parents distracted themselves from thinking about the tragedy by concentrating with renewed vigor on their careers (Dr. Hepburn with medicine, Mrs. Hepburn with her crusades), Kate found herself taking charge of her siblings. "I practically raised the other kids," she would say. "I was a third parent—my younger brothers and sisters were more like my own children than my brothers and sisters."

Looking back, the adult Kate would remark—casually and almost impersonally and certainly without consciously acknowledging its significance—on the effect of parenting being thrust on her at such a tender age: "That's why there are so many oldest daughters who don't marry. By the time they've grown up, they feel as if they've already raised a family." (This self-serving explanation seems to minimize the strong role that the emotional and physical love between husband and wife usually plays in a marriage.)

*　*　*

Among the many lifelong repercussions Hepburn suffered as the result of Tom's sudden death was its stunting of her ability—let alone her desire—to be at all reflective about her attitudes or actions. She ardently adopted her parents' mode of behavior of consciously avoiding introspection or of being deeply analytical about others' motivations. In her contrived way of functioning, it was best to avoid such emotional exploration, for it might reveal unpleasant truths and personality deficiencies. (This applied in particular to her general lack of sexual interest in males and her strong attraction to the comforting companionship—and whatever else might transpire—with female friends.) Lumped together with this methodology of operating in life was the need to stay focused determinedly on the present and not dwell sentimentally, mournfully, or guiltily on the past. Such emotional inspection might reveal too many unconventional elements of one's own nature and that of others. Thus, while Katharine never seemed to have received any guidance or training from her parents on how to be an adult, she mimicked their tactics as a model of how to handle being a grownup.

Over the passing years, as Kate would do with many personal and/or family traits and foibles, she turned her stunted emotional approach to life into a Yankee virtue that she had sensibly adopted. She would twist her (sub)consciously underdeveloped sense of (self-)analysis of motivations, actions, and results, into her having made a levelheaded decision to effectively live life by being constantly busy, never taking time to ponder the past or present. Her modus operandi became: "Go! Go! Go!...Do! Do! Do!" As she explained to longtime friend and biographer Garson Kanin, the film director-writer: "It means you've got to learn to live in the active tense—too many people seem to think life is a spectator sport—it isn't—not at its best, anyway... Be part of it... That's all there is to life—being part of it."

Thus, having lost the companionship of the most important person in her life, Kate set up the mechanism that never again, if possible, would she become so totally invested in another person—male or female—that she could not survive contentedly on her own. (She would come close to breaking that rule with just one person—Spencer Tracy—who entered her life in the early 1940s.)

❉   ❉   ❉

Some weeks after the April 1921 tragedy a deeply affected Kate Hepburn—grown morose and suspicious of others—returned to school. At the Oxford School she had to cope with a new battery of stares and whispers behind her back from her peers as she passed through the hallways. Her grades suffered and, soon, she was failing in her compulsory Latin course. At the end of the academic term in May, it was decided that the teenager would not return to Oxford in the fall and would be tutored at home for the indefinite future. (Kate later insisted the decision was hers.)

That summer of 1921, Kate had two new influences in her life. One was the Britisher William O. Williams, who was on the teaching staff at Kingswood-Oxford. He was hired to coach her in academics. The other newcomer into Hepburn's life was Minnesota-born novelist (Harry) Sinclair Lewis (1885–1951). He had attended Yale University and thereafter achieved literary success with such works as *The Job* (1917) and *Main Street* (1920), (He would later write *Arrowsmith*, 1926, a searing indictment of a man of science for which he was awarded a Pulitzer Prize but declined.) Lewis and his wife moved to Hartford in 1921, intent on partaking of the city's strong literary traditions. However, the author soon discovered that the locals who counted were far more impressed with the world of big business (i.e., the insurance industry) than the creative arts. In growing fury at the priorities of the city's social set, the famed writer—who had a penchant for heavy drinking, which made him more cantankerous—soon insulted most of the local hostesses. In contrast, the Hepburns, long used to and thriving as social outcasts, found Lewis's rebuke by the Hartford gentry to be amusing and a strong recommendation for making his acquaintance.

Before long, Lewis and his wife became frequent guests at the Hepburns', although they drew the line at Sinclair doing any serious imbibing within their house. Lewis was particularly intrigued by young Kate. Like the celebrated writer she had red hair, was the offspring of a doctor, and had a tremendous fondness for chocolates and anything sweet. Hepburn recalls "going on Sunday walks with Red Lewis. We used to shinny up little trees, little willow trees that were very bendable, little birch trees, and he couldn't shinny, but he could look up at me in wonder."

❊ ❊ ❊

During these months, while Kate desperately struggled to mend her wounded psyche and broken heart, she found great solace in going to the movies, both with her father and on her own. While she confided in seamstress Mary Ryan, the teenager kept her cinema excursions secret from the rest of the household. Because, like the other Hepburn children, Kate had no designated allowance, she performed chores in the neighborhood (such as raking leaves and shoveling snow) to earn the pennies needed to gain admission to the local movie palaces. Once inside, she sat entranced, watching dramas and romances unfold on the silver screen. As a result of this constant immersion in the fantasies of the movies, Hepburn developed a thirst for following the careers of her screen favorites, such as Gloria Swanson, Lillian Gish, Pauline Lord, and Leatrice Joy, and to a lesser extent Rudolph Valentino, Ramon Novarro, and the celluloid heroes (e.g., William S. Hart and Tom Mix) of her father's favorite genre: Westerns. On the sly, the girl used leftover change from her paid chores to buy movie magazines, which she read out of her parents' sight.

Finding the escapist entertainment of moviegoing so thrilling, Kate silently determined that one day she would become a movie star. "It seemed perfectly natural for me, and from the very minute I did my first screen test years later, I thought it was a very easy medium because if you didn't get it right the first time, you could do it again."

※ ※ ※

While Kate was quietly settling on her life's work, Kit Hepburn was finding her own escape and satisfaction by throwing herself wholeheartedly into her newest cause: planned parenthood. As with her past involvement in the suffrage movement, Mrs. Hepburn enlisted her children in the cause, having them help distribute pamphlets, walk the picket lines, and so forth. Kit founded the Connecticut Birth Control League and became its first president. Her daunting agenda took her to various parts of the country where she gave impassioned speeches and lectures on behalf of her crusade.

Working avidly for her mother's movement—which went against the legal and moral dictates of most of the nation at that time—Kate found an activity she could share with her emotionally restricted (at least on domestic matters) parent. Hepburn observed later, "Our home was the center for all kinds of things. We were all for birth control and against prostitution. Mother could be very tempestuous. You couldn't tangle with her on certain subjects."

However, as always, it was her father that Hepburn most wanted to please. Whether on the tennis court, on the golf course, figure-skating, or diving in a competition, she was highly motivated to win—especially when her dad chose to be an onlooker at the contest. As Kate observed, "Once I had an audience I *had* to win."

* * *

In September 1921, when Kate Hepburn's peers left Fenwick to return to school, Kate remained at the beach community, where she was home-tutored and had ample time to romp in the healing fresh air. Making life less lonely was the fact that Allie Barbour, a Fenwick friend, was also being home-tutored. Before too many weeks passed, the girls decided they needed something fresh and exciting to break up their daily routine. They agreed it would be thrillingly dangerous to break into the huge, empty homes in the vicinity and explore their contents.

Gleefully—and rather proudly—Hepburn would recount subsequently, "I became a real expert on knowing whether a house was open or closed, whether anyone was in—spotting a window someone may have left unlocked." Sometimes the means of entry would be through the door designated for ice deliveries, which was generally easy to lever open. Of her light-hearted life of crime, Kate insisted that only once did she ever take anything. It was a crocodile-shaped nutcracker. However, once she got this prize home Hepburn was overcome with remorse and quickly snuck back to return the object to its rightful place.

Sometimes these daring escapades required that Kate climb up to the second story of a home and go through an unlocked window. Then she would run downstairs and open a side door through which Allie entered. One of the most dangerous such excursions found Hepburn attempting to lower herself through a skylight of the summer home of Hartford's mayor. As Kate snuck along the roof in the dark, she tripped and plunged through the skylight opening. With great presence of mind and agility, she grabbed hold of the skylight frame. Regaining her strength, she somehow pulled herself up to safety. "*Terrifying*," she said when recounting this adventure, which became one of her favorite anecdotes about herself. "I damned near dropped the whole three stories [to the marble floor below]. It was just by the grace of God that I didn't."

Kate's spree of delinquency came to an abrupt end—thanks to a young man. On one of their planned evening excursions Allie Barbour asked to bring along her new admirer, Bob Post, to which Hepburn (annoyed by this male rival for her friend's full attention) reluctantly agreed. When the trio had cased the target house, Kate decided there was no viable way to gain entry. Bob thought differently. He suggested they use a nearby log to smash in the back door. Once that reckless deed was accomplished, the three made their way through the house. For whatever reason, when they came upon a container of talcum powder in one of the bedrooms, they were inspired to shake a great deal of the powder onto a large feathered muff. They then proceeded to toss the muff around the rooms, leaving in their powdery wake paneled walls encrusted with the white dust. Then the trio nervously fled the premises.

Unbeknownst to them, a domestic in the house next door had witnessed the break-in and brought the activity to the attention of the proper authorities. As a result, substantial restitution had to be made to the householder in question. At this juncture, Dr. Hepburn jumped into the situation and paid for the repairs. To Kate's amazement, she was not punished, but it was the "end to my life of crime." (There was another circumstance, however, in which Kate put herself above the law. Before she reached the legal age to gain a Connecticut driver's license, she would, nevertheless, drive about Hartford in her parents' car. The police, knowing she was Dr. Hepburn's girl, turned a blind eye to her vehicular wrongdoing.)

❋   ❋   ❋

During Kate's troubled years of the early 1920s, she remained frequently a shy and moody loner. She continued to be snubbed by most of the local parents and their conventional children. Hepburn detailed, "The neighbors just regarded me as a different kid. They made me feel it. For example: when I grew to the dancing age, I'd be invited to the big dances but not to the little dinner parties beforehand. Do you know what that means to a girl? Do you know what it means that my father would have to take me to many dances

51

because the mothers and the other girls would have scared off the boys?" The future world-famous luminary also recalled, "We had one neighbor with an extra-grand limousine. She used to send it for all the children when there were parties. Except, she would say, I guess, 'Well, that Hepburn child's always flying about on that bicycle. She can come on it.' And I'd ride home, in the dark on my bicycle, and say to myself, 'I'll show 'em!'"

❊ ❊ ❊

By the time Kate was sixteen she was still being home-tutored. Already she had developed into a striking, lanky five-foot six-inch young lady. She boasted a mane of bright red hair, blue-gray eyes, chiseled cheekbones, and lots of freckles on her lean body. Her voice was higher-pitched and squeakier than in later years, but she already had that distinctive Brahmin New England nasal twang that reflected her upper-class background and her recent tutoring from the British-born teacher.

By now she had reluctantly joined the Hartford Junior Assembly, which helped to ensure that she met the right sort of social equal (i.e., from proper upper-crust Republican families)—even if they were far different from the type of antiestablishment radicals that the Hepburns favored. As Miss Hepburn was still very much Daddy's "little girl," any suitors who courted her were sure to come under Dr. Hepburn's severe scrutiny and tyranny. If the young man proved not to be a freethinking soul who was progressive and individualistic, he was quickly dismissed as a person of no interest by the physician and his wife.

One time in these formative years, Kate brought home a Catholic boy to face parental inspection. "Oh with what chill politeness my father bade him welcome! Sundays I would go with him to Mass. Not that I'd go inside his church. I wasn't that brave. I'd sit on the steps outside and wait for him. Somehow my father would just happen to drive by every time I was sitting on those Catholic steps waiting and he'd smile at me and wave."

In contrast to Kate's half-hearted attempts at conventional social interaction with the opposite sex, she was far more relaxed and enthusiastic at the nearby Hartford Golf Club. Besides learning the sport from her dad, she took lessons from the club's pro, Jack Stait. At fifteen she became runner-up in the state's championship golf tournament for women. When it was suggested Hepburn train for national competitions, Kate said, "Oh, I couldn't. I think golf is just for fun."

* * *

Still determined to carry on as the substitute Tom Hepburn, Kate had not abandoned her ambitions to become a doctor. This meant she must obtain a college degree. From her birth, it was assumed that the future movie star would attend Bryn Mawr College as her mother had. Like her parent, she required a crash course to prepare for the institution's strict entrance exams. Her toughest subject was physics. She managed to cram enough of the bewildering subject matter into her consciousness so that she squeaked by on a re-exam in that discipline with a grade of 71. With that, she was admitted to Bryn Mawr's Class of 1928.

Chapter Seven
COLLEGE YEARS

"I loved it at Bryn Mawr without any boys and I cannot understand our current co-educational system! What do they expect young people to do when they're sleeping in the same corridor? A girl of that age is of fine, ripe, childbearing age and at the peak of her sexuality. The boys are scatterbrained and don't care whom they go to bed with. What a stupid time and place to roll around together as a pastime—and is sex a pastime? The colleges today are practically forcing boys and girls to go to bed together before they're ready. I don't approve of that at all."
—*Katharine Hepburn, 1984*

Martha Carey Thomas (1857–1935), the pathfinding educator, was a founding force at Bryn Mawr College in the mid 1880s. The institution was established at a time when most women did not attend college or were ineligible to do so because most institutions of higher learning only accepted men. Originally Bryn Mawr was affiliated with the Society of Friends (i.e., Quakers) but, by 1893 it had become nondenominational. The first women's facility to offer graduate degrees (including the Ph.D.), in 1912, Bryn Mawr began offering the nation's first doctoral degree in social work

Located approximately nine miles west of Philadelphia, the well-landscaped campus boasted several residence halls noted for their "Collegiate Gothic" architecture. These imposing Victorian-style edifices blended in with the cluster of sturdy structures that housed the administration, classrooms, extracurricular activities, etc. Noted for its high academic standards, its blueblood roster of students, and its growing array of quaint traditions, Bryn Mawr flourished under the diligent ministrations of President Thomas.

By the time Kit Hepburn entered Bryn Mawr in the late 1890s, Miss Thomas was an illustrious, colorful fixture. The faculty and student body (and their parents) had turned a blind (or naive) eye to the fact that the school's guiding force—a visionary, freethinker, and workaholic—was a lesbian and shared her personal life with an adult female. Thomas's abilities as a progressive educator, administrator, and tireless champion of furthering Bryn Mawr's academic reputation made her choice of an alternative lifestyle almost incidental. However, in 1922, having reached the age of sixty-five, she felt obliged to retire, following the tenets of the college staff's pension plan.

Thomas was succeeded, to a degree, by Helen Taft, Bryn Mawr Class of 1915. Taft was the daughter of U.S. president William Howard Taft. Back in 1917, Carey Thomas had requested that Helen become the college's dean. When Taft married an academic, Frank Manning, in 1920, it was a shock—of a temporary nature—to Thomas, for among other concerns she wondered if Helen could successfully combine career and marriage. However, Carey soon recovered her equanimity and fostered the newcomer's career. Because Helen Taft Manning was content to remain the school's dean as well as being an active teaching member of the history faculty and maintaining other duties, she never aspired to be Bryn Mawr's official president.

❋   ❋   ❋

For seventeen-year-old Katharine Hepburn, who entered Bryn Mawr College in September 1924, it was a tremendously difficult period of adjustment. Having been considered such an outsider by many of Hartford's betters and having spent the last three years being tutored at home, Kate had little experience in interacting with girls her own age. Typically excluded by her peers both in and out of school, she had become a shy loner. She had learned to (over)compensate for her lack of social skills by adopting a veneer of independence, indifference, and a nonconformist image in manner, attitudes, and garb. In this way she could convince herself that she was not a victim of ostracism but, rather, was too singular to be appreciated by other young women. Such a posture not only reaffirmed Kate's need to control situations but also helped to guarantee that she remained out of close contact with other females of her age. Was this a method of not having to deal with any "unreasonable" urges she might feel about any young woman? One can only speculate.

Knowing that she needed her privacy and space, Kate finagled an assignment to a single dorm room in West Pembroke Hall for her freshman year. Terribly unsure of herself, Hepburn did everything possible to avoid contact with her classmates outside of the academic halls. For example, she would retire early each evening, then arise before dawn. Thus she could shower in the communal bathroom without others being around to gawk at her.

The first evening Kate entered the Pembroke dorm dining hall, she put on a brave front to hide her extreme nervousness in mingling with so many strangers. Wearing a flame-colored dress, Hepburn mustered up sufficient bravado to make a queenly solo entrance. Midst the stunned silence of the other students, one upperclasswoman blurted out, "Ah, conscious beauty!" Hurt to the quick, Kate did an about-face and hastily departed the facility in tears. So upset was she that it was seven months before she ventured back into the student dining room. Instead, she directed most of her allowance from home into eating inexpensive meals alone in tea rooms and restaurants (including the College Inn) off campus or in stashing nonperishables in her room so she could snack on these instead of dining with her judgmental schoolmates. (Eating alone in public was considered strange behavior in the 1920s, and the fact that Kate brooked convention by doing so showed the degree of her insecurity at returning to the communal dining room.) Sometimes when Hepburn's loneliness got to be too much for her she would ask one of her scant acquaintances on campus—another Hartford girl—if she could bunk in her room overnight. Kate, so she said, would sleep there on the floor.

As Kate proceeded through her first year's courses at Bryn Mawr, she quickly realized that she was never going to master the intricacies of physics or chemistry. Because of this, her chances of eventually becoming a doctor were slim to none. She abandoned this career goal. She rationalized that since there were few females allowed, or dedicated enough, to practice medicine—let alone develop a following in a specialty—it was a lost cause. Hepburn switched her major to world history. Even though no longer over her head academically, she still remained a listless student who left much of her studying to the last minute. She always seemed to freeze up when it came to taking exams, with the result that she achieved only mediocre grades. (In subsequent years, Hepburn had a recurring dream: "I'm sitting in the classroom, facing one of those college exams that used to absolutely paralyze me with terror. And I haven't studied for the test. I've done none of the reading. The feeling is of total impending disaster.... It's the dream of failure, isn't it? I think everyone has a dream of failure and a hope of success.")

As for extracurricular activities, Hepburn joined the swimming team, which did not require much interaction with her equals. When Kate was pushed by faculty advisers to join the Glee Club she deliberately sang off key to get out of this threatening group activity. However, her growing desire to become an actor led her to overcome her fears of dealing with her peers, and she tried out for a freshman stage production. Successful enough in her audition, she was assigned to the chorus. Things, however, did not run smoothly for Kate on this production: "At a rehearsal I happened to say to a girl standing beside me, 'If I could only be an actress!' She was a sharp sort of girl. She looked me up and down and said, 'An actress! You?' I was painfully shy, so I just shriveled up. I vowed to myself that I would never, never mention my idea to anybody—but, just the same, I would be an actress."

❊ ❊ ❊

Moving into her sophomore year at Bryn Mawr and now more adjusted to college life, Hepburn agreed to having a roommate. However, they would part after an unhappy year of living together. Into the new term, Kate developed a severe case of appendicitis and went home for emergency treatment. Going against the custom that a surgeon should not operate on relatives, Dr. Hepburn insisted on undertaking the surgery. The patient made a swift recovery.

Because of Kate's missed classes during her medical crisis and her lackluster academic performance when she was back on campus, the Bryn Mawr administration eventually felt compelled to write Dr. Hepburn a politely worded note suggesting that his daughter might fare better at another academic institution. Never one to be told how he—let alone his family—should handle a situation, the self-centered physician countered in a curt letter to Bryn Mawr authorities: "If I had a patient in hospitalization, and the patient grew worse, I should not discharge him but try to work out a more efficacious treatment." This severe rebuke proved effective, and Kate was allowed to continue her academic program at her mother's alma mater.

Back on campus to stay, Kate furthered her masquerade as a self-sufficient eccentric who seemingly had no concern as to what the school administration or fellow students thought about her. As part of her ongoing pose to hide her shyness and in reaction to her inability to blend in with her more conventional peers, she began to dress in what was then considered a most odd—even outrageous—manner. For one thing, she paraded about the school grounds in slacks, the first girl in the institution's history to do so. Another first on campus was Hepburn's sporting a pageboy hairdo. Over her slacks Kate usually donned a rumpled, worn green coat, hitched together with safety pins in spots to substitute for absent buttons. (Some observers snidely suggested that Hepburn may have yanked off the missing buttons herself.) To add to her bohemian look, she sometimes strolled around the campus barefoot and often sported a bandanna on her head. On occasion, Kate relaxed by sitting on a curbstone, seemingly absorbed in faraway thoughts and pretending to be unaware of the stares or snickers from passersby. Completing her role as a self-made outsider, Kate did her best to remain aloof from everyone. By taking the offensive of not joining any organization or clique she avoided the pain of their possible rejection.

During this difficult academic year Kate made few, if any, acquaintances or friends, rebuffing the overtures of any who were curious to know what made this strange (and to some, intriguing) young woman tick. Self-willed Hepburn also got into difficulties with the administration. Following in the tradition of her mother, Kit, she was caught smoking on school grounds. This led to several unpleasant encounters with the dean, including at least one five-day suspension.

＊　＊　＊

Despite the many miseries of Kate's sophomore year at Bryn Mawr, she had made a satisfying decision that she kept to herself. She was definitely going to become an actor and nothing would stop her. Like many withdrawn individuals with a strong creative bent, she sensed that in playing a role in front of large audiences she could explore and exhibit a range of emotions without fear of intimacy or continued interaction with others. Participation in campus dramatics, however, required that Hepburn bring her grade average up, especially in her double major: history and philosophy. This realization brought a transformation in Kate's attitude toward her class work.

Now she applied herself to her studies. She worked long and hard at them, often staying up all night poring over textbooks in her dorm room or at the library. This excessive about-face and her drive to make acceptable grade scores led her on at least two occasions that school year to sink into near physical collapse. Thrilled by her ability to change and mold the course of her (school) career, Hepburn was overjoyed. "I discovered that although I wasn't that brilliant, I could do it—if I worked. You can do anything, anything in the world if you try hard enough. You've just got to keep on struggling, because everybody gets discouraged, and almost everybody quits, and there are a few who don't—and then they go on and discover gold."

With her academic performance on an upward swing, she began to be noticed at Bryn Mawr as more than just a peculiar loner who so steadfastly refused to partake of the school's traditions, comradeship, and extracurricular activities. Kate actually began to make a few friends. She still lived in Pembroke West Hall, but it was with Alice Palache and a small group of others in Merion Hall that she became pals of sort. (Said Hepburn of her newfound buddies, who called themselves "The Tenement," "I felt safer with them. Safety in numbers.") They helped Hepburn with her studies and in the process became acquainted with as much of the real Katharine Hepburn as the artful poseur dared to share with outsiders. As part of the quartet, Kate soon was sneaking down the dorm fire escape to indulge in post-curfew larks on and off campus, none of which on Hepburn's part involved the normal ritual of dating young men.

Despite these controlled concessions to the social graces, Kate continued to thrive as a unique individualist. On one or more occasions, after a long night of studying in the library, she wallowed in the fountain outside of the building and then rolled herself dry on the grass. (Years later, she insisted her nude dipping was not exhibitionism but practicality: She hoped the brisk morning rinsing would refresh her for the day's classes and that, besides, she lacked a bathing suit in her wardrobe.) It would become Bryn Mawr legend how Hepburn allowed herself to be photographed naked in the snow on her dormitory roof. When the local druggist refused to print the risqué snapshots, Kate pretended great outrage. (One can theorize that, to some degree, this recurrent exhibitionistic activity was a subconscious attempt on Hepburn's part to draw other young women to her.)

* * *

With her scholastic standing at Bryn Mawr now up to par, if not excellence, Hepburn got her wish and participated in the junior class play in early April 1927. For the college's Varsity dramatic group, she took on the key part of Oliver in A.A. Milne's *The Truth About Blayds*. Wearing white trousers, tie, vest, and navy blue blazer, she added to her masculine look by greasing her hair—cut short—and parting it to the left. Said Hepburn decades later, "I thought that I made a damned attractive young man!"

Kate was coached in her taxing role by Professor Samuel Arthur King, who taught speech at Bryn Mawr. According to Hepburn, the veteran instructor "cared desperately how people sounded. Most people make an unattractive noise when they open their mouths, and this is too bad. I learned then to speak with a certain amount of confidence." Kate and the cast also performed the play in Manhattan at the Colony Club as a benefit for the New York Alumnae Regional Scholarship Fund. (The alumnae review of this repeat performance described Hepburn's young Oliver as an "engaging boy, roguish and merry.") Although *The Truth About Blayds* was now history, Hepburn was still too intrigued with her male attire to put it to rest. One evening the unconventional collegian took the train to New York wearing her masculine drag. Her genderless look caused many of the passengers to gape in wonder, all of which amused Kate.

During her third year on campus Hepburn returned to sports. She participated on the swim team, a group that had a championship season. She also played golf, winning trophies in the process. (By now she was so good at the game that she could have progressed into becoming a professional. However, she was too set on becoming a performer to consider this sports option seriously.)

In 1927, during the summer following her junior year, Kate and Alice

Palache treated themselves to a summer on the Continent. Each contributed $500 to the cause and purchased roundtrip passage to England. In London they squandered part of their reserve on a used car. In short order they realized that the luxury of a car and its upkeep was way beyond their budget. Hepburn utilized her burgeoning histrionic skills to convince the seller to repurchase the vehicle for almost what they had paid him for it. Before returning home, the duo dallied in France—particularly in Paris—where they sampled the cultural and bohemian life and its morally unrestrained nightlife.

❋ ❋ ❋

In Hepburn's senior year, for the Yuletide season production of G. Martinez Sierra's *The Cradle Song,* Kate was cast as Theresa. The *College News,* although misspelling Hepburn's first name as Katherine, reported that the student actress was "so extraordinarily lovely to look at that it was difficult to form any judgment on her acting. Her voice had, perhaps, too much of the childish treble, but her little movements, her poses and the contrast of her gaiety with the restrained atmosphere of the convent, could not have been improved. Here was acting not only good, but which seemed to offer really dazzling possibilities of something far better." While this was strong praise indeed, the campus publication lavished its highest admiration for a freshman in the cast whom the reviewer felt provided "the best piece of acting."

The highlight for Bryn Mawr seniors in spring 1928 was the May Day celebration. Instituted by the iconoclastic M. Carey Thomas back in 1900, the every-four-year pageant had an Elizabethan theme and included maypoles, masques, plays, and so forth. The climax of the two days of festivities was to be a production of John Lyllie's pastoral, *The Woman in the Moone.* Dr. King, a staunch believer in Kate's acting potential, chose her for the pivotal role of Pandora in the three-act play. He reasoned, "I find Miss Hepburn has personality, which is essential, and otherwise great powers for unfoldment." He graciously helped her rehearse her demanding part.

As would become her habit in later years, once Hepburn had fixed on her characterization for a performance she was not about to yield to any conflicting authority, including the director's point of view. Now at Bryn Mawr she did what would become her custom in the world of professional show business. Rather than play the role as conceived (i.e., a traditional delicate heroine) she reinterpreted the part to more closely and comfortably match her own inner personality. Thus Pandora, as portrayed by Kate, became a vibrant character, one who, Kate insisted, walked without sandals. (She was so insistent on this particular point that she endured walking barefoot over a perilous gravel path that the cast took to reach the Cloisters to perform their pastoral beneath the arbor there.)

Kate's energetic performance (with her white gown and wreath in her flowing hair) stole the show. She won hearty approval from the audience, which included faculty, students, and relatives of the graduates (among whom were Dr. and Mrs. Hepburn and Kate's siblings). Hepburn recalled, "Dad said that all he could see were the bottoms of my feet—and that they got dirtier and dirtier. For I was lying down, kicking my feet, you see, involved in all sorts of activity."

Receiving her BA degree at graduation, Katharine Hepburn was now ready to spring her career plans on her parents, an event that proved to be a tremendous watershed moment in her life.

Years later, in 1977, Hepburn, by then one of Bryn Mawr's most celebrated alumnae, was awarded the college's highest honor: The M. Carey Thomas Award. In May 1985, at her alma mater's Centennial Commencement Convocation, Kate spoke humorously and affectionately of her years on campus. Earlier, in 1973, she had shared her great feelings for the institution with an audience of Bryn Mawr undergraduates: "I came here by the skin of my teeth; I got in and by the skin of my teeth and I stayed. It was the best thing I ever did. Bryn Mawr was my springboard into adult life.... I feel that I was enormously lucky to come here. I am very proud when I see the name, very proud."

Chapter Eight
THE TURNING POINT

"People can't seem to understand how, if I really am self-conscious (which they doubt), I could become an actress. And I can't understand why they can't understand. It is the most natural thing in the world. Acting, I can get out of myself. No other profession offers me such an exciting way of escape.

"Most people on the stage have a curious kind of self-consciousness. Playing a part, you have smart lines to say, or dramatic lines, or amusing lines—and you move around in a pink spotlight, which flatters you, glamorizes you. But when you step out of the spotlight you're just an ordinary person. Your looks aren't spectacular, you play lousy tennis, and you don't say clever things. You have to have a colossal ego, or be a colossal ham, not to be self-conscious."
— *Katharine Hepburn, 1940*

The trauma of Tom Hepburn's suicide in 1921 shocked Kate into becoming semireclusive for several of her teenage years. During this difficult period of her emotional withdrawal, no one looking out for her welfare questioned why, nevertheless, the maturing young lady did not undergo the typical boy-crazy phase that most young women experience. As Kate passed the age of sixteen and she recovered—to a degree—from the tragedy, she had a few gentlemen callers at the family home on Bloomfield Avenue. However, her heart did not seem to be in this social process. Was Hepburn so restrained because she felt no newcomer could match the range of companionship and emotions she had enjoyed with her dear Tom? Was she afraid to give her heart to someone who might abandon her in one way or another as her brother had? Did she fear that no male friend could match the "admirable" qualities she saw and admired in her dad?

As for strong-willed Dr. Hepburn, he had a supercritical attitude about the few suitors Kate did attract. Looking back on this time, she described her father's attitude on this topic in a lighthearted mode that minimized the man's dogmatic viewpoint. "Dad also used to complain that my beaux were the dullest he had ever known." According to Kate, Dr. Hepburn liked to say in later times: "I used to sit with those goddam men and I'd have to talk to them and I'd think, 'If she marries any of them, it's going to be hell.'" In finishing this telling narrative, Kate would sum up, "Isn't that funny?"

When Hepburn chose to attend suburban Bryn Mawr College (which until 1931 did not permit male students to enroll—and then only on the graduate level), it was viewed by most, and perhaps by Kate as well, as merely a daughter following in her parent's footsteps. During Kate's first three years there she apparently avoided participating in campus socials with students from nearby men's colleges (e.g., Haverford College or the University of Pennsylvania). Certainly, Kate was shy and a devoted oddball in her independent behavior and unorthodox dress. However, had she attended such mixers, her striking looks and bright mind would have certainly prompted some smart members of the opposite sex to (try to) break through her self-created facade of a wallflower. Yet at the time she seemed to have had no interest in availing herself of such heterosexual dating possibilities.

During Kate's senior year at Bryn Mawr, in February 1928, she returned to Connecticut for one of her frequent family visits. While she was there, a local acquaintance persuaded her to attend a dance at Yale University in New Haven—a distance of some forty-two miles from the Hepburns' home on Bloomfield Avenue. At the social event, she met Robert J. McKnight. He was the son of a prominent Springfield, Ohio, family and had grown up in the Buckeye State and on Long Island. He had graduated from Yale in 1927 with a degree in economics. Thereafter, at the time he met Kate, he was studying sculpture at Yale Art School. (McKnight boasted relatives who had been prominent in the creative arts: sculptor John Quincy Adams Ward and painter Edgar Melville Ward.)

During the dance, Kate and McKnight quickly appreciated each other's worth. Bob appealed to Hepburn because he was a smart, vibrant, artistic soul. She was impressed when he told her, "I'm going to be the greatest sculptor in the world." Intoxicated by his great air of confidence, she responded, "I am going to be the greatest actress in the world." When he did not mock her—as that girl had done when Kate made a similar remark during rehearsal for the Bryn Mawr freshman show—Hepburn was doubly impressed by this handsome young man. She lowered her emotional guard sufficiently to invite him to spend time with the Hepburns in Hartford during the coming Easter break. He readily agreed.

McKnight certainly must have been baffled by the unusual mode of life at the Hepburns—just as other suitors for the attention of any of the Hepburn girls had found and would experience over the years. Upon arrival, the parents told Bob, "Just make yourself at home," and then left him to his own devices for long periods at a stretch. At the dinner table, Bob was perplexed by the flurry of diners coming and going and the nonstop discussions where it was extremely difficult for an outsider to break into the debates on politics, planned parenthood, and so forth. McKnight shared a room at the Hepburns' with Kate's two brothers. The morning after Bob's arrival, she dashed into the bedroom and briefly kissed him (for the only time during that visit). Her brothers slept through it all. Although the parents were too self-preoccupied to pay their guest serious attention, they approved of his artistic inclination.

The weekend visit ended with McKnight clearly smitten with the vivacious Kate. However, when he departed he had no sense of how she felt about him because she concertedly spent much of their time together focusing on her family and household tasks.

About a month before Kate graduated from Bryn Mawr, she again was back in Hartford. Bob McKnight asked her to an afternoon picnic at a rock above a tiny lake in middle Connecticut. It was a favored spot he used to visit during his prep school years. The twenty-two-year-old Yalie had half-decided to propose to Hepburn. But, somehow—by her device?—he did not get the opportunity. Garrulous when she felt comfortable with someone, she talked nonstop for nearly three hours on a range of topics (e.g., art, life, love, integrity, and her uniqueness). As sunset descended, she stopped, flung her arms around him, kissed him, and said briskly, "Well, it's time to go home!" The nonplussed McKnight complied.

＊　＊　＊

Also during Kate's final college year she came to know Jack Clarke. Then in his late twenties, Jack came from a socially prominent Pennsylvania family who resided in a large Victorian-style house adjacent to the college campus. With his indulgent father not objecting, Jack allowed Bryn Mawr students to smoke their forbidden cigarettes on his family's lawn, where the shrubbery hid them from the scrutiny of campus authorities. (Sometimes the errant girls congregated in an old tool shed on the Clarke property to have their forbidden smokes.) Congenial Clarke, like his two sisters, had supposedly vowed never to marry because their mother had expired in an insane asylum and they feared passing on bad genes to the next generation. (This provided Jack with an excellent explanation why he had not romanced any of the women in his social set.) Jack's best friend was Ludlow Ogden Smith, with whom he shared a cottage forty minutes away. The duo's closeness prompted speculation that these two wealthy young men were lovers.

Smith, born February 6, 1899, traced his lineage back to Quakers who had settled near Upper Darby (Delaware County), Pennsylvania, in the late seventeenth century. Ludlow's great-grandfather Smith had been a doctor and state senator. Ludlow's father, Lewis, was a prominent Philadelphia attorney and was followed in the profession by Ludlow's younger brother, Lawrence. Ludlow served in World War I in France and returned there for graduate work (in electrical engineering) at the University of Grenoble. The Smiths had their chief residence in a sprawling home on the Main Line (at Strafford, Pennsylvania).

Luddy was tall, balding, with a medium frame, and a bit of a stomach paunch. (Hepburn described him as "an odd-looking man—dark hair, dark eyes far apart. He was foreign-looking. Pink cheeks. An odd nose, long with a hump in it. A long mouth, full-lipped.") Smith was a congenial, passive soul with a wide-ranging cultural background who at times broke out of his somber, patrician mode to be fairly amusing. (One of his diverting tricks was to touch the tip of his nose with his tongue.) If anything endeared Luddy to his blueblood acquaintances besides his patrician background, it was his intense desire to please his friends. He also was a competent musician, which made the unattached man an asset at parties.

Kate was amused by the socially prominent Jack and Luddy. She felt sexually unthreatened by this simpatico bachelor duo and enjoyed spending time with them. Once, when persuaded to visit their country cottage, she agreed to pose nude for Luddy, a devoted amateur photographer. He snapped several pictures of her. While this may have seemed risqué and sexually provocative on Hepburn's part, her daring exhibitionism was not so motivated. Unlike so many women her age in the Roaring Twenties, Kate had no inner urge to rebel against the past generation's Victorian prudery. (After all, she had grown up in an extremely liberal household where social hygiene, planned parenthood, and so forth had been common dinner table topics since she could remember.) Then too, her father was a type who thought nothing of parading nude about the family home, so displaying herself undraped in front of others—especially for something artistic—was not really alien to egocentric Hepburn. In short, for Kate, the photo session was just an entertaining lark.

When asked in 1991 how she had felt about this long-ago modeling turn, Hepburn smiled and said most coyly that it "didn't shock me. I thought I was very attractive." When queried if her dad would have been upset had he known about the revealing photo shoot, she answered, "He wouldn't be a bit surprised, if he had any sense—if she was lovely." As to what happened to those enticing pictures, Kate admitted late in life that the last time she had seen them was many decades ago. They had been in a straw basket that she had carted around from place to place when she first lived in New York City. At first amused by the poses, Hepburn soon found them tedious and inappropriate. She put them out of sight and mind. Later, she must have torn them up, or perhaps Luddy had eventually burned them.

❀ ❀ ❀

In the 1920s, H. Phelps Pelham (1894–1948) was a bright light in American poetry circles. Born in the Jamaica Plain section of Boston, he had graduated from Yale University. His debut book of poems (*Trinc*) appeared in 1927. It was well-reviewed and indicated that he had a bright literary career ahead of him. However, by then, the poet, who lived with his wife in a simple apartment in his parents' home in Jamaica Plain, was on the fast track to becoming a roué. He had a passion for drink and women, and he thrived on living the high life, largely during his frequent treks to Greenwich Village.

(During his frolics in New York, his understanding spouse waited patiently back in Massachusetts for his return.) By this juncture dissolute Pelham was already suffering from asthma as well as other actual and supposed ailments. Floundering under the pressure of producing a follow-up volume of poetry to match his first success and no longer able to recharge his energies in the company of his sympathetic but unstimulating wife, he sought escape by visiting a college chum. The latter was Professor Frederick Manning, who lived in Bryn Mawr with his wife, Helen, the dean at Bryn Mawr College.

Pelham's sister, Frances, was in the Bryn Mawr Class of 1928, and because of this, the poet attended the May Day festivities on campus. He was among those intrigued by the redheaded, freckled senior who played Pandora in *The Woman in the Moone*. Subsequently, he contrived to have Hepburn be a dinner guest at the Mannings. On different emotional levels, Kate and the poet became infatuated with each other. For excitement-hungry Pelham, Kate was a tantalizing potential conquest; for the overly aesthetic, highly imaginative Hepburn, Phelps seemed an intriguing bohemian artist with whom she could communicate on a creative level.

Phelps, however, soon vanished back to Boston to pacify his long-suffering wife. Nevertheless, he had definite hopes of reconnecting with Kate in the near future. He suggested that once she graduated from Bryn Mawr they join up in Manhattan, where he intended to complete his much-anticipated second volume of poetry. He suggested she would be the perfect muse to help him over his writer's block. Despite her own strong career ambitions, Hepburn was thrilled with this romantic notion of being needed emotionally by this established poet. As would become an entrenched habit with Kate, she was strongly drawn to this type of man: self-focused, needy, and alcoholic.

* * *

Looking back on her long life, Kate Hepburn professed it to be one of her "adorable" traits that she had sometimes utilized friends and acquaintances for career networking as well as emotional and financial help. During her senior year at Bryn Mawr she became an energetic practitioner of relying on her circle of acquaintances to lead her to the next step in reaching her life's purpose—entering the world of show business. As she cutely phrased it in

Me, "You can see how wise I was in picking friends." More impartial observers might find it a case of Yankee ingenuity and strong fearlessness in obtaining her objectives without, at the time, worrying much about any repercussions on others.

In spring 1928, Hepburn had became increasingly friendly with undemanding Jack Clarke. One day, he mentioned that a friend of his, Edwin H. Knopf—whose half brother Alfred had founded a publishing firm in Manhattan in 1915—was a young theatrical producer. The latter had a thriving stock company in Baltimore that was now setting up its summer season. Kate immediately asked Clarke to provide her with a letter of introduction. He happily complied.

Because Kate knew that her inflexible father would find her theatrical ambitions frivolous at best, she kept her plans a secret from him. Accompanied by Elizabeth Rhett, one of the Tenement group of Bryn Mawr friends, Kate drove to Maryland, intending to deliver her letter of entrée to Knopf in person. She and Elizabeth stayed at the house of Kate's Aunt Edith. (As a young woman, Edith had been offered the opportunity to embark on a theatrical career by the great stage performer Richard Mansfield but had rejected the offer for fear of entering such a frivolous occupation. However, she remained partial to show business and had great sympathy for her niece's acting ambitions.) That same May weekend, Hepburn celebrated her twenty-first birthday.

Once Kate reached Knopf's office above the Auditorium Theater, she handed him Jack Clarke's note. She stood there speechless, nervously awaiting the man's reaction. In her usual bohemian way, she had broken with the custom of the era and wore no face makeup. Her face was shiny. According to Knopf, "Her red hair was pulled back into a charwoman's bun. Excitement had blotched her skin under her freckles. Her forehead was wet. Her nose shone. Anyone who saw *Morning Glory* [1933] can re-create that scene. She was tremendously sincere, but awkward, green, freaky-looking. I wanted no part of her."

To get rid of this tongue-tied newcomer who stood there with clenched hands, the producer politely suggested, "Write me when you're through college." When Kate nervously asked if she might remain and watch him at work, he said, "No. I don't let anyone watch me direct." She pleaded her case, but he remained firm. She finally left. Knopf recalled, "I felt only one reaction. I was glad to see the last of her." (Some sources suggest that the producer had all but thrown the brazen Hepburn out of his office. When she finally left, it was she who blithely said to Knopf, "I'll be back as soon as school is finished.")

Jubilant that she had successfully navigated uncharted waters in finding the next step in launching her acting career, self-absorbed Hepburn returned to Pennsylvania. She was oblivious to the actual unfavorable impression she had made on Edwin Knopf and that he had actually given her a brush-off.

Back on campus, the remaining school days flew by quickly. She completed her last final exam on June 2. Scrimping together the needed travel funds, she hastened to Baltimore once again. Rushing into Edwin Knopf's office, she found it deserted. She waited, believing he might be out to lunch. Time passed and still no one appeared. Then she heard voices drifting in from the theater. Onstage Knopf was rehearsing Kenneth MacKenna for an upcoming production. She tiptoed quietly into the darkened auditorium to watch, barely able to spot the producer-director seated in one of the front rows. She waited hours for the rehearsal to end, convinced that no one knew she was there. (Actually Knopf had seen her, but did not want to cause a disturbance by throwing her out.) When the run-through concluded, everyone departed. As Knopf marched up the aisle, he stopped and said tersely to Hepburn, "There are four ladies-in-waiting in *The Czarina*. Report Monday morning for rehearsal."

Once again back at school, Kate and her fellow seniors graduated from Bryn Mawr on June 7, 1928. Her parents were in the audience at Goodheart Hall to enjoy the ceremony. As the Thursday morning event concluded, a relieved Dr. Hepburn sighed rather loudly, "Well, that's done!"

En route home—in Doylestown, about thirty miles from Bryn Mawr—the new graduate summoned the courage to inform her parents, "I have a job, Dad. I'm an actress." Dr. Hepburn thought anyone who wished a career involving such personal publicity was unspeakable. When Kate retorted that her mother did public work, the physician countered, "All that was in the public interest! This is nothing but your own vanity!" By now Dr. Hepburn's temper was fast rising. He exploded, "I don't want to hear anything about it! Stop the car! Let me out! I'll go on the train!" To the physician, liberal though he was in some matters, a woman in the acting profession was no better than a streetwalker.

Back in Hartford, Kate refused to give in to her father's demands, insisting she had her own life to live and that she had decided on a stage career. In retaliation, Dr. Hepburn threatened to stop her allowance, shouting that he would not support this ridiculous endeavor. Still she would not yield to his viewpoint. (Meanwhile, Kit Hepburn, no great proponent of the theater or the movies, was pleased that her daughter was sufficiently self-willed to choose a profession rather than follow convention and settle down and wed. Because of this, she supported her offspring's decision.)

Amid this contention, Kate left Hartford for Baltimore. She had persuaded her sculptor friend, Bob McKnight, to drive her to Maryland. Because her Aunt Edith was away for the summer, Hepburn stayed at the almost-deserted local Bryn Mawr Club which had a skeleton crew on hand in the off-season. McKnight took a separate room at the facility. Hardly had Hepburn reached Baltimore than she received $10 from her relenting father. He emphasized that this was not his way of apologizing but that he was merely giving her "ill-gotten gains." (His note explained he had earned the money playing bridge at the University Club.) Kate knew this was his particular way of making amends and still retaining his pride. (Later, she would receive other payments from his sudden winnings at the gaming tables.)

Being within days of starting her stage career, Kate was thrilled. Already she was driven by a growing and consuming ambition to succeed in her exciting new profession. No one and nothing else mattered now that she had settled upon her life's course. This included accommodating Bob McKnight who would soon depart for Europe to further his art studies and continue an already distinguished creative career. As would become habit with Hepburn, she remained on friendly, platonic terms with her ex-suitor, who had never achieved any meaningful degree of emotional or sexual intimacy with her.

Chapter Nine
BEFORE THE FOOTLIGHTS

"I always feel that if something is difficult—as the theatre has always been for me—it must be good for me to do it. That's my puritanical upbringing. When I was a child I loved fairy tales. I suppose acting seemed romantic and thrilling. I haven't changed my opinion at all. It's a delicious way to spend one's life."

—Katharine Hepburn, 1976

In choosing acting as her life's work, Katharine Hepburn was guided by several strong motivations. As a child she had been nurtured by her extremely controlling father to be highly competitive. Thus she was determined to embark on a professional life in which she could and would excel. Having abandoned the notion of following in her dad's footsteps as a surgeon, she sidestepped an obvious alternative: becoming a crusader for improving the social order as her mother had done and continued to do. However, despite professed admiration for Kit over the years, Hepburn seemed to have no strong desire to emulate Mrs. Hepburn—neither in her do-gooder work (which brought a degree of notoriety but also required the individual to have generally selfless motivations) nor certainly as a parent of a large family.

Kate's choice of acting for her life's work was an outgrowth of her childhood love of movies and her bubbling ambition to become a world-famous personality. Such a career choice provided several subsidiary benefits. Her occupational path satisfied any (sub)conscious desire to rebel against her parents. (It would be somewhat of a rebuff to her mother to pick an occupation that Kit Hepburn deemed so superficial. More importantly, her theater choice was so against her father's sense of propriety that her selecting this field of endeavor would not only gain his full negative attention but also keep her sharply in his focus for the future. One might speculate that it was a subtle and strange way of keeping herself closely tied to her dad.

Then too, actors were well-known for being self-focused and individualistic. Such traits fit in admirably with Hepburn's own maturing, eccentric personality. In such an artistic field she would no longer be chastised by her peers for her uniqueness but rather be praised for it. This aspect was especially appealing to Kate, who, despite later protestations to the contrary, was intuitively calculating in shaping a distinctive (offbeat) public image for herself.

Not to be ignored in the equation, Kate's compulsive dedication to her show business career—which at times would climb to near manic levels—offered a perfect hedge against what she most feared: committing herself emotionally and/or sexually to a man. The life of an actor, whether on the stage or on screen, keeps the individual constantly moving and never able to settle comfortably into a normal domestic routine. This would be a perfect buffer whenever a man tried to break through Hepburn's emotional walls and, in the process, demanded physical satisfaction. She could merely plead career obligations to excuse her unavailability to satisfy such typical sexual demands.

By now there was an increasing number of individuals in Hepburn's orbit who believed or assumed that twenty-one-year-old Kate, still a virgin, was drawn to one degree or another to a bisexual or lesbian lifestyle. (Director-producer Edwin H. Knopf would tell a close acquaintance over lunch in New York in the 1930s that he was certain Kate was of "a sapphic" nature. The observation was made in a pleasant, nonjudgmental way.) Being in show business, long a haven for bohemian, creative individuals—many of whom were gay, lesbian, or bisexual—would provide a convenient ambiance for Kate to explore further her latent or actual sexual feelings.

* * *

In the late 1920s theater stock companies flourished throughout the United States, providing stimulating entertainment in the era before the newly emerged talkie movies distracted audiences from such regional fare. Edwin Knopf's company for the summer of 1928 was composed largely of seasoned professionals (e.g., Mary Boland, Alison Skipworth, Violet Heming, and Dudley Digges) and upcoming performers (e.g., Robert Montgomery) about to break out into major film careers. Clearly, Knopf had no need or use for theatrical amateurs like Kate. It was her excessive persistence and her being in the right place at the right time that had won her a very subordinate spot in the troupe at a salary of $25 weekly.

In typical fashion, at the Auditorium in Baltimore, a new production was mounted each week featuring guest notables as marquee lure for theatergoers. The first week's entry was *The Czarina*, starring Miss Boland as Russia's Catherine the Great. By the third day of rehearsal the middle-aged star, then between Broadway vehicles in a busy career, lost patience with Kate. She approached Knopf: "I can't stand it, Eddie! That Hepburn girl's onstage only five minutes, and the rest of the time she sits in the wings staring at me. I feel her every minute."

The producer-director allayed his leading lady's concerns, and rehearsals continued. Kate was as unaware of how her actions bothered the leading lady as she was that her work attire (i.e., faded sweater, loose slacks, bunched hair, bandanna, scruffy tennis shoes, shiny nose, and a shabby felt hat) made her look most odd and affected to the others. Fortunately, for whatever reason— and this proved to be a saving grace for Hepburn repeatedly in the coming years—the star took sympathy on the fledgling and took her under her professional wing.

When the supporting cast was told to report the next morning to select among the period costumes for their wardrobe, Hepburn showed up a few minutes early. She was pleased with herself for having arrived ahead of time. However, to her amazement, the others—veterans of such procedures—had come even earlier and all the best costumes had already been selected. Kate was crestfallen that she would have to make her professional stage debut in a makeshift mishmash of leftovers bits of costume.

One of the other young women in the company noticed Hepburn's utter dejection. She confided that she planned to be married within a few weeks and thereafter her show business career was finished. Since she didn't care if her stage outfit was special, she volunteered to switch costumes with Kate. Hepburn was thrilled by this very unselfish gesture and rapidly accepted the thoughtful offer. (Interestingly, Hepburn, who until her final years had a solid memory for people's names, especially those with whom she had worked in one show business project or another, would have a strange lapse of memory about this colleague who had so graciously saved the day for newcomer Kate. It makes one ponder why Hepburn repressed the name of this helpful cast member. Could there have been more to their association, or was the account a distortion of facts to make Kate seem worthy—even at that early stage in her career—of special consideration from a professional actor?

Now boasting a fine Russian court costume, Hepburn enthusiastically proceeded with the rehearsals for her tiny role as a lady-in-waiting. Boland graciously showed the novice how to apply her stage makeup and to suitably arrange her period attire. (Hepburn's first reaction to such constructive suggestions was to snap back with annoyance, covering her deep insecurities with a bravado. Soon the novice realized the wisdom and good intentions of her mentor and became amenable to the useful tips.) Further into the run-throughs, Mary advised Kate that her golf course stride would best be adapted to accommodate the fancy dress she wore. Kenneth MacKenna, another veteran cast member and a bisexual with whom Kate developed a quick comradeship, kindly pointed out to her that she must learn to speak more slowly so the audience could properly grasp her dialogue.

The Czarina opened successfully for its week's run. Kate delivered her few lines eagerly and adequately. (Hepburn was so inexperienced at acting that she was surprised that the show was reviewed by local critics, although she received no particular mention in the write-ups.) She was invited to stay on for the next week's show. She hid her excitement beneath an airy demeanor, hoping to suggest that all along she expected this vote of confidence. The next production was *The Cradle Snatchers,* a contemporary comedy in which Hepburn was cast in the small role of a flapper. Kate fared less well in this offering, displaying gawky hand and leg movements while onstage.

By the end of Kate's brief stay with the Baltimore stock company she had won the professional interest of several in the company. A few years later Boland (who never married) would recall of her protégée's emergence on the Baltimore stage: "I remember the transformation. We were all awed and excited at the way our ugly ducking blossomed. I have never seen anyone more beautiful than that eager girl, so proud to walk across a stage that she and the costume seemed borne up by light."

Kenneth MacKenna, a suave New Englander who came from an illustrious show business family and had many industry connections, had already concluded that Hepburn was going places in the theater. He volunteered to provide his new pal with a letter of introduction to Frances Robinson-Duff, a leading drama and voice coach in Manhattan, to help the fledgling with the mechanics of speech and stage movement. (MacKenna's note alerted Robinson-Duff that Hepburn "stands awfully and never sits in a chair if there's an inch of floor available.")

Meanwhile, Edwin Knopf told MacKenna, his resident leading man, that he planned to use the profits from the Baltimore season to launch a Broadway production that August of *The Big Pond*. Both agreed that Kate might do for an assignment. Knopf cautioned MacKenna, "Don't say we discovered her. She discovered herself. She wished herself on us. If it hadn't been us, it would have been someone else."

❋   ❋   ❋

From Baltimore, Kate went on to New York, leading Jack Clarke and Luddy Smith to transfer to the city. Hepburn set up headquarters at a relative's apartment, but this was to be short-lived. H. Phelps Putnam had stayed in contact with the striking Kate and was excited to learn that she was now to be based in Manhattan for the foreseeable future. He was again in the city, spending most of his energy and time prowling through the metropolis's fashionable speakeasies and chatting with celebrity acquaintances. Always short of funds, the charming poet turned for help to Russell Davenport, a Yale classmate, who had an apartment on East Fifty-fourth Street. Davenport was then in the throes of writing his debut novel and had decided to leave the city to work without distraction on his manuscript. Putnam borrowed his pal's digs and invited Kate to share the flat with him. She agreed.

When not hanging out with Jack and Luddy, Phelps became her tour guide to the city's sophisticated nightlife. Through Pelham she met Robert Benchley and Dorothy Parker, both of whom had gained fame as part of the distinguished Algonquin Round Table. In contrast to Phelps and the others, Hepburn was a babe in arms among this witty, cynical set. In her usual fashion, Hepburn made no effort to blend in but rather accentuated her differences from this fast, fascinating crowd. She persisted in wearing outré outfits (including the use of her trademark safety pins to substitute for missing garment buttons), refused to wear makeup (continuing her practice of scrubbing her face with alcohol to give it a shiny glow), and talked with what most everyone considered a most affected nasal twang. Unsure how to best converse with this urbane clique, Hepburn interacted in an abrupt, impudent way. When a listener looked askance at her lack of tact, she might react by amplifying her rudeness or suddenly going shy and silent. Despite or because of this peculiar mode of unsocial behavior, Kate made an impression on Phelps's jaded crowd. They soon accepted her as an offbeat addition to their unique group.

❊ ❊ ❊

Meanwhile, Katharine arranged to meet with Miss Frances Robinson-Duff. The veteran coach had gained her reputation from years of training such Broadway personalities as Helen Hayes, Miriam Hopkins, Clark Gable, Ruth Chatterton, Cornelia Otis Skinner, and Ina Claire. Residing at 235 East Sixty-second Street, the single lady held court on the third floor of the old building. (Her aged mother taught singing on the second floor.) The day Hepburn presented herself to the imperious tutor it was raining. Once admitted to the residence, Kate rushed up the three steep flights of stairs to have an audience with the heavy set lady who was seated on a throne. Breathless and dripping wet, Kate dramatically flung herself down on a nearby chest and announced, "I want to be an actress.... I want to learn everything!"

Later, Frances Robinson-Duff would describe her initial contact with the future celebrity: "Sometimes we have an inward vision, a flash. I looked at her, huddled there, bedraggled and wet—at the terrific intensity of that face—and something inside whispered, '[Eleonora] Duse. She looks like Duse.'"

Robinson-Duff agreed to take on Hepburn as a pupil and to train her in the Delsarte style. To pay for the expensive lessons, Kate negotiated with her father for the needed funds. She explained that she had already proved she could have a stage career and that this would be a good investment in her future. He reluctantly agreed with her reasoning and subsidized the classes.

Much of Robinson-Duff's guidance involved exercises to improve the pupil's breathing and in turn make the speaking voice resonate loudly and clearly in a large auditorium. As part of the training, which involved complex study charts, the learner would be repeatedly required to blow out a candle placed at a certain distance. (This was to help the student focus on breathing deeply from the diaphragm.) Another aspect of the coach's curriculum was work on the use of stage gestures, keeping the essential ones and removing the superfluous movements. Duff's ruling principle was "in the end, it can't look like acting."

In Hepburn's case, the experienced teacher felt she must go a step further in her tutelage. It led to the following exchange:

Robinson-Duff: "You're to be an actress. You must dress right. You must look like somebody."

Hepburn: "Teach me to act."

Robinson-Duff: "Katharine, you won't wear clothes fit for a decent scarecrow, but will you do me one favor?… Throw away that old felt hat and get one without a hole in it."

Hepburn (astonished): "Good Lord! What's the matter with people? Can't their imaginations supply enough cloth for that little hole?"

❊   ❊   ❊

During the summer of 1928, Hepburn and Phelps Putnam continued to live together, but they had yet to consummate their relationship. Wanting to introduce "her" man to her family, Kate took the poet on a visit to Fenwick. The parents appreciated Phelps's reputation as an in-vogue poet but had their reservations about his future, let alone his present life, which included a wife back in Massachusetts. During one private talk with the guest, Dr. Hepburn warned the visitor that should Phelps allow headstrong Kate to seduce him, the doctor would shoot Putnam. The artist took the warning to heart. Back in New York, Putnam began work on a major poem ("The Daughters of the Sun") in tribute to Kate. However, their chaste sojourn together rapidly came to an end. Perhaps motivated by Dr. Hepburn's sincere threat, Phelps abruptly departed for Nova Scotia, leaving a perplexed Hepburn to find new lodgings when Russell Davenport returned to town.

One of Kate's now-married classmates from Bryn Mawr was residing at 925 Park Avenue. She and her husband were out of the city for the summer, and Kate took up residence there.

Meanwhile, Hepburn continued her weekly lessons with Robinson-Duff. She also began taking toe dancing classes to tame her unruly arms and legs and to become more centralized in her movements. She studied with the renowned Michael Mordkin (whom she, as a child, had once seen perform with Pavlova) and kept at the discipline for more than three years.

* * *

By August, Edwin Knopf's production of *The Big Pond* was in full preparation for its imminent Broadway bow. The romantic comedy, directed by Knopf, included Hepburn in a small role as a secretary and as an understudy to the actress playing the young American socialite who falls in love with an enterprising Frenchman (Kenneth MacKenna). After days of rehearsal, the ingenue was let go and Kate was substituted in the pivotal female role. (It didn't hurt that one of the play's authors knew Hepburn's family.) Her salary was raised to $125 weekly. She was permitted to visit a fashionable Fifth Avenue shop to select her new stage wardrobe. When the production's publicist asked Hepburn for information to construct her playbill biography, the fledgling actress refused to cooperate. She insisted that all relevant facts about her could be set forth in two lines. She theorized that fame should come *after* success and that advance publicity would merely make her ridiculous if she failed in the venture.

The Big Pond was scheduled for a one-night tryout in Great Neck on Long Island. On the all-important evening Kate took a train out to Long Island, arriving well ahead of schedule. Needing to come to grips with her mounting stage terror, she decided a brisk walk in the nearby woods would be soothing. Thus relaxed, she later stopped at a grocery store to buy her supper: a box of blackberries and a container of milk. Losing track of time, she did not return to the theater until twenty minutes before the show was to start. Having regained her outer composure, she insisted to the irate stage manager and others that everything was fine. Just before she was to go onstage, however, her lace underwear began to chafe. Nonchalantly, she removed the undergarment and flung it to a surprised stagehand. Then she made her entrance.

Within the first act, Hepburn's Barbara Billings was required to do an imitation of the leading man's French accent. She acquitted herself so amusingly that the audience gave her a healthy round of applause. Thinking she had won over the theatergoers, Kate became giddy with exhilaration. In the process, her voice grew shrill and she spoke so rapidly thereafter that no one could understand what she was saying. When the play came to a close Hepburn, unaware of her gaffes, expected her fellow cast members to congratulate her. Instead she was met with stony silence.

That night Kate drove back to Manhattan with Harlan Briggs, who played her dad onstage. Hepburn said, "They all seemed so quiet, didn't they? I'd expected them to come around afterwards and give me some pointers. You know—tell me where I was wrong, and so on." Briggs, a seasoned actor, knew the truth but wanted to spare the young lady's feelings. So he said, "Quiet? It was because they were so busy, I expect."

The next morning Frances Robinson-Duff, at the request of Edwin Knopf, telephoned Kate and asked her to come by the studio. Hepburn declined, explaining she must rehearse all day long for Monday's night performance of the show in Asbury, New Jersey. "You can take time," Frances informed her.

Some minutes later the young actress exploded into her coach's teaching salon. Twirling around the room, Hepburn inquired, "Aren't you proud of me, Robbie? Aren't you proud?"

The older woman said nothing. It prompted Kate to ask, "What's the matter? Didn't I do as well as you hoped? I'm sorry!" When her teacher remained frozen in place, Hepburn suddenly caught on. "You don't mean I'm fired?"

"Yes, you're fired," sighed her coach.

After a moment Kate began whirling around the room again. "Look, Miss Duff! I know you're proud of me now. Look how I'm taking it. *Not* a tear! I didn't cry at all!"

"I'm not proud of you. I'd have some hope if you wept. How can I ever make an actress out of you, if you keep that shell over your emotions?"

Despite being overwhelmed with defeat, Kate was far more concerned with not losing face with her fellow cast members. She insisted upon going to *The Big Pond* rehearsal to congratulate her successor on winning her part.

Said Hepburn, " I was busy being charming and a good sport. I had to show everybody. I ran out of people in New York, so I drove to Hartford and showed my family."

Chapter Ten

LIFE UPON THE BROADWAY STAGE

"The career of Katharine Hepburn is a monument to the keenness and open-mindedness of American theatrical producers. The only trouble has been that, as fast as one man discovered that she was a child genius, another discovered that she was a crude amateur. Both sets of discoverers were approximately right."

—*Alva Johnston, "The Hepburn Legend,"*
Woman's Home Companion, *June 1934*

When *The Big Pond* played its one-night engagement in Great Neck, among the celebrity audience was Lee Shubert, one of the production's chief backers. This famed theatrical figure was one of those displeased by Katharine Hepburn's bizarre stage turn as the leading lady. After the show, he urged Edwin Knopf to discharge her. Shubert reasoned, "[Producer] Arthur Hopkins can take a chance with those Park Avenue amateurs [e.g., Hope Williams in 1927's *Paris Bound*], but I want a real actress." Knopf obediently followed through on the request, but admitted later, "Why blame Lee [Shubert]? My contract with him gave me full authority over the cast. I'd grown scared, too, or I wouldn't have listened. I agreed to throw her out." Hepburn was replaced by Lucile Nikolas. *The Big Pond* made its Manhattan bow on August 21 and lasted only forty-seven performances.

❋　❋　❋

Eager to regain a professional footing, Kate made the round of casting offices and auditioned for *Night Hostess,* a gangster melodrama produced by the well-established John Golden. She was given a tiny background role as a club hostess in the play. The show, written by Phillip Dunning, tried out in Minneapolis. During the warm-up run there, Hepburn received word that she was under consideration for a showier assignment in *These Days,* a study of life at a girls' finishing school. Kate left *Night Hostess* and returned to New York to participate in this preferred Broadway entry. (One source suggests that Hepburn may have been fired from *Night Hostess* because she was too prim and restrained in her role.)

The producer-director of *These Days* was the esteemed Arthur Hopkins (1878–1950), one of those who had seen Kate's disastrous stage turn in *The Big Pond* at Great Neck. Unlike Shubert, who had found no virtues in the novice's gauche performance, Hopkins (as did a few others in the audience, including producer A.H. Woods), perceived that they were witnessing a unique personality onstage. As such, she was an individual worth considering for future stage properties.

Hopkins felt justified in gambling on Hepburn because in look, manner, and breeding she reminded him so much of his recent discovery, Hope Williams (1897–1990). The latter, a Manhattan-born and -bred socialite who the Broadway grapevine insisted was bisexual, had gained initial acting experience in the Amateur Comedy Club and Junior League charity shows. The lanky debutante made her professional stage bow in Hopkins's *Paris Bound* (1927), which was a smash hit. The sophisticated comedy made an "overnight" star of the unique Miss Williams, who stole the limelight from leading lady, Madge Kennedy. As Fanny Shippan, Hope sported a trademark close-cropped boyish hairstyle, a blithe manner, and an aristocratic demeanor that was far more intriguing than annoying. (She had developed a sort of ball-bearing (comical) walk to distract from the fact that her legs were a bit too long for the rest of the body to be in symmetry with them. British playwright-actor Noël Coward was a great admirer of the droll Hope and praised her "charming speaking voice" which had "a sort of beguiling tonelessness.... She was slangy without being vulgar, modern without being brash, and her gaucheries of movement had a peculiar grace." Hopkins was convinced that if Hepburn was properly groomed and showcased, she could become the theater's next Hope Williams.

These Days tried out in New Haven and Hartford with some of the Hepburn clan on hand. Dr. Hepburn still had not changed his mind about his daughter's chosen profession, but felt obliged to show family loyalty by attending the performance. As Kate's younger sister Marion would point out, "My father thought the theater was a place of evil. He really believed his daughter was on the road to perdition." Brother Robert would recall of his father's attitude while watching his eldest daughter onstage (or onscreen): "Dad said to me, 'I hate to go see Kate's performances because she makes me cry, and men shouldn't cry.' That was quite a compliment coming from my father. He didn't give compliments, not easily. Dad was noted not for his tact but for his honesty. He always liked to be in control of his feelings, which is one of the reasons he also hated to go see Kate's pictures because she made him lose control."

These Days bowed at the Cort Theater on November 12, 1928. The critics declared the drama tepid, but a few aisle-sitters took notice of Kate's appearance as Veronica Sims. John Anderson (*New York Evening Journal*) complimented Hepburn for a "perfect passage of repressed deviltry done gorgeously." It was the first time that Hepburn was cited for a New York stage performance. Ironically, while *These Days* was a fast flop (eight performances), *Night Hostess,* which Kate had abandoned, had opened in mid September and enjoyed a 119-performance run.

* * *

Following playwright Philip Barry's tremendous success with *Paris Bound,* which lasted for 234 performances, he collaborated with Elmer Rice on a gimmicky whodunit, *Cock Robin,* which struggled through a far shorter stage run. Then the blueblood author returned to the subject he knew best: the intricate workings of the sophisticated upper crust. Barry wrote *The Dollar* (later retitled *Holiday*) with Hope Williams in mind for the crucial leading role of Linda Seton. She is the millionaire's daughter who falls in love with her snobbish sister's cheerful, middle-class boyfriend, Johnny Case. To her family's bewilderment and/or disgust, Linda applauds Johnny's decision to reject marrying his fiancée and working for her mogul father. When Case embarks on a trip to the Continent to take stock of his life, Linda finds the courage to declare her independence from her aristocratic trappings. She joins up with the antiestablishment hero.

Arthur Hopkins snapped up the rights to produce and direct *Holiday,* and in turn Hope Williams came aboard in the central assignment. With a cast that included Ben Smith, Dorothy Tree, Monroe Owsley, and Donald Ogden Stewart (a Yale classmate of both Philip Barry and H. Phelps Putnam), Kate was hired to understudy Williams. *Holiday* tried out in New Haven on November 18, 1928. Eight days later it opened at the Plymouth Theater. It proved to be one of the season's major hits and enjoyed a 230-performance engagement.

Thrilled to be part of a hit Broadway show, even if she was merely the star's understudy, Hepburn dutifully reported to the 1,000-seat Plymouth Theater for each and every performance. From the wings she intently studied Hope Williams's performance, analyzing the leading lady's every movement and vocal gesture. Kate marveled how the charismatic artist showcased her clipped speech pattern and effectively turned her loping stride into an effective piece of stage business that captivated audiences.

❋   ❋   ❋

While Hepburn progressed from *Night Hostess* to *These Days* to *Holiday* in the last half of 1928, she was participating in an active social life. After Phelps Putnam suddenly vanished from her life, Kate relied increasingly on Jack Clarke and Ludlow Ogden Smith, who were living in Manhattan's Murray Hill district. Clarke ostensibly shared his flat with his unmarried sisters. The bachelor duo gladly squired their former Bryn Mawr pal about town. On her part, it suited Hepburn to be thought of as a chic member of the Park Avenue set who casually hung around with rich, well-bred suitors. It made her feel that she was in the same league with New York's premier club and stage darling, Hope Williams.

In August of 1928, during a weekend trip Hepburn made to Fenwick to view a boat race, obliging Luddy Smith (who had a car) accompanied her. It was his first opportunity to see the Hepburns on their home turf and to be exposed (literally) to strong-willed Dr. Hepburn. (The first night there, Smith witnessed the physician traipsing through the upstairs hallway with only a shirt on.) Luddy proved congenial to Kit Hepburn, who felt, as did her husband, that the meek Luddy would always be overshadowed by increasingly dictatorial Kate. As for the others in the house, Smith tolerated the practical jokes of the especially prankish Dick Hepburn (then seventeen), who was aided and abetted by Kate's younger sisters. That weekend, in the boat race, older brother Bob proved a worthy successor to his deceased sibling, Tom, in championing the family name in the nautical competition.

By September, Phelps Putnam was back on the New York scene and was showing his now-completed poem "The Daughters of the Sun" to his social and literary circles. It was soon gossiped about town that Kate was the subject of his passionate verses, and this buzz strengthened her position as a rising celebrity. Meanwhile, Smith, knowing he was far less colorful or dashing than his rival for Kate's companionship, moved himself into the background of her hectic life. If she required someone to accompany her to Connecticut, he was ready at a moment's notice to do her bidding, oblivious or uncaring how domineering she could be.

Ever the indecisive romantic, Putnam, in renewing his pursuit of Hepburn, did not apparently appreciate how much being an alcoholic, wounded-bird artist appealed to the nurturing—and needy—side of Kate. Phelps continued to hesitate to push his advantage and move their relationship ahead sexually. (This may have been the result of his vacillating nature in all matters, or his reaction to Kate's (sub)conscious setting of sexual boundaries.) For example, when he visited Kate in New Haven during the tryout of *These Days,* he registered at the Taft Hotel. He suggested to Hepburn that after the show's opening that evening they would return to his hotel to properly celebrate. Despite the titillating plans, the sexual consummation did not occur, with Kate perhaps too jittery about the play's future to focus on less essential matters. Phelps soon faded permanently from Hepburn's life.

Back in New York, Luddy took advantage of the poet's latest departure to reinstate himself as Kate's primary escort. One day, while Jack Clarke and his sisters were away, Smith and Hepburn were at Clarke's apartment. Luddy felt it important to prove his masculinity, and Kate thought it high time she lost her virginity so that milestone would be out of the way. The two went to bed together, although Hepburn knew herself sufficiently well to realize that she did not love Smith as more than a compatible friend. Kate would admit in her memoir years later that she was too preoccupied with her desire to become a star to find great meaning in this sexual coupling with Ogden. In short, the duo were great pals who had stepped over the line, if briefly, into an essentially meaningless sexual escapade.

✳   ✳   ✳

After understudying Hope Williams for a few weeks on Broadway, Kate began experiencing a gnawing sense of being a show business failure. The star was parading onstage nightly to great acclaim and seemed far too healthy and stable to ever miss a performance. Hepburn was at a crossroads. She could sit out the play's engagement on the sidelines, or she could give her notice and once again start the dreaded process of making casting rounds.

The show business ritual (and necessity) of presenting oneself at theater managers' Broadway offices in hopes of being considered for a new venture had always been an especially nerve-racking task for essentially shy Hepburn. She abhorred pushing through the crowd of other candidates to gain a disinterested secretary's attention in order to ask that humiliating, stale question: "Anything for me today?" As she recounted, "By the time I had visited one or two offices my face would be moist with perspiration, my hair disarranged and my clothes in disarray. But I was too bashful to ask anyone where the ladies' room was and would spend minutes roaming around the building trying to find it myself."

Another time Hepburn detailed, "I was always fighting fear. Every morning I would start out, determined to walk into a theatrical office and command the attention of the producer. But invariably, by the time I reached the building that housed his office, I would be so excited and wrought up that my first concern was to find a refuge where I could powder my nose and adjust myself mentally." She continued, "After tramping the corridors, I would be so agitated and my makeup would be in such confusion that, in defiance, I would scrub my face with soap and water until it was shiny. Then I would comb my hair straight back and in that guise drive myself into the office, to have the stenographer come out, take one look at me, and then go back in, closing the door behind her." On one unbearable occasion she sat for "three full days…in [producer] A.H. Woods's outer office, watching others come in, get past the girl and into the private sanctum, and then leave again—while I remained. Yet, I was actually afraid to ask how others got in to see Mr. Woods—and finally gave up in despair."

Disheartened by the prospect of making those horrid rounds once again, Kate Hepburn made a decision. She agreed to wed Luddy, which must have surprised her friend as much as it did her. But now there seemed to be no turning back for either of them. They could only hope that great camaraderie would make living together a satisfactory arrangement. The bride-to-be made a particular request of her groom-to-be. She did not want to be known as Kate Smith. Not only did the full name sound too plain (for career or social purposes), but there was a fast-rising, heavy-set performer on Broadway and in vaudeville who bore that same name. Hepburn did not want to be confused with anyone else, least of all with the robust Kate Smith, who soon would claim fame in recordings, radio, and pictures and be known as the Songbird of the South. To the deep chagrin of Luddy's patrician, dominating mother, Smith agreed to the name alteration. Thereafter, he became S. Ogden Ludlow, with Kate and the Hepburns still addressing him as Luddy or Lud.

Having given her notice to Arthur Hopkins, Kate left the cast of *Holiday*. The publicly unannounced marriage took place in the living room of the Hepburns' West Hartford home on Bloomfield Avenue on Wednesday, December 12, 1928. Octogenarian Reverend Hepburn was summoned from Virginia to officiate at the small ceremony. Kate wore a white crushed velvet dress with muted gold embroidery trim. As a wedding gift, Dr. and Mrs. Hepburn presented the bride with a Danish silver hot water kettle.

The couple embarked on a brief, passionless honeymoon to Bermuda. Upon their return, they began house-hunting in the further reaches of suburban Philadelphia, in turf considered part of the swank Main Line. Touring these expensive country houses built for upscale gentlemen farmers, Kate became overwhelmed by what her future would be like—away from the lights of Broadway. Then too, she had already had encounters of the strained kind with the imposing Gertrude Smith. It convinced Hepburn that neither Kate nor compliant Luddy was a match for this imposing matron who looked so askance at her precious son having wed someone in show business.

Scarcely two weeks after they arrived in Philadelphia, Kate and Luddy abandoned their plans for a Pennsylvania life. Hepburn came back to New York and popped into Arthur Hopkins's office. She asked for her understudy's job back. The producer readily agreed, remarking pleasantly, "I expected you. I knew you'd return. But why?"

With her career in motion again, the newlyweds took up residence at 146 East Thirty-ninth Street. It was a small, remodeled house that had once been a stable. They paid $110 a month rent. Deciding he needed a career to preoccupy himself, Luddy became an insurance broker with offices in midtown Manhattan.

Kate should have been pleased that her spouse—still so involved with his pal Jack Clarke—was so obliging in so many matters, but (sub)consciously it bothered her that he was such a pushover. The more he yielded to her wide-reaching demands, the more she expanded her domination over him. It made her realize that what she really wanted—needed—was a man whose nature was more like that of her intractable dad.

Returning to her nightly activity at the Plymouth Theater as Hope Williams's standby, Hepburn utilized the time to soak up whatever she could learn from watching the cast go through their onstage paces. She was determined to be starring onstage one day soon and made no effort to disguise her ambitions. Unused to interacting on an equal level with most anyone other than her family, she came across as snobbish, rude, and cold to the *Holiday* players. She remained unaware, or unmindful, of her negative effect on her colleagues. Meanwhile, after the theater curtain came down each night, she mingled with the Broadway crowd. More often than not, Luddy did not accompany her, as she spent increasing time with those members of the show business–celebrity set who welcomed her into their fold as an entertaining oddity.

As 1929 progressed, Kate wondered if she would have the opportunity to perform in *Holiday* at all before the show closed that June. Hepburn would claim later that Hope Williams graciously offered to call in sick for a performance to give her understudy the chance to go on. Kate insisted, "But of course I wouldn't do that," reasoning that it would not be cricket to showcase herself in such a fashion. Hepburn's rationale seems far too idealistic to be the actual case. It is much more likely that the unique and playful Williams—divorced in 1928 from her doctor husband—had no intention of allowing this often abrasive upstart to play her custom-made role, not even once. Privileged, iconoclastic Williams, who oozed all the confidence that good breeding and a healthy financial portfolio provides, was sexually liberated and had a roving eye that included the same sex but did not seem to fasten on ambitious young Kate. (Free-spirited Hope wandered in and out of bisexual Mercedes de Acosta's social circle, one that included over the years such Broadway names as Katharine Cornell, Beatrice Lillie, Alla Nazimova, and Eva Le Gallienne as well as actor-lyricist-producer Nancy Hamilton, who became a good pal of Kate Hepburn's and would be her understudy in 1932's *The Warrior Husband.* Years later, Hepburn would say of the great Le Gallienne, who was one of her idols and an acquaintance, "I knew she was queer but I didn't think it queer that she was.")

Despite the complicated ongoing dynamics between Hope and Kate, Hepburn acknowledged later of the magnetic Miss Williams: "I stole a great deal from Hope. She was the first fascinating personality from that period, 1929 to 1932, which wasn't really ready for her. She was a woman who blossomed with a little more than she was supposed to."

When *Holiday* concluded its Broadway engagement in June 1929, Kate and Ludlow embarked on a European holiday. Having inherited a tight-fistedness in money matters from her dad, Hepburn insisted they make the trek on the cheap. Luddy disapproved but, as always, did as his wife wanted.

Hardly had the couple arrived back in Manhattan from their Continental lark than Kate received a phone call from Arthur Hopkins's office. The showman was preparing the road tour of *Holiday.* Hepburn was asked if she could immediately take over the play's lead role for one night at the Riviera Theater on upper Broadway. Kate still remembered all the heroine's dialogue and agreed. During the short-notice performance she unabashedly aped Hope Williams's portrayal down to each gesture and every vocal inflection. To Kate's astonishment, she didn't get the laughs as Hope had and, in general, the audience did not respond to her imitation performance. Only then did Hepburn truly appreciate how gifted Hope was and that a real star must bring her own personality to the part.

Chapter Eleven
STAYING THE COURSE

"[Katharine Hepburn's] career in those [pre-Broadway star-dom] days appeared to consist of understudying and getting fired. Yet we all knew (all us hopefuls sitting around in Sardi's or the Penn-Astor Drug Store, standing in Shubert Alley or in the hallway outside [producer] Chamberlain Brown's office) that this high-class broad 'A' broad was going to make it. What is more, she knew it, too."
—actor-director-writer Garson Kanin, 1971

October 24, 1929, became known as Black Thursday. On that day the American stock market crashed with nearly 13 million shares traded and an estimated several billion dollars lost by investors.

For Dr. and Mrs. Hepburn, the start of the Great Depression saw the physician's annual $40,000 income drop to around $10,000, and the family had to tighten their financial belt for the next several years. As Kate was never a big spender and Ogden Ludlow's (and his family's) holdings were sufficiently diversified to weather the economic storm, the quality of their life did not change much. However, the Broadway theater felt the impact of the financial tornado. Fewer plays were being mounted. Investors with discretionary cash were harder to come by, and the typical theatergoer had more pressing priorities than a night of stage entertainment.

✳ ✳ ✳

Steadfast in her determination to make her mark on the Broadway stage, Hepburn overcame her aversion to those dreaded casting rounds. Her repeated efforts paid dividends in the fall of 1929. She was not only hired for *Death*

Takes a Holiday but was chosen for the lead female role at $250 weekly. In Walter Ferris's adaptation of Alberto Casella's poetic fantasy, she would be seen as Grazia, who falls in love with Death. The latter has arrived on Earth to learn why mortals fear him so. When he departs she accompanies him. Originally, the great John Barrymore had hoped to play the challenging stage part of "His Serene Highness." However, prior movie commitments prevented him. Philip Merivale inherited the key role.

Succumbing to the mounting pressures of proving herself in such a major theatrical undertaking—especially in a drama so alien to her unfanciful nature—Kate constantly feuded with director Lawrence Marston. Hepburn wanted to mold the heroine into a tomboy; Marston disagreed. Rather than be guided by the experienced director she challenged him at every turn. The show tried out in Philadelphia at the Adelphia Theater. With her first name misspelled in the program, things went from bad to worse for Kate. One reviewer referred to Hepburn as the "skeleton girl with the raspy voice." She was devastated by the slam, and costar Philip Merivale cautioned her that reading reviews was always a dangerous business.

One night in Philadelphia, during the week of November 25, the stage manger came to Hepburn's dressing room and said, "Will you sign this?" It was a statement that she was resigning. Kate was puzzled until the stage manager explained that in actuality she was being fired. She said, "How can you have the brainlessness to come and tell me that before a performance?" He said it was the rules. (Another variation of the incident had producer Lee Shubert, who wanted a bigger name in her crucial part, offering Kate a face-saving out by resigning rather than being fired. She had exploded, "Resign, hell. If he wants me out of the cast, he can kick me out!" Later in life, Hepburn would retell the story to *The New York Times.* In this rendition she came across as the strong woman affronted far more by the breach of etiquette than from being let go. "I said, 'Well, I'm not taking that privilege [of resigning], so if you want to fire me go ahead, but get out of here because you'll be lucky if I don't kill you.'")

When Kate learned that she would be making her final appearance as Grazia that coming Saturday night she phoned Dr. Hepburn with the bad news. She recalled, "Father drove all the way from Hartford to Philadelphia to catch my last performance. He managed to sit through it. Right after the final curtain, he came storming backstage. 'They're absolutely right!' he shouted. 'You were carrying on on that stage, you were galumphing around there like a maniac! Who's going to believe that my daughter, a big healthy girl like you, could fall in love with death! With death for God's sake!'" The physician helped his daughter pack her belongings and drove her home. At the time she thought her parent had been an insensitive brute in his evaluation of her performance. Later, she admitted, "I see how right my father was, now that I see I've become just like him. I'm a realist now. I like plays and movies about real life."

Rose Hobart replaced Hepburn in *Death Takes a Holiday*, which debuted in New York in late December 1929 and ran for 181 performances.

❉   ❉   ❉

Before Katharine Hepburn had accepted the *Death Takes a Holiday* acting challenge, she had acquitted herself well in auditions for *Meteor*, being produced by the prestigious Theater Guild and starring the prominent husband-and-wife acting team of Alfred Lunt and Lynn Fontanne. The drama by S.N. Behrman was to be directed by Philip Moeller, who thought the young performer would be suitable for a featured part in the prestige vehicle. Since it was understood that the Lunts must pass on the casting of subordinate roles, Hepburn had to be approved by them. Months earlier, Lynn had agreed to give Hope Williams—whom Kate so resembled and aped—pointers about acting. While intrigued with Hope's personality, Lynn felt her acting style was unfathomable and almost immediately abandoned their coaching sessions. In contrast, Fontanne found Katharine a more compatible persona, someone with whom she could work. (The fact that Fontanne, like her spouse, was bisexual, might have factored into the star's decision to want Hepburn to join the troupe.) Having passed muster with both the director and the coleads, Hepburn met with Theresa Helburn, a cofounder of the Theater Guild and a Bryn Mawr alumnus. Initially, Helburn was put off when Kate arrived for their meeting "carelessly groomed," but she soon became impressed by the "electric force" of the applicant's personality. Theresa offered Hepburn a $200 weekly salary to do *Meteor*, but Kate declined the job in favor of *Death Takes a Holiday*. (Hepburn and Fontanne, who developed a polite rivalry in later years, remained in contact over the decades. Kate paid a visit to Lynn at the latter's country home in Genesee Depot, Wisconsin, in 1982, a year before Fontanne's death at age ninety-five.)

Now at liberty, Kate overcame her pride and again called on Miss Helburn at the Theater Guild. It was too late for Hepburn to be reconsidered for *Meteor.* However, Theresa was mounting *A Month in the Country,* a translation of Ivan Turgenev's classic Russian drama. To be directed by Rouben Mamoulian, it was to star the exotic European Alla Nazimova in a cast that included Alexander Kirkland and Dudley Digges. Mamoulian vetoed the applicant for a featured role because of her inexperience. However, he felt that Kate had a special quality and recommended her to his casting director, Cheryl Crawford. In turn, the latter hired Hepburn at $30 weekly to understudy Eunice Stoddard in *A Month in the Country* in the role of Viera Aleksandrovna. Hepburn was in no position to refuse this offer, which was a great comedown from Kate's short-lived important assignment in *Death Takes a Holiday.*

After a week of tryouts in Washington, D.C., *A Month in the Country* premiered at Manhattan's Guild Theater on March 17, 1930. It received decent reviews. As Hepburn had studied Hope Williams intently during the *Holiday* run, now Kate used her new understudy position to observe the great Nazimova in action. Hepburn was fascinated by the famed Russian who mingled a naturalistic, intense acting style with theatrical flourishes that kept audiences mesmerized.

The next month, when Douglass Dumbrille, Leonard Mudie, and Franchot Tone were brought in as cast replacements for *A Month in the Country,* Kate was asked to take over Hortense Allen's part as the maid. Since Hepburn was continuing as Miss Stoddard's understudy, she felt she deserved a $5 raise for doing double duty in the production. Management felt differently and Kate performed her chores at the original fee. (Hepburn would not forget the slight and would have her "revenge" in years to come.) Meanwhile, the highly emotional Nazimova, as passionate about her acting as her assorted same-sex relationships, had no rapport with the uppity-acting Hepburn. At one juncture Alla informed the casting director, "I don't want that girl in the company. She's never on time for rehearsals. Her excuses are that she's been fencing or taking lessons or playing tennis. Fire her." Hepburn was again at liberty. She took the opportunity to take a two-week holiday to Europe with Eunice Stoddard, a young friend from the company of *A Month in the Country.*

* * *

Throughout these roller-coaster years of attempting to overcome the hurdles of Broadway, Hepburn continued studying with Frances Robinson-Duff. Another member of the latter's student entourage was aristocratic Laura Harding, a bright twenty-eight-year-old blonde who had an impressive Social Register pedigree. Harding's maternal grandfather was Jay Cooke, who had helped to finance the Northern cause during the American Civil War. Another of her relatives had founded a prestigious Wall Street brokerage firm. Laura's father was banker J. Horace Harding, chairman of the board of the mighty American Express Co. and a board member of several other major firms. When he died at the start of 1929 he left his family holdings worth several million dollars, which included a country estate, a Fifth Avenue mansion, and a highly valuable art collection.

Laura had attended Miss Porter's fashionable finishing school in Connecticut and traveled on the Continent, and she later became one of Manhattan's most noteworthy debutantes. Deciding to dabble in the theater (as had that other blueblood, Hope Williams), Harding studied acting with Frances Robinson-Duff, apprenticed at the Berkshire Playhouse in Massachusetts, and had gained roles in a few out-of-town theatrical productions. But acting was really only a lark for the patrician single lady who much preferred horseback riding and other strenuous athletic activities. (As a child Laura had been a well-pampered tomboy who looked and acted far more like a male than a female.)

Very soon after starting lessons with Robinson-Duff in 1928, Laura and Kate had met at the acting coach's house, as one was arriving and the other was leaving. Forthright Harding's initial reaction to Hepburn was, "She's not my type.... She had long hair pulled back in a knot, a man's sweater pinned at the back with a big safety pin—what we called a Brooks sweater—and a tweed skirt." On her part, however, Hepburn was immediately drawn to the sophisticated socialite who was so confident about life and so knowledgeable about so many matters. The infatuated Hepburn suggested that the two go out for dinner and become better acquainted. Before long they became great friends, with Laura becoming the fourth member when Kate, Luddy, and Jack went out on the New York nightclub scene. After Kate's impetuous marriage of convenience to Ogden, Hepburn continued to further her special friendship with energetic, decisive Laura, resulting in the two women having a much fuller, more far-reaching dimensional relationship than Hepburn was experiencing with her nominal mate, the passive Luddy.

✳   ✳   ✳

In the spring of 1930, with Kate having no acting prospects lined up, Robinson-Duff suggested that since Harding was returning to the Berkshire Playhouse for the coming summer season, it might do Hepburn good to participate in the same training program. Hepburn promptly agreed.

The Berkshire Playhouse, located in the Bay State's picturesque Stockbridge in the western part of the state, had begun operation in 1928. It was already attracting an impressive array of established performers (e.g., Richard Hale, Edith Barrett, Geoffrey Kerr, and June Walker) as well as up-and-coming talents (e.g., Jane Wyatt, George Coulouris, Leo G. Carroll, and William Tracy). The venue was then operated by executive producer Alexander Kirkland (Kate's fellow cast member from *A Month in the Country*) and director F. Cowles Strickland.

In the summer of 1930 the company of thirty troupers boarded in a one-bathroom sprawling farmhouse operated by a minister, his wife, and two daughters. Kate and Laura, the group's two pranksters, shared a cozy room, which further cemented their status as intense soul mates.

Robinson-Duff had urged Kate to undertake the Berkshire Playhouse experience to sharpen her acting skills and hopefully to learn to interact more harmoniously with fellow actors. Whatever Kate's initial good intentions, she arrived at the New England theater in a posture of arrogance. At the boardinghouse dinners she was constantly argumentative on whatever topic came up for discussion. For example, if someone praised a book of poetry, Hepburn was sure to take the opposite point of view. In particular, Hepburn delighted in baiting the slightly older George Coulouris. On one occasion it prompted him to say, "You're a fool, Katharine Hepburn. You're a fool. You'll never be a star. You'll never be important in the theater. You don't make any sense at all." Kate retorted, "You're the fool. I will be a star before you're ever heard of."

During their Stockbridge sojourn, Kate and Laura became great chums. Hepburn was impressed by the sophisticated Harding, who had great poise and who dispensed practical advice on how best to handle a delicate situation. In contrast, refined Laura was attracted to Hepburn's vitality and to her undisguised obsession with succeeding in show business. It was eye-opening for the socialite to discover from Hepburn that obtaining a role was not the key thing, but getting the star part was. Both of the pals shared a great sense of fun, although Laura had doubts about ever taming her new friend's often brash behavior.

While the two women were forging a strong, complex bond that would last until Harding's death in 1994, reliable, undemanding, and preoccupied Luddy toiled in New York City. Left alone, he found social and sexual diversions to suit his tastes. (By now the Kate-Luddy marriage had long been one of in-name-only, a platonic friendship unencumbered by bothersome sexual interplay.) On weekends, ever the gentleman, he dutifully drove the 175-mile trek to the Berkshire Playhouse, a tiring ride in an era long before superhighways. No sooner would he arrive at his destination than Hepburn would, perhaps, dispatch the exhausted motorist to fetch her and Laura ice cream from the nearby village. Thereafter, Luddy would retire alone at a local tourists' lodging, leaving Kate and Laura to their own devices.

In the Berkshire Playhouse troupe, Kate and Laura were among the subordinate players assigned to very small parts in each week's new stage production. Harding had already experienced this grueling routine, which offered little glory. Never having starred on the stage before, she found the situation amenable. However, Hepburn increasingly bridled at her reduced professional situation. In *The Admirable Crichton* the two friends played titled ladies. In *The Romantic Young Lady* and *Romeo and Juliet* they had equally nondescript assignments.

In one of these productions, Hepburn was directed to walk to the wings and call out the name of a character. Throughout rehearsal week she insisted on shouting the name of her best friend, "Lau-au-ra!" The director argued,

"If you keep doing that in rehearsal, you'll do it opening night." Undaunted, Kate yelled again for Laura Harding. At this, the director lost his temper: "Miss Hepburn, you just can't do that!" "No?" retorted Kate. "Who's going to stop me?"

Throughout these weeks Hepburn told one and all that she was the actress best suited for the lead in every production. "I asked for decent parts," she would remember, "and they gave me strictly mediocre parts in which I was mediocre. After three of them I quit." (Hepburn was scheduled to appear in *The Torchbearers* with Coulouris but left before this show was staged.)

* * *

Back in Manhattan, Hepburn, unrepentant about her poor working attitude at the Berkshire Playhouse, resumed her efforts to find stage work. During this period she spent a great deal of quality time with Laura Harding. When the two were not gallivanting about Manhattan, they might head off on a brief vacation. One of their several intimate treks was to the rural Ogontz Lodge, a small, informal resort in Salladasburg, west of Williamsport, Pennsylvania. The quaint lodge, a rugged outdoorsman's paradise, had been established in 1884 by Harding's great-grandfather Jay Cooke. The out-of-the-way, rustic facility boasted such distinguished past guests as President Warren Harding. (In later years, Kate would return to Ognotz with a new companion, movie star Spencer Tracy, when he needed to dry out from his latest drinking binge away from the prying eyes of Hollywood.) Besides the area's scenic beauty and sporting activities, one of the local attractions was visiting the nearby Cohick's Trading Post, where one could sample the proprietor's delicious homemade ice cream.

* * *

Eventually Kate was cast in *Art and Mrs. Bottle; or, the Return of the Puritan* by Benn W. Levy. The lead role of the middle-aged woman who had abandoned her husband and two children twenty years earlier for the sake of a romantic fling now ended went to Jane Cowl. The veteran stage star was famed for her deeply expressive eyes and delicate, quivering gestures and was ideal to play Celia Bottle, who returns home to find both her adult children (G. P. Huntley Jr. and Katharine Hepburn) embroiled in disastrous romantic relationships.

During rehearsals, Hepburn coped as best as possible with the artistic vision of director Clifford Brooke but quickly aroused the antagonism of the show's playwright. A Britisher used to strict professional decorum, Levy was put off by Kate's bohemian rehearsal togs and in particular by her freckled face, which seemed so distractingly shiny. "What does she use to get that shine?" he asked Jane Cowl. "Cold water and yellow soap?" (In actuality, Hepburn had developed the habit of carrying a small flask of rubbing alcohol on her person. During rehearsals—on the sly—she would repeatedly douse her face with the liquid. This was part of her now-entrenched fetish for cleanliness and a persistent urge to cool herself. Amid her daily routine, she was forever taking cold baths, often eight or nine a day. At night, when she was usually too hyperactive to fall asleep, she often wrapped her feet in wet cloths, hoping to relax herself.)

One day, when Levy was making snide remarks about Kate to Jane Cowl, the star asked the writer, "What don't you like about her?" Levy charged, "She looks a fright, her manner is objectionable, and she has no talent." Thereafter, Jane took Kate aside and persuaded her to try conventional stage makeup. However, the experiment didn't work, as the powders kept streaking because of Hepburn's alcohol applications. It made her skin tone look garish.

As preparations for the Broadway opening proceeded, Levy reached a saturation point and had Hepburn fired. Thereafter, fourteen other ingenues were tried out as replacements but none of them seemed right. Finally, a night before the show was to premiere, Cowl said to Levy, "Remember that Hepburn child?" He certainly did. However, since it was a desperate situation, he agreed to Kate being rehired. (One of the supporting cast with whom Hepburn got along with best was British-born Joyce Carey, a lifelong spinster. Carey was a good friend of Noël Coward and would be one of many friends Kate had in common with the playwright's predominantly gay crowd.)

Art and Mrs. Bottle opened on November 18, 1930, as part of Jane Cowl's repertory season at the Maxine Elliott Theater. The cast, especially Kate, received better notices than the "inconsequential" piece. Alison Smith (*New York World*) reported, "An uncommonly refreshing performance was given by

Katharine Hepburn as the young daughter." Gretta Palmer (*New York World-Telegram*) rated Kate "delightful, if a bit high-strung." Howard Barnes (*New York Herald Tribune*) judged Hepburn to be "agreeable to look at, assured and altogether a proficient actress."

At this particular juncture Hepburn was not sharing the East Thirty-ninth Street accommodations with preoccupied Luddy. She was again staying at a friend's massive eighteen-room Park Avenue apartment loaned while the acquaintance was out of town. Said Kate, "I dashed through the empty rooms, shouting at the top of my lungs!" It was with dedicated Laura Harding that Hepburn celebrated her successful opening night.

The following evening after the play's debut, Cowl rushed into Hepburn's dressing room to congratulate her on her fine reviews, one of which stated it had preferred Kate's performance to that of the veteran star. Jane exclaimed, "My dear, we've done it! I knew you'd sweep them, if you got the chance! I'm so happy and proud for you!" Shocked (and touched) by the star's generosity, Kate answered, "Are you really glad? I thought you'd be sore."

However, onstage there were some growing conflicts between the two performers. Early in the first act, Kate makes her entrance and kisses Cowl's character. Opening night the embrace had left a vibrant Cupid's bow on Jane's cheek. After the performance, Cowl suggested that Hepburn utilize a lipstick that would not leave a telltale mark. The next night the same thing happened again. Cowl reasoned that Kate must have forgotten the advice. When it occurred yet again the following evening, Jane was less forgiving. Confronting the younger talent she asked, "Dear, why didn't you get some of that other lipstick?" Hepburn blithely responded, "Well, I just thought I mightn't like it." For the remaining run of the show, Cowl made sure to keep Kate at arm's length in this particular scene.

Several years thereafter, when Hepburn was reminded of her self-centered response to the star of *Art and Mrs. Bottle*, Kate responded rhetorically—and a bit self-servingly—"Could I possibly have been so rude to so lovely a person? It seems incredible, doesn't it? And unforgivable!"

Chapter Twelve
FAME ON THE GREAT WHITE WAY

"There came a time in my life when I had to face the issue
of motherhood squarely. I was quite young, but it was time
to think about my future. It was a matter of being the best
actress I could be or becoming a mother. But not both: I
don't think I could do justice to both. Acting was right for
me. A career was important to me then as it is now.
"I'm not sure any woman can successfully pursue a career and be
a good mother at the same time. The trouble with women today is
they want everything. But no one can have it all. It's ridiculous to
compete in a man's world on a man's term."
—Katharine Hepburn, 1977

During the late spring of 1931, Kate Hepburn was once more professionally at liberty. She again tried her luck in summer theater. This time it was at
the well-regarded Ivoryton Playhouse in Connecticut where she was contracted to perform in three productions: *Just Married, The Cat and the Canary,* and
The Man Who Came Back. Since the theater was located only nine miles from
Fenwick—and forty-seven miles from Hartford—the proximity made it relatively easy for the Hepburns to attend performances. (The ever-faithful Laura
joined Kate for her latest summer theater excursion, both acting in shows
there and being on hand to encourage and comfort her inseparable companion.) Although not playing lead parts at Ivoryton, Kate had interesting supporting roles. Driven to prove herself, she worked exceedingly long hours to
sharpen her characterizations. (After watching Kate in *The Man Who Came
Back,* a romantic drama involving drug addiction and prostitution, Dr.
Hepburn—a man who rarely complimented anyone—told his daughter, "This
is the first time I've ever thought you might have some talent.")

❋   ❋   ❋

Unbeknownst to Katharine Hepburn, the highly successful playwright Philip Barry (1896–1949) had just returned to New York in the fall of 1931, having been with his family at their Palm Beach, Florida, retreat. (Barry, then thirty-five, was married and the father of two sons.) He had a new play almost ready for production. It was titled *The Animal Kingdom.* Again dealing with the themes of marriage and illicit relationships, Barry's latest work revolved around a love triangle: a publisher, his manipulative wife who convinces him to compromise his professional standards, and the married man's mistress. The sophisticated thesis explored which of the female characters was more a true-loving wife than a calculating mistress. The talented Barry based the married characters on unsuspecting acquaintances of his. As to the inspiration for Daisy Sage, some sources insist it came purely from the author's imagination; others said that it had been written expressly for a Hope Williams–type actress.

The in-progress project was shown to stage and film star Leslie Howard, who was so enthusiastic about starring in the drama that the Britisher offered to coproduce the venture with veteran Broadway presenter Gilbert Miller, the latter set to direct the vehicle. Kay Strozzi was cast as Cecilia, the scheming bride. At the time Hope Williams was involved in a Hollywood film contract (which went nowhere) as well as pending Broadway projects of her own. Remembering Williams's understudy in *Holiday,* Barry suggested Katharine Hepburn as a likely candidate to play Daisy Sage, the hero's intellectual and spiritual equal. Miller was dead set against the casting, recalling all too well the playwright's last project (1931's *Tomorrow and Tomorrow,* a hit show) when Barry had insisted that relatively inexperienced Zita Johann play the female lead and there had been problems with this casting. Despite the producer's objections, the playwright dug in his heels and demanded that Kate be cast as Daisy. She was duly hired.

It took a long three-month process before Hepburn was actually hired for *The Animal Kingdom* in late October 1931. In the interim she auditioned for other upcoming stage productions but turned down all offers because she was convinced that the Barry play—and her sizable part—would be her best showcase. Once Kate came aboard the Barry vehicle, problems proliferated. To begin with, there was little chemistry between the thirty-eight-year-old English-born matinee idol and his fourteen-year-younger colead. Howard complained to the management that this demanding "beanpole" of a woman (whom he found unfeminine and hard-edged) hindered him from doing his best onstage, while she carped that her married leading man—who had a strong penchant for extracurricular romances—"resisted her" in their scenes together. (On one occasion when Kate inquired of her leading man, "What would you like me to do here, Mr. Howard?" he responded, "I really don't give a damn what you do, my dear.") Repeatedly, the playwright arbitrated between the warring forces, but no satisfactory compromise was forthcoming.

Refusing to give in to the disharmony, Kate rehearsed hard for this major assignment. The evening of her fifth day of run-throughs, she was informed by management at quitting time, "You needn't come in tomorrow. It's Saturday and the rehearsal will just be perfunctory." That evening she was at home in Manhattan, chatting with two classmate friends of her brother Richard, then at Harvard. Kate recalled, "We were planning what fun we'd have in Boston if the show opened there... There was a knock at the door... I felt a chill chase itself up and down my spine... I knew...I knew it was my notice. It was...and somehow all the fight suddenly went out of me."

Part of the reason for Hepburn's hasty dismissal was a practical matter. Actors' Equity Association required that if an actor rehearsed as much as six days, the person was thereafter entitled to two weeks' notice with pay. In later years, Kate would explain her summary dismissal with, "Leslie Howard fired me. He said, 'Get rid of that kid fast'...I didn't do anything to him but I was an inch taller..." (Howard's various film studio biographies of the 1930s list him at anywhere from five feet ten inches to six feet tall. Even if part of this height was due to his rumored use of shoe lifts, he still was visually taller than five-foot seven-inch Hepburn, unless she was wearing very high heels.)

What Kate kept a blind eye to then—and later in recalling this phase of her career—was that her real-life general disinterest in the opposite sex was carrying over into her stage work. She was still too inexperienced and without sufficient confidence onstage to effectively disguise her true emotional/sexual orientation. Thus she was ill equipped to play effectively the typical heterosexual heroine that playwrights were creating for audiences of the day. It was this factor that often alienated casting agents or coplayers, sometimes without their being able to pinpoint why the offbeat, strident Hepburn was unsuitable to handle a strongly feminine role credibly.

With Hepburn out of the cast, *The Animal Kingdom* began its pre-Broadway tryout in Pittsburgh. Frances Fuller took over Hepburn's relinquished role, while Lora Baxter soon replaced Kay Strozzi as Cecelia, the wife. The drama premiered on Broadway on January 12, 1932, to positive reviews and ran for 172 performances.

Deeply upset by this latest dismissal, Hepburn brazenly contacted Philip Barry at his Mount Kisco, New York, home. He was then taking a bath, but she insisted she must speak to him immediately. When he came to the phone, she embarked on what the playwright later described as a "a fishwife tirade." Among other things, she shouted, "You can't let them do this to me! You've always said I was ideal for the role. I am! I'm it! They're ruining your play! They're gypping me! I won't stand for it!" Finally, the genteel author lost patience and interrupted, "They're right about you! Nobody with your vicious disposition could possibly play light comedy! You're totally unsuited to the part! I'm glad they threw you out!"

This was not to be the end of the tiff between Kate and Philip Barry. The two encountered each other two years later in Hollywood, where Hepburn was then making a film. The playwright walked onto the set on the RKO lot. When Hepburn completed the scene, she rushed over to Barry and attempted to renew their argument where he had broken it off. Hepburn recalled, "He still thought I was no good. I still know I was good!"

* * *

Concerning her humiliating *Animal Kingdom* fiasco, Kate Hepburn admitted many years later, "That firing was a big blow to me and I thought, I'll never survive this." However, as would be the case throughout much of her life, she had a wonderful support system to buoy her up from her many crashing professional defeats. There was her family, especially her parents. There was also always sympathetic Ogden Ludlow, and now there was ever-present, loving Laura Harding who helped to cushion the emotional impact of Kate's recurrent career missteps.

By now the Ogden Ludlows were living in new headquarters—or, at least,

Kate was. It was at 244 East Forty-ninth Street. It was part of a unique enclave built in the mid to late nineteenth century. By the 1920s the area, known as Turtle Bay Gardens, had fallen into a state of disrepair. A buyer bought all twenty houses at once, ten on East Forty-ninth Street and ten on East Forty-eighth Street. Six feet of land was carved off the back of each property for the creation of a common garden with paths leading to the back of each dwelling. Two tall willow trees and a replica of a Villa Medici fountain became the hallmarks of the garden. Kate's eighteen-foot-wide, four-story brownstone had been built in the 1860s and undergone renovations in the 1920s. The rent was $100 a month. Laura Harding tastefully decorated her friend's new residence.

Having had a sham marriage since shortly after their rash union in late 1928, the Ludlows still felt no need officially to divorce. It served both their purposes to still appear to the world to be a wedded couple, even if now Luddy had been "exiled" to a not distant hotel where he generally resided and carried on his own sexual escapades. (Occasionally, he stayed in a basement room at 244 that had been designated as "his.") For Hepburn, progressive on so many topics but conservative when it came to personal issues involving her unconventional lifestyle, remaining a married woman was important at the time. It provided her with a convenient buffer against the potential advances of theater coworkers or of randy males she encountered socially. Her marital status also provided a distraction to onlookers from the New York social scene wondering why she spent so much time—day and night—with her bachelor pal, Laura.

❋   ❋   ❋

In 1952, Kate Hepburn would recall in a *Time* magazine cover story of her regard in the theater of 1932: "One lot said I was a lovely, graceful young creature. Another lot said I was gawky, hoydenish, gaunt, like something escaped from a tomb." This conflicting career evaluation was sufficient to rob even strong-willed Kate of her professional confidence on many occasions. But whereas other actors in such a rut might have abandoned the theater, Kate persisted, determined to proved to herself and to the world that she was star material.

By early 1932, Kate experienced a bit of good luck—thanks inadvertently to Hope Williams. Arthur Hopkins was producing a stage farce titled *The Warrior's Husband*. In this Julian Thompson comedy set in mythological times in Asia Minor, the action revolved around Amazon women who are the warriors while their rather effeminate men remain at home to keep house. This unusual state of affairs ends when a contingent of Greeks invade the island. Their mission is to grab the sacred girdle of Diana, which will rob the warring females of their physical proficiency. From the start of Hopkins's involvement, it was a given that boisterous, bold (and tomboyish) Hope Williams would play the role of Antiope, the royal Amazon. However, the latter, unable to ignite her Hollywood career, suddenly decided that she wanted to return to Broadway in a more substantial vehicle than *The Warrior's Husband*. So Hopkins showcased Hope in *The Passing Present*, a domestic drama that opened in early December 1931 and then closed after sixteen performances.

Meanwhile, Julian Thompson acquired the producing rights to *The Warrior's Husband* and after casting his net for likely leading ladies decided that Kate Hepburn—that most unfrilly of Broadway's current crop of ingenues—just might do in the tough-to-cast pivotal role. In typical fashion, she was fired during rehearsals—not once but twice. However, the management and director Burk Symon could find no one more suited than Hepburn to play the athletic, butch lead, and she was eventually reinstated.

With a cast that included Colin Keith-Johnston, Romney Brent, and Bertha Belmore, the play bowed on March 11, 1932. From the moment that Hepburn made her first appearance onstage she had the audience in the palm of her hand. Her wardrobe consisted of a silver breastplate over a short tunic (which showed off her lanky figure and her shapely legs). She sported silver-colored leather shin guards and sandals. Her arms, legs, and face were covered in bronze makeup and her red hair was drawn back into a tie, with swirls of little curls breaking loose in front and at the nape of her neck. For her dramatic entrance, she charged determinedly down a narrow, thirty-foot stairway carrying a large (stuffed) antelope on her back. Reaching the bottom, she hurled the carcass at the feet of the Amazon monarch. Next, she dropped to one knee and ordered a nearby attendant, "Get me a bowl of water, will you. I'm in a terrific sweat!" With that the agog theatergoers went wild.

If the critics had mixed reactions to this gimmicky stage offering, they were almost all intrigued by Hepburn's striking looks and especially by her bold, swaggering vitality in *The Warrior's Husband*. Brooks Atkinson (*New York Times*) labeled her performance "excellent." Arthur Ruhl (*New York Herald Tribune*) decided the leading lady "suggests a somewhat tougher and more dynamic version of Maude Adams's Peter Pan." Richard Garland (*New York World-Telegram*) championed that "Katharine Hepburn come into her own" in "a role worthy of her talent and her beauty." Garland further observed, "It's been many a night since so glowing a performance has brightened the Broadway scene."

Energized by the praise she was receiving from the critics and theatergoers alike, Kate found irony in the fact that she gained her first theatrical acclaim in a "leg show." While in its initial Broadway run, *The Warrior's Husband* did terrific business. However, soon the novelty of the gender-reversal story line wore off and attendance began to dip. (In 1932, as the Great Depression deepened, it was increasingly difficult for many Broadway productions to maintain their box-office momentum.) It was not long into the engagement before Hepburn's leading-lady salary—an unremarkable $100 weekly—was reduced to $79.50 as part of the management's economy to keep the large-cast show afloat. *The Warrior's Husband* lasted eighty-three performances.

While Kate was starring on Broadway eight times weekly, she continued her habit of spending every possible weekend (from Saturday night after the show until Monday) with her family in West Hartford. Sometimes doting Laura Harding accompanied her; other times Luddy was pressed into service to shuttle his increasingly famous wife to and from Connecticut.

Breaking into Hepburn's spring 1932 routine was Leland Hayward, a highly personable Nebraskan who had attended Princeton University briefly and then tried various occupations in the Hollywood film business before becoming a talent agent based in Manhattan. Married to a Texas society lady, he nevertheless had a roving eye for interesting women, who in turn were easily captivated by this tall and dynamic individual. With Hepburn now the talk of Broadway, he quickly began courting her to join his talent agency, a business he shared with the Los Angeles-based Myron Selznick–Frank Joyce firm. His plan was to negotiate a movie deal for her.

Laura Harding recalled having met Leland during her debutante days when he had attended fancy Manhattan dances, usually based in the stag line and always chasing after the prettiest girls at the party, intent on seducing them. Initially Hepburn, who had never used an agent for her stage work, found Hayward far too pushy and much too facile. Besides, although her childhood ambition had been to become a great movie star, her intentions now were to stay in the theater and rise in fame up the Broadway ladder. Nevertheless, on June 17, 1932, finally won over by Leland's tenacity, Kate signed a management and personal representation agreement with Hayward and his West Coast associates.

※　※　※

Because of Kate's sudden popularity from *The Warrior's Husband,* movie studios began making token offers of contracts for this suddenly in-vogue stage personality. Hayward had discussions regarding Hepburn with Paramount Pictures. This studio had been particularly successful in recruiting rising stage names (e.g., Claudette Colbert, Fredric March, Kay Francis, and Miriam Hopkins) because the film company maintained a studio in the Astoria section of Queens, which made it easy for theater people to make movies while still appearing on Broadway. At the moment, Hepburn really was not interested in pursuing her luck on the silver screen, and informed the Paramount executive, a Mr. Salsbury, that she truly did not care to make a screen test. She did promise, however, that if she ever changed her mind, she would do a film audition for his lot.

In contrast, RKO Pictures was more persuasive in their pursuit of this red-headed Broadway novelty. Lillie Messenger of RKO's New York office was asked to supervise a screen audition of Hepburn, one of many talents being considered for an upcoming project, *A Bill of Divorcement.* Both disinterested and intrigued, Kate reluctantly agreed on condition that she choose her test scene and the actor to perform the audition with her. She selected willowy Alan Campbell from the supporting cast of *The Warrior's Husband.* (The gay Campbell would soon marry acerbic critic-writer Dorothy Parker, an alcoholic who was ten years his senior.) Hepburn informed the obliging Campbell, "Alan, don't bother to learn you part, because I don't want you to get the part. I want me to get it." Hepburn explained, " I was so egomaniacal that I didn't even have a director for the test. I thought, this I can do. Nothing bothered me. One had a sort of total control." Because she felt everyone else who tested would be doing dialogue from the project in consideration, Kate chose to do a scene from *Holiday,* a show she still knew letter perfect from her days understudying Hope Williams.

Once having made the RKO audition, she felt obliged to follow through on her pledge and do a screen test for Paramount. For that tryout she did a sequence from *The Animal Kingdom,* the Philip Barry play from which she had been fired. She did the test with another coplayer from *The Warrior's Husband,* Colin Keith-Johnston. (There was also talk of Kate testing for Fox Films, which had acquired the screen rights to *The Warrior's Husband,* which for a time was going to be directed by that studio's John Ford. In addition, there was hype that Hepburn, who had acquitted herself so well on the stage in a vigorous, manly type of role, might agree to play the title role in a screen version of *Hamlet.*)

While Hollywood was deciding what to do—or not to do—with Katharine Hepburn, she had other obligations. She had agreed to a one-performance engagement of *Electra* in Philadelphia with Blanche Yurka in the title role. Kate also contracted to team with Henry Hull (repeating his role from the 1931 Broadway comedy) for a production of *The Bride the Sun Shines On* to be done at a summer theater in Ossining, in upstate New York.

Chapter Thirteen
WELCOME TO HOLLYWOOD

"I came along at a point in the movie industry when nothing like me had ever existed—with a loud voice and a very definite personality and a rather belligerent look."
—Katharine Hepburn, 1984

Of the major Hollywood studios (e.g., Columbia, Fox, Metro-Goldwyn-Mayer, Paramount, United Artists, and Universal) in the early 1930s, RKO Radio Pictures was both the newest and the smallest. It was founded in early 1929 as the cumulative result of business negotiations between David Sarnoff, president of Radio Corporation of America (RCA), and Joseph P. Kennedy, a business tycoon involved heavily with film lots like FBO (Film Booking Offices of America Inc). The RKO enterprise was launched with such productions as *Rio Rita* (1929—a big hit) and *Cimarron* (1930—a Best Picture Oscar winner but a financial loser because of its high production cost).

In early 1931 the fledgling RKO combined with Pathé, a preexisting studio and distribution company. Thanks to the merger, RKO acquired the screen services of two major Pathé leading ladies: patrician Ann Harding (1901–1981) and sophisticated Constance Bennett (1904–1965). They and RKO's versatile Irene Dunne (1898–1990) became RKO Pathé's trio of female luminaries. By the fall of 1931, David O. Selznick, the son-in-law of MGM mogul Louis B. Mayer, was placed in charge of RKO studio production. It was part of an ever-changing lineup of RKO regimes, a situation that would prevent the studio from gaining its own personality. However, the frequently shifting control of power at RKO assured a constant infusion of new go-getters.

Thus RKO, with its main headquarters at 780 Gower Street in Hollywood, was equally the most exciting and the most frustrating of film lots for its personnel. One of the chief advantages of being part of this facility was that it was a small enough operation so that workers felt part of a professional family. On the other hand, in contrast to larger moviemaking facilities, there was less margin for a talent to be forgiven for failing.

One of David O. Selznick's initial projects was to give the go-ahead for filming *A Bill of Divorcement,* a successful British play (1921) that had furthered Katharine Cornell's career when she starred in the Broadway edition that same year. (There had been a 1922 British-made silent screen adaptation of the drama.) Initially, Irene Dunne, Anita Louise (a personal favorite of Selznick's), and England's Jill Esmond were in contention for the female lead. When they were not cast for various reasons, Selznick ordered the testing of new candidates both in Hollywood and New York. One of them was Katharine Hepburn.

When Kate's audition was screened for Selznick and the picture's assigned director, George Cukor (1899–1983), the RKO head was unimpressed by Hepburn's unusual look and by her gauche oncamera movements. Cukor, who had a shrewd eye for raw talent suitable for the screen, had to agree with his boss about Kate's offbeat appearance (by Hollywood standards). However, there was one oncamera moment in which Hepburn set down a drinking glass and reacted thoughtfully to the dialogue. This brief footage convinced sensitive Cukor, best known as a woman's director, that he could mold this toothy, aristocratic stage player into a cinema force—even with the obstacle of her decidedly masculine mannerisms. He persuaded the reluctant Selznick to negotiate with Kate to take on the film role.

The bidding for Hepburn's screen services began at $500 weekly. Because Kate was uninterested in a Hollywood career—both from snobbishness at moving from the lofty stage to the more crass film business and because of her fear of failure in a new medium—she instructed Leland Hayward (by now her representative) that she wanted $1,500 weekly for her services. She picked the hefty sum at random, convinced that such a figure would never be met. (She had talked over her pending demand with her parents: Her mother said to accept a lesser fee, while her father insisted she should stick with the higher number.) Now having her heart set on a certain salary, Kate informed Hayward that it was $1,500 weekly or nothing. One day during this negotiation period, Hepburn visited Leland's Manhattan offices three times over a six-hour period. Each time she presented herself in a different outfit. Her scheme was to impress her smooth-talking agent with her financial standing to demonstrate that she was not desperate for money (as were so many other performers during the Depression) and could certainly hold out for her demands. (For Hepburn, who could always count on her family—or even Laura Harding—in a pinch to help out with her living expenses, money was equated with power and her consuming goal of gaining great fame.)

Eventually in the dealmaking, Selznick told Leland, "I like her, but she's got no right to demand fifteen hundred. I won't meet any such figure. That's final!" Hayward, a sly master of bargaining, responded with an inspired suggestion: "She'll never give in, but look here; in the theater she's used to rehearsing free, and she's green. I'll tell her you'll meet the fifteen-hundred figure for four weeks, but that she'll have to give you a rehearsal week free. That's the equivalent of five weeks at twelve hundred." With that, the RKO decision maker said, "I'll do it!" (Other sources state that the weekly sum Hepburn received for *A Bill of Divorcement* was actually $1,250.)

* * *

Hepburn was performing in *The Bride the Sun Shines On* in Ossining, New York, when she received a telegram telling her the movie deal had been made. She was to report to the RKO lot in Hollywood as quickly as possible. Kate arranged to leave her summer stock engagement after Saturday night's performance. The cast gave her a farewell party and Hepburn was Los Angeles–bound.

To accompany her to California for this one-shot picture deal, Kate gave little consideration to her nominal husband, who was still closely tied to Jack Clarke. For one thing, Luddy had his insurance business to run; for another, she realized he might be a professional encumbrance to her in Hollywood. Most people outside of her New York social-stage set were unaware that she was married, and she thought it would be more beneficial when making her first impression with the Tinseltown crowd by appearing to be single and footloose. Kate, however, was used to having a friendly figure close at hand, so she decided it would be comforting to make the trek with the socially prominent Laura Harding, whose Social Register connections would give Hepburn cachet in the new setting. (Besides, it was likely that wealthy

Harding would generously step in to take care of the bills along the way.) Since Laura still nurtured mild aspirations for an acting career, she readily agreed to the trip with her best friend. (In the more naive atmosphere of the 1930s, few people found anything strange about two women traveling together as close companions, so neither Kate nor Laura gave much initial consideration to the possibility that their togetherness would spark rumors in Hollywood about their being more than platonic friends.)

Laura boarded the Super Chief in New York City. She was joined some hours later by Kate, who met the luxury train at a stopover not too far from Ossining. The two happily shared a compartment on the several-day trek to the West Coast. (Also aboard, unknown to Kate, was stage star Billie Burke, who had been hired to play Hepburn's onscreen mother in *A Bill of Divorcement*. She was accompanied by her seriously ill husband, Broadway impresario Florenz Ziegfeld.)

The trip to the West Coast was marred by an oppressive heat wave engulfing much of the country. It prompted Kate and Laura to spend as much time as possible on the open platform of the Super Chief's observation car. Just past Albuquerque, New Mexico, as the inseparable duo viewed the impressive landscape, flecks of steel lodged in Kate's eye and she was unable to remove them. By the time they reached their disembarkation point in Pasadena, California, Kate's eyes were red and puffy. Annoyed by this setback, Hepburn hoped that her designer gray suit and matching pancake hat—selected by Laura from a Manhattan couturier's latest collection—would compensate and allow her to make a good impression.

Kate and Laura were met at Pasadena on July 1, 1932, by Myron Selznick. He was Leland Hayward's partner and the older brother of Hepburn's RKO boss. Myron took one look at his new client—with her outré outfit, her hair pulled back unflatteringly into a bun, and her swollen eyes—and moaned, "This is what David's paying $1,500 a week for?"

As production on *A Bill of Divorcement* was set to start almost immediately, Myron straightaway escorted the two women to the RKO studio. There Kate made a less than stellar entrance onto the lot, given her eye problem, her fatigue from the trip, her distracting outfit, and her singular mannish demeanor. She was ushered into George Cukor's office. The director was aghast when he first set eyes on Kate, now convinced that he had made a dreadful mistake in pushing her cause so strongly with RKO. As the lunch hour was approaching, he reluctantly escorted gauche Kate and the elegant Laura into the studio commissary, where the skinny, freckle-faced Hepburn caused everyone to gape (and snicker) in disbelief. After an uncomfortable luncheon, George ushered Hepburn into Selznick's office, fearing the studio chieftain's reaction to this very untypical candidate for screen stardom.

The disquieting meeting with David was short-lived, with the womanizing Selznick barely hiding his disdain for this arrogant Easterner who, in the flesh, seemed so hopeless a gamble for Hollywood success. Next, George had Kate examine costume sketches for the film. He wanted her reactions to the planned wardrobe for her role as Sydney Fairfield. In her typically contrary and unvarnished fashion, Hepburn blurted out that she had been hoping her wardrobe would have been entrusted to a far more famous designer, such as the internationally renowned Chanel. Annoyed by the newcomer's audacity, Cukor churlishly retorted, "Considering the way you look, I can hardly take your judgment seriously."

Hepburn countered that she thought her outfit was stylish, to which the gay filmmaker rejoined, "I think any woman who would wear such an outfit outside a bathroom wouldn't know what clothes are. Now, what do you think of that?"

Kate froze as she digested this latest volley in the power play between the two. Then she smiled briefly and announced, "You win. Pick out the clothes you want!" It was the start of one of Hollywood's most productive working relationships and friendships—one that endured until Cukor's death in 1983 at the age of eighty-three.

That same day George introduced Hepburn to John Barrymore, the star of her first film. At age fifty, "The Great Profile" remained handsome and dapper. Much in professional demand, he was receiving a $50,000 salary for *A Bill of Divorcement* plus a percentage of the picture's profits. Upon meeting Kate, Barrymore immediately noticed her red, swollen eyes. When an opportunity arose, he took her aside and discreetly handed her a small vial of eyedrops. The notorious heavy drinker confided to his coplayer that he always used them after a night of overimbibing. He explained that it worked magic to make him look clear-eyed on the sound stage the next day. He winked at this assumed fellow substance abuser and bid Kate good day.

Finally, with all the amenities and business of the day taken care, the studio found a doctor to resolve Hepburn's pressing eye problem. Later that evening, an exhausted Kate and Laura collapsed in their room and dined on chicken salad sandwiches that the hotel's bellboy brought them.

By morning, Kate was intent on showing the RKO brass that she knew a thing or two about style and status. So that day she and Harding arrived at the studio in a rented, chauffeur-driven Hispano-Suiza car. The huge and ornate foreign vehicle had been used onscreen by Greta Garbo in *Grand Hotel* (1932) and by this point was considered a clichéd example of affectation even in the excessive Hollywood milieu. When Kate proudly pointed out to Cukor her car parked on the RKO lot, refined George shuddered at her gaucherie. Kate, however, ignored his acerbic criticism and kept the car for months to come.

In short order the studio discovered another unique aspect to the fledgling movie personality. That day she posed for publicity photographs with coplayers John Barrymore and Billie Burke. The trio was asked to autograph glossy copies for visiting film exhibitors. The two senior performers obliged, but Kate refused. Cukor was furious with his protégée, but she would not budge from her stubborn position. The quirk remained with Hepburn throughout her professional life. (Rather illogically, over the years, she thought nothing of sending out many hundreds of hand-signed typed responses to fans, but autographing a photo was always a no-no for her.)

✳   ✳   ✳

Soon after Kate and Laura arrived in Los Angeles, they checked out of the Chateau Marmont Hotel and moved to a rented out-of-the-way cottage in Franklin Canyon, one referred to them by one of Harding's acquaintances. With Hepburn's eye condition now cleared up, she quickly found new ways to attract (un)wanted attention on the RKO lot. She arrived daily at the studio wearing coveralls, a worn man's work shirt, and scruffy sneakers. It was hardly the chic wardrobe of a typical screen leading lady. However, goaded by her unfortunate debut on the Los Angeles scene, Kate's contrariness led her to snubbing Hollywood's fashion demands—let alone other established social customs of the industry. Pushing her image as an eccentric individualist amused her (and Laura) and helped to divert Hepburn from her inner fears of not doing well in her all-important film bow. (In contrast, as a lark, the two friends would sometimes go shopping at a fancy boutique and purchase an assortment of extravagantly priced chiffon peignoirs, items that momentarily amused the inseparable duo.)

❋   ❋   ❋

Unbeknownst to George Cukor, aspects of Hepburn's role in *A Bill of Divorcement* strongly resonated with her. She was playing Sydney Fairfield, a well-bred young British woman engaged to marry. She envisions having a large family. Suddenly Hilary, her long-absent father, arrives at the family estate. She had been told by her mother that he was a victim of shell shock on the World War I battlefields of France. Since then he had been confined to a local sanitarium, too distraught these many years to see his family. In the interim, the mother had divorced Hilary, and she now plans to wed another. In short order, Sydney learns that her father actually is a victim of insanity that runs in his family and that only now has he regained (temporary) mental stability. Convinced that she might pass on such mental defects to her offspring, Sydney nobly breaks off her engagement. Both Hilary and Sydney urge the mother to pursue her marriage plans, with father and daughter agreeing to care for one another for the remainder of their lives.

To understand her character's tragic plight, Kate could refer back to the several suicides on both sides of her own family—including that of brother Tom. Hepburn also had the examples of her friends, Jack Clarke and his two sisters, who claimed their single status resulted from their fear of passing on the insanity that had destroyed their mother. (One can only speculate whether the heroine's reasoning in *A Bill of Divorcement* factored at all into Hepburn's real-life decision never to have children. If so, she hid this key motive. Instead, on one occasion Kate explained, "Right off, before I was married and the minute I started my career, I made the decision never to have children. You see, I was brought up in a very happy family, the second of six children and I could see how terribly difficult it was for a mother to have a family and work. Mothering is the toughest job there is—no Sundays off—and I knew I couldn't get involved in a lot of little creatures I was responsible for and have my work. I'm too self-oriented." Another time, the legend publicly reasoned, "Only when a woman decides not to have children—as many now do, realizing there are already too many children—can a woman live like a man. That's what I've done.")

❋   ❋   ❋

On the first day of shooting *A Bill of Divorcement*, Hepburn and Cukor clashed. An arch stickler for protocol, Cukor was aghast that Kate had dared to arrive on the sound stage wearing what soon became her trademark—slacks. In this era, with the exception of bisexual superstars Marlene Dietrich (at Paramount) and Greta Garbo (at MGM), it was unheard of for a movie leading lady to be so attired. An unamused Cukor spat out, "I will not have my leading lady wear pants!" Hepburn looked her director squarely in the eye to take his measure. She responded with "Fine" and proceeded to remove her slacks. The amusing anecdote made the rounds of Hollywood and made quite a stir in the film colony.

On the plus side, the gay, discreet, and noncontroversial Cukor, particularly sensitive on how to best showcase his leading ladies, did his best to present Hepburn favorably oncamera. (He had already conferred with the makeup and hairdressing departments to ensure that Kate's facial freckles were sufficiently covered over and that she sported a flattering, chic hairdo.) The director also insured that she was given a special entrance within the story line, one in which she makes her way down the steps of the family home to greet her guests. Later in the film, she was provided a sympathetic moment where she smiles at Billie Burke's character as the latter departs for church with her newfound love. Immediately thereafter, Kate's Sidney returns to the living room, where she lies down in front of the lit fireplace to contemplate her future. Such carefully arranged focal sequences gave filmgoers full opportunity to adjust to Hepburn's untypical leading lady looks, to appreciate her beguiling lanky figure, and to become accustomed to her unique, forthright, and mannish personality. (The fact that Kate was playing an upper-class English character, as she would frequently do in her subsequent RKO pictures, helped to explain away Hepburn's overly articulated, high-class vocal mannerisms, which were alien to most American filmgoers.).

During the making of *A Bill of Divorcement*, Kate was sympathetic to Billie Burke's distraction as her real-life husband's physical condition deteriorated. Florenz Ziegfeld Jr. died on July 22, 1932, midway through filming. However, Burke, a trouper, carried on with her screen assignment. Like Cukor, David Manners (cast as Hepburn's fiancé) was homosexual. On the sound stage Hepburn responded to David's gentle, nonthreatening demeanor, and the two became pals during the shoot. One day the two were waiting to shoot a scene. Perfectionist Cukor noticed that one of Manners's shoes had a spot on it. Always the full-blown elitist, Cukor shouted for someone in wardrobe to remedy it. However, before anyone realized what was happening, no-nonsense Hepburn said, "I'll take care of it." She swiftly got down on her knees and cheerfully polished David's shoe with the hem of her dress.

Among this solid cast, however, Hepburn interacted most with Barrymore.

Kate closely watched the great Barrymore as he went through his paces in his melodramatic role. She was impressed that he often redid their sequences, announcing that he was convinced he could bring more subtlety to the part on a retake. (Initially Hepburn was unaware that several of these retakes were for her benefit. They were done in conjunction with Cukor to help Hepburn adjust her stage-trained movements, projection, and reactions to the camera's more intimate demands.)

The much-married Barrymore, a middle-aged, legendary lothario, felt it was his obligation to make a token pass at his leading lady, even though Kate was far removed from the conventional feminine, curvaceous women he pursued. This occurred one day in his sound stage dressing suite, where he suggested Kate come to rehearse one of their upcoming scenes. When she arrived she found him reclining naked on a couch, prepared to seduce her. Miffed, taken aback, and a bit amused, Hepburn diplomatically extricated herself from the potentially embarrassing situation. Once the Great Profile got over this rejection, the two worked in harmony. On more than one occasion Jack Barrymore confided to Cukor that he was convinced Kate was a star in the making and did his best to teach her the tricks of the screen-acting trade.

One other member of *A Bill of Divorcement* cast did not fare so well. As a favor to Kate, Cukor gave Laura Harding, who dutifully came to the set most every day, a brief bit in the film's opening party sequence. She was assigned to be one of the young socialites seen dancing before, and while, Hepburn makes her compelling screen entrance. During one take, as Laura stood at the bottom of the staircase, resting against the banister, the ball-shaped top of the newel post came loose in her hand. She reacted by handing it over to her dance partner, who, shocked by the unexpected bit of business, let out a yelp. An infuriated Cukor rushed over and slapped Laura for having ruined the scene, which had to be reshot.

Unlike Kate's father, who strongly believed in protocol and maintained his professional distance from hospital subordinates, Hepburn from the start found it easy—as well as useful—to develop a camaraderie with the film crew. In fact, she made a point of getting to know them on a first-name basis. She discovered that these blue-collar coworkers shared her directness and distaste for time-wasting formality. In addition, if she made these technicians well-disposed toward her, they would see to it that she was well taken care of during production.

During *A Bill of Divorcement,* Hepburn came to know Emily Perkins, a candid, dour, but sentimental Yorkshire widow employed in RKO's wardrobe department. One day Emily came on the set and found the leading lady perspiring and sitting in a draft. "Trying to catch pneumonia?," she remarked. "You don't look that dumb." Perkins ran off and came back with a shawl. Thereafter, Mrs. Perkins was assigned to Kate on a steady basis and, still later, Hepburn asked Emily to quit her studio employment and become Hepburn's secretary and live-in helper.

After the four-week shoot was completed in August 1932, there were several days of retakes for which Hepburn demanded additional payment. As a result Kate earned a total of $7,125 for her screen debut. By late September 1932, *A Bill of Divorcement* was ready for release, but by then Hepburn had fled back to the East Coast with Laura Harding.

Chapter Fourteen
THE NEW GARBO

"I'm not leery of other people. The explanation for me is I'm leery of myself. I get frightful nervous indigestion. Practically everything or anything can give it to me. But especially throngs of people. At parties I'm in agony. Maybe...maybe I'm terrified I'll be neither the bride nor the corpse.

"All this isn't something new with me. I've been cursed with it all my life. As a youngster, whenever I was invited out to dinner and wanted desperately to create an impression, I'd sit there tongue-tied with self-consciousness, physically unable to talk. Sooner or later I'd have to get away from the table, go somewhere and lie down. I'd be ill. I made up my mind then that I was going to find a kind of life for myself where I'd never have to go to dinner."
—Katharine Hepburn, 1940

Throughout production of *A Bill of Divorcement,* David O. Selznick remained nervous about "his" discovery, Katharine Hepburn, whom many about town mocked as a snotty, horse-faced upstart with a grating voice. However, as the picture's final cut was being assembled and test audiences responded surprisingly favorably to this unusual screen personality, the studio executive had a distinct change of heart. He convened a summit meeting with Hepburn at his Santa Monica, California, beach house. He was represented by several studio attorneys, while Kate had Myron Selznick, Leland Hayward, and the shrewd Laura Harding on her team. The opposing factions hammered out a several-picture contract with options for additional films. Among other terms, it provided Hepburn with a lucrative pay hike, appropriate screen billing, and approval of several facets of each new film assignment. Importantly, she gained the right to perform in a Broadway play once a year.

Hepburn and Harding returned to New York via train. Luddy, keeping up the pretense of being a diligent husband, dutifully rushed to Grand Central Station to meet his celebrity wife, but he was pushed aside by the rush of reporters who were unaware of who he was. While Laura unwound at her family's spacious retreat in New Jersey, Kate and her spouse sailed for Europe with plans to motor through Austria and Switzerland. (Luddy, far more than his wife, hoped to miraculously salvage their marriage of sorts before she returned to the West Coast for more picture-making.) While their significant others were abroad, the left-behind Laura Harding and Jack Clarke cooled their heels on the East Coast waiting for Hepburn and Ogden to return to New York.

The mismatched Kate and Luddy were still on the Continent when *A Bill of Divorcement* debuted in October 1932. While the picture and many in the cast received complimentary reviews, it was Hepburn who proved to be the sensation of the new release. The *Los Angeles Examiner* judged of Hepburn: "That piquant little face and her earnest characterization just about carry off all the acting honors." Harrison Carroll (*Los Angeles Evening Herald Express*) enthused that Kate was "one of the most distinctive personalities to reach the screen in a long time." He reasoned, "Because of her vitality, her temperament, her unusualness...she exerts a peculiar fascination.... It is entirely possible that she may become a star." The *Los Angeles Record* perceived, "She is a remarkable looking girl...not so much beautiful as vividly attractive, and vividly intelligent looking. She is a long shred of a girl who moves with a rather stiff awkwardness which gives the illusion of distinction just because it is highly individual.... Her voice is decidedly metallic, almost brassy at time. While it is not particularly flexible, she achieves the effect of a wide range by sensitive retrained emphasis and delicate shadings."

The New York film critics were also intrigued by the exceptional screen newcomer. Thornton Delehanty (*New York Post*) advised, "All she needs is a little more familiarity with the microphone, some worthy roles and a firm determination not to let her producers exploit her as a second Garbo, a second Joan Crawford, or a second anything." Mordaunt Hall (*New York Times*) extolled, "Miss Hepburn's characterization is one of the finest seen on the screen."

Leland Hayward wired Hepburn that *A Bill of Divorcement* was a big hit in America and that she was to return home at once to start a new RKO picture. Deciding that her new screen status demanded she no longer travel tourist class, Kate and Luddy booked upgraded passage aboard the *Bremen,* which arrived in New York harbor in mid month.

When Hepburn had been making her first picture, RKO's publicity department had little luck in gaining cooperation from Kate, not even to learning the basic facts of her life. Since no one predicted she would make a successful screen bow, no real effort was made to push the issue at the time. Now that *A Bill of Divorcement* was a substantial hit and Hepburn had become Hollywood's hot new commodity, the studio was caught off guard as how best to respond to the media and public's thirst for information on Kate. Since Hepburn was away in Europe, the publicists fabricated a background for their new star. They suggested that she was the heiress daughter of an extremely wealthy New York banker. Rather than hide her eccentricities, the studio flacks exaggerated them. Casting Hepburn in the mode of the elusive Greta Garbo, they touted Kate as the most colorful individual in years to emerge on the Hollywood scene.

When the press discovered that Kate was arriving back in Manhattan by ocean liner, they flocked to greet her. (Luddy obligingly made himself scarce and delayed his disembarking until the ruckus subsided.) A bit overwhelmed by the fanfare, Hepburn gained control of the situation and herself by answering the fawning reporters' questions with—to her mind—ridiculous responses. To her amazement, her bizarre replies were taken as gospel. For example, when one newsman inquired if the rumors were true that she was married, she said, "I don't remember." Another reporter asked if she had children. She shot back, "Yes, two white and three colored." (It was also in this transitional period when both studio and star were fabricating and/or embellishing Hepburn's backstory that Kate established that her birth year was not 1907 but 1909 and that her birthday was *not* May 12 but November 7. The latter was the natal day of her late brother Tom and it was her special way of paying tribute to him—in essence, carrying on in his stead.)

Soon Hepburn left the East Coast to return to RKO. Once again well-meaning Luddy was left behind, and once again Laura Harding accompanied the rising film star to Southern California. This time the much-in-demand Kate was greeted at the Pasadena train station by, among others, handsome actor Joel McCrea. He was the rising RKO hunk who was to costar with Hepburn in *Three Came Unarmed* to be directed by Gregory La Cava. As a promotional strategy, RKO publicists were already concocting a studio-staged "romance" between the intended costars. However, privately, hunky McCrea, still a footloose bachelor, told friends that he found La Hepburn far too masculine for his taste.

No longer novices to the Hollywood landscape, this time the indivisible team of Kate and Laura rented an out of the way home in the Hollywood Hills, which past residents insisted was haunted. Because the two bachelor girls were again sharing digs, the more sophisticated among the film colony speculated anew about this offbeat twosome.

There were many aspects about this pair that Hollywood found baffling, beyond the tantalizing gossip of their being a lesbian couple. For one thing, they rarely participated in any of the numerous industry functions and refused to be part of the town's mainstream social life—at least on any regular basis. For some reason, being together brought out the prankish inner child in these two Easterners. With Laura the boisterous ringleader, the unbridled duo thought nothing of breaking into and exploring the homes of celebrities who happened to be out of town. Before departing the scenes of their crimes, they'd leave notes—unsigned—to document that the house had been invaded.

While the two unconventional women cavalierly refused invitations to glitzy premieres or fashionable dinner parties, they, for example, found it amusing to turn up unannounced at one industry figure's home on the night of a fancy gathering. The zany duo went directly to the kitchen, where they borrowed uniforms from the servants. So dressed, the interlopers served dessert to the perplexed hosts and their famous guests. Another time, Hepburn and Harding secreted themselves in the trunk of director William Wellman's limousine, only emerging after the vehicle reached his estate. Then the two jumped out and made faces at the bemused filmmaker.

Because Kate and Laura rarely—if ever—were spotted about town with dates and spent so much time together away from the limelight, it soon was assumed by an increasing number in the film colony that the two were lovers. Over the decades, the always calculating Hepburn would insist she found such speculation amusing. In contrast, Harding claimed—at least publicly—that she felt caught in a trap: If she denied such talk, it would be assumed she was covering over the truth, and if she ignored the hearsay, it seemed only to confirm the spicy allegations.

In Hepburn's case, there were several factors that when put together gave Hollywood cause to be convinced that she was lesbian or bisexual. Besides her close ties to Laura Harding, there was Kate's rigid refusal to wear feminine outfits; she instead, preferred to stomp about town in men's pants and often masculine-style jackets (designed by Eddie Schmidt, a noted men's tailor in California). Hepburn had a rationalization for her mannish attire: "It seems natural to me to wear overalls to work. I had been doing it for years and nobody had ever criticized me for it. But now, suddenly, my overalls were horrible examples of what no girl should wear. So were my dungarees. They weren't 'feminine.' They were 'mannish,' 'affected' and 'ridiculous.' If I wanted to wear something in the line of trousers, why didn't I wear women's slacks? For the simple reason that women's slacks weren't comfortable. In those days they had crotches down to the knees. Now they're tailored like men's slacks. And every girl in her right mind wears them. I was simply ahead of the times." (Hepburn's explanation changed few people's minds about her sexual persuasion. The local sophisticates were convinced that, like the trousers-affecting Marlene Dietrich, Hepburn was one of Hollywood's several leading ladies—e.g., Greta Garbo, Kay Francis, Claudette Colbert, Lilyan Tashman, Janet Gaynor, Barbara Stanwyck, and Tallulah Bankhead—who were bisexual or lesbian.)

Then there was the matter of Kate's strong friendship with the openly gay George Cukor. While the celebrated director often hosted elaborate parties at his Beverly Hills home for Hollywood's elite and the visiting famous—which Kate sometimes graced—he was also well-known for giving Sunday afternoon pool parties. At these occasions he entertained his male circle: homosexuals in and of the film industry as well as a changing parade of handsome and available young men. Kate, who had many gay acquaintances back in New York, frequently was present at these discreet weekend get-togethers where felt she could be more free to be herself. (There are photos of Hepburn relaxing by Cukor's pool in conversation with such staunch Cukor pals as film star William Haines and screen actor Anderson Lawlor, two well-known members of the Hollywood gay scene.) One weekend when Kate came for a private swim at George's pool, he arranged a treat for her. It was to meet one of her special screen idols, his good friend, the reclusive Greta Garbo. The two women bonded and kept up a friendship over the years. A few sources have speculated that the unlikely duo, who shared many traits (e.g., a thirst for privacy, a shrewd business sense, a fascination with life's basic chores) may have consummated their newfound relationship in a weekend tryst during Hepburn's first years in Los Angeles.

As it slowly became known in Tinseltown that repressed Hepburn actually had a husband back in New York, speculation became rife about why Ogden Ludlow never showed up in Los Angeles to be near his wife. Many observers concluded that his nonappearance indicated the domestic union was a sham geared to distract onlookers from examining the truth about Kate and Luddy's actual sexual orientation. In this viewpoint, they were quite correct.

❋   ❋   ❋

Not long after Hepburn returned to RKO, David O. Selznick abandoned *Three Came Unarmed* (a jungle story) because of unresolved script problems. (By then Kate had grown attached to the Gibbon monkey that was to have been used in the film, and she delighted in going about town with the frisky animal perched on her shoulder.) Instead, Kate was assigned to *Christopher Strong* (1933), a melodramatic vehicle originally intended for the studio's posh Ann Harding. The more urbane industry members arched their eyebrows in amusement at this replacement casting. Not only would Kate—in her first starring film project—be playing an independent (i.e., mannish) aviatrix, but she was to be directed by Dorothy Arzner (1897–1979), a sometimes lover of screenwriter Zoë Akins, who adapted the original Gilbert Frankau novel for the screen. Arzner was one of the few, to that date, women film directors in Hollywood. Known for her successful handling of pictures, the extremely butch-looking Arzner dressed in masculine garb and did nothing to disguise her lesbianism.

Arzner had been displeased when husky-voiced Ann Harding (who was shuffled to another picture) was removed from *Christopher Strong* in favor of Hepburn. The director was even less happy during the late December 1932— early February 1933 shoot when Kate constantly challenged her every directorial decision. (Some on the troubled set called it the battle of the "feminists.") At one point Arzner brusquely informed David O. Selznick that if Hepburn continued to undermine her authority on the set the frustrated filmmaker would quit the project. The peak of conflict between Hepburn and Arzner occurred over the picture's finale. In this sequence the pregnant, unmarried British aviatrix commits suicide by removing her oxygen mask during a test flight rather than force her married lover (played by stiff-lipped Colin Clive) to abandon his family to do right by her. The star was so upset by this death scene—which brought back flashes of her brother Tom's tragic end—that she pleaded illness and was absent from the shoot for two full days and parts of others.

Later in the filming of *Christopher Strong,* Kate came down with influenza and was hospitalized, shutting down the production for days. Meanwhile, widowed Billie Burke (of *A Bill of Divorcement*), who was cast as Clive's neglected wife in the picture, had been jockeying throughout the filming to develop a closer relationship with the leading lady, whom she found utterly fascinating. This led to Burke siding with Hepburn in her battles of wills with Arzner, thus exacerbating further the fires of discontent on the set between Kate and her sapphic director.

When *Christopher Strong* was released in March 1933, the general consensus was that the picture was little more than the "customary emotional orgy" (*New York Herald Tribune*). However, said Regina Crewe (*New York American*), one of those swept up in the Hepburn craze, despite, "That troubled, masque-like face, the high, strident, raucous, rasping voice, the straight, broad-shouldered boyish figure," this leading lady was "a distinct, definite, positive personality—the first since Garbo."

While the film was an artistic disappointment, it established Kate's screen mold (as a strong nonconformist), which she would expand upon thereafter: a bright, independent, and brave woman who nevertheless is wistful that her special standards, attitudes, and desires keep her so apart from the mainstream.

❋ ❋ ❋

Kate was back in New York in mid February 1933, as was ever-reliant Laura Harding. Hepburn felt compelled to deal with the unresolved situation with subservient Luddy, which had grown increasingly complicated. While she was out west, he had continued to be in touch with his in-laws, often driving to Connecticut for the weekend, where he had become almost a fixture at the Bloomfield Avenue home. Always ready to be the family's handyman, he was also their unofficial photographer who happily and constantly snapped photos of the household.

Meanwhile, during recent months Kate's relationship with Leland Hayward had extended beyond the traditional agent-client boundaries. Despite Leland's being married (for the second time) to Lola Gibbs, Kate had succumbed to his many manly charms. It can be speculated that Hepburn followed this emotional path because she felt it incumbent to keep Hayward, a top agent with many rival leading ladies on his client roster, firmly fixed on her as his top professional priority. Another reason for Hepburn's intimacy with Hayward could have been Kate's desire to keep at least a portion of the film colony distracted from knowing her true sexual orientation. Not to be overlooked was Kate's highly competitive nature, which found it an exciting challenge—no matter what it took to win—to make the woman-chasing Hayward her own. Such a victory would (and did) flatter her vanity and, possibly, that part of her psyche that wanted to believe that she truly was heterosexual.

In this period Leland frequently spent the night at the rented Los Angeles house Kate shared with Laura Harding. (One can only imagine how Laura felt being reduced to the third wheel in this surprising new coupling on Kate's part.) Making the cohabiting situation even more complex, Kate and Hayward had entirely different daily schedules. She arose at dawn, spent the day at the studio, came home for an early dinner, and retired soon thereafter to be fresh for the next day's filming. In contrast, he worked hard during the day at his office or in negotiations on the studio lots. In the evening, Leland typically made the round of local nightclubs and industry parties, networking on behalf of his clients and himself. Late in the night, he would return to Hepburn's place where the couple shared a bedroom. Both were so preoccupied with their career priorities that their relationship seemed merely a fun (adulterous) situation for the time being. Besides, from Leland's viewpoint, this special rapport bound Kate, one of Hollywood's currently most in-demand personalities, to him and to his agency. While back on the East Coast, Hepburn revealed to Ludlow her expanded relationship with the married Hayward. In typical fashion, Ogden raised no fuss, apparently hoping this indiscretion would fade and he, once again, would be the key man (if not lover) in her life. Thus, for the present, she let matters ride with her in-name-only husband. It did not seem important enough at the time to make a final break. Besides, as would prove true in the coming years, Kate had a way of hedging her bets when it came to her personal life, often having overlapping "exclusive" relationships so that she would always have ready options when her emotions wavered and situations altered.

❋　❋　❋

Initially, *Morning Glory* (1933), based on an unproduced play by Zoë Akins, was earmarked for RKO's chic Constance Bennett, who had done so well the previous year in another show business yarn, the studio's *What Price Hollywood?* Hepburn, however, was in producer Pandro S. Berman's office, saw the *Morning Glory* script, and liked what she read. She snuck a copy home and concluded the vehicle was *meant* for her. Meeting thereafter with Berman, she convinced him that she and *not* Bennett should play Eva Lovelace, the career-driven heroine. Another version of how Kate won the film's pivotal role was that Berman actually handed the *Morning Glory* script to Laura Harding and told her to read it. She did and in turn convinced her friend that it would be a wonderful screen part.

As reshaped for the screen and directed by Lowell Sherman (a replacement for Dorothy Arzner, who did not want to work with Hepburn again), the film mirrored, in many ways, Hepburn's own valiant struggle to gain a foothold on Broadway. Self-focused, naive, and eccentric Eva arrives in New York from Vermont. Soon she becomes acquainted with a highly successful Broadway producer (Adolphe Menjou), a jaded man-about-town. She also meets handsome young Joseph Sheridan (Douglas Fairbanks Jr.) a rising playwright and an intellectual. Fate quickly leads Eva to taking over a key Broadway assignment at the last minute and proving her acting mettle on stage. Thereafter, the middle-aged producer tells her he will manage her but not become involved romantically with her. Meanwhile, Eva rejects her playwright suitor. Facing her romantically lonely future, Eva vows not to be fearful of becoming a morning glory—a star who shines brightly but briefly on the show business firmament.

With a week of intense rehearsal, *Morning Glory* was efficiently shot in a brief eighteen days, including a re-creation of the balcony scene from *Romeo and Juliet,* which was deleted before the film's release. Hepburn received $2,500 a week for her services. Although the bisexual Akins had based the narrative on her sometimes friend Tallulah Bankhead, Hepburn pushed for script rewrites that softened the heroine's acerbic tone. In building her characterization, Kate looked to her own professional past and also relied on recollections of stage star Ruth Gordon's quirky, effective performance in a past Broadway vehicle.

During production Kate's slightly younger leading man, Fairbanks, long rumored to be bisexual, finalized his divorce from MGM screen star Joan Crawford. Meanwhile, Doug developed a fascination with Kate and finally convinced her to dine with him. (Like many men on the Hollywood scene, Fairbanks may have thought it a titillating challenge to try to seduce Hepburn.) When she pleaded the need to end their night out early, he drove her home. Returning to his car, he reviewed the evening's events. As he sat there, he was chagrined to observe duplicitous Hepburn rushing back out her front door and jumping into a car being driven by a man whose face Fairbanks couldn't make out. (It was Leland Hayward.)

Morning Glory debuted at the studio's New York showcase: Radio City Music Hall. Critical praise and moviegoers' word of mouth quickly turned the film into a substantial hit. For many, especially after Hepburn's hardedged performance in *Christopher Strong,* her starving actress who becomes a determined but vulnerable star was a pleasant revelation. Charles Parker Hammond (*New York Post*) noted, "Eva Lovelace gives her plenty of opportunities to display her more mellow side, which is something for which to be exceedingly grateful." Time magazine was more blunt: "Since *Christopher Strong* she has toned down her strident voice, taken off some of her angular swank in gesture and strut, found other ways to register emotion than by dilating her nostrils."

On February 26, 1934, when the annual Academy Award nominations were announced, Katharine Hepburn was in contention for the Best Actress Oscar with May Robson (*Lady for a Day*) and Diana Wynyard (*Cavalcade*). (It was the first of Kate's lifetime accumulation of twelve Oscar nominations.) Days later, on March 16, at the Fiesta Room of the Ambassador Hotel in Los Angeles, Hepburn was announced the Academy Award winner in her category. However, she had refused to attend the ceremony, as she felt that such industry competitions were meaningless. (In later years, she acknowledged she had been immature to repeatedly ignore such a key event and that her fear of losing had always kept her from being present at such occasions). Many in the audience of 1,000 at the Ambassador Hotel were not pleased at Kate's victory, thinking her too "high-hat" and not deserving of recognition from her peers. To snap the attendees out of their negative mood, movie star Will Rogers, who was that year's awards host, invited the two losers (Robson and Wynyard) to the dais and presented each lady with a rose. The onlookers loudly applauded this gallant gesture, further indicating their displeasure with maverick Hepburn.

Chapter Fifteen
THE ROLLER COASTER OF FAME

"Shoot me as I am, or not at all. I don't care how ugly you make me."

—*Katharine Hepburn's edict to studio publicity photographers in 1933*

Almost from the time that David O. Selznick took over production control of RKO in fall 1931, he intended to produce a new screen version of Louisa May Alcott's 1868 novel *Little Women.* As he developed the property, he decided to modernize the Civil War–era tale so that audiences would better relate to this sentimental drama of a loving family from a bygone century. Subsequently, after several hands fashioned the updated storyline, Selznick abandoned that concept and chose to be more faithful to Alcott's narrative. During this elongated preproduction phase, Selznick moved over to MGM in a key executive capacity. When Selznick departed RKO, he left *Little Women* to the new regime, headed by Merian C. Cooper.

As RKO finally prepared to start *Little Women* (whose budget would soar to $424,000—some sources claimed it eventually reached $1 million), there was general agreement that Katharine Hepburn should star. She would play the boisterous tomboy Jo, one of the four March sisters who optimistically confront life's tribulations in Concord, Massachusetts. Joan Bennett, Frances Dee, and Jean Parker were contracted to portray Jo's siblings, with Spring Byington as their brave mother, Marmee. Douglass Montgomery was hired as Laurie Laurence, the aristocratic next-door neighbor whom Jo, a budding writer, adores. (At one point in the preproduction of *Little Women,* Kate's brother Dick, an aspiring actor, was considered for a role in his sister's new vehicle.)

Since Hepburn first teamed with George Cukor for *A Bill of Divorcement,* the two simpatico friends had wanted to work together again. However, the right opportunity had not arisen, and now Cukor had followed his friend Selznick over to MGM. But the filmmaker still owed RKO another picture. Persuaded by Kate's great enthusiasm for the Alcott project and an unfrilly role that she found especially congenial to her own New England background and strong family views, George agreed to direct *Little Women.*

During the lengthy shoot (late June to early September 1933), RKO allowed Cukor a relatively free hand in mounting this prestigious, intricate production. With location shooting in and around Los Angeles, the sound stage settings were lovingly re-created—at great cost—to effectively reflect the book original. As on *A Bill of Divorcement,* Hepburn and Cukor brought out the artistic best in each other. Because of their close friendship, they trusted each other implicitly and shared confidences that few others knew. Thus, they understood exactly how far they could push each other on the set concerning creative matters without overstepping the proper boundaries between actor and director.

Even with their special kinship, there were times when the two strong-willed collaborators clashed during the making of *Little Women.* For example, as Cukor recounted, "In a technically difficult scene, she [i.e., Hepburn] had to run up a flight of stairs and spill ice cream on her dress. Since we had only two costumes, I warned her I'd kill her if she laughed and ruined the 'take.' Sure enough, she did the scene very skillfully and made the drop of the ice cream seem accidental but then, unaccountably, she giggled. I said 'You damned amateur' and slapped her firmly on the elbow."

On other occasions, George knew when it would be appropriate to kid his leading lady's growing status as a great cinema star—all for the benefit of the cast and crew. Cukor detailed, "She had this rather fancy scene in which she twirled around in a beautiful dress and spoke extravagantly of her dreams of becoming a great author or an opera singer. On that line, to everybody's delight, especially Kate's, we had a large ham lowered onto the set at the end of a rope." Another instance of Cukor's constructive wit occurred after the director demanded thirty takes of a difficult scene featuring Hepburn. She became so frustrated by the situation that she threw up. His response was, "Well, that's what I think of the scene too."

As *Little Women* wrapped production, George was extremely pleased with the results. He told one and all that Hepburn had been "born to play Jo" and that "she's tender and funny, fiercely loyal…Kate and Jo are the same girl."

When a rough cut of *Little Women* was assembled, Cukor invited Hepburn and some of his crowd to a private screening at his home. Following the showing, the always outrageous Tallulah Bankhead rushed over to Cukor. She emitted a terrible scream as she threw herself into George's arms. Then she gave a Kate a big hug and finished by falling to her knees in front of the nonplussed Hepburn. In that posture she gushed teary praise for her peer's screen performance. The director, long accustomed to such outbursts from freewheeling Bankhead, quipped, "Tallulah, you're weeping for your lost innocence."

Little Women enjoyed a highly successful premiere engagement at Radio City Music Hall in November 1933. The critics heaped praise on Hepburn, with *Time* magazine predicting that her star turn "is likely to place Katharine Hepburn near the top of the list of U.S. box-office favorites." The feature went on to gross $2 million in worldwide rentals. While named Best Picture of the Year in many polls and festivals, *Little Women* lost out in the Oscars' Best Picture Category to Fox's *Cavalcade*. That season Hepburn was nominated for (and won) Best Actress for *Morning Glory* and thus was not in the running at the Academy Awards for *Little Women*.

Years later, on the set of *The Rainmaker* (1956), Earl Holliman, one of Hepburn's coplayers, asked Kate about *Little Women*: "What did you play in that?" She replied, "My dear young man, you never ask a star what she played in a film for which she's famous." The role of vim-and-vigor Jo March remained among Hepburn's favorite screen performances. In fact, she said later in life, "I would defy anyone to be as good as I was in *Little Women*."

❋ ❋ ❋

During Hepburn's busy year of filmmaking in 1933, in which she became RKO's top female star, she furthered her reputation as one of Hollywood's most unconventional players. Besides the strangeness of her wearing coveralls or men's pants when not oncamera, she also broke with convention for a rising screen star by driving an unadorned station wagon. She insisted the plain vehicle was far more practical than being shepherded about town in a fancy limousine.

The movie fan magazines, so frequently rebuffed in their efforts to interview this elusive "New Garbo," got their revenge on uppity Kate by finding fault with the renegade leading lady, even after she won her *Morning Glory* Oscar. They made sure to publish such undiplomatic Hepburn pronouncements as, " I cannot understand why the private life of an actress should intrude in her public work, or why her public character should be forced into her private life." These same journalists gleefully underscored to their readers how shocking Hepburn's behavior was. For example, one day Kate had been spotted sitting on the curb outside the RKO administration building reading a letter. Was this proper decorum for a leading lady, these often sanctimonious magazine writers asked?

Kowtowing to the class structure of the Hollywood studio system, these fan publication scribes were also aghast that Hepburn broke with tradition by preferring to mingle with the blue-collar crew workers in the RKO commissary—behavior certainly not befitting a proper luminary. On location and sometimes at the studio, it was duly noted that Hepburn frequently brought picnic lunches prepared by her staff (or the omnipresent Laura Harding) for favorite members of the cast and crew to enjoy, leaving the others to suffer the menu provided by studio caterers.

The movie magazines delighted in detailing in print how temperamental—even by Hollywood's standards—Hepburn was on and off the set. It was recorded that one day in the commissary she said to an associate, "Do you suppose they gave me that frightful [serving] girl on purpose, to make me late in getting back to work?" Reportedly Kate behaved so outrageously to a studio hairdresser that the woman told her superiors, "I'd rather lose my job than work on Miss Hepburn." (When told of these past remarks years later, the mellowed Hepburn offered, "If I behaved like that, I was a stinker!")

In short, reckless Hepburn was building a cadre of adversaries among the fan press. Their bemused and/or sarcastic published coverage of Kate's actual (and rumored) doings would cause readers increasingly to reconsider their initial fascination with the iconoclastic Hepburn, a unique personality whom some fan magazine writers had already labeled "Katharine of Arrogance."

* * *

When not working at RKO or secreted at her rented Los Angeles home with Laura Harding and/or Leland Hayward, Kate kept in close touch with her family back east. (By now Dr. Hepburn was handling all of Kate's income. He invested the proceeds and doled out a "sensible" allowance to his obedient eldest daughter, who still thrived on being her father's best girl.)

While it was considered an established part of a star's duties to pose for publicity photos on the movie sets of other current leading players, Kate abhorred such time wasters. However, when she invited herself to Fox Films to watch scenes of the screen version of *The Warrior's Husband* (1933) being shot, she readily consented to be snapped by the publicity photographers. On this occasion, rather than being annoyed by the shutterbugs, Hepburn was too busy observing how Elissa Landi was faring in the butch role of the warrior princess that had made Kate a Broadway name. (At one point Fox had attempted to borrow Kate for *The Warrior's Husband,* but RKO chieftain Merian C. Cooper rejected that offer as he did a bid to have Hepburn star in a biography of dance great Anna Pavlova.)

Exotic Landi had been born on the Continent in 1904, the daughter of a cavalry officer in the Austro-Hungarian army. Her mother, touted as a blood relation to a monarch, Elizabeth of Austria, divorced her military husband and married an Italian count who adopted Elissa and her sister. Later Landi wed a British barrister and drifted into novel writing and acting. By the early 1930s the attractive blond performer with the intriguing Continental accent was separated from her stodgy spouse, had performed on Broadway, and had been placed under contract at Fox Films. The fair-haired, unconventional Landi—already pegged by the film colony as one of those leading ladies who often preferred offscreen to have sexual involvement with women—struck up a special friendship with Hepburn. The infatuation burned brightly and briefly on the Hollywood scene.

Kate had first met "double-gaited" Elissa at one of George Cukor's weekend parties, and the two vibrant personalities had been immediately intrigued with one another. (Hepburn was particularly drawn to the fact that Landi was a published novelist as well as an accomplished pianist.. There was also a narcissistic aspect to Kate being beguiled by charming Elissa, as the latter's profile bore some resemblance to the sharper-featured Hepburn's.) They each had experienced lavender marriages (i.e., unions of convenience) and respected one another professionally for having succeeded on the stage and screen without resorting to playing weak-willed heroines. In the late summer of 1933 Elissa found herself on loanout to Kate's studio. Landi came to RKO to costar with Francis Lederer in *Man of Two Worlds* (1934).

Although Hepburn's private life was already complicated by balancing her nonwork attention between demanding Laura Harding and vain Leland Hayward, Kate happily rearranged her busy schedule to share secret private time with arresting, strong-willed Landi, whom more than one film critic of the day described as "gorgeously boyish." At the time Elissa was living with her mother on a ten-acre estate near the Pacific Ocean.

There is a very telling press photo taken in this period of Kate and Elissa— draped in lush, full-length fur coats—as they are about to step aboard a plane for a short trip away from Los Angeles. Rather than staring at the cameras (which was the expected thing for a star to do when posing for the media), the striking duo were snapped gazing at one another with undisguised, rapt admiration. When this telltale photo was published in the press, Laura Harding was crushed to discover that her growing suspicions that Kate had taken up with Landi were apparently true. It caused a new rift between Hepburn and Harding that did not heal for some time. Meanwhile, as with so many of Kate's emotional and/or sexual flings, the infatuation for lovely Landi (whose screen career soon stagnated) quickly sputtered out. (Some sources suggest that randy Elissa had found a new sexual conquest—this time a man. According to these sources, when Kate discovered the embarrassing deception on her lover's part, she quickly ended her brief affair with Landi.)

❊   ❊   ❊

In the midst of her meteoric rise in Hollywood, Katharine had an urge to return to Broadway and prove to the world that she could be a great lady of the theater. She would not be dissuaded from this dream, not even when RKO insisted that to be given the time off for a play, she must first star in a most unlikely screen vehicle. The project was *Spitfire* (1934), an outdoor drama based on a Broadway play (*Trigger*).

Single-minded about returning to her theater roots, Kate gave in to the studio's blandishments. Besides her hefty *Spitfire* salary, it was a touch of conceit and/or indifference that led upper-crust Hepburn to believe she could carry off this particular film assignment. She was to play a quaint, illiterate mountain girl who becomes involved with an engineer (Robert Young) and his supervisor (Ralph Bellamy), both working on the construction of a nearby dam. Under John Cromwell's direction, the $223,000 entry was rushed into production by mid October 1934, which was cutting it close. As Leland Hayward frequently reminded the RKO hierarchy, the leading lady was due back in New York in mid November to start rehearsals for her stage project.

The film shoot, which took the cast on location to Hemet, California, and elsewhere, ran relatively smoothly. On Wednesday, November 15—the last day of filming before Kate's scheduled departure—the director called it a wrap at 6:15 P.M. However, two scenes, including the ending, remained to be lensed. Hayward was on the set at the time and hastily conferred with producer Pandro S. Berman. The agent informed Berman that Kate's *Spitfire* contract had now expired and that she intended to fly to New York at eleven that night. Berman quickly conferred with his lawyers. He then advised Leland that the day was *not* officially over until midnight. Therefore, RKO was entitled to five-and-three-quarters hours of Hepburn's time on the following day. If she did not appear, she would be considered in breach of her legal agreement.

On Thursday a frustrated Kate was present for the last scenes of *Spitfire*. However, things did not go well that morning. After an hour lunch break, she was back at work. About 3:30 P.M., Frank O'Heron, RKO's assistant treasurer, appeared on the sound stage with several Eastern visitors—important stockholders. Pointing in Kate's direction, he bragged to his group, "There's the new type of girl we're getting in Hollywood. Fine family. College education. Manners and charms. One of the most delightful girls in America. You'll meet her in a few minutes."

Meanwhile, Kate performed a few lines in front of the cameras. Suddenly she looked at her watch and broke away from the scene. She headed over to O'Heron and his entourage. "Excuse me," she said. "You'd better read this—now." Hepburn handed him a letter stating that it was now 3:45 P.M. and she had fully complied with the studio's definition of its legal rights. As far as she was concerned, *Spitfire* was through.

In short order Kate was in Berman's office, telling the executive, "You make other people live up to the conditions you write into contracts. It's time you learned to do so too." There was still an hour left to shoot on the script and Hepburn demanded $10,000 for her further services. She received it, giving $1,000 of the amount to the Community Fund. (Later Kate explained, "I didn't care so much about the money. I wanted to show them that when we set a definite date, I meant to keep it, even if they didn't. Time means nothing to Hollywood, but it means a lot to me. The same for promises.")

* * *

Finally unburdened of *Spitfire,* Kate flew to New York. She was to start rehearsals for *The Lake,* based on a recent British play that had been a London hit. For this production she had chosen to work under the aegis of Jed Harris. It was a bizarre professional career move for the screen star, guided by even stranger personal motivations.

Born Jacob Horowitz in 1900 in Austria, Harris was still an infant when his parents immigrated to the United States. His shopkeeper family scrimped and saved, and he attended Yale University where future playwright Philip Barry was a classmate. Upon graduation, and now known as Jed Harris, he moved from being a newspaper reporter to working as a theatrical press agent and on to producing mainstream plays. Within a few years he launched such major stage hits as *Broadway* (1936), *The Royal Family* (1927), and *The Front Page* (1928). Meanwhile, he had wed and divorced. But Harris was rarely without a female companion The physically unprepossessing man had a magnetic way of attracting talented leading ladies—each of whom proved useful to progressing his career. His affair with Broadway figure Ruth Gordon led to her giving birth to their out-of-wedlock child in 1929.

By 1933, Jed, who had a reputation of being extremely difficult professionally and was regarded as a bad sort personally, had suffered a severe downturn in his theatrical fortunes. In a wild gamble, he gained the American stage rights to two recent British plays (*The Green Bay Tree* and *The Lake*). Next he sought name talent to star in these pending Broadway productions. Having previously met Hepburn as she seesawed through her Manhattan stage apprenticeship, he was aware of her current desire to return to the footlights.

Harris offered Kate the choice of his two plays. She rejected *The Green Bay Tree* not only because the heroine's role was subordinate to the male leads but because of her reluctance regarding its controversial subject matter: homosexuality. Instead, she agreed to star in *The Lake*, a highly melodramatic study of a spoiled British society miss who abandons an involvement with a married neighbor to agree to a loveless marriage. By her wedding day she realizes she actually loves her kind fiancé. Before their happy life together can commence, however, he dies in an auto accident. She is left with bittersweet memories and an emotionally bleak future. (This downbeat plot line was somewhat autobiographical, as one of its two playwrights, Dorothy Massingham, committed suicide a few days after the drama bowed on London's West End.)

In past occasional conversations with Harris in New York, the hypercritical producer had always managed to make Kate question her acting abilities. She was now determined to prove him wrong. Another part of her enjoyed the notion that she had the box-office power to restore Jed to his lofty Broadway position. These intertwined feelings, plus the man's charismatic vitality, led Hepburn to feel somehow romantically drawn to Harris. As a result, Kate contracted to do *The Lake*. She made her impetuous decision despite warnings she received from stage greats Helen Hayes and Ruth Gordon, each of whom had suffered through bad working (and/or personal) experiences with irascible, petty Jed.

❋   ❋   ❋

When Kate (and Laura) reached New York following the delayed wrap of *Spitfire*, rehearsals for *The Lake* were already under way. Because of Harris's perilous financial situation, he had foreshortened the usual preproduction schedule and had already booked the play to open on Broadway in late December—only a month away. There was to be a brief out-of-town tryout in Washington, D.C.

Hepburn threw herself energetically into preparing for her role as Stella Surrege but quickly sensed that she had no affinity for this woebegone character. The movie star's bravado barely hid her insecurity as she struggled through rehearsals, a nerve-racking situation accentuated by being surrounded by so many established (and intimidating) stage veterans: Frances

Starr, Blanche Bates, Lionel Pape, and Colin Clive (Hepburn's *Christopher Strong* costar). Several days into the process, Harris fired the director and took over the directing chores himself

If Harris had been indifferent to Hepburn's needs up to this point, he turned dictatorial once he became the show's official director. He forbade tag-along Laura Harding to attend further rehearsals, claiming she was distracting his star. When Kate arrived one morning in her usual rehearsal outfit (men's slacks and a loose-fitting shirt), Jed barked out in front of the entire company, "Please do be good enough to find a skirt and put it on." Hepburn disappeared backstage. After rummaging around, she reemerged in a piece of ragged burlap. "All I could find," she muttered matter-of-factly. Her remark set the cast to snickering, but she found nothing funny about the situation. The hostilities between Kate and Jed mounted daily. One witness observed of the tense rehearsals in which Harris increasingly berated Hepburn, "If she turned her head to the left, he didn't like it. If she turned it to the right, he liked it still less."

The star became so distraught that she had screens placed in the stage wings so that she would not be distracted by fellow cast members before making an entrance. (This prompted playwright George S. Kaufman to quip, "She's afraid she might catch acting.") But even with these unorthodox safeguards, she still found it upsetting to be close to the other players offstage. During one run-through she screamed, "Get those people away from there! I can't work with those people staring at me." Harris, relishing Hepburn's discomfort, responded rancorously, "If you're to become an actress, you must learn the stage tradition of courtesy. Every one standing at that line, obeying orders, is a better trouper than you."

When *The Lake* moved to Washington for its December 18 debut, Hepburn's nerves were badly jangled, even with Laura Harding on hand to provide moral support. Kate barely maneuvered through the opening performance. After the curtain calls, Jed Harris came backstage and announced, "Perfect! I can do no more!" Hepburn was convinced he was being sarcastic because she felt—correctly—that her stage portrayal was far from perfect. She begged the producer-director to take *The Lake* on tour before launching it on Broadway. Jed refused, claiming the Martin Beck Theater was already booked. Besides, he mentioned, ticket sales were brisk.

Like a condemned prisoner about to meet her doom, Kate suffered through the next days. At the December 26 New York premiere, the leading lady thought seriously of quitting the show after the first act. But Hepburn persisted through the traumatic evening. During the intermissions, Kate's African-American maid placed a Bible in the star's hand. Hepburn clutched it during the breaks, but it didn't help her recover her nerve. Years later Kate recounted, "I just fell apart on the opening night.... I failed the people who believed in me and depended on me.... My trouble was that I froze in my tracks—I couldn't do a thing."

The reviews for *The Lake* were unpromising, but particularly devastating in assessing its star. Brooks Atkinson (*New York Times*) chided, "There is no point in pursuing Miss Hepburn with her limitations as a dramatic actress. The simple fact is that as a result of her sensational achievements on the screen she has been projected into a stage part that requires more versatility than she has had time to develop. She still needs considerable training, especially for a voice that has an unpleasant timbre." Another aisle sitter complained, "The second act's climax demanded high emotion from the leading woman. Miss Hepburn began the first act in full hysteria. By the time she reached her big moment, she could climb no higher. She was washed out, flat."

Perhaps the most demoralizing criticism came from Dorothy Parker (who had recently wed Alan Campbell, Hepburn's former *Warrior's Husband* coplayer). Quipped the Algonquin Round Table wit of Kate's star turn: "She ran the gamut of emotions from A to B." The quip—printed in newspapers across the nation—haunted Katharine Hepburn for the rest of her life.

Chapter Sixteen
RECLAIMING HER THRONE

"[Katharine Hepburn] tells nothing, permits her studio to tell nothing and denies anything anyone else tells. Furthermore, she does it in such a way that you feel she is not being truthful—and that's exactly the way she wants you to feel. It creates the impression that she is saying, in a very polite way, 'None of your business' and in Hollywood where anyone's business is everyone's business, you sort of resent it, and vow to find out anyway."
—True Confessions *magazine, February 1934*

While Katharine Hepburn was enduring her Broadway calamity, another Hepburn, her mother, was much in the national news. Kit Hepburn was in Washington, D.C., attending a caucus at the House of Representatives. In public sessions she debated Father Coughlin of Detroit on the highly controversial topic of birth control.

Meanwhile, Kate rallied in New York, refusing to give in to defeat. With the mostly unfavorable reviews of *The Lake* to goad her onward, Hepburn worked with acting coach Frances Robinson-Duff to revamp her performance. It was also during this nerve-racking time that performer Suzanne Steele introduced herself to Kate and volunteered to work with her on honing her stage portrayal. Despite all of Hepburn's Herculean efforts to improve her characterization in *The Lake*, none of the critics bothered to revisit the show and reevaluate Kate's restructured interpretation of the bereft heroine.

As the February 10, 1934, closing of the play loomed, Jed Harris advised Hepburn that he intended to take *The Lake* on tour. He was convinced that audiences in the hinterlands would be more interested in seeing the star of *Little Women* in person than in judging the quality of her performance.

Hepburn, worn out from this catastrophic stage experience, pleaded with the sadistic Harris to reconsider, but he remained firm that she uphold her contractual commitment. Kate asked the ogre what it would take for him to drop the tour plans. He inquired, "How much do you have in your bank account?" She answered, "$15,461.67." He said, "OK, I'll take that."

So ended Hepburn's association with twisted Jed Harris. The bitter experience of this failed heterosexual romantic fantasy, however, haunted her forever.

❋ ❋ ❋

After Hepburn returned alone to New York in March 1934 following her abortive trip to France with Suzanne Steele, Kate persuaded brooding Laura Harding to please forgive this latest defection on Kate's part. As had happened several times over the past few years, the emotionally needy socialite did so.

After spending a week back at the Turtle Bay house, Kate, with Laura Harding once again her faithful traveling cohort, headed to Miami. Hepburn hoped to visit in Key West with her new pal Ernest Hemingway, but he claimed to be unable to break away from his writing. The two women boarded the *Morro Castle,* an American cruise ship that was bound for Mexico via the Panama Canal. Once the American duo registered at their hotel in Mérida, Yucatan, on April 24, news began to leak out that Hepburn was in Mexico to divorce her husband. Two days later appropriate legal papers were filed by the star's local legal representative. On April 30, with Harding serving as Kate's witness, the divorce was granted. (Luddy did not make an appearance, having hired an attorney to represent him in court and to make everything as easy as possible for Hepburn.)

Kate and Laura flew back to Miami and then went by train to New York City. Once back at her east side brownstone, Hepburn remained in seclusion, ignoring the media mob who wanted details about her divorce. Her privacy, however, was broken due to her new household pet, a kitten. One day the little Persian feline escaped from the Turtle Bay house with Hepburn shouting to a nearby reporter to retrieve the scurrying animal. He did so, and as a reward the International News Service earned an interview with the elusive star. Kate said of her antimedia stance, "I always tried to be helpful to newspaper men but they go away dissatisfied and perhaps prejudiced. I fear this prejudice will affect my career and shorten it." She noted, "Success and fame are all too fleeting" and sighed, "Somehow I wish I could paint pictures play music or write books. Alas, I am not talented at all." When pressed about her future personal plans, she answered, "I won't discuss my personal affairs ever. They wouldn't be personal if I made them public."

✳   ✳   ✳

When Hepburn obtained her Mexican divorce, it had been noted that the thirty-day waiting period for either party to remarry had been waved. This led the press to assume that perhaps Kate intended to wed Leland Hayward (who divorced his first wife, once again, in 1934). Neither party would confirm or deny the assumption, which only caused the media to further speculate in print.

Meanwhile, RKO, already transitioning into a new regime, wanted Hepburn to return to the screen as quickly as possible. To entice her, RKO agreed to a highly lucrative $300,000 pact (negotiated by Leland Hayward) for six films to be made over the next two years. Since *Little Women* had done so incredibly well (unlike the follow-up, *Spitfire*), the studio reasoned that her next vehicle should be another period picture. This led to Hepburn doing a color test for a projected *St. Joan* to be directed by George Cukor, but that vehicle did not come to be. Nor did a touted celluloid biography of George Sand, the nineteenth-century French novelist who had a penchant for wearing men's trousers. A planned adaptation of Edith Wharton's *The Age of Innocence* was offered to Kate. When she declined, Irene Dunne took on the costume role. There was also talk of Kate headlining a screen rendition of John Galsworthy's *The Forsyte Saga,* but that came to naught, as did a suggested screen account of seventeenth-century English actress, Nell Gwyn.

Next, Theresa Helburn of the Theater Guild, who had developed close personal ties with Hepburn, suggested that Kate would be ideal for a screen version of Eugene O'Neill's *Mourning Becomes Electra,* which had costarred Alla Nazimova and Alice Brady on the stage in 1931. Helburn thought Kate would be well showcased as the father-obsessed Lavinia, with Greta Garbo cast as the adulterous mother. The notion of working with her screen idol excited

Hepburn, and she made overtures to MGM mogul Louis B. Mayer about casting his prized leading lady, Garbo, opposite Hepburn (on loanout from RKO). Mayer, who wanted to present only wholesome-type families onscreen, responded to this proposition with, "Over my dead body!" (Knowing Hepburn's tenacity when a favored project was involved, several insiders jokingly wondered why she didn't follow through on the mogul's quip.)

Meanwhile, despite Kate's failed attempt to capture Broadway glory, there was conjecture that she might star for producer Arthur Hopkins during the 1934–1935 season in a stage edition of Jane Austen's *Pride and Prejudice.* In the interim Hepburn, now headquartered at the family's beach house, was at loose ends.(Following their divorce Kate and Luddy reestablished their great comradeship from bygone days, and he was frequently on hand to console her, run errands, and buoy her confidence.) To fill the void in her career, she agreed to play the lead in *Dark Victory,* one of the new offerings of the 1934 summer season at the nearby Ivoryton Playhouse. She rehearsed this teary drama with colead Stanley Ridges, but Hepburn found playing the heroine of an unabashed tearjerker uncongenial to her temperament. A few days before the scheduled opening, Kate informed the theater owners that she could not go forward with the production, unfairly thrusting the blame (for the show not coming together as a cohesive whole) on her costar, a well-regarded British character player. The tryout had to be canceled. It ended plans for Hepburn to take the new drama to Broadway. (*Dark Victory* was staged that fall in Manhattan with Tallulah Bankhead and Earl Larrimore. It lasted fifty-five performances. Bette Davis scored a great hit in the 1939 film adaptation.)

❋ ❋ ❋

Returning with steadfast Laura Harding to Los Angeles in the summer of 1934, the pair rented yet another house, as Hepburn stubbornly still refused to put down roots in the movie colony. By now, many of the fan magazines—who dared not in those conservative times overtly reference the emotional or sexual bonds between the movie star and her woman friend—felt comfortable in describing imperial Laura as the true power behind Kate's lofty throne. These movie publications detailed that it was well-bred Laura who passed on the proofs of all publicity pictures, helped to design the costumes that gave the

actress such glamour onscreen, sat in on story conferences, and was "a constant companion and coach in the long hours of rehearsals before each production." It was said that it was well-bred Harding who was the instigator of
her friend's well-publicized screwball antics and that it was the level-headed
Laura who provided Kate with a needed sense of balance amid the craziness
of the Hollywood scene. Left as only subtext in many of these published references to Hepburn and Harding's close-knit friendship was the suggestion
that the multidimensional relationship went far beyond the platonic.

Years later, in 1973, Harding, still extremely sensitive on the subject of the
real nature of her much-publicized relationship with Hepburn and how gossip had labeled her a lesbian, would tell *Ms.* magazine, "Hollywood is a kind
of a great big red-light district. And it's assumed that if you're not sleeping
with men, you must be sleeping with women. This was something that was
really shattering to us. And Kate used to say, if anyone would come around
me, 'Keep away from her. She's my woman.' We, in our innocence, did things
like that all the time."

✳   ✳   ✳

Especially during Hollywood's Golden Age of the 1930s and 1940s, each
year saw an influx of exciting new screen personalities, many of them drawn
from the Broadway stage. One of filmdom's brightest imports in 1933 was
Universal Pictures' Margaret Sullavan. She made a great impression in *Only
Yesterday* and in the following year's *Little Man, What Now?* The petite
actress, with her captivating throaty voice and sparkling eyes, was born in
1909 in Norfolk Virginia, the offspring of a prosperous, well-established family. She began her acting career in winter and summer stock companies. In
1931, the year she made her Broadway debut, she married fellow actor Henry
Fonda. Four months later the couple separated (they divorced in 1933). By
then, the sexually voracious and aggressive Sullavan had come under the spell
of producer Jed Harris, who provided her with useful career advice. Once she
made a conquest of Harris, Sullavan was ready—and did—move on to several other men, but Jed remained dogged in his attention to her. Jed was still
besotted with Margaret at the time of *The Lake*. (It deeply annoyed Hepburn
to discover that Sullavan had been Harris's first choice for the play and that

Jed cast Kate in the challenging lead part only because of her screen popularity. These belated revelations—as well as Jed's natural nastiness—helped to turn Hepburn against this theatrical powerhouse whom she had chosen to "rescue." In the process, Kate grew increasingly angry with Sullavan, who publicly gloated over Kate's uncomfortable situation.)

Once the free-spirited Margaret Sullavan was established in Hollywood, she made it clear she would not play by the usual film colony rules. Like Kate, she often wore men's slacks in public, avoided the press, and ignored attending premieres. Despite her rebellious, highly flirtatious nature, moviegoers and critics alike found Sullavan enchanting (which made Hepburn further dislike her). In short order, Margaret was much in demand for major film projects—often up for the same role as Kate. It did not hurt Sullavan's career trajectory that high-powered Leland Hayward (who had a deep crush on this star) was her talent agent.

While the career backgrounds of Kate Hepburn and Margaret Sullavan had intertwining parallels, their natures differed greatly (although they were both born under the sign of Taurus). Outgoing, completely heterosexual Sullavan was strongly drawn to a wide variety of men, while she had few women acquaintances. In contrast, self-possessed, Hepburn felt far more at ease with her small circle of women friends, able to relax with them and not feel she had to prove herself in a battle of the sexes. They were her family. (In Hollywood circles, sophisticated Sullavan enjoyed poking fun at "Krazy Kate and her Giddy Girlfriends" and found it amusing to imitate her highly mannered, nasal-voiced rival. On occasion, no-holds-barred Maggie referred to Hepburn as "that dykey bitch.")

Kate and Maggie again crossed professional paths upon Hepburn's return to Los Angeles. RKO suggested Hepburn star in a new screen adaptation of Sir James M. Barrie's *The Little Minister.* At first Kate thought the period drama, a great stage hit for her idol Maude Adams decades earlier, was far too whimsical for her forthright Yankee personality. When Hepburn brusquely rejected RKO's offer, the studio let it be known that Margaret Sullavan was quite interested in starring in the production. Soon thereafter Kate said yes to portraying Lady Babbie in *The Little Minister.* As she admitted later, "I really didn't want to play it until I heard another actress was desperate for the role. Then, of course, it became the most important thing in the world for me that

I should get it. Several of my parts in those days I fought for just to take them from someone who needed them." (Both Leland Hayward and Laura Harding had counseled Hepburn against accepting the fanciful Babbie role, but she turned a deaf ear to their sage advice.)

So convinced was RKO that Kate could provide the studio with another major screen hit that it lavished a whopping $648,000 budget on this period feature directed by Richard Wallace. In this highly sentimental tale of 1840 Scotland she appeared as an unhappily engaged woman. While disguised as a flirtatious gypsy wench so she can mingle with the common folk of the village, she finds true love with the new local clergyman. Hepburn wanted Franchot Tone (her former Broadway coplayer) to take on the title role. However, Tone was committed to another production elsewhere. Stage actor John Beal, recently signed to a RKO pact, was substituted. Unfortunately, Beal lacked the physical charisma or emotional vitality for the assignment.

At a lengthy 110 minutes, the dated *The Little Minister* had difficulty in finding a sufficiently wide audience. Eileen Creelman (*New York Sun*) summarized, "Miss Hepburn, gauntly handsome and spirited, makes no attempt to become that elusive, charming creature, a Barrie heroine. She is just Miss Hepburn, arch, vivid, varying little…wistfulness is not a Hepburn characteristic." Despite a better reception for *The Little Minister* abroad, the picture lost money for RKO.

Now deciding that perhaps Hepburn would fare better with the moviegoing public in a contemporary story, Hepburn was assigned by RKO to *Break of Hearts* (1935). This modern soap opera would be a pale imitation of Kate's swirling private life in the coming months.

Chapter Seventeen
THE HOLLYWOOD TREADMILL

*"Because Hollywood does certain things is no reason I must
do them. I tell you, I am one person who is not going to let
Hollywood make me over!"*
— *Katharine Hepburn, 1935*

RKO was constantly exploring options as how best to showcase Katharine
Hepburn, its high-salaried resident leading lady. For example, the studio had
thought of reteaming her in 1934 with John Barrymore in an updated version of Edmond Rostand's *Cyrano de Bergerac*. (This projected casting of
Kate as a modern-day Roxanne led one Hollywood columnist to ponder sar-
castically, "Is RKO trying to feminize the slim, boyish Katharine Hepburn?")
That high concept project evaporated and the studio announced that the
costars of *A Bill of Divorcement* would rematch for *Break of Hearts*. However,
by the time *Break of Hearts* went into production in early February 1935,
Czechoslovakian-born Francis Lederer, a new addition to the RKO actor stable, was set as Hepburn's vis à vis. Hardly had filming begun than fireworks
erupted between demanding Kate and her handsome leading man. He was
strong-minded and full of himself, which did not set well with Hepburn, who
was used to being the focal point of everything on her sets. When Lederer got
into arguments with assistant director Edward Killy (a pal of Kate's who had
worked on three of her past pictures) over which camera angles best flattered
his profile and mentioned his annoyance at being subordinated to his colead,
Hepburn and Killy marched into the offices of studio president J.P.
MacDonald. After they recited their grievances against the interloper, Lederer
was removed from the picture and Charles Boyer substituted. (The French-
born Boyer and Kate got along famously both on and off the set. Although he
had recently wed—a marriage that endured until his actress wife's death in

1978—Kate would suggest later that the two stars had supposedly sparked romantically offcamera, including cuddling together in her car on the studio parking lot.)

By now, Hepburn was showing increased dedication with each new screen job. For *Break of Hearts* she was cast as a struggling composer in love with a celebrity orchestra conductor. This led her to meeting with musicians to understand better their craft and their artistic commitment. Originally John Cromwell (*Spitfire*) was to direct this romantic drama, but Kate pushed for Philip Moeller instead. As he was a cofounder of the Theater Guild, he had come to know Hepburn during her New York stage days. RKO had already brought Moeller to Hollywood—partly at Kate's encouragement—to direct her onscreen. They were to have worked together on *The Age of Innocence* (1934), but she had eventually rejected that entry. Now she made it known she wanted Moeller to guide her through *Break of Hearts*.

As Kate quickly discovered during the nearly seven-week shoot, Moeller had no flair for screen directing. The Hollywood newcomer was too inexperienced with the special requirements of filmmaking. In making his creative choices, he relied heavily on Jane Loring, who was associate director on *Break of Hearts* as she had been on *The Age of Innocence*.

Loring was born on June 6, 1890, in Denver. By the time she was sixteen the ambitious adolescent had set a goal of breaking into the film business and becoming a director (a challenging ambition for a woman in such a male-dominated industry). As a teenager she relocated to New York, using her skill as a violinist as an entrée to finding stage work. Before long, go-getting Jane was shadowing the theater director's every move, eager to learn each aspect of his craft. Meanwhile, she mastered the skill of stenography, knowing it would make her more useful to future employers. Thereafter, she became a secretary to a New York film exhibitor. This paved the way to her becoming a script girl on a movie set, where she quickly absorbed filmmaking techniques. Her growing experience allowed her to move into the cutting room, where she began editing film trailers. For a time after moving to Los Angeles she edited movie comedy shorts. Then, in 1927, Paramount Pictures promoted her to assistant editor on feature films. Soon Loring became highly in demand on important studio productions.

By 1933 workaholic Jane had transferred to RKO Pictures, where she soon became a key assistant to energetic producer Pandro S. Berman. Quickly demonstrating her wide-ranging moviemaking knowledge, she was asked to assist Philip Moeller in his directing debut. She was so tactful in providing him useful on-the-set guidance—and he was so grateful for her being so willing to share her skills—that he requested her to work in a similar capacity on *Break of Hearts.*

In describing curly dark-haired, bespectacled Loring in a mid-1930s profile, *The New York Times* detailed, "Jane is a frail slim little thing, who dresses in slacks [blue in winter; white flannel trousers in summer], sport coat, rubber-soled shoes, a beret and dark glasses. She moves with unhurried poise and her voice is low and mellow. She is the most inconspicuous person on the set with ne'er a hint of the arrogance of achievement." The dynamic Loring was noted for arriving at the studio daily around 8:30 A.M. and staying till 11:30 P.M. She scurried unobtrusively about the lot during her hectic work day, moving from the sound stages to the casting office and on to script conferences, then, perhaps, heading to the projection rooms with a stopover in the makeup department. As she had become such an able jack-of-all-trades, her salary escalated to a lofty $750 weekly, which allowed her to live (alone) in one of Hollywood's fanciest apartment buildings. With her androgynous look both on and away from the studio lot, it was little wonder that a Los Angeles newspaper interviewer would remark of Loring, "They never think of her primarily as a woman." Such a statement was the reporter's coded way of noting subtly that Jane was likely a lesbian.

During *Break of Hearts,* Hepburn spent a good deal of time on and off the set with Loring, whom she found a fountain of useful moviemaking knowledge and whom Kate appreciated for being such a worshipful companion. Soon the diminutive Jane became an increasingly important member of Kate's studio family—as had Hepburn's protégée, former vaudevillian Pat(ricia) Doyle, Kate's stand-in for several films (who later married film editor–turned–director Robert Wise), and fledgling performer Eve March. This new Hepburn-Loring alliance that carried over away from the studio made the excluded Laura Harding quite jealous. Rightly, she felt her importance in her famous friend's life was once again being usurped.

✳   ✳   ✳

With Hepburn's forceful, mannish personality and her inability to project the submissive, romantically alluring aspects of the typical 1930s Hollywood heroine, *Break of Hearts* proved unconvincing fare and barely squeaked by at the box office. This was Kate's third disappointing movie vehicle in a row. RKO was becoming justifiably concerned that their costly Oscar winner might not pull out of her extended career slump. However, Hepburn had a firm multipicture commitment, and the studio had to move ahead on her next project. (As producer Pandro S. Berman would say in retrospect, "We turned out so many Hepburn pictures every season—right or wrong, ready or not. We hadn't found Kate's right formula.")

In bandying about properties suitable for Hepburn's particular talents and very specific screen persona, Kate suggested that Booth Tarkington's *Seventeen,* once a Ruth Gordon stage hit, might be worth considering for her. Before long it was decided, instead, that her next 1935 release would be a fresh screen adaptation of another Tarkington work, *Alice Adams.* This biting satire of small-town America concerned a pretentious young lady who aspires to mingle with the local upper class. While RKO was angling to borrow Randolph Scott or Fred MacMurray from Paramount Pictures to be Hepburn's leading man, producer Berman conferred with Kate (who had final approval) regarding the proper director for this romantic drama. It boiled down to two choices: William Wyler or George Stevens. The former was an experienced filmmaker whom George Cukor (busy on his own films at MGM) thought could properly guide Kate. In contrast, Stevens was a young director of mostly comedy shorts and a few minor features who had recently come to RKO. Berman favored using Stevens because he was under studio contract at a relatively low salary. The negative of employing Wyler was that he commanded a much larger fee. Also, he had been born in France, and Berman felt Wyler might not relate as well as Stevens to the film's Americana ambience.

One account of how the film's director was finally chosen had Berman and Hepburn flipping a coin to see which director would be picked. According to the coin toss, Stevens was the winner. However, there was actually another factor at work. Despite her professional partiality to Wyler, Hepburn could not bring herself to accept him for this venture because he was then married to her nemesis, Margaret Sullavan. (The couple had met while Wyler directed Sullavan's 1935 entry *The Good Fairy* and had eloped soon thereafter.)

From the start of filming *Alice Adams* there was an obvious tug-of-war between Hepburn and ruggedly handsome, stocky, and quiet Stevens (1904–1975). Kate soon came to appreciate his keen sense of timing for comedic sequences (e.g., the memorable dinner scene in which the Adams clan attempt to impress Alice's wealthy suitor). However, Kate could not resist making constant suggestions on all sorts of matters throughout production, which threatened to undermine Stevens's authority with the cast and crew. These two forces particularly feuded over the handling of a crucial crying scene involving the heroine. Stevens won out by persistence, and later Hepburn acknowledged he had been artistically sound in his creative choices.

While making *Alice Adams,* rumors abounded of the growing romantic connection between Kate and her married film director, who was then already a father. Less discussed was the on-the-set presence of Berman's assistant, Jane Loring. On the RKO financial books Loring was listed as part of the "directorial" budget and was paid $3,500 for her services on this feature. Increasingly, Hepburn was counting on the adoring Loring as a pivotal member of her team and someone with whom she was simpatico. Jane became so overawed by her new colleague and friend that their growing bond became far more of a priority than her own burgeoning career (which many in the industry were predicting would lead to her directing features in the near future).

When *Alice Adams* was released in August 1935 it received glowing reviews: "It is a performance that is superb in every detail, well sustained, carefully modulated and accurately pitched to the keys of humor and wistful pathos which define the character." (Thornton Delehanty, *New York Post*) The picture made a healthy profit, and Kate was Oscar-nominated for her telling performance (which owed so much to her childhood experiences in Hartford when she had so often been a social outcast.) Hepburn lost the Academy Award for Best Actress to Bette Davis (*Dangerous*).

❄   ❄   ❄

With *Alice Adams* doing so well at the box office, RKO felt confident that Katharine Hepburn was back on the right commercial track with moviegoers. Because of this, producer Pandro S. Berman did not argue too strenu-ously when the star announced that she and George Cukor wanted to reteam for her next picture (*Sylvia Scarlett*). It was to be based on a Compton Bennett novel (1918) that had long intrigued Cukor. Because Kate and George were so enthusiastic about this offbeat venture, Berman overrode his initial concerns that the story line would repulse or baffle mainstream movie-goers: Kate, the daughter of a debt-plagued widower, shaves her hair and dis-guises herself as a boy to help her dad flee his creditors. Relocating to England, the duo team with a Cockney confidence man (Cary Grant). Hepburn's character, still masquerading as a male, is drawn to a well-to-do artist (Brian Aherne) who finds himself strangely attracted to this androgy-nous newcomer. However, it is the conniving con artist whom Kate's alter ego really loves, and she eventually wins him away from his aristocratic Russian girlfriend.

With its unconventional sexual overtones and its very strong gay under-tones, *Sylvia Scarlett* was far from the usual fare, especially in the mid 1930s, when Hollywood had such a strict industry production code in force. However, because of the obliqueness of its plot twists, self-indulgent Hepburn and Cukor recklessly thought they could carry off successfully their barely disguised screen excursion into homosexuality and lesbian themes. Halfway through this daring experiment, though, a new beginning and clos-ing to the picture were suddenly tacked on, hoping to make the heroine's digression into cross-dressing more palatable to audiences and to give Kate's character a more sympathetic persona. Unbilled, faithful Jane Loring served as the film's editor and was Hepburn's unofficial advice-giver and confidant throughout filming.

By the time *Sylvia Scarlett* was ready for test previewing in late 1935, Hepburn and Cukor were uncertain if their bold venture would satisfy the average moviegoer. At a prescreening dinner hosted by Kate and George, another George—Stevens—was among those invited. During the meal, Cukor, having half-convinced himself that he had created a cinematic mas-terpiece, announced, "I can quit the business now and rest on my laurels." Overhearing this, the more levelheaded Stevens wondered aloud, "Wouldn't it be funny if you had a flop?"

At the screening, Kate was seated near to French-born Natalie Paley, who played a seductive Russian aristocrat in this comedy drama. Part way through the showing, Paley asked, "Why aren't they laughing?" Hepburn answered glumly, "Because they don't think it's funny." By now Kate was convinced that *Sylvia Scarlett* was a dreadful miscalculation and not only would she never see a penny of profit participation on the venture but the film could be a great setback to her already badly fluctuating movie career. Cukor would say later of this extremely uncomfortable evening: "The way the audience looked at us, we felt as if we were being stoned."

With their egos badly deflated after the disastrous preview, Hepburn and Cukor meekly met with Pandro S. Berman and offered to make amends for their calamitous misstep by making a new RKO picture for free—if only Pandro would shelve this obvious fiasco. The producer declined their too-late offer but did advise Cukor that he never wanted to work with him again. (It was a threat that practical Berman rescinded in the years to come.)

When released, *Sylvia Scarlett* was roasted by many major reviewers. Eileen Creelman (*New York Sun*) judged, "The picture is a tragic waste of time and screen talent." *Time* magazine concluded, "*Sylvia Scarlett* reveals the interesting fact that Katharine Hepburn is better looking as a boy than as a woman." The public stayed away in droves from this untraditional offering. As a result the extremely expensive project registered an enormous loss at the global box office.

During the shooting of *Sylvia Scarlett*, Hepburn had had the satisfaction of continuing her track record of performing all her own oncamera stunts. On this project the athletics included the sequence in which she swims into the ocean waves to save Paley's character from drowning. Kate was also pleased to have started a working relationship with reputedly bisexual Cary Grant, who had been borrowed from Paramount Pictures for $15,000. In contrast to the other primary participants in this picture (including the gay British character actor Edmund Gwenn), handsome Grant came out unscathed. His performance as the jocular con artist gave his movie standing a tremendous boost. Previously relegated to being a well-groomed, bland leading man, here he displayed a forte for high and low comedy. It paved the way for a major career as the king of screwball comedy and thereafter as one of Hollywood's premier debonair superstars.

On his part, Grant would be forever grateful to Cukor and Hepburn for choosing him for such a showcase role. In assessing Kate, with whom he would make a total of four pictures, the British-born actor would say, "She was this slip of a woman, skinny, and I never liked skinny women. But she had this thing, this air, you might call it, the most totally magnetic woman I'd ever seen, and probably have ever seen since. You had to look at her, you had to listen to her, there was no escaping her. But it wasn't just the beauty, it was the style. She's incredibly down to earth. She can see right through the nonsense in life. She cares, but about things that really matter." (Left unsaid is that Grant and Hepburn shared a common bond in their sexual proclivities.)

As the years passed, the bizarre *Sylvia Scarlett* developed a cult status. As mores became progressively less structured and far more tolerant of alternative lifestyles, the film's themes were now appreciated as being sophisticated and forward thinking. Whereas at the time of release Hepburn and Cukor thought they would never live down this embarrassing commercial flop, in subsequent decades they were praised for their audacity in instigating this project. In (re)evaluating this entry in 1986, Hepburn praised Grant's performance as being "beyond belief" and noted that he was "such fun to work with, an actor with lots of energy." Interestingly, she also pointed out, "I thought I made a mighty attractive boy."

When Katharine Houghton, Hepburn's niece and her costar in *Guess Who's Coming to Dinner* (1967), appeared on cable TV's *Larry King Live* in June 2003, she observed intriguingly of *Sylvia Scarlett* and her legendary aunt: "I think that the film and her whole ambience in that film is just quintessentially who she is."

✳ ✳ ✳

While *Sylvia Scarlett* was sinking at the box office, the RKO corporate powers (which were already shifting and would soon put Pandro S. Berman in charge of studio production), decreed that Hepburn would next star in the title role of *Mary of Scotland* (1936). This high-prestige production was based on the Pulitzer Prize–winning Broadway success (1933). It had featured Helen Hayes as Mary Stuart, Queen of Scotland (1542–1587), who engaged in a deadly contest of power with England's Elizabeth I (1533–1633). (Hepburn had seen the stage hit in New York and felt immediately that she was immensely suited to playing Hayes's role oncamera.)

The studio hierarchy was so convinced that this illustrious property could not fail to lure moviegoers that it lavished a mighty $864,000 on the historical production. In rationalizing this business gamble, RKO executive Ned Depinet enunciated, "Sex has definitely lost its place in the movies. The public doesn't give a hang about sex anymore if we feed it good, clean wholesome pictures with a plot." When these pompous remarks were published in the trade press, a journalist for *Motion Picture Herald* responded, "If Mary, Queen of Scots, didn't have sex, and lots of it, we have been grossly deceived. And doesn't Mr. Depinet know about Elizabeth, the virgin queen? Virgins just have to have sex. They cannot do or be without it. No sex, no virgin."

While this duel of words over Hepburn's upcoming movie raged onward and casting for Kate's coleads was being negotiated, the star was dealing with the ever-shifting sands in her complex personal life.

Chapter Eighteen
SHIFTING LOYALTIES

"It became clear to me that my presence in Hollywood was increasingly inessential to myself, to Kate [Hepburn], and to pictures. I had no interest in going into the industry, Kate was firmly established as a huge star and was no longer dependent on me, and I was tired of the rather meaningless, sterile life of Southern California."
—*Laura Harding, 1975*

Several of Kate Hepburn's pivotal personal relationships were in tremendous flux as 1935 moved into 1936. For a time after Hepburn had divorced Luddy Smith in spring 1934 it seemed that she and talent agent Leland Hayward might fulfill the media speculation that they would soon wed. But their individually busy professional lives, their essential inability to commit to one another, and Kate's undiminished sexual preference for women kept getting in their way. As 1934 ended, Hayward became seriously ill with a prostate ailment that might be cancerous. A deeply worried Kate—always at her most effective and contented when her bossy maternal instincts came into play—insisted that her father operate on Leland back in Hartford. The surgery was a success. When the couple returned to the coast, Hepburn again became oblique with the press about when or if she and her beau would marry. Throughout 1935 the couple experienced alternating periods of closeness and then separations (as each partner dabbled romantically with others or became preoccupied with their fast-paced careers).

By late 1935, Hayward had come back under the spell of beguiling Margaret Sullavan. Her impetuous marriage to director William Wyler was fast coming to a close, and she would file for divorce in Mexico on March 13, 1936. (Wyler later said of his ex-wife, "She castrates a guy—she makes him feel like two cents—and two inches.") Never for long without men dancing attention on her, Sullavan cast her alluring net over her frequent movie costar Jimmy Stewart. Among her other suitors was still-persistent producer Jed Harris. Finally, during 1936, Jed accepted the fact that she was far more intrigued with Leland than he, and Harris bowed out of her life. Hayward and Sullavan grew closer in New York, where she was preparing for her theater return in *Stage Door*. When Hepburn heard rumors of this escalating relationship it severely wounded her pride, which far overshadowed her sense of relief that fate was rescuing her from an unrealistic union with Leland.

Meanwhile, Laura Harding had fled back east. After a few years of living in Kate Hepburn's movie-star shadow—and being the subject of endless film colony and media guesswork as to her actual role in the star's private life— the socialite had had enough. As she explained later, "I came from a totally different social milieu from either Hollywood or Kate. Our family was in railroads and the travel business, our friends were East Coast old money people, and I never even approved of Kate's bohemian ways. I adored her and still do, but in 1935 it had become obvious that I did not belong at the center of her life." (Left unstated was that Laura, still smarting from Kate's several past romantic strayings, had now been replaced by the shadowy Jane Loring. The latter, at both RKO and away from the studio, had become Hepburn's chief sounding board and primary companion. It forced Harding to accept that she was no longer Kate's significant other.)

When the rebuffed Harding returned home, she established a new life for herself, one that revolved around herself and not Hepburn. The wealthy Laura purchased a sixty-acre farm in Holmdel, New Jersey. (Her uncle already owned a twenty-acre property nearby.) Naming her spread Bayonet Farm, Laura gradually expanded her rural property and in the process built new barns, cottages, and sheds. The main house was renovated in the colonial revival style, and soon Harding had a proper country estate complete with maids and other staff. She raised cattle, kept over thirty dogs on the property, and maintained a large stable so she could go horseback riding frequently. As time wore on she and Kate managed to forge a new rapport, as good friends who shared a rich past and wanted to somehow remain friends. Thus, whenever Hepburn returned east she generally visited Laura in New Jersey; Harding kept a room in the main house for Kate's special use. (Over the years, Harding went into Manhattan on a near-weekly basis and volunteered to watch over Hepburn's brownstone whenever the movie star was out of town.)

Another of Harding's occasional visitors at Bayonet Farm was movie producer David O. Selznick. He had first met Laura while he was in charge of RKO and Hepburn was the studio's bright young star. Reputedly, because of Selznick's recurrent fascination with wealthy Laura, David's wife, Irene (who became a staunch Hepburn friend in later times), refused to entertain Harding at the Selznicks' home. In later years, Laura's niece (Christine Tailer) recalled delightful holiday stays at Bayonet Farm and "riding in an open sleigh with her Aunt Laura cracking a whip and dogs barking at the horses' hoofs." Said Tailer of Harding who always remained unmarried, "I never saw her in anything but slacks, ankle boots and broadcloth man-tailored shirts. Kate [Hepburn, when she visited]...was always dressed very similarly."

❋   ❋   ❋

When RKO put *Mary of Scotland* into production, Hepburn urged Pandro S. Berman to have her pal George Cukor direct the vehicle. Still coping with the fallout from that duo's last collaboration (*Sylvia Scarlett*), the request was refused. Instead, the producer assigned John Ford (1894-1973), who, when not working at Fox Films, had made RKO's *The Lost Patrol* (1934) and *The Informer* (1935). (In March 1936 the latter picture would win Ford a Best Director Oscar.) Berman believed that the manly, rugged Irish Catholic Ford would provide a positive change for the floundering Hepburn and hopefully instill some earthiness into her generally very airy screen vehicles.

Ford was well aware of Kate's special screen personality and unique looks, both of which demanded proper showcasing. To research his star, he and his staff screened each of her past films. "We studied every angle of her strange, sharp face—the chiseled nose, the mouth, the long neck—and then adjusted the [costume] sketches to fit her personality. We planned photographic effects, decided how best to light her features and what makeup to use in order to achieve for her a genuine majesty."

With Fredric March cast as the Earl of Bothwell (a historical character whom RKO publicity touted was a very distant relative of Hepburn) and his wife, Florence Eldridge, set as Elizabeth Tudor, *Mary of Scotland* got under way in February 1936. While Kate exhibited little screen chemistry with her randy leading man and there were insufficient sparks between her character and that of Eldridge's Virgin Queen, Hepburn and Ford generated great rapport from the start. She treated him with good-natured amusement based on her great respect for his talent. This was evidenced on the first day of shooting. He arrived on the set to find his leading lady seated in his director's chair with her feet propped up on a nearby table. She was puffing on an Irish clay pipe. If anyone else had dared to poke such fun at Ford's filmmaker image, he most likely would have banished the person from the set. But with Kate, John, thirteen years older than she, was alternately entertained or diplomatically silent when her playful jibes punctured his solemn outlook on life and work.

Like Leland Hayward, Ford was a married man. (He had wed Mary McBride Smith in 1920; their son was born in 1921 and their daughter the following year.) Like Hepburn's future mainstay (Spencer Tracy), Ford was Irish Catholic and a heavy drinker. There had been rumors of the director occasionally carrying on with one of his leading ladies (e.g., Madeleine Carroll in 1934's *The World Moves On*). John, however, had always returned to his wife, as much for the sake of their two children as his own emotional stability. He found outlets for his wanderlust and frustrations by escaping on weekend or longer seafaring trips aboard his yacht with his equally heavy-drinking buddies (usually actors from his "stock" company). Talented and prolific, Ford was considered a member of Hollywood's higher echelon of directors, with his best and most personal screen work yet to come.

During the making of *Mary of Scotland,* Ford quickly became disenchanted with the unwieldy historical production. He felt the final shooting script was insubstantial, a judgment with which Kate soon came to agree. Bored with his task, John diverted himself by lavishing his star with carefully lit, flattering close-ups. He made a special point of constantly looking out for her welfare on the production. (One day on location, as Hepburn was rehearsing a scene that required her to ride through a forest, it was Ford's last-minute warning to duck that saved her from a possibly fatal injury from a dangerous overhead branch.)

As filming continued, Ford rushed through the several dialogue-heavy sequences between Hepburn and March. Meanwhile, the director's lack of interest in this cumbersome period vehicle became increasingly obvious to everyone. One day, as another of the scheduled love scenes between Kate and Fredric dragged on, the director exploded in frustration—or perhaps with jealousy—and walked off the set. Before departing, John suggested to Kate that if she valued this particular sequence as much as she claimed, she should direct the segment herself. Accepting the challenge, Hepburn did so. (Over the years there was recurring talk that Hepburn would direct a full feature, but it never came to pass.)

By the time filming on this costumed spectacle wrapped in mid April 1936, Ford was so entranced with Hepburn that he accompanied her back east. He even joined her at Fenwick, where he was exposed to her distinctive family, especially the imposing parents who wondered what their famous daughter was doing with this older, married, Catholic man who seemed so unsophisticated compared to her past suitors or spouse. For her part, Kate was intrigued by John's creative talent, his arrogant self-sufficiency, and his conflicted outlook on life, which found release in alcohol. Perhaps, because this guilt-ridden, emotionally unavailable family man was so realistically unattainable (as she was, in actuality), she regarded her association with Sean (as she called him) to be safely in her control and an enticing challenge. (From his point of view Ford appreciated the duality of Hepburn's sexual nature and sensed the many emotional barriers that caused her to push away several men in her past. He referred to Kate as "half pagan, half Puritan.")

To this day it is uncertain whether Hepburn and Ford ever physically consummated their affair. However, for the next year, they carried on an elaborate but playful cat-and-mouse game in which each attempted—often through letters or phone calls—to pin down emotionally the other individual without making any true commitment on his/her part. A major setback to their unrealistic alliance occurred in June 1936 when the director's eighty-two-year-old father passed away. It cast a strong shadow of pending mortality over John and led him to seriously reevaluate his moral and religious obligations to his wife and children. (At one juncture in the seesawing association between Hepburn and Ford, which included weekends together on his yacht, Kate allegedly offered his wife, Mary, $150,000 if she would divorce John and let Ford retain custody of his beloved daughter, Barbara. As would be the case with Spencer Tracy's wife, Mrs. Ford enjoyed her assured status in

Hollywood as the spouse of a famous talent and had learned to weather her husband's indiscretions with great fortitude—at least publicly.)

If the depth of the strong emotional connection between Catholic Ford and WASP Hepburn—both New Englanders—bewildered those in the know at the time, a new wrinkle would be added decades later when Maureen O'Hara published her memoir, 'Tis Herself (2004). O'Hara, who was counted with Hepburn and Anna Lee as one of Ford's favorite actresses to direct, recounts a disturbing incident in her long professional and emotionally perplexing association with the irascible filmmaker.

One day in the 1940s, without knocking, Maureen walked into John's film office on a studio lot to discuss wardrobe for their upcoming picture. To her surprise she discovered Ford kissing a movie actor ("one of the most famous leading men in the picture business"). The incident prompted the redheaded Irish-born star to ponder if this possible penchant for an alternative lifestyle had caused the strongly Catholic Ford overwhelming feelings of guilt. She postured that such "conflicts were manifested as anger toward me, his family, his friends, his heroes, and most of all himself. His fantasies and crushes on women like me, Kate Hepburn, Anna Lee...all of whom he professed love for at one time or another—were just balm for this wound." O'Hara further theorized, "He hoped each of us could save him from these conflicting feelings but was later forced to accept that none of us could."

* * *

By the time *Mary of Scotland* was in postproduction, Ford was already involved with his next project—RKO's *The Plough and the Stars* (1937). Film editor Jane Loring was left to make many final decisions on continuity and pacing. When released in late summer 1936, *Mary of Scotland* received somewhat respectful but unenthusiastic reviews. *Time* magazine stated, "That, outside the narrow range in which she is superb, Katharine Hepburn often acts like a Bryn Mawr senior in a May Day pageant; that Fredric March's Scottish burr has Wisconsin overtones; and that Director John Ford tried to symbolize the somber qualities of his story by the over-simple expedient of shooting in the dark, are circumstances which do not heighten the film's dramatic impact." The unwieldy *Mary of Scotland* lost $165,000 in worldwide distribution.

Blinded by the failures of Hepburn's recent period entries (e.g., *The Little Minister, Mary of Scotland*) to draw in filmgoers, RKO amazingly shoved its high-priced star into yet another such stuffy costumed venture. Perhaps the decision was inspired by the success other studios were having with the historical genre. There is also some indication that Kate agreed to this new entry as a tribute of sort to her crusading mother.

In *A Woman Rebels* (1936), Kate was presented as a beacon for women's emancipation during England's Victorian era. She was Pamela Thistlewaite, who gives birth to a child out of wedlock, becomes the crusading editor of a women's periodical, and eventually weds her long-patient suitor (played by Herbert Marshall). Hoping to inject verve into the expensively mounted historical drama, the studio assigned Mark Sandrich to direct. He was notable for inventively helming several of RKO's Fred Astaire–Ginger Rogers musicals that had proven so enormously profitable. In contrast, *A Woman Rebels* lost $220,000, making it Kate's third box-office fiasco in a row.

※　※　※

Shortly before *The Little Minister* opened to poor results in late 1934, RKO acquired the screen rights to *Quality Street*. This was another Sir James M. Barrie play in which Maude Adams had scored a sizable Broadway success (in 1901). For this latest Hepburn showcase—a whimsical comedy-drama of mistaken identity and unreciprocated affection set in bygone times—Kate suggested Charles Boyer should be her leading man, the physician who enlists in the British Army during the Napoleonic wars. This casting did not occur, nor did RKO's efforts succeed to in contracting Douglas Fairbanks Jr. as the object of the outspoken, spinster heroine's enduring love. However, the studio did borrow Franchot Tone from MGM to portray Dr. Valentine Brown, with Fay Bainter cast as Kate's spinster older sister.

Hoping to turn around her run of bad professional luck, Kate convinced George Stevens—with the studio backing up her request—to direct the overly precious *Quality Street*. Stevens reluctantly agreed, but it meant he had to relinquish supervising the allegorical Broadway drama *Winterset* in its bigscreen translation. George was resentful about being pushed into this RKO assignment and proved unable to provide Kate with the degree of creative support she sorely needed to make her performance less potentially cloying. One regular member on recent Hepburn screen projects who was now missing from the lineup was Jane Loring. Stevens believed she was a distracting force on the star and he wanted to be fully in charge of guiding Kate through the tricky waters of *Quality Street*. Thus he ordered that Jane not appear on Hepburn's set. Reluctantly Jane returned to her duties as Pandro S. Berman's special assistant and awaited her chance to direct a feature.

If Hepburn was not already under enough stress trying to make *Quality Street* into a much-needed hit, she had to cope with distressing personal news during the two-month shoot. On November 15, 1936, Leland Hayward wed Margaret Sullavan in Newport, Rhode Island. While Hepburn knew the couple had been dating, she had not realized (or accepted) the seriousness of their love. (She also did not know that Sullavan was already pregnant with Leland's child, Brooke, who would be born in 1937.)

Also unknown to Kate at the time was that before the ceremony took place, Hayward, an experienced aviator, had flown his plane to Los Angeles to tell Hepburn in person of his pending nuptials. He drove to Kate's home but got no farther than her driveway. There he suddenly realized he just could not confront her with this news. He returned to the airport and flew back to New York, a lengthy trek in those days. He then sent Kate a telegram. When Hayward recounted this narrative years later to his son, William, the offspring registered disapproval of his dad's lack of courage in the delicate situation. Leland brushed off the reprimand with, "Once Kate is your friend, she's your friend for life."

Hepburn forced herself to send the newlyweds a note of congratulations, one the bride openly mocked and then crumpled and tossed into a wastepaper basket. For days after "losing" Leland—a man whose marriage offers she had previously rejected—Kate was distraught. She was literally sick to her stomach and moved about the *Quality Street* sets in a daze. Nothing seemed to be going right for Hepburn. George Stevens was not working any miracle with their new picture, while Jane Loring was preoccupied with other duties and she and Kate were not as close as before. Then too, Hepburn's fanciful bond with John Ford was stuck in gear and going nowhere. Moreover, Laura Harding was back east just when Kate needed her counsel the most.

When *Quality Street* was released in late March 1937, Kate's histrionics won mixed reactions. (One New York reviewer noted, "Her fluttering movements and the strained intensity of her emotional scenes evoke the full flavor of the work's genteel whimsy." In contrast, a *Los Angeles Times* reviewer observed that the star's "Phoebe Throssel needs a neurologist far more than a husband.") The film's exaggerated artifice and overly genteel shenanigans did not amuse many audiences, and *Quality Street* lost a massive $248,000 in worldwide distribution.

With Hepburn's further-diminished status at RKO, it required all her determination and caginess to convince Pandro S. Berman to consider her for a key role in an upcoming major picture. The studio had acquired expensive screen rights to the Broadway hit *Stage Door* and was planning this as a pivotal release of its late 1937–early 1938 distribution season. Kate had to cajole the studio's top executives to give her the key role of Terry Randall, the haughty neophyte actress. Because it was the part that irksome Margaret Sullavan had originated on the New York stage, Hepburn was determined to obtain this screen assignment at any cost. When it was announced that Kate had snagged the role Sullavan told friends, "I have never been 'desperate' for any part; I have had my pick of the best; as for having 'needed them,' it's *Miss Hepburn* who needs good parts, as the public is getting fed up with her."

Chapter Nineteen
FLYING HIGH

"Howard [Hughes] and I were indeed a strange pair. He was sort of the top of the available men—and I of the women. We each had a wild desire to be famous. I think that this was a dominant character failing. People who want to be famous are really loners. Or they should be."
—*Katharine Hepburn, 1991*

Like Claudette Colbert, Joan Crawford, Bette Davis, and Marlene Dietrich, four other enduring major stars of Hollywood's Golden Age, Katharine Hepburn developed a remarkable skill for professional self-preservation. In a cutthroat industry where the average leading lady (e.g., Helen Twelvetrees, Ann Dvorak, and Sidney Fox) had a success expectancy of four to five prime years, this quintet had the knack for continuously reinventing themselves to suit the changing times and to fashion their own maturing screen look. Tenacious Hepburn was as crafty and manipulative as her Tinseltown rivals. However, no-nonsense Kate made her career and life choices seem to be natural extensions of her practical New England personality and not unsubtle desperation moves to retain a glorious industry standing. As Hepburn became more adept and amenable at manipulating—rather than ignoring—the media, her reputation as America's most self-sufficient and lasting star became more entrenched in the minds of her adoring public.

✻ ✻ ✻

In the wake of the disastrous *The Lake,* Kate was understandably cautious about returning to the Broadway stage. However, she often pushed herself to tackle what she feared most. At the time she was convinced that theater critics and playgoers were not rooting for her to succeed, and that gnawed at her psyche.

Because of her cumulative concerns about appearing on the stage and due to film commitments Kate bowed out of headlining a 1935 adaptation of Jane Austen's *Pride and Prejudice.* (To her chagrin, the show, starring Adrianne Allen enjoyed a healthy run.) The next year Hepburn almost had the opportunity to portray Napoléon Bonaparte's sister, Pauline, in a new play being written by Louise Perkins. Louise was the wife of famed publishing house editor Maxwell Perkins and a neighbor of Kate's on Manhattan's East Forty-ninth Street. However, the novice playwright never solved script problems and the venture evaporated.

Meanwhile, the Theater Guild approached Hepburn to star in a new adaptation of Charlotte Brontë's novel *Jane Eyre,* which had recently opened in London to qualified approval. Since Kate's latest RKO pact had been completed with *Quality Street,* she was at loose ends professionally. In this frustrating career limbo Hepburn agreed to the offered stage project on condition that she receive a $1,500 weekly salary (her payback for the Guild not giving her a $5 raise when she took on double duty during the 1930 run of *A Month in the Country*). She also decreed that the play must tour the country until such time as she felt it was ready for Broadway scrutiny. (To some onlookers, it seemed illogical that Hepburn would agree to appear in a costume drama after the failure of her last three period screen outings.)

* * *

A backdrop to Hepburn's planned return to the stage was Kate's personal life. Fortuitously, she always had her family as a support group to fall back on and always had a clique of women friends to provide companionship, encouragement, and, sometimes, romantic diversion. However, it was rare for Hepburn to have several male figures intertwined so integrally into in her daily life. In 1936 there were three (discounting her discarded but still loyal, congenial, and always available ex-husband, Luddy). What is unique, and to Hepburn's credit, is that even after matters sorted themselves out, this trio of diverse, famous men were still so impressed and entertained by Kate that they remained friends with her for life.

First and foremost was Leland Hayward. He had been both her chief negotiator with RKO and her favored man in private life, outlasting her brief distraction with director George Stevens while making *Alice Adams*. That the charming, high-energy Hayward meant a great deal to Kate cannot be denied.

Being a woman of many different moods and needs, Kate had continued to see Hayward. Meanwhile, she dallied with the married John Ford during *Mary of Scotland* and thereafter. Whether Hepburn would ever have traveled with John to Ireland, as they so often discussed, and/or settled down with him into a conventional domestic situation, if he divorced, remains moot. Eventually the filmmaker would chose not to abandon his existing family life. But that pivotal decision was not reached until sometime in 1937. After that Kate and John transitioned into a wistful platonic friendship that endured until his death in 1973.

Meanwhile, in 1936, as the novelty of Kate's friendship with the shadowy, subservient Jane Loring was losing its luster, Kate believed she still had Leland Hayward on her string. She thought he was ready to marry her when and if she so chose. In this same period the star was still exploring her personal ties to John Ford, not sure how far she and/or he should allow the situation to progress. Then into the mix came enigmatic Howard Robert Hughes Jr.

※　※　※

In the course of Howard Hughes's most bizarre life, the bashful Texas-born billionaire would be associated amorously with a long string of glamorous movie actresses and fetching debutantes and would be twice wed. However, none of his many romantic associations over the decades would receive the amount of publicity and speculation afforded his lengthy courtship of Kate Hepburn.

In the early 1930s, Hughes won prestige within the film industry by producing such important features as *Hell's Angels* (1930), *The Front Page* (1931), and *Scarface* (1932). After that he had temporarily abandoned the movie business. Instead, he redirected his focus to expanding his aircraft corporation and building his global reputation as a record-breaking aviator. Remaining based in Los Angeles, Howard continued to pursue women with a reckless abandon. One of his few male friends was film actor Cary Grant, whose marriage to movie performer Virginia Cherrill had just ended. (Both Grant and Hughes were reputed—but never proven conclusively—to be bisexual and to have enjoyed a togetherness that extended far beyond conventional male bonding.) With his good looks, dazzle, and outgoing posture, Cary had little difficulty attracting desirable women. This enviable knack intrigued the emotionally reticent Hughes, who was increasingly restrained on the social scene. (Howard had an accelerating hearing problem that he refused to acknowledge publicly and that increasingly inhibited his interaction with others.) The two men soon developed a routine in which Cary would make social entrées with those females who appealed to the idiosyncratic Hughes. This procuring routine bound the two men even closer together.

In August 1935, Grant began filming RKO's *Sylvia Scarlett*. As an amateur matchmaker, Cary thought that Hughes would be an interesting choice for Grant's current leading lady, Katharine Hepburn. (Both adored golf, had a fascination with flying, and enjoyed associating with bright, well-mannered individuals. Each had a fetish for cleanliness and bathed several times daily. In addition, each was reputedly bisexual.) Thus Cary, always eager to do favors for his wealthy and powerful pal, offered to introduce Hughes to Hepburn. The British actor encouraged his entrepreneur friend to temporarily forgo tinkering on his racer plane on a particular day and instead fly to Trancas, ten miles west of Malibu Beach. *Sylvia Scarlett* was currently on location there. Howard reluctantly agreed. It was decided Grant would not alert Kate or director George Cukor as to who would be Cary's special guest at the next day's lunch break.

The following day, as Kate, Cukor, Grant, and a few other primary figures of the cast and crew spread out their picnic lunch, they heard a roar in the sky. Soon a biplane landed and out stepped six-foot three-inch, lanky, and handsome Hughes garbed in dashing flight togs. The Texan ambled over to Grant and introductions were made. Cukor was impressed to have Hughes as his lunch companion and was amused by Cary's matchmaking efforts. However, Kate thought Howard's presence was an intrusion (or, perhaps, she was deliberately playing hard to get). During the light meal she pointedly ignored the newcomer as she, Cary, and George exchanged Hollywood gossip. Howard was in awe of the opinionated leading lady and remained silent.

1.

2.

1. The young Katharine Hepburn.
[Courtesy of Photofest]

2. Kate Hepburn, second from right, playing a man in a Bryn Mawr college production (1927's *The Truth About Blayds*).
[Courtesy of Photofest]

3. At Bryn Mawr's 1928 May Day festivities, Hepburn played the lead of Pandora in *The Woman in the Moone*.
[Courtesy of Steve Campbell]

4. With Frances Dee, Jean Parker, and Joan Bennett in *Little Women* (1933), one of Hepburn's most popular films of the 1930s and a personal favorite of the star's.
[Courtesy of JC Archives]

3.

4.

5.

7.

5. Starring in *The Warrior's Husband* (1932), the Broadway sensation that brought Hepburn to Hollywood.
[Courtesy of JC Archives]

6. With Billie Burke in Hepburn's film debut, RKO's *A Bill of Divorcement* (1932).
[Courtesy of JC Archives]

6.

7. A miscast Hepburn as a hillbilly tomboy in *Spitfire* (1934).
[Courtesy of JC Archives]

8. Hepburn with socialite Laura Harding (right), the longtime friend who frequently lived with Hepburn in 1930s Hollywood.
[Courtesy of Photofest]

9. Hepburn embraced by costar Elizabeth Allan in the period drama *A Woman Rebels* (opposite page, 1936).
[Courtesy of JC Archives]

8.

9.

10. Actor Anderson Lawler, one of Hollywood's more flamboyant personalities, chatting with Hepburn poolside at the home of film director George Cukor in the mid 1930s. [Courtesy of Photofest]

11. Katharine Hepburn with Ginger Rogers—her greatest RKO studio rival—on the set of their costarring vehicle, 1937's *Stage Door*. [Courtesy of JC Archives]

12. On the set of her comeback film vehicle, MGM's *The Philadelphia Story* (1940) with Jimmy Stewart (center) and director-friend George Cukor (right). [Courtesy of Photofest]

13.

14.

13. Katharine Hepburn carrying the burden of China during the Japanese invasion in *Dragon Seed* (1944).
[Courtesy of Professor James Fisher]

14. Hepburn literally sitting at the feet of Humphrey Bogart in *The African Queen* (1951), another of her many Oscar-nominated performances.
[Courtesy of JC Archives]

15. Spencer Tracy with his wife, Louise Treadwell.
[Courtesy of JC Archives]

16. MGM attempted unsuccessfully to kindle oncamera chemistry between Hepburn and screen idol Robert Taylor in *Undercurrent* (opposite page, 1946).
[Courtesy of JC Archives]

15.

17.

18.

20.

19.

17. Katharine Hepburn on the set of *Guess Who's Coming to Dinner* (1967) with Spencer Tracy, who died a few weeks after filming was completed. [Courtesy of Photofest]

18. A very relaxed moment on the set of the British-filmed telefeature *Love Among the Ruins* (1975) with colead Sir Laurence Olivier and director George Cukor. [Courtesy of Photofest]

19. As Eleanor of Aquitaine in *The Lion in Winter* (1968), for which Hepburn garnered her third Academy Award. [Courtesy of JC Archives]

20. Hepburn sharing screen time with another enduring cinema legend, John Wayne, in the Western *Rooster Cogburn* (1975). [Courtesy of JC Archives]

21. Teamed with Henry Fonda in *On Golden Pond* (1981), Hepburn earned her fourth and final Best Actress Oscar. [Courtesy of JC Archives]

21.

Later, as Hughes was being escorted back to his plane, Kate told Cary she *thought* they had agreed to bring only "interesting people to lunch." Despite Hepburn's pointed remark, Grant continued to promote Hughes to Hepburn and vice versa.

Several weeks later Hepburn was enjoying a relaxing game of golf at the Bel Air Country Club. She was at the seventh tee when she heard the roar of an aircraft flying low overhead. The craft landed on the golf course (much to the consternation of the club's administrators) and out popped Hughes. Kate told her golf pro partner to ignore the approaching intruder. Howard was carrying his golf bag and asked to join Hepburn as she played out her game. After belittling Hughes for his lack of decorum on the links, Kate reluctantly agreed. When it came time to leave, Howard found he needed a ride home. (The club had decreed that he could not fly his plane from the green and further tear up the well-manicured course. Hughes nonchalantly phoned his crew to come and disassemble the craft, which was then carted away in pieces and later put back together at the hangar—all at a premium cost). Hepburn was flattered by her new suitor's persistence and offered Hughes a ride home. Thus began their dating of one another.

The Hughes involvement could not have come at a more strategic time for emotionally beleaguered Hepburn. Leland Hayward soon "betrayed" Kate by marrying her archrival, Margaret Sullavan. The liaison with John Ford was not picking up the momentum she had anticipated and wanted in order to satisfy her fantasy. Now here was one of America's—in fact, the world's—most eligible males paying special court to her.

Hepburn found Hughes's pursuit of her to be very flattering, and that in turn piqued her interest in this prized playboy. Then too, as she smartly anticipated, the growing public knowledge of their coupling would certainly help to divert Hollywood and the public from the fact that Kate's movie career was in rapid decline. At this juncture, Kate was thinking ahead to the fact that in May 1937 she would turn thirty. She was keenly conscious of this chronological milestone and pondered how she should spend the next three decades of her life. (In coming months Hepburn would write a long note to John Ford discussing this very topic.)

With boyish Howard constantly yapping at Kate's heels she knew that her being seen socially with this internationally famous bachelor would grab a great deal of media attention—all the more because the duo went to enormous lengths to avoid the press, which in turn made reporters pursue the couple all the more. Then too, a fanciful part of Kate may have hoped that her involvement with Hughes would spark jealousy in Ford and push him into actually leaving his family. Moreover, the hoopla over Kate dating Howard could only help the box office for *Jane Eyre* and her upcoming RKO release, *Stage Door*. And certainly, being associated with Howard, regarded as a virile man among men, could only help to dispel recurring rumors about Kate's lesbianism or bisexuality (or, as some observers were now coming to believe, her growing *asexuality*).

❊ ❊ ❊

Between orchestrating the boundaries of her overlapping involvements with John Ford and Howard Hughes—and making a great show of bemoaning Leland Hayward's "defection"—Hepburn began preparations for her stage appearance in *Jane Eyre*. On the plus side, she found Worthington Miner a congenial director. On the downside, Kate had reservations about British character actor Dennis Hoey being given the key role of Mr. Rochester. She felt he was not a sufficiently strong stage presence. It also bothered Kate that the Guild insisted on billing her above the play's title rather than as part of the ensemble. (If the theatrical venture failed, the blame would rest squarely on Hepburn's shoulders. As she reasoned to the producers, "I just don't want to stick my neck out!") More upsetting to Hepburn was the fact that playwright Helene Jerome refused to adjust her script to better suit American audiences and to showcase the leading lady's best qualities.

After run-throughs in Manhattan, *Jane Eyre* played in New Haven, Connecticut, on December 26, 1936. Impulsive Hughes had followed Hepburn to the East Coast, but he deliberately avoided attending the debut performance. He feared his presence in the audience would distract from Kate's stage showcase. The show opened, and it became clear immediately that the drama still had structural flaws. Nevertheless, theatergoers flocked to see the unique Hollywood star perform onstage.

While the show continued its tour (with Laura Harding often along to bolster Kate's spirits, as was the rather mannish Emily Perkins, ever present in her combined functions as secretary and maid), Hughes made sensational headlines of his own. On January 19, 1937, he piloted his *Flying Bullet* plane from Burbank, California, to Newark, New Jersey. He flew at a particularly high altitude to increase his speed and to minimize fuel usage. While zooming over Winslow, Arizona, he suffered from hypoxia, an inability to breathe properly in the rarified atmosphere, and became almost too dizzy to navigate the craft to a lower altitude. He finally overcame the problem by biting through the oxygen mask tubing and gulping quantities of air.

For a time during the perilous flight Howard was out of communication with ground control, and newspapers reported that the famed pilot was feared lost. However, seven hours and twenty-eight minutes after he took off from the West Coast, Hughes landed safely at his destination. He had made the most sensational long-distance flight to that date, beating his own cross-country flight record of a year earlier. He immediately wired the good news to a much-relieved Kate, who was performing *Jane Eyre* in Chicago.

Americans—and the world—wildly cheered this new aviation hero, and no one was more pleased by Howard's success than proud Hepburn. (It greatly bolstered her ego to know the world's most dashing, glamorous playboy was courting her.) Hughes joined her in Chicago, where they had separate suites at the Ambassador Hotel. The media frenzy was tremendous, with newspapers declaring that Hepburn and Hughes would definitely wed in the Windy City. Hemmed in by the pursuing press and onlookers, the couple barricaded themselves in their hotel accommodations. Kate required a police escort to get her from the Ambassador Hotel to the theater for her daily performances. Although the Cook County clerk was quoted in the press as being excited that the celebrity duo would soon be arriving to obtain their marriage license, hours later it was announced by a hotel representative that "Miss Hepburn will not marry Mr. Hughes in Chicago today."

From Chicago (where *New York Times* critic Brooks Atkinson wrote a special pre-Broadway review complimenting the star for her "exquisite grace of movement"), *Jane Eyre* moved on to engagements in Indianapolis, Pittsburgh, Washington, D.C., and Baltimore. There the show closed on April 3, 1937. It was decided not to bring the play to Broadway at this time, a decision that both pleased and frustrated perfectionistic Kate.

While Hughes spent a great deal of time with Hepburn on her tour, he seemed unaware that she remained in touch by phone and letter with John Ford. When the director still refused to commit himself to Kate, she went on vacation to Key West, Florida. Her companion on the train trip south was her secretary, Em Perkins.

By the time Hepburn returned to California that May she had accepted that her private situation with Ford would not improve (even if she really wanted it to). With that in mind she made the rash and bold gesture of moving into Hughes's thirty-room mansion at 201 South Muirfield Drive in the Hancock Park area of Los Angeles. Kate was accompanied by her entourage of a personal maid (Johanna Madsen) as well as her cook and chauffeur (Ranghild and Louis Prysing). They joined Hughes's existing house staff of three. In addition Hepburn brought along her menagerie of dogs (two cocker spaniels and a French poodle).

Both Kate and Howard had been married previously but each had from the start established unconventional rules for those domestic unions—typically living apart from their mates and finding emotional support and physical comfort from others. From the beginning of their cohabitation Hepburn and Hughes were unsuited to each other. If they had thought seriously about it, neither one was about to submerge his/her distinctive personality, public image, and career for the other, as those facets represented too much of who they were. Kate returned to filmmaking while Howard was preparing for his next airborne feat.

Hepburn was content to slip back into her spartan social schedule while making films. She found sufficient outlet in channeling her tremendous energy and concentration into her role in *Stage Door*. On a late afternoon free of the sound stage, sometimes she and Howard would sneak through the fence on the Muirfield Road property to the adjacent golf course and enjoy a highly competitive game on the empty links. They also enjoyed trips on his luxurious yacht, and he taught tomboy Kate how to fly a plane. Hughes's pet name for Hepburn was "City Mouse" and for himself "Country Mouse."

As Hepburn fought to regain her industry standing, she paid little heed to Howard's frequent disappearances; he sometimes vanished for days at a time. She was apparently unaware—or did not care—that Hughes was often busy pursuing new female conquests. Occasionally, Kate agreed to play hostess when Howard entertained business associates. However, she was put off to discover that his dealings included meeting with disreputable figures—including gangsters.

Kate was always most happy when she could control situations, whether on the sound stage or on the home front. It caused growing dissension between the oddly matched couple as she realized Hughes intended to be the final arbiter of decisions involving them. Possibly, if each had not been so distracted by other, higher-priority pursuits, their romance (with whatever scant sexual interaction that encompassed) would have ended much sooner than it actually did. As it was, the increasingly tenuous links between these two eccentric, fascinating individuals lasted into 1938. By the middle of that Hepburn was between pictures and at another career fork in the road. Unsure of her next step, she retreated to Fenwick to be nurtured by her family.

During their time together, Howard once visited the Hepburn tribe, but it was an unsettling occurrence for him. Hughes was baffled by the presence of Ogden Ludlow, who insisted on following everyone around snapping pictures. This bothered photo-shy Howard, but Dr. Hepburn took his ex-son-in-law's side and sharply reprimanded Hughes for being snide to Luddy. Then too, finicky Howard was accustomed to a special diet, and he found the cuisine at the Hepburns' not to his liking, With his hearing handicap Hughes was especially distracted by the noisy, circus-like atmosphere at the Hepburns' dinner table, where everyone—but he—chimed into the heated discussions. Hughes was relieved to say goodbye to the Hepburn clan.

When Howard set out on his record-breaking flight around the world on July 10, 1938, Kate and her family were impressed that he dipped his wings over the Hepburn home in acknowledgment of his girlfriend. Upon returning to New York City in mid July, Hughes received a ticker-tape parade befitting the great hero he was. Thereafter, like a lovesick schoolboy he rushed to be with Kate at her Manhattan brownstone. (She had closely followed his daring global jaunt by listening to the frequent radio news bulletins.) Between avoiding the hounding press and coming down from the exhilaration of his spectacular plane trek, the couple finally admitted that they were unsuited to one another. It brought about the end of their grand association, one that had done so much to glamorize each participant's romantic image. Because of this, the courtship had provided some elements of what each had hoped to gain from the unrealistic union.

In typical (and practical) fashion, Hepburn ended her involvement with Hughes on a civilized note, one that paved the way for she and her ex-intimate to continue being friends of a sort over the coming decades.

Meanwhile, during the final period of Hepburn's cohabitation with Howard Hughes, she and RKO had come to a parting of the ways. The breakup of star and studio had begun its final course when Kate returned to the Gower Street facility to film *Stage Door*. In that picture she had to deal daily with a new professional adversary. The latter was blond, four-years-younger Ginger Rogers, whom RKO now celebrated as its biggest female moneymaker. Rogers received all the pampering and respect on the lot—just as Hepburn had a few short years earlier.

Chapter Twenty
A HOLLYWOOD FAREWELL

"The times I failed, on stage or screen, didn't depress me because of career; they worried me because I hadn't mastered myself and made myself do correctly what I'd set out to do."
                                        —*Katharine Hepburn, 1940*

Returning to the RKO lot in early June 1937, Katharine Hepburn was caught in a most peculiar career situation. She had enjoyed a qualified stage success with the *Jane Eyre* road tour. However, the script-weak play had not opened on Broadway as anticipated, and this counted against her professional standing. Adding to this show business failure were Kate's quartet of recent feature film flops. As a result her worth had dimmed considerably in the eyes of RKO studio executives and with moviegoers. (In 1993's *Hollywood Androgyny*, Rebecca Bell-Metereau said of the 1930s Hepburn: "Audiences of her day found her a bit unconventional, probably in exactly those features that make her ideal for male impersonation—a wide, strong jaw, rather large teeth, prominent cheekbones, and relatively small eyes. Moreover, her brusqueness, outspoken manner, and forceful, abrupt gestures...combined to make her unpopular for the period in which audiences rankled at her aggressiveness and apparent disdain for convention.")

On the plus side, Hepburn was the media-touted object of Howard Hughes's continuous affection. Although it was not officially publicized that she and the Bashful Billionaire were actually sharing digs (for fear of upsetting the country's moral conservatives), her well-covered romance with the elusive playboy gave her special cachet with the enthralled public. It suggested that despite Kate's recent screen roles failing to capture the star's unique personality, she obviously had an abundance of real-life charms that appealed to the world's most eligible bachelor. Therefore, it was theorized, if Hughes was so smitten with Kate, then she still had marketable box-office worth. Because of this, Hepburn was able to negotiate a new RKO pact, with *Stage Door* to be her first picture at a $75,000 fee.

❊ ❊ ❊

As preproduction began on *Stage Door,* Hepburn coped with the disquieting fact that the studio was hedging its bets on Kate's marquee lure by placing Ginger Rogers in top billing on this ensemble project. Well aware of the value of one's screen billing, Hepburn complained to her mentor, Pandro S. Berman. He told her only semijokingly, "You'd be lucky if you played seventh part in a successful picture."

Thus, Hepburn began *Stage Door* in a vulnerable mood that she masked with her usual gilt-edged bravado. Beneath her surface equanimity Kate was extremely leery of her pretty, highly feminine costar. In actuality, Hepburn had many reasons for her increasingly negative feelings about the popular Rogers. Four years younger than Kate, Ginger had been on a career fast track since she and Fred Astaire had been the surprise sensations of RKO's *Flying Down to Rio* (1933). Since then the elegant song-and-dance team had been rematched profitably in several prestigious RKO entries. Occasionally, workaholic Rogers appeared oncamera without Astaire, as with *In Person* (1935). In that popular screwball film she had revealed a delightful comedic persona capable of maneuvering through lighthearted fare. This particular Ginger Rogers success gnawed at Hepburn because Kate had earlier rejected the role as being unsuited to her refined personality.

When Rogers and Astaire made the lilting *Swing Time* (1936) director George Stevens had become enchanted with the effervescent Ginger. Although each was then married—Ginger for the second time—a romance had blossomed. It accelerated when they worked together again on 1938's *Vivacious Lady.* Stevens's "disloyalty" to Hepburn upset Kate, who felt her rapport with the director both on and off film sets entitled her exclusively to his special attention. However, because Kate had such high regard for George as a talent, she instead directed all her hostility toward Rogers. Hepburn's growing dislike of her perky studio challenger was accentuated because another of Kate's former beaus, Leland Hayward, not only represented Kate but also guided Ginger's career moves.

Then there was the matter of *Mary of Scotland*. When that 1936 picture was being prepared RKO had considered casting Tallulah Bankhead or Bette Davis as Kate's oncamera adversary. After those negotiations fell through, other talent was tested. While this was happening Ginger demanded to be considered for the highly dramatic role. RKO considered her request frivolous and denied her request. Undaunted, Rogers wangled an audition using the name Lady Ainsley. Wearing a disguise and sporting a thick British accent, Ginger arrived on the sound stage for her test opposite Hepburn. By then director John Ford, producer Pandro S. Berman, and even Hepburn knew of the ruse. Kate was not amused. During the audition, according to Rogers, Hepburn constantly kicked her coplayer under the table at which they were seated for their oncamera scene together. Later, when the studio confirmed that Florence Eldridge would play feisty Queen Elizabeth I, Hepburn chortled at the outcome. Her snide reaction was made known to Ginger.

Adding to the contention between these two ambitious women, just before Hepburn began seriously to date Howard Hughes he was busy escorting Ginger around town. (After Howard and Kate broke up, Hughes proposed to Rogers, but she decided such a union could not last and rejected his offer.) Further intensifying the enmity between RKO's two prime leading ladies was the presence of Ginger's mother on the film lot. To distract Lela Rogers from her annoying micromanaging of her daughter's career, RKO established a studio talent school for Lela to operate. With this role the powerhouse mother was a constant presence at the filmmaking facility. As Hepburn unavoidably crossing paths with the formidable Lela, there had to be times when Kate must have compared her own mother—always preoccupied with her planned parenthood crusades and totally uninterested in ever visiting her daughter in Hollywood—with Ginger's overly devoted parent and career manager. Thus there had to be occasions when Hepburn wished she had such a loyal family member as Lela in her corner as she struggled for survival amid the ever-changing RKO regimes.

Not to be overlooked in the battle between RKO's chief women stars were two other incidents. One day Rogers returned from vacation and proudly paraded about RKO showing off her new full-length mink coat. Passing an administration building, she waved to George Stevens, who had just stuck his head out the window to see what the commotion was all about. Suddenly, a torrent of water poured forth from a neighboring window and drenched Rogers's expensive mink coat. According to Ginger, she looked up to see prankish Hepburn smirking and yelling down, "If it's real mink, it won't shrink!" Another time, trying to make peace with Kate the Great, Rogers purchased a platinum pin inlaid with small diamonds as a birthday gift for her formidable rival. She never had any response from Kate regarding the present. Years later, Ginger went backstage to say hello to Hepburn, who was then appearing on Broadway. When Rogers inquired what Hepburn had done with "my little birthday gift," Kate replied, "Oh, I don't really remember. I must have given it to someone."

❋ ❋ ❋

Directing *Stage Door* was Gregory La Cava, a long-time Hollywood talent who had recently scored exceptionally well with his screwball comedy *My Man Godfrey* (1936). Renowned as a heavy drinker, La Cava was also famous for his working habit of rewriting the script of his current production on a day-to-day basis and then urging his cast to work relatively impromptu with the just-completed material. He believed this created the necessary spontaneity within a scene to make it fresh to filmgoers. *Stage Door*'s original story line—which was essentially anti-Hollywood—was revamped to such an extent that some industry observers quipped it should be retitled *Hollywood Door*. To help in restructuring the screenplay, La Cava and his staff had gathered the cast together for two weeks of getting acquainted, recounting show business backgrounds, and working improvisationally on dialogue exchanges and scenes that sprang from these rehearsals.

One of the most intriguing creative results of this preproduction effort was La Cava's inspiration—and Kate's surprising willingness to go along with the problematic notion—to develop her new screen role by mingling aspects of Hepburn's real-life stage career with fragments of her Oscar-winning *Morning Glory* characterization. La Cava even utilized Hepburn's flop *The*

Lake as a springboard for *Enchanted April.* In this play-within-a-play Hepburn's Terry Randall tearfully says, "The calla lilies are in bloom again. Such a strange flower, suitable to any occasion. I carried them on my wedding day and now I place them here in memory of something that has died." (The maudlin lines subsequently became essential dialogue for anyone doing a Kate Hepburn impression.)

One of Kate's more congenial coplayers on *Stage Door*—the cast of which included Eve Arden, Constance Collier, Lucille Ball, and Adolphe Menjou—was teenage Ann Miller. Years later the veteran performer–tap dancer recalled of Hepburn: "Well, she was a terrific woman. I liked her so much. You know, when we did *Stage Door*, every afternoon she had it in her contract that at five o'clock [actually four o'clock] she would have her tea, and it didn't matter whether Gregory La Cava was in the middle of a huge dramatic scene with Ginger Rogers or what. Everything stopped and in came the tea cart and in came the cookies and all the doughnuts, and the crew just loved her. Of course, all the actors did. And we'd have our tea and after all that was over, we'd go back to work."

By the time *Stage Door* completed production at the end of July 1937 not only had Kate's part been built up considerably, but she was awarded top-billing in the screen credits. (La Cava would say of working with Hepburn, "She is completely the intellectual actress. She has to understand the why of everything before she can feel. Then, when the meaning has soaked in, emotion comes, and superb work.")

When released the ensemble film was well appreciated. Kate registered effectively as the smug, wealthy neophyte who becomes a humbled stage worker able to interact with her wisecracking roommate (Rogers) and the other aspiring talents at Manhattan's Footlights Club. Her sterling performance resonated as forthright, honest, and realistically determined. Rose Pelswick (*New York Journal*) reported that this film "brings Katharine Hepburn back to the spot she occupied before a series of monotonous performances dimmed the memory of *Morning Glory.*" That was true, but the acting honors in this picture were divided among several: Hepburn, Rogers, and Andrea Leeds (as the disappointed actress who commits suicide). Therefore the picture could not be regarded (by the industry or the public) as purely a Katharine Hepburn vehicle, Moreover, although *Stage Door* did quite nicely at the box office, it had cost an enormous $952,000 to mount and earned only a modest $81,000 profit.

*　*　*

As *Stage Door* awaited release, RKO had a brainstorm. Wanting to show-case its once-prized leading lady in a new screen posture and hoping to rein-vigorate her now-spotty career, the studio assigned Hepburn to her first con-temporary screen comedy. It was the screwball entry *Bringing Up Baby* (1938). Veteran director-producer Howard Hawks (1932's *Scarface,* 1934's *Twentieth Century*) nurtured this long-brewing project into reality. He had a penchant on and off the screen for lanky, self-confident women. Howard agreed with the studio that Kate might function well in this celluloid account of a flighty heiress who becomes attracted to a nerdy paleontologist. Unfortunately, the more that daffy Susan Vance tries to help the dinosaur expert sort out his career and love life, the more she unintentionally causes the man a cascading series of misadventures. Eventually, the hero recognizes that the well-meaning but bungling socialite is his true soul mate.

After efforts to cast Robert Montgomery or Leslie Howard in the male lead failed, Hawks eventually hired the much-in-demand Cary Grant to play bespectacled Dr. David Huxley. As production got under way in the fall 1937, Hawks soon discovered that Hepburn was treading on professional quick-sand. She was trying too hard to be comedic rather than approach the role seriously and let the comedy—both verbal and physical pratfalls—proceed unforced. In desperation Howard turned to Walter Catlett, an old hand at stage and film merriment. Catlett was brought onto the set to offer Hepburn a few pointers. After the two conferred for a short time, Kate approached Hawks and said, "Howard, hire that guy and keep him around here for sever-al weeks, because I need him."

One of the key gimmicks of *Bringing Up Baby* was its title character played by Nissa, an eight-year-old leopard. Unlike Grant or the others on the set, Kate exhibited no fear of the animal and got along well with Nissa. Relaxed with each other, Kate and Cary displayed great rapport in this well-oiled screwball comedy, which included the two undertaking many athletic stunts as well as harmonizing on "I Can't Give You Anything But Love."

As *Bringing Up Baby* wound up production in January 1938, RKO executives learned that the Independent Theater Owners of America were about to circulate an open letter to the film industry asking the studios to please stop featuring low-grossing stars of the moment in their releases. Among the indicted luminaries were Fred Astaire, Joan Crawford, Bette Davis, Marlene Dietrich, Kay Francis, Greta Garbo, Katharine Hepburn (who led the list), and Mae West. With Hawks's film already way over budget, RKO executives panicked. They reacted by making a snap decision to shelve the production rather than spend additional sums on editing, scoring, and advertising. It was at this critical juncture that Hughes, still much involved "romantically" with Hepburn, took a risky gamble. He acquired distribution rights to *Bringing Up Baby* from RKO and arranged for its release through the Loew's theater chain.

In later years critics would hail *Bringing Up Baby* as a true classic of the screwball comedy genre. At the time of its release, however, it was but one of a long procession of such cinema amusements, and the public was tiring of such zany fare. The brewing world war was already affecting America's priorities, and moviegoers' interests were fast changing. Thus this second Hepburn-Grant vehicle received mixed reviews. For every positive response ("the new Miss Hepburn...should find favor with a new audience as well as her old following") to Kate's contributions to the proceedings, there were unpleasant digs at her screen presence ("Miss Hepburn has a role which calls for her to be breathless, senseless and terribly, terribly fatiguing. She succeeds, and we can be callous enough to hint it is not entirely a matter of performance.") When the financial books on *Bringing Up Baby* were tallied, the feature had lost a gigantic $365,000, despite having earned $1.109 million in worldwide film rentals.

Publicly labeled "box-office poison" by the Independent Theater Owners, Kate was in a major career pickle. She attempted to treat the demoralizing situation lightheartedly. She was quoted as saying, "They say I'm a has-been. If I weren't laughing so hard, I might cry." (In actuality, being taunted so publicly by the critics mortified Kate and pushed her to a near-breaking point. There are accounts that the dreaded "box-office poison" label led her to an abortive suicide attempt on the RKO lot when she supposedly threatened to jump out of a second-story window of one of the studio's buildings.)

Declared persona non grata at RKO, Hepburn eventually willed herself to fight back and not slink away from Hollywood in defeat. She learned that Columbia Pictures had acquired screen rights to *Holiday* and planned to remake the 1930 film, which had costarred Ann Harding and Mary Astor. Eager to show everyone that she could successfully handle the rebellious rich girl role that she had once understudied on Broadway, Hepburn used her business skills (learned from her father) and her ingenuity under pressure to negotiate a deal with Columbia's mogul, Harry Cohn. Eventually, it was arranged that on loanout to Columbia she would costar with Cary Grant (for the third time), while MGM's George Cukor would be borrowed to direct his favorite leading lady for the fourth time. Lew Ayres (Ginger Rogers's ex-husband) was hired to be Hepburn's onscreen brother and Doris Nolan to play their older sibling.

When the picture was released, *Time* magazine reported that in *Holiday* Kate "gives her liveliest performance since appearing in *Little Women*." Philip Barry's decade-old play, however, seemed out of touch with life in the late 1930s. Filmgoing audiences, still coping with the real-life Depression, could not relate easily to a screen hero who abandons a lucrative position and embarks with the heroine on a European lark to find himself. The feature failed at the box office.

RKO now totally gave up on Kate, the "box-office deterrent." Rather than gamble any additional company funds on future Hepburn vehicles, studio executives used a familiar industry ruse to embarrass the once-lofty star into ending her studio contract. They decreed that her next starring role would be in a B picture, *Mother Carey's Chickens*, a bucolic domestic drama set in the 1890s. Unlike Warner Bros.' Kay Francis, who was pushed into similar dismal celluloid fodder but worked out her contract to guarantee continuation of her lofty salary, Kate immediately terminated her ties to RKO. She still owed the studio two additional pictures at $100,000 per film. To end her agreement, she agreed to relieve RKO of its obligation to pay her the contractual $200,000. Anxious to extract full revenge on the once-haughty Hepburn, the studio also demanded reimbursement for the sizable overtime pay she had received for *Bringing Up Baby*. An angry Hepburn immediately directed her father back in Connecticut to issue a $20,000 check to the studio. With that, she had her freedom. Katharine Hepburn would never work for RKO again.

By mid May 1938 the usually resilient Hepburn concluded she was washed up in Hollywood. As she phrased it, it was time to "start looking at airline schedules." In this bleak period one studio offered her a low-salaried multipicture contract, which she rejected, as she did an offer to do a film at MGM for a mere $10,000. She vowed "never to be under contract and have to do something I didn't want to do. I could afford it because I didn't need the money. I wasn't rich, but I wasn't poverty-stricken, and I could say no. That's the luckiest thing that can happen to you." As she further explained her brash stand in being so choosy about accepting film roles at this low ebb, "If people think you're independent, they trust you with a lot more respect. If they know you're their victim, they're apt to push you around. They thought I was terribly rich. I wasn't, but they thought so, and that's all that mattered."

When Kate vetoed these "rotten offers," studio executives asked, "Who are you to make demands?" The still-proud Hepburn replied, "I'll always make demands." During this mortifying time, Kate kept up a brave face while on the Hollywood scene. (By now Laura Harding had returned once again to the Coast to bolster her good friend during this period of crisis.) George Cukor, watching his dear friend flounder in the tricky Hollywood waters, recalled, "We could only suspect what she was going through at that time. Certainly Kate never showed it. She came to our small parties and was funny, gay; she made herself the butt of a great many jokes about her position. She certainly maintained her dignity. It wasn't until her plans for survival were perfected that she even revealed that she had been fighting, with courage, intelligence, and tenacity."

Chapter Twenty-one

PROVING HER
NEW ENGLAND METTLE

*"I think [Katharine] Hepburn has two strikes against her—
first, the unquestionable and very widespread public dislike
of her at the moment, and second the fact that she is yet to
demonstrate the sex qualities which are probably the most
important of all the many requisites of Scarlett [O'Hara in*
Gone With the Wind*]."*

—*producer David O. Selznick, 1938*

Once back east, Kate Hepburn, now a Hollywood pariah, busied herself
with catching up with her large family in West Hartford and at Fenwick.
Channeling her career frustrations into an exhausting regimen of sports
activities, she devoted her days to golf, tennis, swimming, and sailing. The
routine made her recent Hollywood mortification seem far less important in
the scope of life. In fact, many thought she appeared happier now than she
had been in a long time.

Meanwhile, the deposed movie star had the additional distraction of her
unresolved relationship with Howard Hughes, who in the summer of 1938
would embark on his thrilling round-the-world flight. In the coming months
there would also be the excitement of the preparations for sister Marion's wedding to Ellsworth S. Grant. Marion, a graduate of Vermont's Bennington College
(where youngster sister Peg was currently a student), had followed in her mother's social-reformer footsteps. She had recently worked on behalf of the
Congress of Industrial Organization in Washington, D.C., assisting the labor
union in picketing for improved wages for hotel workers. Kate's brother Bob was
completing medical school training in preparation for his career as a urologist.

As for artistic, sensitive, highly unconventional Dick, he was devoting himself exclusively to radical playwriting, squirreled away in his attic retreat in the family home. Inspired by Howard Hughes's visit with the Hepburns during 1938, Dick constructed a satirical play whose main characters—full of foibles and quirks—bore a conspicuous resemblance to Kate and Howard. The Hepburns were affronted that he would dream of making their private life public for his own aggrandizement. When Dick in a frenzy insisted on circulating the script to stage producers, Kate made it clear that if he did not abandon the project, she would cease her substantial contributions to his monthly allowance. The crestfallen brother eventually withdrew his controversial play. However, this widened the gulf between the two siblings. In the coming years Kate felt guilty that she had perhaps hindered Dick from making his modest creative place in the world. She continued to look out for him but developed a self-protective attitude in which she viewed this extremely puzzling, impractical soul with thinly veiled skepticism. It was also silently understood that in the Hepburn family there was room for only one show business star.

✻   ✻   ✻

In spring 1936, Lillie Messenger, the New York–based RKO talent scout who had once guided Hepburn in the screen test that first brought her to movies, read the galleys to a sprawling new novel. It was a sweeping epic of the American South before, during, and after the Civil War. Messenger was deeply impressed with Margaret Mitchell's *Gone With the Wind* (due for publication in mid June). She thought the property ideal for resolute Kate and had the studio take a short option on it. Lillie immediately sent a copy to Hepburn, another to producer Pandro S. Berman (who was heading back to Los Angeles from New York), and a third to Leo Spitz (RKO's then-president). Hepburn told Spitz of the forthcoming book: "It grows on you, and I'd like to make it." When Spitz agreed to buy the property as a vehicle for Kate, he mentioned that the option would cost RKO $52,000 [actually $50,000]. She reacted with, "It's too much for a picture for me."

Despite Hepburn's honest appraisal of her shaky current box-office worth, Spitz ordered Messenger to put in a formal bid which would hold the property for RKO for a short while. As Berman read the galleys on the way to the West Coast, his misgivings over the project escalated. Because Pandro became so opposed to this costly venture—especially given the poor returns on Kate's recent releases—Spitz suddenly became negative toward the proposition. Summarily RKO's bid was withdrawn.

Thereafter, Hepburn went on to make a string of big-screen flops. Meanwhile, producer David O. Selznick, who had left MGM to form his own independent studio, became interested in the Mitchell saga. However, he was particularly concerned that he had no stars under contract who could properly handle the pivotal roles of willful Southern belle Scarlett O'Hara and dashing blockade runner Rhett Butler. While Selznick was equivocating over the project, Kate assured David that the novel would make a marvelous picture and that he was the right man to bring it to the screen.

By early July 1936 Selznick had purchased the screen rights to *Gone With the Wind*. Soon thereafter he negotiated for his longtime friend and professional associate George Cukor to direct the complex vehicle. It would take nearly two-and-a-half years before the massive undertaking was ready for actual filming. Early on it had been decided that Clark Gable was the ideal star to play Rhett, and eventually he was hired on agreement that his studio (MGM) receive distribution rights. On the other hand, casting Scarlett—and the other pivotal screen characters—was no easy matter for the supremely finicky Selznick. From day to day he pondered his choices regarding who should play the headstrong Miss O'Hara.

At one point in this intensive casting process—which Selznick ballyhooed into an international talent hunt—Kate met with her former RKO boss. The formidable star told David, "The part was practically written for me. I am Scarlett O'Hara!" Reputedly Selznick, who had always thought Hepburn lacked the requisite sex appeal for a leading lady in the cinema, responded, "I just can't imagine Clark Gable chasing you for ten years [in the plot line]." As time went on, vacillating David had a change of heart (a decision not particularly favored by Kate's pal George Cukor, who felt Hepburn was wrong for the lead female role). Selznick intimated that if Hepburn would make a screen test for the Technicolor feature, she could indeed be in the final running. The Oscar winner was taken aback by this affront but continued over succeeding months to press her cause with the filmmaker. By mid 1938, as her RKO career crashed to an end, Hepburn still clung to the belief that she was in realistic contention for the coveted part.

At this juncture the casting of *Gone With the Wind* had captured world-wide attention, with the media reporting hourly on the latest contenders for key assignments and the newest speculations of who would be the likely victors. For the plum role of Scarlett, it had boiled down unofficially to Paulette Goddard, Jean Arthur, Loretta Young, Joan Bennett, and a few other finalists. Still beating her own drum, Kate suggested to Selznick—who was yet reconsidering her anew for the pivotal assignment—that with her filming slate empty, she could be ready at two days' notice if the producer should finally cast her as the Dixie vixen. However, she did not want to be announced as a final official choice if there was any possibly that David might suddenly favor an unknown for the role (as he had asserted for some time was his ideal alternative). Hepburn explained that it would be too devastating to suffer such a new career embarrassment if she lost out on *Gone With the Wind* after being labeled in final contention for the screen role of the decade.

When Kate decamped from Hollywood in May 1938, she had convinced herself that eventually Selznick would decide in her favor on the matter of Scarlett. However, unbeknownst to Hepburn and most of the world, Selznick had already been in negotiations with another major contender for *Gone With the Wind*. It was London-based Vivien Leigh (1913–1967), who had appeared on the West End stage and had already made several movies in England. Six years younger than Kate, Leigh had more obvious sex appeal than Hepburn, and her highly charged personality better suited the capricious nature of flirtatious, selfish Scarlett O'Hara.

From her Connecticut base Hepburn kept hoping that *Gone With the Wind* would become a reality for her. Such a casting coup would solve her movie career crisis, guaranteeing her a grand comeback. Kate kept abreast of the pending West Coast shoot, which was scheduled to finally commence on December 10, 1938—even though a leading lady for the project had yet to be formally announced. On that memorable Saturday night the "Burning of Atlanta" was to be filmed on the back lot at Selznick International Pictures with a stuntperson substituting for the still-uncast Scarlett O'Hara. Film lore has it that Myron Selznick brought his client Vivien Leigh to the set and there introduced her to David for the first time. As a result, according to

Hollywood "history," Leigh was quickly signed for the much-prized film. In actuality, contract negotiations for Vivien to step into the key role had been under way well before she left England to come to Los Angeles.

Losing *Gone With the Wind*—considering how extremely well this milestone film turned out—was a deep disappointment to Hepburn. But relying on face-saving spunk, Kate insisted to one and all that the part had, in actuality, not been that important to her. (As late as 1991, Hepburn informed the *Hartford Courant*, "It wasn't something I was dying to do. I thought it was a damn good book when I read it. I would have liked to have done it, but I wasn't that mad to be Scarlett O'Hara. I thought I was right, that it was extremely important they get somebody new [for the part].")

* * *

While Hepburn was vying for (and eventually losing) *Gone With the Wind* and turning down S.N. Behrman's upcoming Broadway production *No Time for Comedy*, Philip Barry was at work on fresh play ideas. One that appealed to him revolved around a wealthy family being profiled for *Fortune* magazine. He envisioned a romantic comedy centering around the spoiled socialite daughter who has yet to learn humility, leading her to faltering relationships with family, friends, and the men in her life. Barry gained inspiration for his lead figure from a real-life Main Line heiress named Helen Hope Montgomery Scott (who would died at age ninety in 1995). As the playwright worked on his script concept it struck him that this might be an appropriate vehicle for Kate, who had recently filmed a remake of his stage hit *Holiday.*

Barry met with Hepburn at Fenwick. He told the at-liberty star he had two play ideas that might appeal to her. One concerned a forty-two-year-old man who has failed in a suicide attempt and is saved by his daughter, a virtual stranger to him. The other concept was the in-progress *The Philadelphia Story.* With her family history of suicides, it was little wonder that Kate gravitated to the latter as her favorite of the two possibilities. That agreed, she and Philip tossed around notions for reshaping the embryonic comedy of manners into a tailor-made Hepburn vehicle. During this and later Connecticut conferences Barry scrutinized Kate's personality to observe her assorted pluses and minuses. He also studied the Hepburns during the family's get-togethers to inspire his shaping the personalities of her onstage family.

With Kate's useful feedback, Philip refined the plot and characters to effectively showcase Hepburn's physical and vocal mannerisms and minimize her annoying (to some) quirks. For much of that summer, Philip worked at his Maine retreat. Sometimes when Howard Hughes was available he flew Hepburn to confer with Barry as the latter polished the now-completed first two acts of his three-act play. Already star and playwright were discussing how best to launch *The Philadelphia Story* on Broadway. Kate repeatedly cautioned Philip that if her *Gone With the Wind* part should be confirmed, their play would have to be placed on hold.

❋ ❋ ❋

On Wednesday, September 21, 1938, a hurricane was centered east of Cape Hatteras, North Carolina. According to the weather forecasters, the storm was reaching a speed of sixty miles per hour but supposedly posed no real threat to New England. At the time Kate was at Fenwick. That morning she played a round of golf, scoring a hole in one on the ninth. Next, she took an invigorating swim. (Later she would recall, "It was great in the morning. It was full of life and wind.") As the day progressed and weather conditions worsened about Old Saybrook, brother Dick suggested they really should evacuate the beach house. However, Mrs. Hepburn insisted Fenwick was safe. (That day Dr. Hepburn was back in West Hartford at his medical practice.) Before too long, as the storm's momentum accelerated, shards of glass began blowing into the house, then one and then another of the building's chimneys collapsed. Finally the family reluctantly abandoned their beloved house, making their retreat through the rapidly rising waters. As they waded to safety on higher ground, the trio used a rope to stay together. At one point Kate and Dick turned and saw their adored cottage slowly spin about and float away, breaking apart in the process. Once out of harm's way, the Hepburns vowed to rebuild their summer home on the same spot. (They did so in 1939, creating an even more elaborate structure: an 8,000-square-foot, three-story white-brick home with nine bedrooms, eight bathrooms, and five fireplaces—all largely financed by Kate, to whom this home meant so very much.)

When Howard Hughes, then on the West Coast, heard of the storm back east, he contacted Kate to see if she and her family were all right. He had a supply of fresh bottled water flown to her but made no real offer to be at her side during this crisis. This is when Hepburn recognized that her special relationship with Hughes was over.

✳ ✳ ✳

Now passed over for *Gone With the Wind* and able to proceed with *The Philadelphia Story*, Kate arranged for the Theater Guild to produce the stage offering. At the time the Guild was undergoing a serious financial crisis, Barry had just suffered through several of his plays failing on Broadway, and Hepburn was a movie star without a film career. They each badly needed the other, and once their creative differences and priorities were resolved, the play moved into rehearsal. Kate's leading men included Joseph Cotten (from Orson Welles's Mercury Theater group) and Van Heflin (Hepburn's coplayer from *A Woman Rebels*), with smart and sassy Shirley Booth in support as one of the tabloid reporters who invades the heroine's Main Line home. Instead of taking a guaranteed salary, Hepburn agreed to receive 10 percent of the gross profits from the New York run and 12.5 percent on the road.

During the pre-Broadway tour there was a point where the powers-to-be on *The Philadelphia Story* almost threw in the towel, so dissatisfied were they all with the play's third act and other smaller structural problems. Clearer heads prevailed, and the play debuted at Manhattan's Shubert Theater on March 28, 1939. Kate had such jitters about this opening pivotal to her career that, accompanied by her secretary, Emily Perkins, she took rooms at the Waldorf-Astoria Hotel. No one knew where Hepburn was. She kept the shades drawn, refused to take calls, and so forth. As the momentous night approached, the traumatized star paced the floor of her hotel rooms telling herself over and over, "This is Indianapolis. This is Indianapolis." This mantra was to convince herself that she was merely facing one more road performance and not the all-important Broadway bow. On the way to the theater that premiere night Kate kept her eyes closed, refusing to acknowledge that she was indeed in Manhattan.

When the third-act curtain came down on *The Philadelphia Story* that evening, all concerns for the comedy's future evaporated. The audience and critics alike had responded heartily to the new offering, which was deemed a clever blend of irony and playfulness and lauded for being both comic and reflective. John Mason Brown (*New York Post*) enthused of the star, "If it is difficult to take one's eyes off of her, it is because she is also blessed with an extraordinary personality. Slim and lovely as she is, Miss Hepburn likewise possesses a voice which in her emotional scenes can be sheer velvet." Brooks Atkinson (*New York Times*) reported of the lilting leading lady making her first Broadway appearance since the calamitous *The Lake*, "Miss Hepburn skips through the evening in any number of light moods, responding to the scenes quickly, inflecting the lines and developing a part from the beginning to its logical conclusion." In short, said Atkinson, "She acts [the play] like a woman who has at last found the joy she has always been seeking in the theatre."

From being a Hollywood castoff, thirty-two-year-old Katharine Hepburn was suddenly the toast of Broadway. Ensconced at her east side Manhattan brownstone, she settled into a fulfilling life of performing her hit play eight times weekly. As was her custom, she avoided the social scene, preferring to rise early, exercise (including taking tennis lessons on Joe Sawyer's East River courts), have occasional acting classes with Frances Robinson-Duff, tend to household business, and have dinner (usually steak with ice cream for dessert), and then arrive at the theater well ahead of time to relax before the upcoming taxing performance. (During this period she was also involved in supervising the reconstruction of the Fenwick beach house. Sometimes when she had days off, she relaxed at Laura Harding's spread in New Jersey. There, Kate thrived on romping about the farm, picking wildflowers, and absorbing the beauty of the delicious landscape.)

Ever-faithful Laura Harding, Ogden Ludlow, a few other long-standing pals, and the Hepburn clan made up the special group for whom Kate entertained and who made her feel secure—as did her three dogs. She also had the familiarity of her loyal Manhattan household staff, which included secretary Emily Perkins, cook Wei Fung (who only spoke Chinese), and her faithful chauffeur-bodyguard-handyman, Charles Newhill, known unofficially as the Mayor of East Forty-ninth Street. (One of Newhill's chief duties was to ensure that the police never ticketed Hepburn's car in front of her brownstone.) What made life most delicious for Hepburn throughout 1939 and early 1940 was the unabashed adoration she received nightly from theatergoers enchanted by her beguiling performance. For the first time she felt that audiences actually might like her. It was reassuring after so many years trying to succeed on Broadway. (Nevertheless, Kate continued to have preperformance jitters and often vomited before she forced herself to go onto the stage. Once she was in the limelight, however, everything magically became okay for her.)

* * *

When *The Philadelphia Story* was being mounted, Kate and Philip Barry had been among the show's backers. At the strong suggestion of Howard Hughes, who proved an adept and helpful business adviser to his ex-amour, Hepburn acquired the screen rights to the property. Once the comedy was launched successfully in New York, the studios began bidding for the film rights, initially unaware that Kate controlled them. When they learned they must go to Kate to make the deal, they were charming to her but usually skirted the issue of who they envisioned starring in the screen adaptation.

Of all the Hollywood representatives who bargained with Hepburn over this hit play, which ran for 417 performances, Kate was most impressed with MGM's veteran chieftain Louis B. Mayer. (It was Mayer's studio, just two years earlier, that had offered Kate a paltry $10,000 to star in a feature for them.) Once the stage star made it clear that she would be re-creating her leading role onscreen or no deal, Mayer abandoned thoughts of Norma Shearer taking on the Tracy Lord character. It was finally agreed that for $250,000 (which included the screen rights and Kate's salary) *The Philadelphia Story* would be made at MGM with Kate repeating her stage part. She and Mayer tacitly agreed that the vehicle required two strong movie leading men (i.e., to provide box-office insurance against her lingering "box-office poison" reputation). Hepburn suggested Clark Gable and Spencer Tracy as her coleads. Mayer rejected using his two top male stars in this already costly production. The executive countered by offering her the studio's Jimmy Stewart and providing her a budget for signing a second suitable leading man. Her choice was Cary Grant, who came aboard the project, then donated his salary to the British War Relief Fund.

With George Cukor already at MGM, it was quickly decided that he would direct Hepburn's comeback vehicle. Utilizing a restructured plot line and sharpening of characters, the gilt-edged production was completed by late November 1940. Thereafter, Hepburn returned to the road tour of her beloved show. The hit stage comedy came to a final end on February 15, 1941, suitably enough in Philadelphia. In a farewell speech Hepburn tremulously told the audience that *The Philadelphia Story* would never end and thus there would be no final lowering of the curtain. Luddy was on hand to help her pack up personal items from her dressing room, and he drove her to Hartford (where he still frequently stayed with the Hepburns).

As the glossy screen rendition of *The Philadelphia Story* went into release into early 1941, the film critics equaled their Broadway compatriots in heaping praise on Hepburn's charismatic performance. *Life* magazine proclaimed, "*The Philadelphia Story* fits the curious talents of the redheaded Miss Hepburn like a coat of quick-dry enamel.... Its shiny surface reflects perfectly from her gaunt, bony face. Its languid action becomes her lean, rangy body. Its brittle smart-talk suits her metallic voice. And when Katharine Hepburn sets out to play Katharine Hepburn, she is a sight to behold. Nobody is then her equal."

The movie version of *The Philadelphia Story* made a profit of more than a million dollars, giving Hepburn a glorious screen return and once again putting her much in demand with the Hollywood film studios. The picture was nominated for six Oscars and won two: Best Actor (James Stewart) and Best Screenplay (Donald Ogden Stewart). Kate had been nominated in the Best Actress category but lost to her old RKO rival Ginger Rogers for *Kitty Foyle* (a potential screen property Hepburn had rejected as drivel when she had read the original novel in galley format).

Having now achieved professional success on both coasts, Kate announced her future career plans: "I'm going to try to go back and forth between the stage and screen—combine the two. Change of scenery, I've always heard, does things for a person's vitality. And I place a high value on vitality."

Chapter Twenty-two
MR. TRACY, I PRESUME

"Here's what's most important about Katharine Hepburn: not her career and not her brilliance and not her talent— it was her profound, unconditional love for Spencer Tracy. That was her greatest achievement. She and Spencer were one of the greatest love affairs in the history of America."
—The Glass Menagerie *costar Michael Moriarty, 2003*

During Katharine Hepburn's RKO stay (1932–1938) she had quickly outranked her biggest on-lot rivals: Constance Bennett, Irene Dunne, and Ann Harding. Once the queen bee there, Kate got whatever she wanted: closed sets, company acquiescence to her ignoring the press or doing the usual publicity chores expected of a star, and most important of all—besides her sizable salary—script and director approval. Each of the new RKO regimes quickly learned that Hepburn was tenacious and would not surrender to the usual industry games employed to control contract stars. In this imperious, self-indulgent mode, Kate reigned supreme. It was only in her final years at the film factory that another RKO star, Ginger Rogers, who now outranked her in box-office popularity, became the studio's primary focus of pampering.

At MGM, Hepburn was in an entirely different environment. The huge Culver City lot was the crème de la crème of Hollywood facilities. Its huge, well-oiled organization was guided by Louis B. Mayer (1887–1957), the crafty mogul who had been in continuous charge of the studio since its founding in 1924. With its large cash flow, MGM contracted an extensive array of top-flight screen personalities, making the company's catchphrase ("more stars than there are in the heavens") not such an exaggeration.

When thirty-two-year-old Kate stepped onto the Metro lot in 1940, she was no longer the biggest fish in a small pond. There were already many other major personalities ensconced at the sprawling, efficiently run operation. Among the current group of distaff talent were seven (Joan Crawford, Greta Garbo, Jeanette MacDonald, Maureen O'Sullivan, Eleanor Powell, Rosalind Russell, and Norma Shearer) veteran leading ladies who would leave the fold by 1942. (Another Metro leading lady, Hepburn's longtime rival Margaret Sullavan, would depart the lot in 1943.) But there was a host of other bright lights on hand, including Judy Garland, Hedy Lamarr, Myrna Loy, Ann Sothern, Lana Turner, and Mayer's new favorite, Irish-born Greer Garson. (Throughout the 1940s several younger female contractees joined the swelling MGM ranks, including June Allyson, Cyd Charisse, Ava Gardner, Kathryn Grayson, Deborah Kerr, Janet Leigh, Jane Powell, Donna Reed, Elizabeth Taylor, and Esther Williams). By the sheer number, diversity, and glitter of Hepburn's rivals, even iron-willed Kate had to acknowledge that she was in a far different working situation than when she ruled the RKO roost.

Then too, Kate's self-protective hauteur of the 1930s had been punctured by her "box-office poison" label, just as her near-miraculous comeback on the stage and in film with *The Philadelphia Story* had given her a fresh perspective on her relationship to the world. Moreover, unlike the ever-changing RKO facility, stable MGM had a seasoned publicity staff, and it provided more malleable Hepburn with a new—more viable—public image. It was geared to remove the taint of patrician exclusivity than had hounded her in the past.

Not that opinionated, stubborn, individualistic Kate was about to do a 360-degree change of personality. However, now she was actually willing (with a little cajoling by studio officials) to talk with—and not at—the press. Taking its signal from powerful MGM, which controlled a lot of advertising dollars and provided cooperative reporters with gifts and favors, the fourth estate displayed a new approach to the cinema's comeback queen. No longer were most journalists and columnists taking potshots at the former "Katharine of Arrogance," nor were they gleefully reporting upon her quirks, temper tantrums, and excesses. Now they—with her cooperation—were apologizing for the "old" Hepburn and setting the stage for the new public-friendly movie star.

For example, the December 1940 issue of *Modern Screen* magazine headlined an article on Kate as "The Most Maligned Woman in Hollywood." In the piece reporter James Reid bent over backward to help the star explain away her past "bad' behavior. He quoted her as saying, "I've been guilty of a lot of things but one thing I can't be accused of is thinking up stunts to attract attention. I don't have the right kind of stomach for that sort of thing. Remember my nervous indigestion. Nothing brings it on so fast as a feeling being conspicuous.... But—there's a large amount of stubborn Yankee in me. If I'm criticized for doing something that seems natural to me, nothing can make me stop doing it—no matter how conspicuous it makes me, or how much bicarbonate of soda I have to swallow."

* * *

After the success of *The Philadelphia Story,* MGM wanted Hepburn to make another picture for the studio, but she was in no rush. (Meanwhile, other studios considered Kate for a variety of properties, including *The Little Foxes, Kings Row, The Gay Sisters, Reap the Wild Wind,* and *Take a Letter, Darling.*) While choosing among her options, Kate, a great supporter of President Franklin D. Roosevelt and his humanitarian wife, Eleanor, agreed to narrate *Women in Defense* (1941). Written by the first lady and produced by the Office of Emergency Management and the U.S. government, the short subject was released a few weeks after America's official entry into World War II.

Meanwhile, synergy came into play and changed Hepburn's entire life. While in her final stretch at RKO, Kate had met actor-turned-director Garson Kanin who recently had been put under studio contract there. The two became friendly. Soon the obsequious Garson became part of Kate's Hollywood private social circle. Now, in 1941, when she returned from a vacation in Florida with Laura Harding, it was Kanin who told her of a script he was shaping, along with his brother Michael and Ring Lardner Jr. It was a vehicle custom-made for Hepburn's screen qualities, and she agreed to propel it into reality. Hepburn submitted the script to Louis B. Mayer and producer Joseph L. Mankiewicz, not revealing that the work was by two unknown young scripters. So successful were Kate's negotiations that MGM bought the screenplay for a mighty $100,000, gave her a $100,000 salary to star in the project, plus an additional $11,000 as her "agent's" commission and for expenses. Her remarkable business acumen at a time when most female stars were mostly arguing over billing, costumes, and their number of close-ups made Hepburn a wonder of the film industry.

As part of the deal to star in *Woman of the Year* (1942), Kate decided that George Stevens—her past brief amour—would be ideal as its director. (She felt the project demanded a man's man and thus was not in favor of George Cukor helming the romantic comedy. This sharp snub bothered Cukor, but his friendship with Kate remained intact.) Stevens was borrowed from Columbia Pictures. Next, Kate requested Spencer Tracy (1900–1967) as her leading man, not realizing he was already busy filming *The Yearling* in Florida. However, technical problems on that location shoot led to the project being abandoned for the time being. Suddenly Tracy was back in Culver City and available for work. He agreed to make *Woman of the Year.*

Hepburn always insisted she had never met Spencer before preparations began for *Woman of the Year* but that she had greatly admired his past screen work, especially his Oscar-winning performance in *Captains Courageous* (1937). As preproduction on the new project got under way in summer 1941, Kate was strolling on the MGM lot one day. She spotted Spencer near the writers' building. He was in conversation with Joseph L. Mankiewicz, the producer of their new film. Hepburn was wearing her "power" shoes—footwear with extremely high heels that made her tower over such studio executives as Mayer and literally gave her a position of authority. Mankiewicz introduced stocky, five foot ten-and-a-half-inch Tracy to his new leading lady. After a brief chat, Hepburn blurted out, "I'm afraid I'm a bit tall for you, Mr. Tracy." Reputedly, it was the producer who cracked, "Don't worry, he'll cut you down to size."

Later, Hepburn learned that Tracy had a preconceived notion of her. He thought her highfaluting (in manner and speech) and had misgivings about working with a woman of "ambiguous sexuality." A great lover of film colony gossip, Spencer had heard for years the rumors about Kate and her special circle of close women friends. Because of this he had a definite image of her as a staunch lesbian with dirty fingernails. (As late as 1992 when an interviewer asked Hepburn if those sexual orientation rumors had bothered her (of still did), she neatly sidestepped the delicate question by joking, "Well, I cleaned my fingernails this morning so you wouldn't think that." Notwithstanding these rumors, it should be noted that, regardless of her bisexual nature, Kate never hesitated to go to bed with men who attracted her, either to advance her career or just for her pleasure.)

* * *

As *Woman of the Year* got under way, Hepburn and the still-married George Stevens briefly rekindled their closeness from *Alice Adams*. However, from the first days of shooting scenes involving Kate and Spencer, it became evident the two costars generated great chemistry together oncamera and off, and George was quickly shunted aside to just being the director. While each colead initially was wary of the other, they had mutual professional respect for each other and had studied the other's past films carefully. Unlike in her RKO starring vehicles, here Kate was not only receptive to her leading man's script suggestions and acting choices but subordinated herself to him both oncamera and on the set. Those on the sound stage were agog that the mighty Kate—once branded as a snooty egotist—could make such a dramatic turnabout in her dealings with Tracy. (She herself would admit, "I knew from my first day of working with Spence...that I had met my match—and then some." Later, she would rhapsodize of her new leading man: "He's like an old oak tree, or the summer, or wind. He belongs to the era when men were men."

There was much in taciturn Tracy's personality that appealed to complex Hepburn.

Born in Milwaukee on April 5, 1900, Spencer was the second-born son of a devout Irish Catholic (with a heavy drinking problem and a strong penchant for violence) and a Protestant mother. As a youngster, Spencer had frequently changed schools not only because his family often moved but because of his repeated truancy and/or recurrent disruptive nature. At one juncture, feeling contrite, he briefly considered becoming a priest. Later, after serving in the Navy during World War I, he attended Wisconsin's Ripon College. There he participated in the campus debating team, which inspired his interest in acting. Eventually he quit college to attend the American Academy of Dramatic Arts in Manhattan, and he made his Broadway debut (1922) before graduating. Thereafter, while working in stock, he fell in love with an up-and-coming coplayer, Louise Treadwell, an Episcopalian. The couple wed in 1923. The next year their son, John, was born. Later it was discovered that the boy was incurably deaf, a fact that changed the Tracys' lives forever.

Louise dealt with her grief by devoting herself to her boy's welfare, including learning to teach her impaired offspring to communicate with the world. In contrast, Spencer was too guilt-stricken and impatient to aid in the laborious, frustrating educational process. As an escape, Tracy turned to ferocious bouts of drinking and to carousing with women. Ultimately he got in control of himself sufficiently to focus on his career so he could support his family, which now included a daughter, Susie, who had normal hearing.

After a major Broadway success in 1930's *The Last Mile*, John Ford hired the actor to make his screen debut that year in *Up the River*. Spencer signed a contract with Fox Films, where he remained for five years. During his stay on the lot he was frustrated by the mediocre quality of most of his movie roles and took out his anger in heavy drinking, violent, self-destructive behavior, and hard-fisted polo playing with his movie-star pal, Will Rogers. Spencer's most publicized extracurricular romantic relationship was with Loretta Young (who had not long before annulled her yearlong marriage to actor Grant Withers). The Tracy-Young affair became so serious that Spencer moved out of his family's home. However, Loretta later broke off their ties, saying that because they were both Roman Catholics they had no realistic future together. Tracy and his wife reconciled eventually, although their domestic situation had now become primarily a marriage of convenience.

In 1935, Tracy left Fox and joined MGM, where he quickly proved himself adept in major screen assignments, winning his first Academy Award nomination for *San Francisco* (1936). While Spencer was far happier professionally on the Metro lot, he was still an exceedingly heavy binge drinker who might be set off by any little matter. It was not uncommon for him to disappear for days at a time or turn up in some obscure town where he was creating mayhem to a hotel room. Spencer continued cheating on his wife, sometimes with costars such as Jean Harlow or Joan Crawford, on other occasions with non-celebrities.

During the making of *Dr. Jekyll and Mr. Hyde* (1941), Tracy developed a strong crush on his leading lady, Ingrid Bergman. However, the married actress was already enamored of their director, Victor Fleming. By now Tracy spent little time at his family's San Fernando Valley ranch except to visit his children on weekends. Usually he stayed in a suite at the Beverly Hills Hotel and socialized with his Irish drinking pals (including movie stars James Cagney and Pat O'Brien). To maintain a respectable image with the filmgoing public, Spencer lent his name and occasional presence to his wife's fund-raising efforts on behalf of her John Tracy Clinic, a Los Angeles–based center for deaf children.

* * *

When *Woman of the Year* premiered in February 1942, it displayed a more accessible and far sexier Kate Hepburn as she cavorted oncamera as aristocratic journalist Tess Harding. (Her character's surname was a tribute to Hepburn's longtime pal Laura Harding.) The media were quick to compliment the leading lady: "The title part is played by Miss Hepburn, who has never looked more beautiful" (*New York World-Telegram*). "Her performance...shows even more subtlety and depth...[and] is a constant pleasure" (*Baltimore Sun*).

Woman of the Year was also the first celluloid effort of a delightful, resourceful new screen team. *Time* magazine reported of Tracy and Hepburn: "They take turns playing straight for each other, act one superbly directed love scene, succeed in turning several batches of cinematic corn into passable moonshine." *The Christian Science Monitor* confirmed, "Miss Hepburn and Mr. Tracy are admirably paired. Mr Tracy's easy style with an undertone of firmness convinces one that his [sports reporter] Sam is the man to cope with Miss Hepburn's combination of detachment and restlessness as Tess, the career woman [i.e., international affairs columnist]."

Woman of the Year made a remarkable profit of three quarters of a million dollars, with Kate receiving her fourth Oscar nomination. A thrilled MGM wanted Hepburn to make another picture immediately, but she had other plans. She was committed to returning to the Broadway theater.

* * *

After Hepburn's huge success on Broadway with *The Philadelphia Story* both the Theater Guild and playwright Philip Barry were eager to reteam with

Kate for a new venture. Barry wrote *Without Love* with Kate in mind. To reflect the worsening world situation, the romantic comedy was overlaid with political topics relevant to the current battle against the Axis forces of Germany and Japan. The play's premise involved the nonphysical courtship between a young widow and Pat Jamieson, the latter a man with high political connections. He hopes to awaken the Allied forces to the dangers of the Third Reich using Ireland as a launching-off point to invade England. The heroine proposes that she and Pat enter into a platonic marriage so she can better help him with his noble cause. Once wed, the two fall romantically in love. Kate signed on to star in the play in February 1942, accepting a $1,000 weekly salary and agreeing to purchase a 25 percent share in the production.

One of the inherent problems with the new stage property was that its political themes were not resolved within the plot and many of its elements quickly became dated as the ongoing war rapidly changed the world situation. Another basic failing was the casting of bland Elliott Nugent (who suffered from a drinking problem) as Hepburn's love interest. The forty-six-year-old actor had earlier in his career specialized in playing the proverbial onstage worm who turns. In more recent years, multitalented Nugent wrote and produced Broadway plays and became a successful Hollywood film director, concentrating on turning out Bob Hope screen farces. He and Kate, who had conflicting artistic approaches to the show, displayed far too little romantic chemistry together which damaged the production's overall mood.

Without Love had its pre-Broadway debut on March 4, 1942, in Princeton, New Jersey. During its tour of thirteen cities, which included Wilmington, Delaware, and Philadelphia, Hepburn was not pleased by either the play or her performance but persuaded herself that the show must go on. She hoped that the constant rewrites would cure the production's many ills.

When *Without Love* played Pittsburgh's Nixon Theater in mid May, Hepburn was in a particularly tense mood. When a news photographer from a local journal snapped a photo of the star arriving backstage to prepare for a matinee, Kate was angered by the unauthorized picture-taking. Resorting to the tomboy within, the irked star wrestled the man to grab his camera and the offending photo. Later, during the Hartford engagement, a more relaxed Kate hosted a party for the entire cast at her parents' home. In the course of the get-together, the star mentioned to her father that Elliott Nugent and a local girl pal of hers had beaten Kate and the club professional at tennis that week. Dr. Hepburn was amused by his daughter's loss and advised Nugent, "Never let my daughter beat you…or she'll never play with you again. That's what happened when she won her first golf match against me."

Weeks later, the extended pre-Broadway tour disbanded for the summer and Hepburn rushed back to Hollywood to join Spencer in making their second film collaboration, *Keeper of the Flame* (1942). Then in late October with the new movie completed, Kate returned to *Without Love* as she had promised. The production—with Robert B. Sinclair's direction restaged by Arthur Hopkins—played Detroit for ten days. With a continued healthy box office, it seemed the show would be a major hit in New York. However, when it opened at Manhattan's St. James Theater on November 10, 1942, the critics had many justified reservations. Brooks Atkinson (*New York Times*) complained, "As the unloved wife Miss Hepburn is giving a mechanical performance that is not without considerable gaucherie in the early scenes. In both the writing and the acting, *Without Love* is theater on the surface of a vacuum." Other reviewers were equally unenthusiastic.

Thanks to Hepburn's renewed film career standing, audiences ignored the negative reviews and flocked to see her star turn in this perfunctory stage vehicle. Wearing Valentina outfits she performed for 113 performances before the show closed, as she had contracted, on February 13, 1943. The Guild had begged her to extend her limited-run engagement, but she refused. It was not so much that MGM was pressuring her to return to picture-making. Rather, Spencer Tracy had gone off the emotional deep end without levelheaded Kate on hand to comfort him.

Hepburn was so convinced that she had to rush back to Los Angeles to be at Spencer's side that she bypassed any consideration of what her decision might do to her career momentum. Instead, she thrilled at the golden opportunity to play Miss Fix-It to the man who had, in such short order, come to symbolize all the needy men in her life (e.g., brother Tom, husband Ogden Ludlow, and so forth). Kate had convinced herself—subconsciously or otherwise—that through unstinting devotion to massively self-destructive Spencer, she could somehow make amends to those males in her past whom she thought she had let down.

To appease the Theater Guild and Philip Barry for leaving them in the lurch, Hepburn persuaded MGM to acquire *Without Love* as a future screen property for herself and Tracy.

Chapter Twenty-three
SHAPING A NEW LIFE

"We all knew but nobody ever said anything. In those days it wasn't discussed. They were totally hand in glove, totally comfortable and unself-conscious about their relationship. She [Katharine Hepburn] wasn't the sort of woman that many men would be attracted to—the snuggly, cuddly woman in the movies at that time. And yet because of her enormous affection and love for Spencer [Tracy], she had the ability to subjugate this almost manly quality she had at times and became this wonderfully warm, irresistible woman."
—State of the Union *coplayer Angela Lansbury, 2003*

In describing the new, improved Kate Hepburn in early 1942, *The Saturday Evening Post* detailed, "In repose she is still boyishly awkward, but she has learned to move with grace. Her voice is slower and richer; its old stridence returns only with her frequent profanity. Her clothes are unique as before, but she carries them with distinction; on a woman less assured, they would seem grotesque. She wears no jewelry and uses no off-stage make-up except lipstick, which emphasizes the droop of her mouth and the fact that her upper and lower lips are exactly alike." For the same magazine piece George Cukor described his long-time friend Kate with the astute, if waspish, comment, "She is an actress who has succeeded in spite of her personality, not because of it."

❃　❃　❃

While the press of the early 1940s were marveling at Kate's reinvented movie star image, the public was largely unaware that she and married Spencer Tracy had begun an offcamera relationship. Had this special rapport become generally known in the morally conservative 1940s it could have easily cost them both their MGM affiliation and destroyed their gilt-edged film careers. However, due to Metro's extremely careful control of the media, the excessive discretion of both actors, and the press's respect for the two Oscar-winning celebrities' professional reputations, even the broad facts of the Kate-Spencer offscreen association remained a secret to most of the world for several years to come.

Those industry folk in the know about the Hepburn-Tracy relationship were divided as to its real nature. On one hand, people such as MGM leading man Gene Kelly would recall—in rosy terms—of the studio's famous duo during the 1940s: "At lunchtime they'd just meet and sit on a bench on the lot. They'd hold hands and talk—and everybody left them alone in their little private world." Perhaps this uncharacteristic lightheartedness on the part of usually emotionally reserved Kate and generally gruff and undemonstrative Spencer did actually occur in the earliest days of their discovering one another. However, such a scene would seem untypical of either of those stars.

In contrast, there were those, quite familiar with both parties, who insisted that the Hepburn-Tracy bond was (nearly) from the start largely or entirely platonic. Publicist and book writer Stanley Musgrove stated to an industry colleague that George Cukor once told him that Kate and Spencer's relationship was always platonic. Constantly prying Garson Kanin certainly knew the famous screen team well over the decades and wrote a book about the celebrated duo (1971's *Tracy and Hepburn*). When Kanin was asked years later by writer Patrick McGilligan (then preparing a biography of George Cukor) if the pair really had as great a love affair as Garson's tome suggested, Kanin snapped back, "I didn't say they MADE love, did I?" Irene Mayer Selznick, who knew Hepburn from her very first days in Hollywood, insisted to writer A. Scott Berg (2003's *Kate Remembered*), "You can't drink as much as Spencer did and maintain a relationship built on sex."

Then, of course, there were the long-recurring rumors or accounts of Kate's continuing bisexuality, including her intimate associations with Laura Harding, Elissa Landi, Jane Loring, and others. Even the reputedly virile man's man, Tracy, came in for speculation occasionally as an individual who was drawn both ways sexually. The British-born Richard Gully, part of the Hollywood upper echelon social scene for decades and a onetime minor member of the Warner Bros. studio staff, was a dedicated gay man about town. He claimed to know a great deal about many of the Tinseltown famous. In an April 2001 *Vanity Fair* piece, Gully (who died in 2000) devoted a section of his spicy recollections of Hollywood's good old days to the sexual lifestyles of the town's celebrities. He noted, "There were some who were bisexual. Spencer Tracy was." Gully added, "Spencer Tracy was never sober. I don't think he functioned as a man. He and Katharine Hepburn had chemistry only on-screen." (Angered by these allegations in the new millennium, a generally incapacitated Kate mustered enough strength to tell the media, "Spencer Tracy was not a homosexual.")

The possibility that Hepburn and Tracy experienced a mostly platonic affair prompted Axel Madsen, who wrote of Hollywood's lesbian movie personalities in *The Sewing Circle* (1995; updated 2002), to inform the media in 2003, "Katharine Hepburn was afraid her lesbianism would come out. Tracy was a nice cover and painting this picture of their romance was very clever. Tracy was married and Catholic, so divorce was out of the question.... If you were found to be gay, either your career was finished or you were subjected to blackmail. Hepburn didn't not want to be subjected to either, so she used Tracy for the grand cover-up."

Anne Edwards, author of *Katharine Hepburn: A Remarkable Woman* (1986; updated 2000) would comment to *Publishers Weekly* in July 2003 of her now-deceased biographical subject, "She was a woman who fictionalized her life to the public. She romanticized and fictionalized her relationship with Spencer Tracy, a bisexual, abusive alcoholic—not so much physically as verbally abusive.... She and Spencer were great beards for each other throughout their lives. I can understand why she would have to keep her sexuality a secret, but in later years I felt it was less moral of her to never make some sort of gesture to the gay community. This was, after all, a woman who married a gay man."

✻　✻　✻

While a full understanding of the physical dynamics between the bisexual Hepburn and Tracy may always remain open to debate, there was little doubt of Kate's extremely strong emotional ties to SPEN-suh (as she always pronounced it). She bragged—for public consumption—that he taught her what love was truly about. Her definition seemed a radical departure from her long-held belief of gender equality (or female superiority), self-sufficiency, and putting one's own needs first. To the nearly middle-aged Hepburn, being in love meant "total devotion" in which "I put you and your interests and your comfort ahead of my own." Thus, according to her new guidelines, if "he didn't like this or that I changed this and that. They might be qualities which I personally valued. It did not matter I changed them." In practicality, life for Kate with Spencer encompassed: "Food—we ate what he liked. We did what he liked. We lived a life which he liked." She insisted, "This gave me great pleasure. The thought that this was pleasing him." (One has to wonder at the power of the inner forces that drove thirty-something Hepburn into advocating—and allowing herself to fall into—such a claustrophobic emotional captivity and subversion of her independent spirit.)

On a more constructive note, Kate claimed that she learned a good deal about her craft from Tracy; she rated him and Laurette Taylor (1884–1946) as the greatest performers she had ever seen. "Much of what I know about acting I learned from Spencer Tracy," Hepburn said. She admired Tracy's simplicity of performance, which he made seem natural and impromptu (even though he always prepared for a filming by carefully memorizing the script and thoughtfully crafting his characterization). Through Spencer's example and goading, Kate learned to be far less mannered both on and offcamera and to keep more in check her compulsive habits, including her abrupt manner of conversing.

But it was not all a one-way street in this bizarre personal entanglement between the two world-class stars. From Hepburn, Spencer, always a great reader, learned to broaden his cultural interests, to expand his intellectual viewpoints, and to take up the relaxing hobby of painting (which Hepburn first adopted in the mid 1930s to help pass the time on film sets). Through Kate's influence, Spencer now saw less of his longtime drinking buddies and widened his social circle to include some of Hepburn's close friends, such as George Cukor, Ethel Barrymore, and Fanny Brice.

❊   ❊   ❊

With extreme fervor and fortitude, Hepburn appointed herself caregiver supreme to Tracy, this enigmatic man who suffered bleak periods of self-doubt and self-destruction, and who frequently lashed out at anyone handy with his verbal and/or occasional physical abuse. (There was at least one occasion of this hands-on mistreatment when, one evening, Kate was administering to a drunken Tracy back at his hotel digs. As she was cleaning him up and putting him to bed he—accidentally—struck her, but he was too inebriated to know at the time or recall later what he had done. She never mentioned the humiliating incident to him for fear of the remorse it might generate in the actor and how that in turn might affect their togetherness.)

Hepburn's full-steam-ahead decision to make a lifetime career of protecting and nurturing Spencer not only served her emotional and practical needs but was also useful to MGM. Louis B. Mayer and his staff soon realized that in compulsive Hepburn they had a resourceful force far stronger than the real Mrs. Tracy or Spencer's older brother Carroll to keep Tracy relatively under control. Kate's devotedness to this mission gave her far more worth on the studio lot than merely her leading lady capacity. Just as RKO had occasionally turned to Hepburn to help sober up John Ford when the director went on a drinking binge during a film shoot, so MGM relied similarly on Kate regarding Spencer. She could be counted on, more often than not, to snap Tracy out of his debilitating black moods. If need be, she would gamely track him down late at night at the various seedy Los Angeles bars he frequented and escort the inebriated man back to his Beverly Hills Hotel accommodations to get him in condition for the next day's filming. There were even occasions when Hepburn cheerfully kept vigil outside his hotel room all night— sitting outside his door—waiting for the insomniac actor to finally fall asleep or, if he had been drinking heavily, to pass out in a stupor.

Later in life, when discussing Tracy's pervasive substance abuse, Hepburn insisted in very black-and-white terms, "His drinking was no problem between us. Drinking is your own problem, and the only person who can do anything about it is you." When writer A. Scott Berg, Kate's friend and chronicler, asked Hepburn why Spencer had never turned for help to a support group such as Alcoholics Anonymous, she rationalized that Tracy was afraid of letting his problem be known publicly. (This seems to be a strange answer since such organizations pride themselves on confidentiality about their memberships.)

Summarizing in retrospect her cherished avocation as Tracy's self-appointed protector, Hepburn asserted, "Spencer was a fascinating man to me. I was not able to solve his problems, but I was able to help him by seeing that he didn't fall down the stairs, you know, or break his God-damned neck or just be miserable. So that was my pleasure." She also pointed out—almost proudly, "I've known several men who drank too much and they were all extremely interesting."

* * *

On the studio sets or at the small private social gatherings Hepburn and Tracy sometimes attended with industry friends like Garson Kanin and Ruth Gordon, the Nunnally Johnsons, or the Chester Erskines, Kate the Egalitarian was shamelessly deferential to the chauvinistic, self-centered Spencer. She often sat at his feet, looking girlishly at her dear one and laughing heartily as he retold familiar stories. She ignored his brusqueness—or caustic rudeness—when he felt she was momentarily stealing his limelight or acting particularly haughty.

However, for Hepburn, Tracy could do no wrong, as she had concocted an ideal image of this man—which she would not allow troublesome realities to shatter. For her, Spencer was "a sturdy oak buffeted by the wind—a throwback to an age of rugged heroism...that vanishing American, the self-made man. He was what we imagined our grandfathers to be." Having constructed such an obsessively romanticized vision of Tracy, she determined very early in their association that "if you are going to help anybody who is in trouble, this is not a two-hour-a-day job. It is a 24-hour-a-day job. You won't do anything else if you decided that you are going to resurrect and rearrange a human being...I was his."

But as Hepburn pointed out all too frequently in the years following Spencer's 1967 death, despite their closeness and her slavish attention to his least need, she never really understood what motivated the inner man who found acting so easy but living so interminably difficult. "Who was he?" she wondered repeatedly. "I never really knew. He had locked the door to the inside room. I have no idea whether even he himself had the key. I only suspected that inside that room was a powerful engine that ran twenty-four hours a day at full speed."

In a rare moment of astute self-observation, Hepburn—who generally refused to analyze her own motivations, let alone those of others—said, "The human animal is so complex. I don't think I've ever understood anyone fully in my life, however much I loved them. Which is tragic, because you can't really help when you don't understand."

* * *

If Hepburn loved Tracy as much as legend would suggest, why did the couple not wed? Some said it was because of Spencer's strict Roman Catholic background, which generally forbade divorce. However, in the late 1950s former MGM player Jean Porter (married to Edward Dmytryk, who directed Tracy in two features) asked the star, "You really didn't marry Kate because of the Roman Catholicism?" Spencer replied, "Hell no, I wanted to divorce Louise and marry her when we first met, but that's when John was a young kid and had all these problems, he had polio, he had the hearing thing, and I wanted him to have a secure family support system until he got old enough to be on his own, which he eventually did, becoming an artist at the Disney Studio. By that time Kate didn't want to marry me anymore, so we just kept going the way we were going."

On the other hand, over the years Kate's pat explanations varied for why she never legalized her relationship with Tracy. One time she suggested, "Long ago I had already decided that I could not be, at the same time, a great actress and a good wife and mother." (As an example, she had her mother, Kit, who sacrificed many of her career ambitions to remain a dutiful house-wife and mother.) On another occasion Hepburn reasoned, " I don't approve of marriage unless you have children. I really don't. I think people behave so badly with each other. It's a tough, tough relationship. Any deep friendship is a tough relationship and I think it's thrilling that as many relationships work out and I think usually it's because the people are held together by the kids." In *Me* she offered, "I was not in the business of capturing anyone into a mar-riage.... I liked the idea of being my own single self." She also stated in her carefully constrained memoir, "We never really thought about or discussed marriage. He was married, and I wasn't interested." Then there was the time she spelled out why the two had not shared living quarters even on a sub rosa basis (except in the very last years when Tracy was extremely ill), "I don't like living in a house with anyone."

✻   ✻   ✻

In 1991 Hepburn wrote, "People have asked me what was it about Spence that made me stay with him for nearly thirty years. And this is somehow impossible for me to answer... I can only say that I could never have left him. He was there—I was his. I wanted him to be happy... I liked to wait on him... I struggled to change all the qualities which I felt he didn't like... I found him—totally—totally—total!"

Whatever the full actuality of Hepburn's long-term personal relationship with the enigmatic Tracy, and regardless how much she and the media masterfully embroidered the association over the decades into a grand sexual romance of dynamic dimensions, two things remain sadly clear. Kate never remembered Spencer ever saying specifically he loved her. She also admitted that she was not even certain of his true regard for her.

Chapter Twenty-four
HOLLYWOOD'S GREAT LOVE TEAM

"A critic in the East who praised very highly our work in various pictures together also indicated that he hoped the matching of our personalities would not be carried to the point where audiences might ever weary of us.

"Therefore, I believe it is safer that we should rest on laurels gained, rather than try for new ones, and that probably Sea of Grass, *which I believe will be a very great picture, should be the final one for a time."*

—*Spencer Tracy, 1946*

Having established a successful formula for Spencer Tracy–Katharine Hepburn pictures in the urbane *Woman of the Year,* MGM was happy to have the well-liked pair back on the screen, even if their follow-up vehicle was not up to par. The George Cukor–directed *Keeper of the Flame* (1942) was a somber and overly melodramatic tale of blind hero worship (a subject close to Hepburn's heart). Again, as in all their joint pictures, Tracy insisted on top billing over Hepburn, and she obliged. Kate received a $100,000 fee for this picture.

In *Keeper of the Flame,* Spencer played a crusading reporter deeply attracted to the widow (Kate) of a national hero who was actually a fascist out to subdue America. The *Citizen Kane*–inspired narrative bypassed any real love scenes between America's newly minted cinema team. (Actually, in only a few of Hepburn's films did she and her leading man ever exchange anything resembling Hollywood love clinches. Often the inevitable screen kiss between Kate's stiff-necked heroine and her oncamera hero would be merely a perfunctory peck on the cheek. Or sometimes the sequence would be filmed with Hepburn's profile almost hidden behind the male actor's face to distract viewers from her usually rigid response to scripted moments of affection. This pattern for Kate's minimalist love scenes onscreen persisted even in her several movie outings with Tracy. These celluloid sequences would seem to further the idea that their personal relationship did not depend on physical or sexual interplay.)

❋   ❋   ❋

After completing *Keeper of the Flame* in fall 1942, Hepburn returned east for the Broadway startup of *Without Love*. As usual, she had trepidations about appearing before a live audience. In addition, she was on constant alert for downbeat news from the West Coast about Tracy's state of being. She was rightly fearful that if left to his own devices, Spencer would spiral into another substance abuse rampage. As a precedent she had remembered his indulgently destructive behavior while he was making *Tortilla Flat* (1942). This was his childish revenge for her daring to leave his side to do the *Without Love* pre-Broadway tour.

Meanwhile, having embarked on her save-Tracy crusade, Kate finally set free ex-spouse Ogden Ludlow. Since their 1934 Mexican divorce Luddy had remained firmly in Hepburn's galaxy. He still spent quality time with her family and was always at autocratic Kate's beck and call when she was back east. Now in wartime Luddy was a civilian employee of the Navy Department in Washington, D.C., and was living in nearby Alexandria, Virginia. At age forty-three, the bisexual man was dating divorced Boston socialite Elizabeth K. Albers and the couple wanted to wed.

Since there was some question as to the legitimacy of Kate and Luddy's earlier marital dissolution, the groom-to-be filed for divorce in Hartford, Connecticut. On September 19, 1942, superior court judge Patrick B. O'Sullivan rendered judgment for the plaintiff on grounds of desertion (with Luddy stating "she had decided that she couldn't continue her career and be married too"). Because the case was on the docket as *Ogden Ludlow v. Katharine H. Ludlow*, it was not until the brief hearing was nearly over that the presiding judge realized the defendant's identity. (Kate did not appear in the courtroom, but Dr. Hepburn testified on her behalf to establish Connecticut as her legal residence.) A week later, Luddy and Elizabeth were united at All Souls' Unitarian Church in the nation's capital. (In coming years the couple had two children, a boy and a girl.)

With Luddy largely out of Kate's orbit for the time being, Laura Harding remained one of the few from the old crowd to keep a major position in Hepburn's life. As the New Jersey–based socialite-farmer had for years, she remained always available whenever Kate beckoned her to be at her side.

※　※　※

After completing her *Without Love* stage engagement in winter 1943, Hepburn hastened back to Los Angeles to be at needy Tracy's beck and call. While Spencer proceeded to make a trio of successful war-themed pictures, including 1944's *Thirty Seconds over Tokyo,* Kate was content to go before the cameras for a mere cameo—along with such unique notables as Tallulah Bankhead, Katharine Cornell, Lynn Fontanne, and Gypsy Rose Lee—in United Artists' *Stage Door Canteen* (1943). Thereafter, Hepburn returned to Metro for *Dragon Seed* (1944). (In this period Kate was touted for lead roles in MGM's *Madame Curie* and Paramount's *Our Hearts Were Young and Gay,* but other stars were utilized instead for these big-screen presentations.)

Regarding *Dragon Seed,* many of MGM's leading ladies (including Hedy Lamarr, Greer Garson, and Judy Garland) had been considered for the pivotal role of Jade in the ambitious screen adaptation of Pearl Buck's best-selling, patriotic novel. However, most of these candidates looked far too unconvincing as Asians in their screen tests. In contrast, with Kate's high cheekbones and the application of special makeup to slant her eyes, she gave a surface impression of being Chinese. While Hepburn knew that such peculiar casting would subject her to ridicule, she accepted this lead assignment at Louis B. Mayer's special request.

By the time *Dragon Seed,* budgeted at a hefty $3 million, went into production in October 1943, the project's original producer had left the studio. Pandro S. Berman took over the film's supervision. It was a professional reunion not only for Kate and her onetime RKO mentor but for Hepburn and onetime compatriot Jane Loring, who had joined MGM in 1939 as Berman's assistant. (Because Kate had deliberately so enmeshed herself in

Spencer's frenzied life, there was no way for Jane to wedge herself back into Hepburn's restructured intimate social circle.)

If Hepburn found this war drama about China's resistance to the invading Japanese blatantly specious, her film assignment did offer a few enticing pluses. Not only did she wear trousers (Asian-style) throughout the ambitious chronicle, but she played a highly progressive, take-charge Chinese woman who believed females should not be subjugated to males. During the lengthy shoot, which extended through the spring of 1944, director Jack Conway died and Harold S. Bucquet took over control.

When released, the 148-minute *Dragon Seed* received mixed reviews; it was "often awkward and pretentious" (*Time* magazine). In contrast, Hepburn was generally appreciated for a warm and sincere performance. *Newsweek* magazine reported, "Miss Hepburn reveals a fine understanding, particularly those moments when she finds courage to drop her Bryn Mawr accent." Leo Mishkin (*New York Morning Telegraph*) commented, "She is in herself such a splendid actress when given the opportunity that she even overcomes her own personality to give a shining, glowing performance." With its extremely high production cost ($3.07 million), the popular release still registered a $281,000 loss.

* * *

With Spencer Tracy and Katharine Hepburn finally available to make a picture at the same time, Metro-Goldwyn-Mayer placed *Without Love* into active production. In its transition from stage to film, the leading man's role was changed into an inventor working on a secret military project for the U.S. government. Hepburn's character remained the grieving widow who finds fresh meaning in life when she is drawn to Tracy's Pat Jamieson. For this Harold S. Bucquet–directed project Lucille Ball and Keenan Wynn provided comic relief.

The studio assigned veteran producer Lawrence Weingarten to oversee *Without Love*. He quickly learned what a monumental handful Hepburn, the control freak, could be on the film set. According to Weingarten, "Kate was 'into' everything.... We were building the sets and dressing them when the decorator came up to me in a fury and said, 'I quit.' I asked him, 'What's the matter?' He said, 'She doesn't like the set—she wants it like it was on the stage.' I didn't know what to do to resolve the problem. As she was leaving, late that night, after sniffing her disapproval of everything down to the cushions, I said to her, 'Kate, if you've got time before you go, go down and see Buddy Gillespie in Special Effects to see how the miniatures are coming along.' She got the message. She didn't interfere anymore. People always said to me, 'She's trying to do everything.' And my reply was, 'The thing I'm afraid of, and you should be afraid of, is that she *can* do everything.'"

Unable to fully overcome the story's original shortcomings, *Without Love* still did very nicely at the box office but did not match the lucrative financial returns on *Woman of the Year*. In contrast to Tracy's approved brand of mugging, Kate performed her celluloid role in a straightforward manner, getting out of focus only when she had to portray giddiness. Eileen Creelman (*New York Sun*) reported, "Miss Hepburn caricatures her part, perhaps not always intentionally. It still was as good a way as any to play the neurotic young widow." *The New Yorker* judged of the screen team: "The somewhat metallic and stylized quality of Miss Hepburn's acting is almost perfectly suited to a role that is largely a vehicle for fashionable humor, and Mr. Tracy's homespun behavior seems just about right for a man who really prefers airplanes to dames."

※　※　※

During World War II, Tracy, too old to be drafted for military service, felt guilty that he had not enlisted as had others among MGM's mature contract stars (e.g., Clark Gable, Jimmy Stewart, Robert Taylor, Melvyn Douglas, and Robert Montgomery). While Spencer participated in some USO activities on behalf of the armed forces, he was deeply disappointed when a secret government mission he was asked to undertake never materialized. As he sank into recurrent funks, Hepburn hoped to divert him by suggesting his return to stage acting. The play in question was *The Rugged Path*, a patriotic drama written by the distinguished Robert E. Sherwood. The couple's mutual friend Garson Kanin was set to direct. The venture proved to be a nightmare both in its out-of-town tryouts and its New York bow in November 1945. It was the actor's first time appearing on Broadway since 1930, and he was extremely nervous about passing muster with theater critics. This led to his being irascible and moody during the pre–New York engagement, repeatedly threatening to quit the production. Kate, ignoring her own career, was on hand, however, to bolster his fragile confidence, keep his drinking under relative control, and maintain peace of sorts between the moody leading man, the director, and the playwright. Sometimes, Laura Harding was also present to provide needed moral support for Kate when dealing with the obstreperous Tracy when he became too much even for Kate to handle.

When *The Rugged Path* debuted, critics expressed great reservations about the drama but lauded Tracy's sincere portrayal of the liberal newspaper editor who joins the Navy. The production might have lasted well beyond its eighty-one performances. However, nerve-racked Tracy could not wait to abandon the show, and he vowed never to set foot on a stage again. (He never did.) During the run Tracy (and his watchdog brother, Carroll) stayed at a midtown hotel while Kate was in residence at her east side brownstone.

Once freed of *The Rugged Path,* Spencer embarked on a giant-size bender in Manhattan. Eventually the studio located him and had its errant leading man admitted to Doctors Hospital. To keep the media from discovering the star's whereabouts, Tracy was assigned to a private room on the maternity floor. A well-meaning friend snuck a bottle of liquor to Spencer, which propelled him into delirium tremens. During the traumatic drying-out process, the out-of-control Tracy had to be restrained in a straitjacket. This misadventure caused the actor to be off the screen for a year.

❋   ❋   ❋

Ensconced in a leased Bel-Air home with her secretary-companion Emily Perkins, Hepburn signed a new three-year contract with Loew's Inc. (MGM's parent company) in mid September 1946. Its terms (which provided for a $3,512.59 weekly salary) allowed Kate to return to the stage upon mutual agreement with the studio. Meanwhile, there had been discussion of Kate appearing with Gene Kelly in a skit ("Shakespeare in Tap Time") for the studio's gargantuan movie musical revue, *Ziegfeld Follies,* but the concept never became reality for either of them. Instead, she took on the paper-thin role of a hysterical heroine in the unsatisfactory thriller *Undercurrent* (1946). Directed by Vincente Minnelli (with whose wife, MGM's Judy Garland, Hepburn was extremely friendly), the film was Robert Taylor's first postwar feature.

By now approaching forty, Kate was increasingly concerned about her physical appearance oncamera. In particular, she was fixated on the belief that her neck was ungracefully long and revealed telltale age marks. Special camera lighting and angles were devised to minimize her concerns. For added insurance the hypersensitive star began demanding that her onscreen wardrobe feature high necklines, that she wear scarves, and that her character's actions allow her fluttering hands to distract from her "annoying" neck. (In contrast, Hepburn was thrilled when the studio costumers found ways to give her the appearance of having cleavage. ("You darlings, I love you all," she gleefully exclaimed to the wardrobe designers. "Me, with cleavage!"))

* * *

There was discussion that Kate might accept the heroine's role in the glossy saga *Green Dolphin Street,* but it was fourteen-years-younger Lana Turner who claimed that 1947 major assignment. Hepburn was wanted by John Ford to star in *The Ghost and Mrs. Muir* (1947) at Twentieth Century-Fox, but it was Gene Tierney who eventually played the whimsically romantic celluloid part for director Joseph L. Mankiewicz.

Instead, Kate reteamed with Spencer Tracy for 1947's *The Sea of Grass.* It was based on Conrad Richter's novel of rugged nineteenth-century life on the desolate plains of the New Mexico Territory. Elia Kazan came over from Twentieth Century-Fox to direct this account of a ruthless cattle baron (Tracy), his ignored well-bred wife (Hepburn), and her refined attorney lover (Melvyn Douglas). From the start of production, director Kazan and the Kate-Spencer team were definitely at artistic cross-purposes. (The director said later, "Hepburn had a star complex and believed in 'personality.'") Kazan was disgusted that the movie was not being shot on location and he found his star team resistant to utilizing the earthy, more realistic acting style for which the director was justly famous. (The director later said of his leading lady: "I was scared of Kate—I was overpowered by her. After all, she was 'royalty.'")

At a two-hour running time, *The Sea of Grass* was rarely convincing or entertaining film fare. (*Cue* magazine's Jesse Zunser remarked, "The script is weak, and the acting varies between dramatically effective and artificially slick—with Miss Hepburn chief offender in her lately acquired highly stylized patronizing fashion.") Made on a hefty $2.349 million budget, the heavily promoted feature pulled in a $742,000 profit, much to the surprise of its key participants. *The Sea of Grass* marked the final time that Kate worked at MGM with producer Pandro S. Berman. (During preparations for *The Sea of Grass,* ubiquitous Jane Loring participated in script conferences for the Western, and she showed up on the set occasionally, much to the consternation of Kazan and Tracy. It was the last occasion that Kate and she crossed professional paths at the studio. Loring, who never achieved her goal of becoming a full-fledged film director, remained at MGM until her eventual retirement. She died in Los Angeles of a heart ailment on March 15, 1983, at the age of eighty-two. She was long forgotten by the movie industry, and her passing went largely unnoticed. On the death certificate of this unsung, highly productive individual, who in bygone years had played such a meaningful role in both Hepburn's professional and private life, was the surprising notation that once—probably in her pre-Hollywood years—the woman who had seemed to only have eyes for Kate had been married to a man.)

❋   ❋   ❋

While Spencer Tracy had been enthusiastic about Democratic president Franklin D. Roosevelt during his four-term tenure, he remained largely nonpartisan He believed actors should not use their fame on behalf of politics. (Tracy's favorite remark on the subject was, "Remember who killed President Lincoln.") In contrast, opinionated, outspoken Kate had been encouraged from childhood onward to be an advocate of causes. During the late 1930s and early 1940s, Hepburn had contributed to ultraliberal groups, some of which later proved to have socialist overtones. Although a staunch Democrat she was unimpressed by President Roosevelt's successor, Harry S. Truman. When Henry A. Wallace, who had served as U.S. vice president (1941–1945) became a Progressive Party candidate for U.S. president, she wholeheartedly supported his running. Considered to be far too left-wing by both the Democratic and Republican parties, Wallace found that these major political camps were hamstringing his efforts to communicate his campaign platform to potential voters.

When Wallace was denied the use of the Hollywood Bowl for speechmaking in the spring of 1947, an anticensorship rally was staged at Los Angeles's Gilmore Stadium. The keynote speaker at this May 20 gathering was Hepburn, replacing a previously scheduled Edward G. Robinson (himself a great liberal). Various individuals, including playwright-screenwriter Arthur Laurents, helped Kate with the text of her address. She delivered her impassioned message in front of a crowd of 20,000. Instead of wearing her trademark slacks and man's jacket, she appeared that crucial evening in a dress. Of all possible colors for her outfit, she selected red. (Later she acknowledged with deep chagrin, "At first I was going to wear white. And then I thought they'd think I was the dove of peace.... How could I have been so dumb!")

The repercussions of Kate's political misstep were enormous, especially in that highly paranoid era when the House Un-American Activities Committee was launching its investigation of Communist Russia's infiltration of the movie business. Hepburn's speechmaking led the FBI to maintain a detailed file on her. For a time there was a possibility that she (as well as Spencer Tracy who had remained on the sidelines throughout this rhubarb) would be made to testify before the forceful instigators of the congressional witch hunt as to her loyalties to the United States. Cooler (or more practical) heads prevailed, and the blunt Kate—who might well have given that investigatory body an embarrassingly severe verbal thrashing—was never subpoenaed, unlike so many others of the Hollywood work force.

However, Hepburn's endeavor on Wallace's behalf did not escape the wrath of MGM's Louis B. Mayer, an archconservative Republican. In their private conference on the lot, a contrite Kate admitted that as a studio employee she had no business circumventing her employer's wishes by making her surprise appearance at Gilmore Stadium. She volunteered to do penance by quietly going off her studio salary. The angered but eventually forgiving mogul chastised her for her behavior but chose not to punish her further. He had shown and she had accepted that he was the boss of his domain.

Nevertheless, there was still a whiplash from patriotic filmgoers of the day, who felt that movie star Hepburn was far too much in sympathy with the Russian Reds. As a result, the American Legion, among other irate groups, boycotted her current film release—*Song of Love* (1947). In this lumbering vehicle, directed in heavy-handed fashion by Clarence Brown, she played

Clara Wieck Schumann (1819–1896), the noted pianist-composer who devoted her life to championing the musical works of her German composer husband, Robert (played by Paul Henreid), who died insane.

What especially fascinated Hepburn about starring in this romantic claptrap was the stimulating challenge of learning to play the piano sufficiently well that moviegoers could not tell where her "keyboard banging" left off and the dubbing of noted pianist Artur Rubinstein took over. To prepare herself properly for the demands of *Song of Love,* she studied devoutly and obsessively several hours daily for many weeks with Laura Dubman, a pupil of Rubinstein. While Kate's keyboard technique proved to be was impressive oncamera, especially in the "Carnival" showcase number, it did nothing to help the unwieldy narrative. Nor did her keyboard prowess distract viewers sufficiently from the distinct lack of chemistry between her and Henreid or with Robert Walker (as young composer Johannes Brahms, who adores the married Clara). The tedious 119-minute film lost more than a million dollars.

* * *

When Frank Capra planned his Liberty Films production of the Broadway hit *State of the Union,* he envisioned reteaming his *It Happened One Night* (1934) costars, Clark Gable and Claudette Colbert. Gable proved to be unavailable, as was alternate choice Gary Cooper. However, a deal was made to borrow Spencer Tracy and other MGM players and make this a Metro-Goldwyn-Mayer release. On the Friday before filming commenced in late September 1947, Colbert walked off the picture, upset over last-minute contractual negotiations. Capra thought the project would have to be abandoned. However, Tracy mentioned that Kate, who had been rehearsing Spencer's part with him, was familiar with the script, and she readily agreed to substitute in the lead female part. (Most likely, without this fortuitous happenstance, Hepburn would have continued to remain sidelined professionally due to her recent political indiscretion in the Gilmore Stadium matter.)

While the *State of the Union* shoot was under way, the House Un-American Activities Committee was conducting its anti-Communist hearings in Los Angeles. A key friendly witness was ultraconservative Adolphe Menjou, who was a featured actor in *State of the Union.* Menjou's personal political stance caused great friction on the set between him and Kate. When they were not oncamera he constantly attempted to bait her with derogatory remarks. Her response was to glare icily at him.

Within *State of the Union,* Tracy appeared as a Republican presidential candidate. Hepburn was cast as his estranged wife. Idealistic and outspoken, she is aghast at his attraction to a shapely newspaper publisher (played by Angela Lansbury) and by his sacrificing his righteous political principles for expediency. Breaking with the formula in the Tracy-Hepburn entries, which usually had Kate's uppity character getting her comeuppance from salt-of-the-earth Spencer, here it is Tracy's Grant Matthews who is goaded by his clear-headed wife, Mary, into withdrawing from the presidential race.

Thanks to the still-potent box-office magic of the Tracy and Hepburn team and the fame of the play original, *State of the Union* drew many moviegoers.

※　※　※

While *State of the Union* had more than respectable financial returns, Louis B. Mayer wanted to rematch Tracy and Hepburn in a comedy that would duplicate the success of *Woman of the Year.* First, however, Spencer was committed to making *Edward, My Son* (1949) on location in England with director George Cukor and producer Edwin H. Knopf (Kate's first stage producer-director, who had been a Metro producer since 1941). Hepburn went abroad with Tracy. As always, the duo stayed at separate hotels and remained discreetly out of the limelight whenever they wished to be together. While based in London, Hepburn made time for luncheon with her longtime friend Noël Coward, enjoying catching up on his circle of gay friends in the creative arts. On one of Tracy's weekend breaks from filming, Kate and Spencer went for a weekend visit to their actor friends Laurence Olivier and his wife, Vivien Leigh.

Once back in the States, Tracy and Hepburn prepared for their next screen match in *Adam's Rib* (1949). This time, Garson Kanin and his actress wife, Ruth Gordon (with her getting top billing), provided the witty screenplay. Again dependable George Cukor was at the helm, directing the couple in a scintillating comedy that gave fresh meaning to the age-old battle of the sexes. The deft narrative concerned a happily married couple, both New York City attorneys, who finds themselves on the opposite sides of a case involving a housewife (played by Judy Holliday) who has wounded by gunshot her straying husband. (It was Hepburn, fascinated with the talented, bisexual Holliday, who convinced Cukor, Kanin, and Gordon that they should combine forces to do all they could to build up Judy's role in the new screen comedy.)

By now, it was customary on a Kate-Spencer picture that he would sit complacently on the sidelines until the cameras were ready to roll, then step forward casually and steal the scene. In contrast, Hepburn, who funneled so much of her life's passions into her acting, was a firebrand on the sound stage, offering rapid-fire suggestions to one and all. She would rehearse and worry a scene until she knew it inside out. While the sets of the Tracy-Hepburn films were closed to outsiders—to accommodate her exceedingly private nature and need for extreme concentration—Metro players often snuck onto the sound stage to witness these two professionals going through their well-modulated paces.

Strongly bolstered by a quartet of New York actors (Judy Holliday, Tom Ewell, David Wayne, and Jean Hagen) and the use of actual Manhattan locations (which allowed a delighted Kate to often walk to the day's shoot from her Turtle Bay home), the sophisticated *Adam's Rib* was a sizable commercial success. It restored luster to both stars' box-office standing, which had been declining. The classic comedy appeased the cultural climate of the times by having Tracy's chauvinistic assistant district attorney point up in a postcourtroom confrontation the illogic of Hepburn's defense strategy (which had won her the case). But not to be overshadowed, the game wife, Amanda, continues to nip at her spouse's self-satisfied male superiority. She intends to challenge him in the upcoming run-off for a county court judgeship. The plot neatly pointed up that if the male insisted on being the master at home, the bright female could be an equal or better in the workplace—as long as she let the man feel superior.

Having ended the decade on a professional high note, Hepburn took a sabbatical from filmmaking and the burden of being Spencer Tracy's full-time caretaker. She was returning to Broadway.

Chapter Twenty-five
REACHING FOR NEW GOALS

"I'm not sure Mother always admired what I did on the stage or on the screen—not sure she ever did—I'd like to think she did. She'd come, of course, to everything, and sit through it and come back and say all the right things. But I couldn't help noticing a difference in her reaction to other theater things she'd go to—odd things, downtown avant-garde agitprop theater.... I think she thought of most of the things I did as being sort of la-di-da commercial— he was one who believed you had to plunge your arms into life right up to the elbows, but she didn't think the things I did...had enough to do with what really mattered in the world."
—Katharine Hepburn, 1971

The 1940s had been a decade of many transitions for Katharine Hepburn. She was no longer the oddly striking movie newcomer but an established, more conventional film star at Hollywood's most prestigious studio (MGM). Having minimized her oncamera hauteur, Kate had become more humanized for the average audience and in the process gained a degree of refined, conventional sex appeal. Her 1940s cinema image was that of the smart woman brought to bay by Spencer Tracy, who personified a well-meaning, traditional man of the people. It was a mainstream image moviegoers of the era could accept and appreciate, unlike her too rarified personae in most of her 1930s pictures.

As the 1940s ended, Kate was approaching her mid forties. Like her peers (including Claudette Colbert, Joan Crawford, Bette Davis, Marlene Dietrich, Irene Dunne, and Greer Garson), Hepburn was finding it increasingly difficult to land showcase screen assignments in an industry increasingly obsessed with youth and fresh beauty. Moreover, by 1949, the long-established studio system was crumbling. At MGM, Dore Schary had been brought in as chief of production, and Louis B. Mayer was on his way to being dismissed in 1951. Kate had little affinity for the overly intellectual Schary and his penchant for "message" pictures.

On a personal basis Hepburn found herself in a frustrating quandary, revolving around her offscreen life with Spencer Tracy. The complex relationship had long ago become a demanding codependent situation in which neither individual could or would exist "successfully" without the other. Dealing repeatedly with Tracy's drunken binges and catering continuously to his egocentric needs had left her increasingly restless. Her frustration with the situation into which she had thrown herself only grew more so when she took Spencer to meet her family. Tracy and the Hepburn clan had not hit it off when he accompanied her to Fenwick for a brief stay. Her family found this troubled, married Catholic man as unsociable and unappealing as he judged them to be eccentric, overly opinionated, and far too influential over Kate.

As balance to her consuming and frequently enervating association with Spencer, Kate counted on several sources. There was her family. Their continuity of devotion to the internationally famous Hepburn provided Kate with a sense of inflated well-being that she would increasingly romanticize over the decades. There was also steadfast Laura Harding, whom Kate repeatedly visited on trips back east to regain her sense of self, bask in her friend's continued adoration and support, and partake in this bit of connection with her past.

On the West Coast, Kate's beacon of compatibility was erudite, fussy George Cukor, with whom she chatted on a constant basis concerning both intimate and trivial topics. Through the years Hepburn and her favorite director hinted at and/or divulged to one another details of the most personal aspects of their private lives, including their lifestyles and their succession of romantic interests. However, because both had too much to lose career-wise by such confidences leaking to other friends or to the press, they largely kept such delicate information to themselves. Moreover, both parties were from an older generation who had been taught the virtue of discretion, indirection, and formality about sensitive subjects, even when conversing with one's best friends.

Hepburn also indulged herself by frequently attending George's elaborate dinner parties, where she met an array of sparkling personalities, especially from the old guard of show business. It was through Cukor that Hepburn developed an enduring friendship with the great stage star Ethel Barrymore (1879–1959), who had returned to moviemaking—through George's aegis—in the mid 1940s. Kate became a devoted friend to the aging Ethel, who had been ravaged by bad marriages, financial reversals, career downturns, and recurrent alcoholism. When Barrymore was bedridden toward the end, Hepburn considered it an honor to visit and pay her court. Playing Florence Nightingale to this illustrious legend gave Kate a great emotional lift.

Since they had made *Stage Door* together in 1937, Kate had become close with matronly performer Constance Collier (1878–1955), a mutual friend of George Cukor. The grand Constance, a lesbian, was a knowing member of the director's gay and lesbian crowd, as she had been of the gay circle of England's show business notables (including Noël Coward and matinee idol Ivor Novello). The imposing, intense, and energetic Constance was a dazzling conversationalist who had a delicious and wicked sense of humor. The British-born stage and film talent had been widowed since 1918.

By the time Kate met Constance, the latter—never a conventional beauty—was an established part of the Hollywood scene. Noted for playing grande dames onscreen, the portly performer with those wide, expressive eyes was an authority on Shakespeare and frequently coached players on the Bard. For Hepburn, Collier was a handy, West Coast substitute for her New York drama coach, Frances Robinson-Duff, who had guided her star pupil through many rough professional waters. Constance quickly became part of Hepburn's inner circle. For Kate, the arresting Collier was a delightful mixture of surrogate mother, drama teacher, confidant, idol, and ardent devotee.

The portly Constance had long mingled with the glittering sapphic circles of New York and Los Angeles. She was on intimate terms with such lesbian and/or bisexual personalities as Alla Nazimova, Mercedes de Acosta, Katharine Cornell, Greta Garbo (a longtime acquaintance and icon of Hepburn's), and scenarist Zoë Akins (who wrote two of Kate's early movies). In typical fashion of those far more closeted times, gay, lesbian, and bisexual celebrities rarely dared to frequent the few established gay clubs in Los Angeles, such as the International, the Montmartre, and those watering holes run by, among others, Jane Jones, and Bruz Fletcher. Instead, they generally mingled with one another at the usual traditional mainstream clubs or, more often, preferred (like George Cukor) to entertain one another with dinner parties and other gatherings at their plush homes.

In the 1940s randy Collier developed a lustful yen for glamorous, married movie star Paulette Goddard, with whom she made two features. Meanwhile, Constance had a longtime live-in companion-secretary, the British-born Phyllis Wilbourn, who had once been an aspiring stage performer. The unmarried, compliant, prim Phyllis was devoted to the freewheeling, dominating Constance.

*　*　*

One of Hepburn's more colorful and most complex friendships was with bright, sophisticated, complicated Irene Mayer Selznick (1907–1990). When Kate first came to Hollywood—to make *A Bill of Divorcement*—Irene was then wed to the film's producer, David O. Selznick. Initially Irene thought Hepburn affected and "wacky" but admired the fact that "the girl had class and plenty of spunk." (In contrast, in *Showman: The Life of David O. Selznick*, biographer David Thomson described the always dramatic Irene with, "She could not pick up a knife and fork without being the actress.") At the time the two remained casual acquaintances.

It was not until the mid 1940s, by which time Irene and David—the parents of two sons—had separated and Kate was employed at MGM by Irene's father, Louis B. Mayer, that the two women developed a significant friendship. (Hepburn signed her correspondence to Irene Selznick "Sister Kate.") Several on the Hollywood scene believed highly analytical Irene, obsessed with proving to the world (including her sister, Edith, with whom she had a most difficult relationship) that she was much more than merely the daughter and wife of film moguls, was bisexual.

Both Kate and Irene were pals of George Cukor, and at one of his smart gatherings in the 1940s they had been seated next to each other. By then witty, judgmental Irene was embarking on a highly successful career as a Broadway stage producer. As Kate and Irene's bond deepened, their activities ranged from holiday trips (such as one to Bermuda to visit Noël Coward) to larks on the Hollywood scene where they might take refreshing dips in a progression of Beverly Hills swimming pools—whether invited or not. As Selznick observed ambiguously in the early 1980s—before their intricate attachment suffered a fatal breach: "We entered a lifelong conspiracy which we haven't yet either defined or implemented." There were those film colony observers who speculated that Kate and Irene (who envied Hepburn's genius for keeping her career alive so spectacularly and who was very sensitive as to her ranking among Kate's select group of intimate friends) may have shared a sexual bond as another facet to their comradeship. The two women were also linked creatively and intellectually by their mutual involvement in Broadway theater: Kate as a gilt-edged star and Irene as a shrewd producer.

※　※　※

The Theater Guild's Lawrence Langner had suggested repeatedly to Hepburn that while she was still at a proper age, she should stretched herself artistically by returning to the stage and in particular tackling Shakespeare. He suggested that with her trim, boyish figure, she would be ideal to play Rosalind in *As You Like It*. Before long Kate, recurrently restless at playing second fiddle to Spencer Tracy in their joint movies, agreed. She reasoned, "The part of Rosalind is really one of the great tests of how good an actress you are, and I want to find out."

In preparation for her stage return as a titled young woman who disguises herself as a man, Kate spent three hours daily for eight months studying the Bard with her good friend Constance Collier. (When preproduction for the play got under way in Manhattan, Collier, along with her companion, Phyllis Wilbourn, came to New York so Constance could continue to tutor Kate, a process that carried on after the show opened.)

Under the direction of Michael Benthall (a Britisher), a cast was hired that included William Prince, Jay Robinson, and Cloris Leachman. In a bit of benevolent nepotism, Kate employed her brother Richard to understudy Robinson, do a walk-on, and be an assistant stage manager in the prestigious Shakespearean offering. The well-mounted production opened at the Cort Theater on January 26, 1950. Reviewers were more appreciative of Kate's fetching appeal in tights than in her overall mastery of the Bard. (Brooks Atkinson of *The New York Times* pointed out, "Her acting is tight; her voice is a little hard and shallow for Shakespeare's poetry; she has to design the character too meticulously.") Nevertheless, thanks to Hepburn's movie-star allure, the play drew in theatergoers.

During the run Hepburn kept in trim shape by energetically playing tennis and golf, walking, and biking. One weekend she went skiing and brother Dick was part of the support group in attendance. By then Dick had developed a strong fascination with striking coplayer Jay Robinson and invited him to tag along on the ski trek. While on the slopes, young Robinson injured himself and was forced to wear a neck brace for a few days thereafter. Feeling unable to perform, he advised the management accordingly. This meant that Dick must go onstage in his stead. As curtain time approached Robinson received a frantic call at home that Dick had locked himself in his dressing room and refused to come out. Kate demanded that Jay—ill or not—rush to the theater and resume his role. He did. (Dick's stage fright episode did nothing to endear him to demanding sister Kate. Thereafter Dick returned to his playwriting efforts. In this period he became chummy in Manhattan with actor Lon McCallister, who had begun his acting career in the mid 1930s when still a child. Over the years the good-looking Lon had become part of George Cukor's social set. McCallister had had a leading role in 1943's *Stage Door Canteen,* in which Kate had played a star-turn cameo.)

After a 145-performance stand, *As You Like It* closed and Hepburn returned to California to spend the summer with the still-difficult Tracy. In the fall she escaped the difficult situation with Spencer by embarking on a national tour of the Shakespearean comedy. By March 1951, Kate was back in Hartford visiting her family. On Saturday, March 17, she and her father took a late afternoon walk. When they returned home, they found seventy-three-year-old Mrs. Hepburn dead from a heart ailment. The shock of losing her parent—albeit not her favorite one—was profound. It foreshadowed the gradual disintegration of the Hepburn family in the coming years. The star was also dismayed to discover that soon after Kit's passing, Dr. Hepburn destroyed all her personal papers. It was as if she had never existed. Within months the always self-focused physician married Madeline Santa Croce, one of his hospital nurses. She was twenty-two-years younger than her widower groom. When Kate learned of the rushed nuptials she had mixed feelings: upset that her mother had been replaced so quickly but in a way relieved that there was someone else to care for her cantankerous septuagenarian dad.

* * *

Kit Hepburn's unexpected death almost made Kate cancel her upcoming film project. However, she was always willing to find a ready rationalization to keep a-goin' with her all-important career—no matter what. She told herself that the location shoot would be distracting and healing, especially since it would take her to the exciting wilds of Africa. Accompanied by doting Constance Collier, Hepburn sailed to England aboard a small passenger-freighter ship in mid April. There Kate met with movie producer Sam Spiegel to finalize preproduction arrangements for *The African Queen* (1951), her first movie to be lensed in color. Kate quickly discovered that the film's director, John Huston, was full of blarney and bravado. It made the star wonder at her judgment in agreeing to go into the hazardous wilderness of the Dark Continent with this boozing braggart. In addition, she was unprepared as to how she might respond to her leading man, Humphrey Bogart. She soon discovered that while the actor had a deeply sarcastic nature and could match Huston in guzzling booze, he was a gentleman at heart. Most impressive of all, he was proud to be an actor and thoroughly enjoyed his craft. Besides, he was traveling with his screen star wife, the stylish Lauren Bacall. She and Kate quickly became boon companions and remained pals throughout the remainder of Hepburn's long life.

Having left Constance to visit with friends in England, Hepburn went on to Rome. There she met up with Spencer Tracy. Their days of sightseeing were marred by his annoyance that she was once again deserting him, leaving him to return to Hollywood alone. Next, Hepburn flew to Africa. Her destination was Léopoldville in the (Belgian) Congo (now known as Zaire) and then to Stanleyville before moving on to the isolated film camp near the banks of the Ruiki River. Kate had to adjust mightily to work effectively with Huston under such primitive filming conditions. She was won over to his talents when he insightfully suggested how she might better play Rose Sayer, the repressed spinster missionary in *The African Queen.* (With Kate's naturally turned-down mouth, Hepburn was coming across in the initial footage as too somber.) John told her to envision how Eleanor Roosevelt, the president's wife, had looked in newsreels when visiting injured soldiers in hospitals. It gave Hepburn the needed clue to interpret her middle-aged character caught in 1914 German East Africa with an alcoholic Canadian riverboat pilot (played by Bogart). As they share many (mis)adventures the unlikely couple fall in love, marry, and—amazingly—survive their perilous mission to blow up a German gunboat.

In her best-selling book (1987) about the extremely difficult production of *The African Queen*, Hepburn would colorfully describe the many wonders, hardships, and dangers of their hectic existence in the African brush. During the nearly three-month shoot Kate (and the others) survived daily battles with the oppressive heat, poor food, pesky insects, and bothersome animals. However, she got deathly ill from contaminated bottled water. As a result of contracting dysentery she lost several pounds from her already-thin frame and had to take three days off from filming for complete bed rest. Much as she always enjoyed undertaking her own stunt work, in *The African Queen* she was forced to allow the production's script-continuity girl, Angela Allen (who bore a great resemblance to Kate), to substitute in the long shots of the decrepit boat shooting down the dangerous rapids.

There were times on the difficult location when Bogart found Kate's over-size enthusiasm and curiosity for everything—mingled with her refined superiority—to be exceedingly irritating. Nevertheless, he came to respect her professionalism as a performer and to accept her eccentric, compulsive nature. Some of the crew, however, were not thrilled that Kate refused to allow them usage of her private portable toilet, which she demanded be carted down the river from one filming location to another, or her insistence that a jerry-rigged, cumbersome, full-length mirror (for checking her costumes) be laboriously transported from one remote location to another. As usual, imperious Kate was at her best when giving orders or suddenly called upon to nurse an injured member of their party (as with David Lewin, a reporter on special assignment from the British *Daily Express* who suffered a severe reaction to a bite from a poisonous insect).

After completing the remaining scenes of *The African Queen* on sound stages at the Worton Hall Studios in England in early November 1951, Kate returned to the United States loaded down with mementos, photographs, and wonderful anecdotes of her great adventure (during which, besides contracting dysentery, she had developed skin cancers from overexposure to the tropical sun). While it would take several months to recover from her hazardous moviemaking safari, she never regretted the challenging experience.

When released, *The African Queen* garnered great praise, was a terrific box-office success, and emerged an enduring cinema classic. It won Bogart an Academy Award and Hepburn her first Oscar nomination in nearly a decade. She lost the coveted prize to Vivien Leigh (*A Streetcar Named Desire*). However, at forty-four, by bravely shunning her past Hollywood image, Hepburn opened up a whole new set of movie roles for herself.

❈   ❈   ❈

Back in Los Angeles, Hepburn engineered Tracy's moving from his current hotel accommodations to one of the three secluded guesthouses on George Cukor's Beverly Hills estate. While Spencer preferred living in austerity and avoided mingling with the film director's diverse crowd, taciturn Tracy and gregarious Cukor furthered a very close friendship that had developed over years of joint moviemaking. Kate felt more at ease knowing that Cukor would be nearby should Tracy need companionship or help. She also counted on ever-obliging George to provide frequent reports on the current state of Spencer's physical and emotional health.

Owing MGM one more picture under her existing contract, Kate teamed with Tracy for the seventh time in *Pat and Mike* (1952). With Cukor directing a script by Ruth Gordon and Garson Kanin, the comedy was tailor-made to what audiences expected of a Tracy-Hepburn outing. In this broad romance she was the college physical education instructor who abandons her stuffy fiancé for a fast-talking, colorful sports promoter. By the finale the oddly matched duo are in love and seal their professional (and personal) partnership not with a kiss but with a handshake.

During filming Tracy brought his two children onto the set, and reputedly it was the first time they met Hepburn. When Kate proved headstrong about dealing with the press during the shoot, the studio convinced Spencer to persuade his recalcitrant costar to be more amenable toward the useful media. To everyone's surprise, she followed her friend's request. When released, *Pat and Mike* was a critical and commercial success.

✳   ✳   ✳

By the time *Pat and Mike* was in release in mid 1952, Hepburn was on the British stage starring in George Bernard Shaw's *The Millionairess* under the direction of Michael Benthall. (Constance Collier, as always, had come along to coach Kate in her new stage role. Collier, Hepburn, and Constance's companion, Phyllis Wilbourn, shared digs at Claridge's.) For Hepburn, performing Shaw in front of an audience was the realization of a childhood dream. It made her feel even closer to her dad, for Shaw was Dr. Hepburn's favorite playwright.

The difficult play had never before met with audience enthusiasm. However, thanks to Hepburn's robust performance, *The Millionairess* attracted large audiences at London's New Theater. Critics either marveled or were taken aback by Kate's full-throttle portrayal in the demanding lead role of the wealthy woman who obliterates whatever she cannot possess. Some aisle-sitters suggested that she was performing in a state of near hysteria. In actuality Hepburn was in a real-life emotional turmoil. A combination of the aftereffects of her mother's death and the increased pressure to maintain her star status in a changing entertainment industry had, among other factors, put Kate into a state of total exhaustion. This midlife crisis (which verged on a full-blown nervous breakdown) was accentuated by news that back in Hollywood, reckless, selfish Spencer was having an affair with Gene Tierney, his beautiful costar in *Plymouth Adventure* (1952). While recently divorced Tierney thought she and the much older Tracy might one day marry, the relationship soon ended—much as had Spencer's several other sexual diversions or attempted romances.

Not fully recovered from her London ordeal and her efforts to keep her perilous emotional condition from the press, Kate brought *The Millionairess* to Broadway in October 1952. She was hoarse from shouting out her many lines of dialogue and never felt on top of her performance during the limited engagement, which garnered mixed reviews. Undaunted, Hepburn obsessively worked on packaging a film adaptation of the property. She collaborated tirelessly over many months with veteran scripter-director Preston Sturges, who planned to helm the property. However, proper financing could not be found.

* * *

After the Manhattan run of *The Millionairess*, Kate caught up with her Broadway theatergoing and, among other new productions, saw *The Time of the Cuckoo*. This major stage success concerned the wistful romance of a middle-aged American schoolteacher on vacation in Venice who is drawn to a married Italian shopkeeper. It was written by Arthur Laurents, whom Hepburn first met in 1940s Hollywood through Irene Selznick. It starred Shirley Booth, who had supported Hepburn in the stage edition of *The Philadelphia Story*. Visiting Shirley in her dressing room after the performance, Booth asked Hepburn's advice about the advisability of re-creating her role (for which she won a Tony Award) onscreen when, and if, the time came. According to Arthur Laurents, Kate talked Shirley out of the "dubious" notion.

Several months later—lo and behold—Hepburn was in Venice starring in *Summertime* (1955), the screen version of *The Time of the Cuckoo*. Her director was respected English filmmaker David Lean (1908–1991). Less than a year older than Kate, David was in the midst of a difficult marriage to his third wife, British leading lady Ann Todd. Lean already had great admiration for Hepburn before filming began, and during the shoot he became enamored of her talent, persona, and great moviemaking knowledge. (In tribute to his leading lady, Lean gave meticulous attention to presenting his freckle-faced, angular star in a glamorous, adoring mode.)

Kate arrived in Venice in the heat of summer with her girls (Constance Collier and Laura Harding) in tow. The screenplay had been altered considerably from the stage original. The heroine's cynicism had been excised, and her summer romance was now a touching, laughing-through-tears love story rather than a comparison of two cultures, with the teacher choosing between a short-term love affair or nothing at all. While Hepburn was not charmed by her slick leading man, Italy's Rossano Brazzi, she found perfectionistic David Lean endlessly fascinating—even when he repeatedly lost his cool at her constant bossiness on and off the set. (Despite her annoying habits, Lean had such high regard for Kate that he allowed her to direct a sequence within the film: one that featured Isa Miranda and Hepburn's characters having a heated discussion.)

One of *Summertime*'s most famous scenes involved Hepburn's distracted Jane Hudson tumbling into the dirty canal as she snaps photos of picturesque Venice. Thereafter, Kate would insist that this oncamera dunking—done for the sake of her art—resulted in her lifelong case of conjunctivitis, which in turn caused her eyes thereafter to tear constantly. However, several individuals involved in the Italian-shot production recounted that the star sometimes ended her daily *Summertime* tasks by recklessly taking a brisk swim in the polluted canals.

Released in the United States in June 1955, *Summertime* was a substantial hit with both filmgoers and critics. Lee Rogosin (*The Saturday Review*) commented, "Miss Hepburn has labored long in the service of her art, and like many grand actress personalities, she has now created herself in her own image. Everything superfluous is gone, the elements are refined and complete." Both Hepburn and Lean were Oscar-nominated, and each lost the prize (Kate to Anna Magnani of *The Rose Tattoo*). While Kate and David never made another picture together, they remained in frequent touch and never stopped bragging about the other's greatness. (David would say of Kate, "She's just about my greatest friend. I love her." In return, Hepburn demonstrated her tremendous affection and respect for the British director by introducing him to Sam Spiegel when the producer was desperately seeking someone to helm 1957's *The Bridge on the River Kwai*.)

❋   ❋   ❋

On April 25, 1955, Kate's longtime pal Constance Collier died at age seventy-seven. Sorely missing her coach and confidant, Hepburn would hire Collier's veteran secretary-companion, Phyllis Wilbourn, to serve her as the now-retired Emily Perkins once had. It began an association that would last until the reserved, self-sacrificing, tremendously considerate Phyllis passed away in 1995, then in her nineties. Similar to when Wilbourn had been Constance Collier's inseparable friend, confidant, lackey, and possible sometime lover, now gossipers suggested that Phyllis played a similar role in Hepburn's life.

Meanwhile, still requiring more emotional freedom and artistic growth away from selfish Tracy (who was annoying Kate by dallying with Metro contract star Grace Kelly), Hepburn undertook an Australian trek from May through November 1955. She went Down Under to perform a repertory of Shakespeare's *Measure for Measure* (as Isabella), *The Merchant of Venice* (as Portia), and *The Taming of the Shrew* (as Katharine). This multicity engagement featured Kate and her gay friend Robert Helpmann (of *The Millionairess*), supported by members of England's distinguished Old Vic Company. The showcase proved overall to be relatively successful. As always, hyperactive Hepburn thrived on exploring novel landscapes and local sights. However, she was greatly distracted during the Australian stay when she learned that Tracy had been fired from a new MGM picture and then let go from his studio contract. MGM had grown tired of Spencer's drunken rampages and ended his twenty-year tenure at the Culver City lot. Initially, Tracy was convinced that this setback would finish his movie career, but he soon found screen offers elsewhere.

* * *

Back in America, Kate rejected a request from friend Noël Coward to star in his unproduced play *Volcano*. However, she accepted producer Hal B. Wallis's offer to portray another movie spinster. This time it was in *The Rainmaker* (1956), based on a recent Broadway play that had showcased Geraldine Paige. In this entry for Paramount Pictures, Kate took second billing to Burt Lancaster, who was cast as the boastful con artist who brings precipitation to a dusty southwestern town and a romantic spark to an arid middle-aged woman. Once the aggressive, athletic, and overly cerebral Lancaster realized that his few-years-older leading lady made no artistic demands of others that she would not make of herself, the two worked in relative harmony. It was hard-drinking Wendell Corey, cast as her sheriff beau, with whom Hepburn felt absolutely no rapport.

While filming *The Rainmaker,* authoritarian Kate was up to her old elitist habits. As *Hollywood Reporter* columnist Mike Connolly penned on August 6,

1956: "Poor Kate Hepburn hasn't advanced much temperament-wise since a critic poison-penned that she 'ran the gamut of emotions from A to B'.... How do you publicize a picture without [promotional] stills, Kate? As your old pal Fanny Brice would say, 'Come off it, kid!... Paramount had to open a side door for Kate so that she wouldn't have to rub elbows with the hoi polloi."

During the shoot, for which Kate received $750 weekly just for living expenses (for her and Phyllis Wilbourn in their rented Los Angeles home) director Joseph Anthony, who had already had his star to his home for afternoon tea, invited Hepburn out to dine. He recalled, "She replied, 'I can't go anywhere. I can't do anything. I can't appear in public; people would follow me.' I realized then what it meant to be a star. The loneliness...to have to live as a recluse." Anthony added, "Ten minutes later, she called and said, 'I'd be enchanted if you and your wife would come to lunch.' And then she wouldn't let us go! I think she had a moment of regret that she had turned me down, that she had acted a little impetuously. She didn't want to feel she was being 'used' by her guests inviting themselves over, but really she was lonely, she wanted friends, and once they arrived she wanted them to stay with her. Her graciousness, her warmth and pleasure in entertaining were unforgettable."

Largely shot on Hollywood sound stages as an economy move, the color feature did moderately well in the constricted film marketplace. Her performance in *The Rainmaker* as Lizzie Curry earned Kate her seventh Oscar bid. (She lost the Academy Award this time to Ingrid Bergman of *Anastasia*.) Later Hepburn would comment to veteran gossip columnist Louella Parsons, "I get the nominations because I'm always playing freaks. The awards generally go to the sad, dramatic freaks."

Continuing to field professional offers, Hepburn flew to England to shoot *The Iron Petticoat* (1956) at Pinewood Studios. Her improbable costar was wisecracking comedian Bob Hope (who replaced an earlier choice: Cary Grant). In this quasiremake of 1939's classic *Ninotchka,* which had starred Greta Garbo and Melvyn Douglas, Kate was cast as a sexless Communist, Captain Vinka Kovelenko of the Russian Air Force. (The part allowed her to dressed in masculine uniforms, a gambit that amused her.) With a screenplay by veteran talent Ben Hecht and direction by Ralph Thomas, Hepburn thought the venture could be fun to make and entertaining for moviegoers to watch. She was wrong on both counts.

Egocentric Hope brought in his personal writing staff to punch up his lines and enlarge his part at the expense of Kate's. While she struggled to deliver a credible Slavic accent and to make her brusque military officer blossom through love, Hope sabotaged Hepburn's performance and ultimately the entire film. (At one point during the coleads' tug-of-war Bob said of Kate, who was in a snit, "If she's not careful, I'll spread it around that she's Audrey Hepburn's father!" The costars continued to feud throughout filming and their lack of rapport showed onscreen. The picture proved a creative and financial misfire.

Having spent so much time abroad during the 1950s, Hepburn could not wait to return to the United States. Her energy revived, she was once again prepared to help restore Spencer Tracy's spirit and career.

Chapter Twenty-six
A DEVOTED WOMAN

"I think back to my mother and father now. We were so close, and I wonder, Why didn't I ask them more questions? But we all hide things, you know. Even from those we love most. Even from ourselves. We say, 'I'll put this part of me in a box where no one can see it, and I'll never open that, never step on that one, ever.'"
—Katharine Hepburn, 1985

By the late 1940s, Leland Hayward, divorced in 1948 from Margaret Sullavan, had become bored with the rigmarole of being a film talent agent–manager. He turned to becoming a Broadway and film producer. One of his pending ventures was bringing Ernest Hemingway's short novel *The Old Man and the Sea* to the screen. He hired Fred Zinnemann to direct and Spencer Tracy to star. (Leland's continuing admiration for Kate was a factor in Tracy's being contracted for the project.)

In spring 1956 the Warner Bros. release got under way in Cuba, where Hemingway then lived. Knowing that Tracy, a devout creature of comfort and routines, hated filming on location, Kate accompanied him. Besides, it would provide an opportunity to visit with her old friend Ernest. (During her spare time on this extended holiday Hepburn amused herself by painting several sea- and skyscapes.) Things got off to a bad start on the moviemaking front when outspoken Hemingway grumbled about Spencer being "too fat, rich and old" for the lead part.

As the technically difficult shoot lagged behind schedule, cranky Tracy and demanding Zinnemann became increasingly dissatisfied with one another. Eventually the director quit the project and was replaced by John Sturges.

Thereafter, the jinxed production regrouped back in Hollywood, where newly shot scenes in indoor studio tanks were blended with specially shot footage. The difficult undertaking did not wrap until months later and was not released theatrically until October 1958. With the budget having reached a then-astronomical $6 million, the specialty picture was doomed at the box office, made worse when Tracy's reviews were largely unenthusiastic. The extended, unhappy making of *The Old Man and the Sea* left Tracy emotionally shaken and his once-sterling movie-star reputation besmirched. As usual, Kate was always present to coax him through this latest ordeal and to smooth things over with coworkers.

While Spencer was anguishing through the last of *The Old Man and the Sea*, Kate was offered the lead in the film of *Desk Set* (1957). It was derived from a hit Broadway show starring Shirley Booth that dealt with the repercussions to employees when high technology (i.e., newfangled computers) came into the workplace. For a $150,000 salary plus a percentage of profits, Hepburn was amenable to playing Bunny Watson, the head of a TV network's reference library, who in middle age find a satisfying romance. (One can only imagine how bad Booth felt losing out once again to Hepburn, having already had her *The Time of the Cuckoo* stage part turned into a hit role for Kate onscreen in *Summertime.*) As part of the deal Hepburn "requested" that the play's role of the methods engineer be expanded and tailored for Spencer's special talents. Twentieth Century-Fox agreed and the CinemaScope color comedy was placed into preproduction.

While bossy Kate urged that *Desk Set* utilize New York location filming, the studio vetoed this added expense. Stymied but not beaten, Hepburn persisted in making other aspects of her characterization and the story line as valid as possible. One day she argued that a large plant used to dress the set was neither genuine nor sufficiently large. To prove her point the next morning she dragged in from her rented home a humongous real plant and proudly set it in place on the sound stage. On another occasion, coplayer Joan Blondell broke an earring her character was wearing in a particular scene. Rather than wait idly on the sound stage while the wardrobe department found a suitable replacement, Kate marched over to a decorated Christmas tree on the set, pulled off a trinket, and fashioned a new earring for Blondell. This accomplished, the cameras rolled.

As the first Tracy-Hepburn screen collaboration in five years, *Desk Set* was warmly received by their many fans. However, several critics noted the obvious: the long-term screen love team had settled into middle age. (While Kate still looked pert and vibrant, decades of heavy drinking had turned Spencer into an old man before his time: white-haired, stocky, and wrinkle-faced.)

❋   ❋   ❋

On May 12, 1957, Katharine Hepburn turned fifty. As Charles Higham pointed out in *Kate: The Life of Katharine Hepburn* (1975), "For Kate, in middle age...life became more and more a discipline, less and less the madcap, eccentric jaunt of her youth. She had come to understand her own nature, had come to terms with her faults and accepted herself frankly." Further, according to Higham, "For all of her shrewdness and piercing wisdom, she was still a child at heart. Her secret as an artist was that she never lost her sense of wonder. Each day was both an adventure and a challenge. Each person she met was utterly intriguing."

Seeking to further challenge herself artistically—and gain recuperative time away from Tracy—Hepburn accepted stage producer Lawrence Langner's latest offer. He invited her to be a guest star in the summer 1957 edition of the American Shakespeare Festival in Stratford, Connecticut. Taking minimum salary and shunning star treatment in her basic accommodations, Kate threw herself devotedly into her work.

With her entrenched, mannered acting style, which did not allow for much modification, Kate often had difficulty interacting with the established New York actors (e.g., Alfred Drake and Morris Carnovsky) playing in tandem with her. (The younger set of players, including Lois Nettleton, were in such deep awe of Oscar-winning Hepburn that they kept their distance respectfully from her when not onstage. Nearly half a century later Nettleton distinctly recalls the fervor of Kate's determination to excel in her latest stage turn. Lois also remembers Hepburn providing her with a gratis piece of useful acting advice regarding how to better shape her portrayal.)

At Stratford that year Kate starred in *The Merchant of Venice* (as Portia) and in *Much Ado About Nothing* (as Beatrice) and earned respectful reviews. (John Chapman of the New York *Daily News* wrote that her Portia was "a girl of intelligence, humor and iron determination—which is almost type-cast-ing.") During the weeks of performance Hepburn lit up brightly whenever she confided to cast members that her friend Spencer Tracy was due any day to attend a performance. To her great disappointment, the man for whom she had sacrificed so much over the years never came.

*　*　*

Over the decades, John Ford never lost hope of working again with his adored Kate. When the director, now in his sixties, was preparing *The Rising of the Moon* (1957), he hoped Hepburn would accept a key assignment in the picture. She declined the offer to appear in this trio of tales about Irish rural life, but did have a casting notion for another of his upcoming projects, *The Last Hurrah* (1958). She suggested Spencer for the key role of Frank Skeffington, the veteran Irish-American political boss embarking on his last mayoral campaign. Ford cast Tracy in the part to a great success.

Meanwhile, another of Kate's past professional associates, Joseph L. Mankiewicz was preparing *Suddenly, Last Summer* (1959), based on a one-act play (*Garden District*) by Tennessee Williams. Producer Sam Spiegel (for whom Kate had made *The African Queen*) wanted Hepburn for the part of wealthy Violet Venable once Vivien Leigh, the original choice, had declined. (The unsympathetic role was that of an embittered New Orleans widow who had an unnatural fixation on her sensitive son, who had died recently in Spain under mysterious circumstances.)

Hepburn respected Williams's enormous writing talent but not his per-sonal life, full of substance abuse and destructive gay relationships. Later she claimed to have had absolutely no affinity for his excessive allegorical tale that dealt with homosexuality, cannibalism, repressed incestuous feelings, and unnecessary lobotomies. Because of this, it was a wonder that Hepburn par-ticipated at all in this dark screen project that centered so heavily on a gay poet and his overly possessive mother. In the narrative the latter had long pimped for her offspring with young men encountered on vacation trips to exotic locales. When Kate's character grew too old for the task, a beautiful cousin—played by Elizabeth Taylor—took over the chore.

As Hepburn packed to fly to England for the *Suddenly, Last Summer* shoot, she was extremely keyed up. Actor–theater reviewer Travis Michael Holder, a friend of Kate's through his performer mother (June Travis), was twelve at the time and happened to be visiting at Hepburn's New York brownstone. He recalled of the agitated star: "She was in a state, and Phyllis [Wilbourn] told her to wait and get into character when she got there and the cameras started rolling."

Arriving in England, Hepburn and Elizabeth Taylor, her former MGM studio mate, were immediately wary of one another. Taylor was concerned that she might well be overshadowed as a performer by this veteran talent. As a result she was cool and distant to Kate. On her part Hepburn, who for the first time ever oncamera had a female colead billed over her, was miffed that everyone—including the director—was paying court to Elizabeth rather than to her. (At one juncture during the tense shoot Kate—known to some on the set as "Katie the autocrat"—shouted at Mankiewicz: "You are treating me like an *old* actress!") Hepburn was also concerned that she was being photographed unflatteringly, which was a point of great sensitivity for a leading lady then already in her early fifties.

Then there was the matter of emotionally distraught Montgomery Clift, the third member of the star trio. Ironically, he played a psychiatrist in *Suddenly, Last Summer* but in reality was in tremendous emotional chaos. Engulfed by entrenched alcohol and drug habits, intense insecurity over his damaged looks from a mid-1950s car accident, and unable to come to terms with his bisexuality, Montgomery was in constant turmoil. Rather than cater to his ailing leading man, highbrow Mankiewicz showed only disdain toward Clift on and off the set, which further battered the actor's depleted confidence.

Oncamera Clift emoted in a most disoriented manner. While his good friend Taylor constantly pampered and protected him, Kate was bewildered, then sympathetic, and finally annoyed by his highly unprofessional behavior. In her typical manner caregiver Hepburn attempted to help her coplayer regain a grip on his mangled life. She coaxed him to try to sleep normal hours without medication, to deal with the residual pains of his auto accident, but the no-nonsense approach of this doctor's daughter fell on deaf ears. (Hepburn detailed later, "None of my arguments did any good. I thought he was weak. Simpatico but weak.") At one juncture Mankiewicz threatened to close down the filming because of Montgomery's erratic behavior when he would belatedly show up on the set—with his face contorted in fear and his body covered in perspiration. However, Elizabeth pressured the filmmaker to proceed with the production.

At one of the many crisis points in the making of this troubled undertaking, a frazzled Hepburn condemned the entire venture, again questioning Williams's unique set of extremely disturbed characters. She insisted, "I'm far too healthy a person to be in something like this. Who are these people?" (This outburst prompted Gore Vidal, who had adapted the play for the screen, to think, "But she knew exactly who they were, and she gave easily her best performance.")

By the time the shoot ended, Kate was furious with Mankiewicz, who had offered her so little direction and who had treated Clift so severely. She stalked into the filmmaker's office. Once being assured that her final scenes had indeed been shot, she spat in his face (the director claimed she spit at his feet.) That done, Hepburn stormed into Sam Spiegel's headquarters and repeated the same contemptuous gesture at the producer. Her chores done, Hepburn returned to America. (Later Kate said, "I didn't spit just for Monty Clift. I spat at them for the way they treated me.")

When released in late 1959, the $2.5 million *Suddenly, Last Summer* proved controversial and took in nearly three times as much at the box office. Photographed unglamorously, Kate looked matronly in her Norman Hartnell wardrobe. Nevertheless, she gave a forceful performance as the emotionally corrupt Southern matriarch who is rapidly descending into madness. Arthur Knight (*The Saturday Review*) judged, "Katharine Hepburn uses every ounce of the Hepburn charm (and every one of the Hepburn mannerisms) to make her portrait of an egocentric matron and too-doting mother ring true." Both Hepburn and Taylor were nominated for Oscars in the Best Actress category but lost to Simone Signoret (*Room at the Top*).

* * *

In the summer of 1960, Kate returned to the American Shakespeare Festival in Stratford, Connecticut. This season she did *Twelfth Night* (as Viola) and *Antony and Cleopatra* (as the Queen of the Nile). Among her coplayers were Morris Carnovsky, Sada Thompson, Earle Hyman, and Robert Ryan (whom Hepburn particularly admired).

During 1960, Hepburn visited England and Ireland with her longtime stalwart friend Laura Harding. In a postcard to George Cukor, Kate insisted in mock horror that beloved Laura "has bought all of Dublin." However, most of Hepburn's energies during this period were devoted to dancing attention on the increasingly ill Spencer. For 1960's *Inherit the Wind* filmmaker Stanley Kramer took a chance on the ailing Tracy by having him team with Fredric March in the screen version of *Inherit the Wind*. Although Spencer was crabby and had grown more sedentary, he got along famously with the younger Kramer. The two developed a strong friendship, and the producer-director utilized Spencer in as many of his subsequent vehicles as possible.

When Mervyn LeRoy suggested Spencer for a colead in 1961's *The Devil at Four O'Clock*, the sixty-year-old star could not resist the offer because it would allow him to play a priest again and a chance to work with Frank Sinatra. On the Hawaiian location Kate's full-time occupation was sitting attentively on the sidelines. She was constantly vigilant for Spencer's professional and personal well-being on the set and always ready to soothe his ego if the day's shoot sparked problems. To keep herself occupied she knitted furiously.

On *The Devil at Four O'Clock,* Sinatra was highly deferential to the legendary Tracy. However, the famed crooner could not keep from being his usual prima donna self. Frank had a habit of staying up most of the night drinking with his cronies. In Hawaii he would often be returning to his quarters just as dawn was breaking. On a few such occasions he encountered Kate, who was heading to the ocean for a brisk early morning swim. Typically she wore a see-through tank suit. According to George Jacobs, valet to Frank for over thirteen years, this sight prompted Sinatra to have "erotic dreams" about Hepburn "being the hottest fifty-something star in the business." As production progressed Frank became increasingly obsessed with Kate. One night he nervously invited her and Spencer for a pasta dinner at his quarters. By the time the spaghetti was served, Frank was keyed up. Tasting the main course, he screamed that it was not cooked properly. He picked up the serving dish and flung it in the direction of his valet, making a huge mess. The guests of honor were so taken aback by this outburst that they departed immediately, while Sinatra cleared the dinner table by smashing all the dishes.

* * *

For *Judgment at Nuremberg* (1961), Kramer hired Tracy to be the chief Allied judge at the post–World War II trials of key Nazi leaders. The part appealed to Spencer. However, typically, as filming drew very near he suddenly wanted to back out as he waited at the Los Angeles airport to fly overseas. It took all of Kate's coaxing to get her longtime friend to board the plane for the location work in Germany. Later, at the end of 1961, when the prestige feature had a special premiere in Berlin, Kate and Spencer attended the festivities. They made sure, however, to never to be seen traveling in public together.

* * *

For the sake of remaining at Tracy's side, Hepburn rejected an offer from producer Hal B. Wallis to star in the screen version of Tennessee Williams's *Summer and Smoke* (1961). Instead, Geraldine Paige re-created her stage performance as the spinster in 1916 Mississippi. Kate also turned down a pivotal part in the Broadway-bound *The Night of the Iguana* (1961), a role that Williams had written especially for her. Instead, Bette Davis claimed that theater assignment. In contrast, Hepburn could not resist the chance to star in a film adaptation of Eugene O'Neill's *Long Day's Journey into Night.* Although the low-budget feature would pay her only a modest salary plus a percentage of profits, the artistic challenge of playing the drug-addicted Mary Tyrone was too inviting to decline (once she overcame her fears about tacking such a demanding role). That decided, Kate and producer Ely Landau agreed that it would be exciting if Tracy appeared as her oncamera spouse, a renowned stage star whose glory days have long past.

Regarding this casting possibility, Landau was invited to meet with Tracy and Hepburn in Los Angeles. The producer remembered, "It was extraordinary to watch her with Spence. She was a totally different person. She turned really submissive…and hardly opened her mouth, other than introducing us.

She smiled, laughed at everything he said... Finally, when we got down to business, I explained to him, 'I don't have to tell you what it would mean to have you.' He replied, 'Look, Kate's the lunatic. She's the one who goes off and appears at Stratford in Shakespeare. I don't believe in that nonsense—I'm a movie actor. She's always doing these things for no money! I promise you this: If you offered me this part for five hundred thousand and somebody else offered me another part for five hundred thousand, I'd take this!" And Kate exclaimed, 'There he goes! No! It's not going to work' And we just went ahead and had a charming breakfast."

Before filming began in New York City, director Sidney Lumet insisted on three weeks of rehearsal. Lumet said, "We had the read-through, and at the end of it, Kate just looked at me and said, 'Sidney, help.' She had used up her instinct, which was superb, and now all of a sudden she needed help because you can't keep going on instinct. She needed help and she was bright enough to ask for it."

Shot in economical black-and-white, *Long Day's Journey Into Night* was made over thirty-seven days at a film studio on Manhattan's West Twenty-sixth Street. An old house on City Island in the Bronx substituted for the Tyrone family's seaside cottage in 1912 Connecticut. With Britisher Ralph Richardson, instead of Tracy, as the father, Jason Robards Jr. as the elder son and Dean Stockwell as the tubercular younger offspring, the cast went through their paces in this account of one dreadful day in the family's sad life.

Director Lumet recalled, "There was a moment when Edmund [Dean Stockwell] stops her [i.e., Hepburn] from ranting and says, 'Mama, listen, I've got consumption,'" and he grabbed her and shook her, trying to get through to her. I said, 'Kate, I want you to haul off and whack him across the face as hard as you can.' She said, 'Sidney, I don't think I could do that because I'm not a physical person. Can I try it?' I said, 'Let's go,' and she whacked him. I think the poor bastard still feels it. It was just brilliant. What it released in her emotionally—it was the breakthrough that she made in the part. I never rehearsed it again until we shot it because I didn't think Dean would be able to take it."

Long Day's Journey Into Night (which ran nearly three hours) had an art-house release in the fall of 1962. Rarely had Hepburn ever received such glowing movie reviews. "Katharine Hepburn caps her distinguished career in the role of the pitiful, dope-addicted mother, groping back to the past for dimly remembered moments of happiness" (Arthur Knight, *The Saturday Review*). "She emerges as a superb tragedienne" (Dwight Macdonald, *Esquire*). A dissenting vote came from Bosley Crowther (*New York Times*). He opined, "She is put to so much repetition in the first hour or so of the film, in hinting at the ultimate revelation that narcotics have her hooked, that she strains her own gifts of airy acting and the patience of workaday folks."

Hepburn was nominated for yet another Oscar but lost the Best Actress Academy Award this time to Anne Bancroft (*The Miracle Worker*). Kate, however, did claim a Best Actress trophy at the Cannes Film Festival.

What was all the more remarkable about Kate's sterling performance in *Long Day's Journey into Night* was that during the concentrated filming her aged father was in precarious health. She used her free weekends to visit with him in West Hartford. To do so, she put aside, temporarily, concerns for Spencer Tracy who was dealing with an emphysema attack on the West Coast. On November 20, with his family at his side, Dr. Hepburn died. Kate, in particular, was especially bereft.

After her dad's death, the Bloomfield Avenue home was donated to the University of Hartford. Kate detailed, "There was a lifetime of living in that house and we had quite a job of cleaning it up. I was cleaning the toilet in the library. I was covered with filth, crawling around the floor thinking the thousand thoughts you can imagine I might be thinking of this place where I had been brought up. Then in comes my sister Marion with a strange man, both of them looking down at me and Marion saying, "Oh, Katty, this is Dr. Woodruff, the chancellor of Hartford University.' I was at a loss for words." Still grieving over her father's passing, Hepburn returned to Los Angeles. She vowed to take such good care of Spencer Tracy that he would not desert her through death.

Chapter Twenty-seven
THE END OF A ROAD

"It's the most extraordinarily delicate and strong face but as a human being she [Kate Hepburn] is growing all the time and that is written in her face. She wears very odd things and she certainly doesn't give herself a break, because she looks wonderful when she wears dresses, but she can't be bothered and she doesn't."

—George Cukor, 1963

From the time that Katharine Hepburn and Spencer Tracy forged their emotional bond in 1941 on the set of *Woman of the Year*, the Hollywood press had avoided publishing direct references to the couple's close friendship. (One can only imagine how long that policy would have lasted in today's world of tell-all tabloid newspapers, TV programs, and the Internet.) Occasionally a Tinseltown columnist such as Sheilah Graham would make an oblique remark about the illustrious star duo, such as her report in February 1942 on the just-released *Woman of the Year*. She informed readers that the costars of this MGM comedy "got on like a house afire" and that "the love scenes in the picture are extremely convincing." Or *Daily Variety*'s Mike Connolly might include a blind item in his trade paper gossip column such as a February 1951 squib about Hepburn being in London's Mayfair "with an old flame."

Generally, however, the famed movie costars, who studiously avoided being seen in public together, remained off the press's radar regarding their togetherness. As Hepburn recalled of her modus operandi in the Tracy years: "I never went out in public with Spencer, never, ever did. Ever. Mrs. Tracy lived in California and he was married to Mrs. Tracy and I didn't think it was my place to be seen all over town with him. The press respected it for the reason that I respected it and Spencer respected it. We went out of our way to be reticent. And I think people thought, 'Well, if it means that much to them, let's shut up.'"

While reporters remained mum on the Hepburn-Tracy tandem, they were urged—again by MGM and for the sake of not shattering the film colony's status quo—to play up whatever residue of a normal marriage Spencer and Louise Tracy had. Thus Dan Senseney could write in *Photoplay*'s September 1956 issue, "Spence and his wife have the kind of warm, affectionate relationship you find between two people who have shared both happiness and sorrow—who understand each other completely and have found their way to a mature, undemanding love…. But since there has always been a streak of restlessness in Spence, he could never be happy as a full-time gentleman farmer. He needs the stimulation of people and activity and new scenes. So, while he is working on a picture, he lives from Monday to Friday in a small, comfortable Hollywood apartment, spending only his weekends at the ranch."

The same *Photoplay* magazine article referenced Spencer's circle of friends as including such married couples as Humphrey Bogart (who would die in January 1957) and Lauren Bacall, Stewart Granger and Jean Simmons, baseball coach Leo Durocher and Laraine Day, Garson and Ruth Kanin, Pat and Eloise O'Brien, as well as acerbic (and very gay) movie star Clifton Webb, England's Richard Burton, writer Ernest Hemingway, directors George Cukor and William Wyler, MGM executive Benny Thau, and talent agent Bert Allenberg. (No mention was made of Katharine Hepburn.) Naive fan magazine readers accepted the text at face value, especially since the press continued to feature photos of Mr. and Mrs. Tracy posing proudly together at fundraising functions on behalf of the John Tracy Clinic for deaf children.

Then in the January 30, 1962, issue of *Look* magazine veteran journalist Bill Davidson bylined an extremely revealing—for the times—profile of Tracy. One late evening the reporter had cornered Tracy at Chasen's restaurant in Beverly Hills and pushed for a few usable quotes from the usually taciturn star. Spencer was feeling no pain that night and was most revealing in his conversation with Davidson. The lengthy piece that ensued focused on five telling facets of the enduring star: 1) as great actor; 2) as reluctant star; 3) as Hollywood hermit; 4) as a man who didn't live with his family, and; 5) as a tragic success. The article suggested that Spencer's guilt over son John being born deaf both split the Tracys apart and "led him to seek the companionship of Katharine Hepburn." Davidson cited that out of their working relationship and "professional admiration grew genuine friendship. A woman who has known Tracy many years says that Miss Hepburn understood his problems and gave direction to his restless yearnings. She is a woman of great quality and from a wonderful family.... She rubbed off the rough edges and led Tracy into a world of culture and art that he didn't know much about."

The *Look* account also called attention to the fact that, until she met Spencer, Kate "was considered a cold woman with no sex appeal. Little by little, she could have become a typical old maid. However, her friendship with extrovert, down-to-earth Tracy, who knew a lot of people she didn't know anything about, was good for her." The paragraphs on the celebrated costars concluded with "The Tracy-Hepburn friendship has lasted for 20 years.... With Miss Hepburn, Tracy moved into the Hollywood intellectual set.... Tracy found himself in lively discussions about Shakespeare, D.H. Lawrence and Renaissance art. Later, he spent weeks touring art museums in the United States and Europe with Miss Hepburn."

When that *Look* magazine issue appeared on newsstands, it created a furor in the film colony. Said Davidson in 1968, "There was a gentleman's agreement in Hollywood then that you don't write these things. I broke that for the first time, both the drinking and the long romance with Katharine Hepburn, and then everybody who had been screaming and yelling at me started doing the same thing." Left unexplored in the aftermath of the Tracy exposé was the real possibility that the Kate-Spencer situation had been (almost) from the start a highly platonic involvement of two friends who satisfied their strong needs for companionship and emotional support by enabling each other. The cloak of their decades-long "hidden" romance also provided, possibly, a cover for their clandestine bisexual lifestyles, which they feared coming to light and destroying their extremely lucrative acting careers. If this was true, there was actually a well-calculated dual layer of secrecy at work in the Hepburn-Tracy bond.

❋   ❋   ❋

In the 1960s Tracy contentedly continued residing at George Cukor's guest cottage in Beverly Hills. According to the highly cultured, trend-conscious director, "The bedroom of this house is almost like a monk's cell. It has an oak chest, one chair, a bed—and that's all. It has the air of a place where a man might do penance." Meanwhile, Hepburn was staying in John Barrymore's spacious old Beverly Hills home, the lower part of which hung over a cliff, cantilever-style. With its many large windows and skylights, the house was admirably suited to her relaxing avocation of painting and her new hobby of sculpting. (This craft was the occupation of Hepburn's long-time chum Frances Rich, a graduate of Smith College and the daughter of former movie star Irene Rich. Frances, a noted artist, created several pieces of sculpture in which she captured her buddy's likeness in various acting roles.)

In past years, Tracy and Hepburn had occasionally vacationed together in Palm Springs, California. Sometimes they stayed at the Racquet Club, where the management was famous for being discreet regarding its VIP guests. When Spencer was filming Stanley Kramer's *It's a Mad Mad Mad Mad World* (1963), portions of the shoot were done not too far from the desert resort. This time Spencer and his famous companion rented Kirk Douglas's Palm Springs home at 515 Via Lola, a house they had leased at other times.

Sporadically the celebrated duo vacationed in Santa Barbara. According to Mark Rydell (who directed Hepburn in 1981's *On Golden Pond*), Hepburn "was always the one who carried the luggage. One day after the weekend he told her to put the luggage in the car. She looked outside and it was full of people loading luggage from the cabin next door, and she said, 'I can't do this, Spencer. I'm embarrassed that I'm carrying the luggage.' He said, 'Don't worry, I'll take care of it.' So she carried the luggage and then he came out limping like a cripple."

In July 1963 the professionally inactive Hepburn was renting a beach home in Trancas, near Malibu and close to the spot where Howard Hughes once had set down his plane to meet Kate on the set of *Sylvia Scarlett*. On Sunday, July 21, as Hepburn was loading up the car for her and Tracy to go on a picnic, he collapsed with severe chest pains outside the house. Kate called the Zuma Beach fire department. Meanwhile she summoned a doctor from his nearby home and he administered an injection to the fallen star. While awaiting the ambulance Hepburn held Spencer's hand and told him to relax. As his condition stabilized to a degree, he remarked to her, "This is a heck of a way to spend a picnic." Minutes later the ambulance arrived at

30842 Broad Beach Road and Tracy was rushed to St. Vincent's Hospital in Los Angeles.

At the hospital Tracy's doctor, Karl Lewis, took over the case. Once Spencer was settled into his air-conditioned private room, Kate alerted Garson and Ruth Kanin and the Chester Erskines of Spencer's pulmonary crisis. Louise Tracy was notified of her husband's perilous condition and an arrangement was made so the two women could split shifts in watching over Spencer and never have to cross paths. When pressed for information on the movie star's condition, Mrs. Tracy told reporters she was confident her husband would be returning (to his real) home any day now. This did not sit well with Kate.

After ten days Tracy was released from St. Vincent's. By then his medical problem had been diagnosed as temporary congestion of the respiratory tract. However, three weeks later Spencer was back in the hospital for additional tests. It proved that he had a prostate condition. (In September 1965, Tracy would undergo prostate surgery for removal of what proved to be a noncancerous growth. For a time it was touch-and-go if he would survive the ordeal.)

As Spencer recuperated at his guest cottage, Kate did everything possible to encourage him to live more healthfully. She convinced him to change his diet and cooked special meals for him. The two went on short walks or to fly kites—all to get the physically inactive Tracy to exercise in moderation. Following Kate's example, Spencer had taken up painting, which seemed to distract him from his constantly troubling thoughts.

Anxious to return to his craft, the actor accepted a guest role in John Ford's *Cheyenne Autumn* (1964) but had to drop out due to a fresh decline in his health. He was replaced in that Western by Edward G. Robinson, who also substituted for Tracy in *The Cincinnati Kid* (1965). Although there was no appropriate role for Spencer in Stanley Kramer's *Ship of Fools* (1965), it was arranged for Tracy to have his own armchair on the set at Columbia Pictures so he could observe the shoot and chat with the cast between scenes. (Kramer had wanted Hepburn to play the aging divorcée Mary Treadwell in *Ship of Fools,* but she begged off and the part went to Vivien Leigh, who was then in fragile mental health. Both George Cukor and Kate made it their special mission to help the distraught Leigh through what proved to be her final picture.)

❋　❋　❋

To keep physically active during these caretaker years, physical fitness addict Hepburn continued her nearly daily ritual of playing tennis at the Beverly Hills Hotel. One observer described, "You always knew when Katharine Hepburn was playing.... Even if you were outside and the green wind screens prevented you from looking in, you knew those sudden flights of laughter or startled exclamations of dismay meant Katharine was working out with Harvey Snodgrass, the hotel pro." In the 1960s a more relaxed Kate—who for health reasons had cut way back on her cigarette smoking—began playing doubles on the courts with club regulars. This led to the formation of the Katharine Hepburn Memorial Lawn Tennis Association, an informal group of Kate and several men. During its three years of existence, the members awarded, annually, a deliberately large and garish trophy to the winner of their playoffs. Kate thought it all great fun and didn't grouse about contributing to the prize, something unusual for Hepburn, who was notoriously close with her money.

During this period Marion Kubichan, a struggling, attractive young actress, was taking lessons from Harvey Snodgrass at the hotel. One day Marion was asked to join in a court foursome. Kate turned out to be one of the players, a surprise for Kubichan, who was a tremendous Hepburn fan. In the coming weeks Kubichan became a mascot to the star's group, which played at least twice weekly. Marion recalls of Kate: "At one point, I had mentioned to her about wanting to finish my studies with [acting coach] Stella Adler in New York, and she promptly offered her guest room for my use. I was overwhelmed and very grateful. Within three weeks, her N.Y. Forty-ninth [place] was robbed, and she became very uneasy about allowing me to stay alone in that home. Meanwhile, she arranged an introduction to [actress] Jane Wyatt's mother's home, around the block at 310 East Fiftieth.... I never knew Kate that well, but she was a most generous and giving person, and we corresponded for many years."

※ ※ ※

Continuing her soul-satisfying vigilance over Spencer Tracy, Kate bypassed a lead role (as a repressed lesbian missionary) in John Ford's *7 Women* (1966), which proved to be the filmmaker's final movie. However, after much prompting from a friend, Hepburn took time to write an essay for *The Virginia Law Review*. It was on one of her pet topics: "The Right of Privacy." In the piece, which took two years to prepare, Kate stated, "Polite pornography is no longer interesting—No more subterfuge—The naked fact—Tell it… Don't hide it—Talk—tell it—It is never your fault—We'll fix the blame—Mama—Papa—Uncle Sam—Teacher—Employer—They are responsible."

When asked once why she utilized dashes so often in her writing, the star explained, "I can't bear a period. I correct my letters sometimes when I'm writing to people who think I'm totally uneducated if I send them out unpunctuated and I put a period in and it hurts me. It absolutely hurts me. I love a dash. A dash…pleases me. And I write it that way. You see; I write it longhand and then I tap it out on the typewriter.

"I don't think in sentences. It's probably a terrific indication of confused thinking, isn't it? But I don't feel a period. Clipped! Clipped thoughts! Pinned together—and an occasional change of paragraph and I think I think that way. I look at what I'm writing with periods and it's as if somebody had felled an enormous tree and put it across my path. It's funny, isn't it?"

For the book *Double Exposure* (1966), which featured celebrities penning brief essays about famous friends along with actor Roddy McDowall's photos of the notable subjects, Hepburn wrote about Lauren Bacall. Kate observed of Lauren, "No zulac from the bazaar has a sharper knife." When asked what "zulac" meant, iconoclastic Hepburn answered, "Just made up that word. It sounded the way I wanted it to sound. There is no such word, but I thought that people will think they're wrong and it had the feel I wanted. There should be such a word."

* * *

In 1966, George Cukor announced a planned screen biography of pioneer Hollywood film director D.W. Griffith, with Gregory Peck to play the late filmmaker and Hepburn to undertake an as yet unspecified role. The project never came to fruition. There was mention that Kate might undertake the lead role in *A Very Special Woman*. However, when Ruth Gordon's Broadway play reached the screen as *Rosie!* (1967) it was Rosalind Russell who starred as the madcap grandmother.

Finally, in late September 1966, Hepburn's several years of career inactivity ended. It was announced that Kate and Spencer would reteam for Stanley Kramer's *Guess Who's Coming to Dinner,* scheduled to start at Columbia Pictures on February 1, 1967. When Tracy was asked what it was like filming with Hepburn, he quipped, "Gee whiz, I can't remember. What's it been? Ten years? *Desk Set* was the last one. No, we worked well together. We didn't mind cutting one another off now and then."

William Rose (1918–1987), who had scripted *It's a Mad Mad Mad Mad World,* had come to Stanley Kramer in the fall of 1966 with a new film idea on a then-controversial subject an upper-class white girl who falls in love with a black man. Kramer knew: that to make this interracial story sell he needed Sidney Poitier in the cast. The Oscar-winning African-American actor had a track record of recent mainstream box-office successes (e.g., *To Sir, With Love* and *In the Heat of the Night*).

To persuade Poitier to play the idealized black hero (a noble, highly educated physician who works for the World Health Organization), Kramer told the actor that already he had commitments from Tracy and Hepburn to play the heroine's San Francisco–based liberal parents. When Sidney agreed to the assignment, Stanley rushed to Kate and Spencer to persuade them to join the venture. (He was to receive $300,000 and she would earn over $200,000.) Tracy was dubious, declaring that his declining health made him an unlikely candidate for the movie. However, the director and Hepburn quickly decided that it would be better for the veteran leading man to spend his days on a film set than brooding at home about his failing physical condition. To appease studio officials, who had legitimate concerns about Spencer making it through the production, Kramer and Hepburn quietly deferred their salaries. This sizable sum would remain in escrow until filming was completed and there was no longer any possible need to pay for Tracy's replacement.

There was much speculation as to who would play Joanna, the love-struck heroine. Eventually a relative unknown was selected—Katharine Houghton, the twenty-two-year-old daughter of Hepburn's sister Marion and her husband, Ellsworth Grant. Not only was the Sarah Lawrence College graduate a budding actress, she bore a striking resemblance in looks and speech to her Aunt Kate. This casting brought the film an extra dollop of publicity, with

Hepburn constantly on hand to supervise her niece's interactions with the media and to coach her through her impossibly sweet movie role.

Before filming began Hepburn and Tracy hosted a small dinner for Sidney Poitier which the latter perceived as the Hollywood legends' way of evaluating up close their non-Caucasian colead.

Kate would say later of her nonwhite costar: "I can't consider Sidney as Negro. He's not black, he's not white, he's nothing at all as far as color is concerned." Accepting the appraisal as well-meaning if not enlightened, Poitier was highly respectful to Kate and Spencer throughout production.

Because the ailing Spencer tired so easily, Kramer arranged the shooting schedule (without Columbia Pictures realizing it) to have Tracy shoot for only half-days and avoid strenuous oncamera activity. If Kate had been deferential to Spencer in recent years, she was nearly obsequious to the often crabby man during this latest movie teaming. Her devotion to him on the set was all the more remarkable in that she was also overseeing her niece's performance as well as dealing with her own major characterization.

While Hepburn's contemporary chic wardrobe, good lighting, and artful makeup disguised the fact that she was nearly sixty, it took more skill to hide a new aging problem. In recent years she had fallen victim to a genetic palsy—not Parkinson's disease—which occasionally caused her head and hands to shake and her voice to tremble. The debilitating condition had been somewhat apparent in *Long Day's Journey Into Night* but had become more pronounced in the intervening years. (The disability would become even more accentuated in the future, but Hepburn refused to let this derail her performing career.) It required careful editing to showcase Kate at her physical best.

Three days before principal photography was completed in May 1967, Tracy told Kramer, "You know, kiddo, I've been looking at this script, and if I died tonight at home, it wouldn't make any difference—you could still release the picture." At the end of the picture, there was a cast party. Hepburn gave a lengthy speech. Next a teary-eyed Houghton delivered her sobbing thank-you. Finally Kramer came front and center. The director emotionally told the assemblage that this was the "last film in which we will be able to see the greatest motion picture actor who ever lived."

Several days later, on June 10, 1967, Spencer Bonaventure Tracy, age sixty-seven, was dead.

Chapter Twenty-eight
CARRYING ON—ALONE

*"The thing that sustains everyone in life is to dream the
impossible dream, isn't it?... You dream. That's the come-on.
That's what keeps you going. That's what keeps me going, in
both my career and my relationships with people. One ide-
alizes people. Do you see people whom you admire exactly as
they are? No. You see them through your own eyes."*
                                        —*Katharine Hepburn, 1967*

In the last months of Tracy's life, Katharine Hepburn had taken to staying
in the second bedroom of Spencer's guesthouse in order to be always near at
hand. On Tracy's final day he had gotten up early and trudged to the kitchen
for a glass of milk. Listening from her room to Spencer's movements, Kate
heard a strange noise and went to investigate. When she reached him, he was
dead—bent over the kitchen table.

Although Hepburn understood that Tracy had been living on borrowed
time, his sudden death was nevertheless,a tremendous shock. After alerting
George Cukor, Laura Harding, and others of the sad news, Hepburn debated
about clearing out her possessions before Mrs. Tracy, her children, and the
press arrived. Eventually, Kate chose not to. When she and Louise passed each
other at the small house there was a chill in the air as the two met face-to-face
for the first time. The atmosphere was unthawed by Kate's offer to make a
breakfast of bacon and eggs. Later the widow became annoyed that Hepburn
had already decided in what clothing Tracy should be buried. Unwilling to
argue, Kate wearily conceded to Louise's own choices.

On the morning of the requiem mass for Tracy, Hepburn arrived early at
the funeral home with docile Phyllis Wilbourn in tow. Having placed a small
painting of flowers under Spencer's feet in the casket, she and Phyllis helped
the morticians hoist the box into the hearse. The two maiden women fol-

lowed the vehicle for blocks, driving behind at a discreet distance. As the hearse approached the Immaculate Heart of Mary Roman Catholic Church in Hollywood, Kate and Phyllis bid their farewells and turned off. (In the 1960s it would have been considered indiscreet for the "other woman" to attend the funeral service and burial.) For weeks thereafter Hepburn visited Tracy's crypt in the Garden of Everlasting Peace at Forest Lawn Memorial Park in Glendale. Sometimes she made the pilgrimage twice daily. Coping with her loss, Hepburn told friends, "Spence was the only pure person I ever met in all my life. No affectations, not a selfish bone in his body. He took his work seriously—never himself—and such a good, clean brain. I'll miss him every day of my life."

Hepburn was well aware that Tracy's will, finalized on May 6, 1961, left everything to his family. She was not upset by this proper disposition of his estate. On the other hand, Kate was taken aback when she later phoned Louise Tracy. In this call Hepburn again extended her condolences and suggested that there was no reason the two could not be friends. Louise Tracy responded coldly, "I always thought you were a rumor." End of discussion.

* * *

In Hollywood a dear one's death is never sufficient reason to avoid business as usual. Within days of Spencer Tracy's passing Hepburn was receiving movie offers. They were politely couched as helpful distractions from her grief.

Thanks to Dr. Hepburn's careful investments of his daughter's income and her own prudent spending over the years, Kate could have easily retired in 1967. Yet, despite her accelerating palsy and the usual aches of older age, she felt too physically fit and full of high energy to sink into private life.

One bid for Hepburn's acting services was for her to star in the screen version of the theater hit *The Killing of Sister George*. However, playing an openly lesbian character who engages in intimate onscreen moments with her youngish lover was not Hepburn's cup of tea. She declined. Another professional proposal was more appealing. It was from producer Martin Poll.

Poll had already contracted James Goldman to adapt his recent play, *The Lion in Winter*, for the big screen. The producer thought Hepburn would be ideally suited as Eleanor of Aquitaine (c. 1122–1204), daughter of the duke of

Aquitaine, queen of France and thereafter of England. Poll contacted Kate's agent, Abe Lastfogel, at William Morris. The script was dispatched to Hepburn, who was then preparing to visit Garson and Ruth Kanin on Martha's Vineyard. While in seclusion Kate read the screenplay and was impressed. She contacted Poll and expressed her interest in the project. He advised her such a production would have to wait until after he made *The Ski Bum*, a movie to star Peter O'Toole and to be distributed by Joseph E. Levine's Avco Embassy Pictures. During further discussions Poll learned that Hepburn had recently committed to star for John Huston in *The Madwoman of Chaillot* and there was already a firm start date for that venture. Besides, she told Poll, she was anxious to do this dream part while she was alive and well. Before long O'Toole was switched from *The Ski Bum* to playing the king in this Avco Embassy release of Goldman's play. Hepburn was thrilled with the casting because she was a great fan of the Irish actor. (In fact, a few years earlier she had recommended Peter to David Lean for the lead in *Lawrence of Arabia*, a casting that took place.)

When O'Toole met with Hepburn he charmed her and suggested they consider Britisher Anthony Harvey to direct. The thirty-something Harvey, a former film editor, had made his film directing bow with *Dutchman* (1966). When Kate saw it she invited Harvey to meet with her. The filmmaker recalled, "I took her a bunch of roses, which she immediately threw on the floor and said they were terrible. 'They've got wires in them.' I thought, this is very difficult." Nevertheless, the two quickly developed a viable working relationship that turned into a lifelong friendship.

＊　＊　＊

Before *The Lion in Winter* started production, Hepburn dealt with the opening of *Guess Who's Coming to Dinner* in mid December 1967. Surprisingly, Kate was almost amenable to promoting her new picture. She explained, "I have a much more objective feeling about publicity now than I did, say thirty years ago, when I was leading the kind of personal life that would be sort of titillating to the public. Then I would go to absolutely endless trouble to fix it so that the reporters knew nothing... I didn't like people to see the inside of my house. And I certainly still don't like people to see the inside of my brain."

Kate was the focal point at a pivotal press conference held in Manhattan. She demonstrated that she had not altogether forsaken her old imperious ways. As one attendee described, Hepburn talked touchingly about Tracy. However, her tribute was "only minutes after she had reduced to tears a young woman from *Newsweek* by ridiculing the reporter's then-fashionable miniskirt that showed off her spectacular tights, circled in bands of red and white like barber poles. To the howls of the members of the press, Hepburn bellowed, 'Does your mother know you dress like that?'"

While reviewers found *Guess Who's Coming to Dinner* too simplistic in its message of racial tolerance, Tracy and Hepburn's contributions were treated with extreme reverence.(Already the *Los Angeles Times* had eulogized the couple as "a remarkable legacy of an association as beautiful and dignified as any this town has ever known."). The duo received lavish tributes: "Their performances in this movie are beyond the bounds of criticism" (Richard Schickel, *Life*). "A lump rises in the throat on the realization that they will never appear together again" (Leo Mishkin, *New York Morning Telegraph*). Made for $4 million, the picture grossed a then-stellar $56.7 million at the box office.

When the Oscar nominations were announced the following February, both Hepburn and Tracy were among the film's ten nominees. Only William Rose (Best Screenplay) and Hepburn (Best Actress) won. George Cukor accepted Hepburn's trophy, as she was then abroad filmmaking. When told she had won, she asked if Tracy had also won. When informed he had not she said, "I guess, then, this is for both of us." Later, she proudly told *Forbes* magazine, "They don't often give...[the Academy Award] to old girls like me."

❋ ❋ ❋

Hepburn and Phyllis Wilbourn flew to London for the two weeks of rehearsals that preceded filming *The Lion in Winter*. The star stayed at the Connaught Hotel and traveled daily by chauffeured Rolls-Royce to the Haymarket Theater for the run-throughs. For some members of the noteworthy cast (e.g., Anthony Hopkins and Timothy Dalton), this was their debut movie. For others, such as Jane Merrow (cast as Eleanor's much younger rival for King Henry's affections), she had been making movies for seven years. Nearly all of the troupe had stage experience.

During the first rehearsal at the Haymarket, a thick metal door slammed on Hepburn's thumb. She vetoed having emergency medical attention, reasoning, "They'll put stitches in, it won't heal on time and I can't wear bandages. My father was a doctor. I'll care for this myself." Once again she proved to be correct.

Part of the shoot was accomplished at the Gray Studios outside of London, with additional lensing done at Ardmore Studios in Kilbride, Ireland. Exteriors were shot in Ireland, Wales, and around Tavasoon and other parts of France. In true Hepburn style, when not oncamera she wore an eclectic outfit: trousers, a tattered red sweater, her brother's World War II Army jacket, and a blue seaman's cap. She spent her off time exploring nearby sights, swimming, and indulging her penchant for gathering colorful wildflowers in the countryside.

Hepburn could be bossy on the set, as when she demanded that the production schedule be from eight A.M. to five P.M. and not the later schedule O'Toole, the nocturnal carouser and top-billed performer, preferred. Jane Merrow recalled another instance of Kate showing her mettle. "Peter and I were going through lines in his trailer, and Kate thought he had kept the hair and makeup away from her during one very difficult scene. (He hadn't, but obviously they had taken their time between trailer and set, and Kate came storming into Peter's trailer, face red with rage and tears streaming down her cheeks. She gave him two good hard smacks across both cheeks and said, 'You SOB, don't ever keep hair and makeup when I need them again!' and stormed out again... He sat in silence for a rather long moment and then burst out laughing. He adored her. And her feistiness. Later Peter went onto the set with his arm in a sling, on a crutch, and with a bandaged head; everyone had heard about the scene and were fearful of what would happen next between these two huge stars. Kate stared at him and then fell about laughing as did the rest of the crew. Tension broken and no hard feelings." As a result of this episode, Peter jokingly called Kate "Old Nags" and she referred to him kiddingly (at least most of the time) as "Pig." (A screenwriter, not attached to *The Lion in Winter* but in the British Isles at the time, insisted that during filming

O'Toole and Hepburn underwent a rivalry of another sort as both became interested in the same female in the production's company, but this assertion has never been verified.)

In Arles, France, Anthony Harvey came down with the flu and it was Hepburn who nursed him. The star also had a whimsical side. Hepburn's film entrance had her arriving at Chiffon Castle on a barge. She was convinced the cumbersome vessel might turn over during the approach. So she wore a bikini-style bathing suit underneath her heavy costume in case she had to shed it in a hurry, jump overboard, and swim to safety.

After completing *The Lion in Winter*, Kate visited Joseph Levine at the producer's New York offices. He inquired what she thought of the film. She admitted that she never looked at her own pictures but did agree to see this effort in the filmmaker's private screening room. Levine left her alone as the picture unspooled. When it was over he returned to find Hepburn sobbing. She embraced him and said amid her tears, "I was very good, wasn't I, Joe?"

When released in the fall of 1968, *The Lion in Winter*—especially Kate—impressed the critics greatly. *Variety* enthused, "Whether coldly scheming some political coup, sincerely or insincerely remorseful over a failed marriage, or—at one dramatic highlight—crying out that people, not abstract causes and marital things, are the breeders of war and tumult, she is terrific." At Oscar time the commercially successful *The Lion in Winter* won three awards, including a Best Actress prize for Hepburn (who tied with Barbra Streisand for *Funny Girl*). In the annals of the Academy Awards, Kate was first to win three trophies for lead assignments and only the third performer to ever win consecutive accolades.

In customary fashion, Hepburn was not at the Oscars, preferring to remain at her Manhattan brownstone. It was Anthony Harvey in Los Angeles who informed the star of her victory. "I called Kate in New York about four in the morning, because I thought she'd be thrilled to know that she had won... 'What time is it? Oh, for God's sake, I am asleep. Just put it in a bag or something,' she said. I put it in a brown paper bag and ten years later, we were sitting around one evening, and she was looking for some chocolates, and there was this bag, with the Academy Award still there."

❋　❋　❋

Because of Kate's start date on *The Madwoman of Chaillot* (1969), *The Lion in Winter* required everyone to work at full pace. Immediately wrapping one vehicle, she moved on to the other. Originally John Huston was to direct this screen adaptation of Jean Giradoux's 1945 play. However, when the executives at Warner Bros. insisted that the story be updated to create a more commercial appeal, Huston bowed out after several days of filming. British director Bryan Forbes took over. By then Kate felt it was too late to abandon ship.

A strange mix of international talent—some old, some young—was assembled for the project, including Richard Chamberlain, Paul Henreid, Charles Boyer (Kate's movie costar back in 1935), Edith Evans, Yul Brynner, Nanette Newman (the director's wife), and Danny Kaye. An intricate Parisian street set was constructed at a Nice studio. Only belatedly did the production staff realize that the set was so near the local airport that filming had to be interrupted whenever planes flew overhead.

As always, Kate valued her privacy above all else. She stayed in a villa some distance from where the rest of the cast was housed. As usual her day began and ended early. After her nighttime ritual of drying her freshly washed hair she went to bed. Occasionally a visiting friend joined her on weekend countryside excursions. One time writer Peter S. Feibleman was in Nice and went with her to explore nearby Monaco and find the palace of ex-movie star Grace Kelly (now the princess of Monaco).

When the pair reached a particularly steep hillside on their trek, Hepburn was convinced that the royal domain was just over the horizon. They hauled themselves over a high wall only to discover they were looking at a local park. Undaunted, Kate persisted. Her exhausted companion suggested they ask a passersby for guidance. She replied, " I never ask directions if I can help it. It depresses me to ask. So defeating. Come along." Eventually they spotted Princess Grace's domicile in the distance. Hepburn groused how dark and uninviting it looked. Nevertheless, curiosity got the best of Kate. "I wonder what's it like inside?" However, it was late in the day and they had to head back to Nice. Later the writer learned that weeks earlier Kate actually had been invited to Grace's palace. When the friend asked if that was true, and if so, why she did not visit this intriguing building then. Kate answered, "Oh, good heavens, no. I couldn't possibly have gone. I never go out."

During the *Madwoman* shoot, as a scene involving Hepburn and Richard

Chamberlain was being lit, the coplayers relaxed on the set. According to Chamberlain, who finally acknowledged his own homosexuality publicly in his 2003 memoir, "I was lying on the bench with my head in Kate's lap, and she became very fascinated by my hair. She started fooling around with my hair, and it had been streaked blond for the part, and she wanted to know how it was done and everything, and then she uncovered my ear and she said, 'Uh-oh…little pig ears close to your head just like mine.' She said, 'That means you're very, very selfish, just like me.' "

One evening after the work day several of the movie's company were at a hotel café. As Chamberlain described, "In this vast expanse of empty chairs and tables…were Danny Kaye, Federico Fellini [the famed Italian moviemaker married to Giulietta Masina, a member of the cast of *The Madwoman of Chaillot*], and Kate Hepburn with a bottle of champagne. They invited me to join them, and they were in the middle of this conversation about [Fellini's 1965 film] *Juliet of the Spirits*." Hepburn was saying, "I mean, please, what was that all about? You and Picasso were just alike. You started out great and then you got really off-track." Chamberlain continued about Kate, "And then it was time for her to go home. Fellini watched her walk off, and with a kind of sadness, he said, 'She's afraid of the night. She's afraid of her dreams.' And it seemed terribly accurate."

For all the effort and expense put into *The Madwoman of Chaillot*, the fantasy did not work on screen. Vincent Canby (*New York Times*) complained, "At heart, of course, the madwoman is just as authoritative and no-nonsense a personality as Miss Hepburn, but she should mask her sanity behind a façade of dead-panned lunacy. Miss Hepburn's madwoman is as sentimental…as her mannerism of gently clenching her perfect teeth, looking into the middle distance and weeping through her tears." The film quickly passed from distribution.

❋   ❋   ❋

It had been seventeen years since Katharine Hepburn had last been on the Broadway stage. Not that she did not have offers along the way. When her still-close friend Irene Mayer Selznick was producing Enid Bagnold's *The Chalk Garden* (1955), Kate was asked to star and George Cukor to direct.

Hepburn said no, and Cukor, who accepted, was soon fired from the project. Now Hepburn was being asked to portray famed French couturier Coco Chanel (1883–1971) in a Broadway show. If playing that high-fashion European designer was a stretch for Kate, it was no greater a challenge than the fact that this was a musical!

Up to that point Hepburn had never been noted for memorable melodic outbursts on or off the screen. However, as she recalled, "I can't imagine a life without challenge, without danger. Like when I appeared in *Coco*. Now, that took some nerve!… I dared to sing—although I'm still not sure that what I did could be called singing."

Kate rehearsed several Noël Coward and Cole Porter songs with music composer–adapter Roger Edens, who was famous for having coached Judy Garland over the years. When Hepburn felt ready she flew to New York and auditioned in front of a small audience at Irene Mayer Selznick's apartment suite at the Hotel Pierre. Among the elite group there was Alan Jay Lerner (the famed librettist-lyricist of such hit musicals as *My Fair Lady* and *Camelot*) and producer Frederick Brisson. Refusing to dress up for this important occasion, Kate wore men's pants, turtleneck sweater (in this case two of them, rolled up to the elbows), and scruffy sandals. Completing her mini-concert, she said to Lerner, "You didn't think I could do it, did you?" Whatever Lerner told Hepburn at the time, he later informed reporters, "She does sing—she doesn't just talk to music. And she's really musical if a strident voice can be called musical. There's steel in that voice."

The complicated origins of the *Coco* musical went back to the late 1950s when Brisson was seeking a new vehicle for Rosalind Russell, his movie-stage star wife. He thought Coco Chanel's colorful life (which included a range of male lovers and female interests) would make an interesting basis for a Broadway musical. By the time the idea germinated with Alan Jay Lerner, he and his usual show partner, composer Frederick Loewe, were on the outs. Eventually Lerner teamed with André Previn for *Coco*. Also by then, Russell was suffering from severe arthritis and other medical problems and was not up physically to tackling the strenuous part. That's when Hepburn came to mind. Days after Spencer Tracy died she was contacted about the possibility, which led to her January 1968 audition in Manhattan.

In between Hepburn's filming schedule, she and others of the *Coco* project flew to Paris to meet with the tough-minded French designer. After the chat Chanel found the little gift that Hepburn had quietly left for her. The Frenchwoman thought that was a tremendously kind gesture. When asked her reaction to Hepburn, the frank Parisian, who was then in her mid eighties, remarked that Kate, at nearly sixty-two, was far too old to play her. (The original plan had been to unfold all of Chanel's life in the musical.) Kate said of Mademoiselle Coco, "She's the real article. She's not stupid." She also noted that she and the fashion designer shared similar traits: "We're two females who have never been intimidated by the world, who have never shifted our styles to conform to public opinion…her capacity for survival is what really fascinates me."

With Chanel's blessing now obtained and Kate agreeing to a weekly salary of over $14,000 plus a percentage of the profits, *Coco* went into preproduction. Paramount Pictures provided much of the financing. (Eventually, the studio would decide against bringing Broadway's *Coco* to the big screen.) Lerner and Brisson had already determined that England's Cecil Beaton would provide the costumes and sets. This went against Hepburn's grain because the two had been feuding since the 1930s. Back then, in his *Cecil Beaton's Scrap Book* (1937), the waspish photographer-designer-diarist had described her cruelly as the woman "with the rocking horse nostrils and corncake, cockney voice" who is "freckled, with semaphore gestures and a nasal twang." Beaton, himself bisexual, also took pains in his bitchy 1930s piece to make unsubtle references to Laura Harding as Kate's traveling companion, letting the more sophisticated readers make of this what they would. Despite Hepburn's protests, Beaton stayed on the show, leaving the two enemies to continue their private war.

Beaton wrote many vicious diary entries on Hepburn during the frantic *Coco* period. Among his unflattering, perceptive remarks were, "But in spite of her success, her aura of freshness and natural directness, she is a rotten, ingrained viper…. Completely lacking in feminine grace, in manners, she cannot smile except to bare her teeth to given an effect of utter youthfulness and charm."

On her part, Kate, wanting familiar faces around *Coco*, insisted on hiring her old pal Michael Benthall to direct. However, it quickly proved that the Britisher, who had a nagging drinking problem, was in over his head. But loyal Kate would not allow him to be dismissed. Instead, talented choreographer Michael Bennett restructured much of the show's staging.

Because of the elaborate, unwieldy staircase set that Beaton had created for *Coco,* it was decided not to undergo a pre-Broadway tour. Instead, after five weeks of previews the $900,000 musical debuted at the Mark Hellinger Theater on December 18, 1969. The consensus was that the show had a weak book, undistinguished songs, and a most unremarkable ingenue (Gale Dixon) cast as Coco's special interest, but that Rene Auberjonois (as the calculating gay fashion designer) was flamboyantly amusing. However, all the hosannas were reserved for Hepburn, who wore a black wig, oversize glasses, and striking outfits (including conspicuous hats). She played heartily to the audience (including her memorable saying of the expletive "shit"), underscored funny ripostes ("What God hath wrought is often better bought"), did shameless double takes, and shouted out with verve the lyrics to her talk-songs. The fact that Kate presented Chanel more like a sports figure than a dress designer apparently bothered few viewers.

Reviewers endorsed Hepburn as a great living legend. John Chapman (New York *Daily News*) offered, "Miss Hepburn generates an amazing lot of steam as she dominates a lavish and visually beautiful show." Richard L. Coe (*Washington Post*) summarized, "Without Miss Hepburn and the stage splash, *Coco* would be a no-no."

During the show's run Hepburn demanded that even in the midst of winter the theater not be heated and stuffy and that side exit doors be left open to waft in fresh air. Although the cast—especially the dancers—disagreed with her dictum, her wish was the production's command. This extended to forces outside the theater. Across the street from the Mark Hellinger, where *Coco* was playing, the Uris Theater building was being constructed. During Wednesday matinees, the street racket carried over to the stage musical. Determined to remedy the situation, Hepburn donned a hard hat and took the workmen's elevator to the top of the Uris steelwork. Kate walked onto a girder and approached the flabbergasted construction workers. She charmed their supervisor into taking an extended coffee break every matinee at the time when a quiet, important scene was under way in her show. Also, during the *Coco* run, the horrifying massacre at Kent State University occurred. Cast member Rene Auberjonois convinced Kate to make a special curtain speech decrying the tragedy. She agreed if he would write her words. However, when it came time to talk directly to the audience she relied on her own heartfelt thoughts.

As was her custom, Kate worked keenly on enhancing her characterization during the show's Broadway stay. One of those who saw her performance more than once was New York–based writer Sandford Dody. He recalled, "In the few weeks since I had seen the play, Katharine Hepburn had made the part her own. Not able to become Coco under any circumstances whatsoever, she did the next best thing, that which came naturally to her. She made Coco become Hepburn. From curtain to curtain, this extraordinary woman did the impossible. Her energy, her style, her very will pulled the whole, impossible thing together. She was as sharp as a seamstress' shears and she cut the material to her size and pattern. It was absurd and wrong and she was marvelous, capturing the entire paying audience."

Hepburn's original *Coco* contract called for her to remain with the show for six months. She extended her stay to help the backers regain more of their investment and because she enjoyed starring on Broadway in her personal success. (During the run she was nominated for a Tony but lost to Lauren Bacall, who was headlining *Applause!*) On Kate's final night, after 332 performances, she gave an emotional curtain speech which ended with, "Well, I love you and you love me and that's that." Before the cast left that night they received gifts from Hepburn: a small framed painting she had done for each member.

Chapter Twenty-nine
ON THE MOVE

"Ruth Gordon said you never learn to act—by the time you
learn how to act you're too old to do it. Well, by the time you
learn how to live, you're practically at the end of the trail."
—*Katharine Hepburn, 1967*

One reason Katharine Hepburn needed to exit *Coco* was her agreement to star in director Michael Cacoyannis's screen version of Euripides's *The Trojan Women* (1971). Heading a cast that included Vanessa Redgrave, Irene Papas, and Genevieve Bujold, Kate, accompanied by Phyllis Wilbourn, flew to Spain. (The two senior citizens adored their all-expenses-paid opportunities to see the world. Thus, in choosing new vehicles, Kate examined submitted scripts to determine which were being shot in locales that pleased her.)

The Trojan Women was filming in the arid, hilly turf of Atienza, a three-hour drive north of Madrid. One of the journalists who braved the elements to visit Hepburn on location was celebrity interviewer Rex Reed. He described the difficult on-set atmosphere: "Cast suffered from sunstroke, diarrhea, nausea and every kind of local disease imaginable, except for Kate, who nursed them all." Iron-willed Hepburn told Reed, "I'm working as hard as any human being can. The climate hates me, and there is no money, but I am hired to deliver the goods no matter what the circumstances, so I'll do the best I can. I owe it to the people who have supported me through the good years and bad. Spencer taught me to play the material, come hell or high water, never jazz it up. He never even seemed aware of whether the role was good or not."

When the difficult moviemaking concluded, Kate and Phyllis returned to the U.S. having shipped home several mementos acquired initially to decorate the fifteenth-century manor house in which they had stayed in Spain. In release, the stagy *The Trojan Women,* with its cast speaking a jarring array of accents, proved too high-flown for filmgoers. However, Hepburn felt reward-ed by the challenge of interpreting Hecuba, another of her many portrayals of strong, lonely women. *The New Yorker* observed of Kate's most recent screen appearance: "Perhaps our awareness of her as Hepburn makes us a lit-tle impatient with the weak, resigned side of the character." Kathleen Carroll (New York *Daily News*) suggested, "We could have done with a little less of the wet-eyed look she has perfected."

❋   ❋   ❋

In the late 1960s, Hepburn had became fascinated for a time with William Rose, her *Guess Who's Coming to Dinner* screenwriter. With Irene Selznick tagging along, Kate visited Rose at his home on the island of Jersey off the coast of France. Later, Hepburn was seen strolling about London with the about-to-be-divorced writer. Thereafter Kate and Willie flew to Italy to pick up his new claret-colored Maserati car. Their subsequent unpleasant car trek proved that these two strong-minded individuals were incompatible. The trip ended Kate's relationship with her hard-drinking "beau." She returned to the United States to spend the remainder of the summer months at Fenwick with Phyllis Wilbourn on hand to tend her needs.

In actuality, at this point in life Kate much preferred orbiting in a world where she was in absolute command. Because of this she thrived on the *Coco* road tour, which began on January 11, 1971, in Cleveland and ended on June 26, 1971, in Los Angeles. When the musical played Baltimore, Hepburn coyly allowed, "I'm just getting sweeter and sweeter. I'm not so objectionable any-more." When asked why she did not watch her old movies on TV, she responded, "There's a certain melancholy in watching yourself rot… I don't want to sit and study the process."

When *Coco* was presented in Hartford the star suffered a bizarre experi-ence. She had recently discharged her female chauffeur, a former nurse who purportedly was angry that Kate had not allowed her to take over Phyllis Wilbourn's responsibilities. Returning to her Connecticut house late one evening, Kate was confronted by this former employee, who was wielding a hammer. In the ensuing struggle the agitated woman bit off the end of one of

Hepburn's fingers. (Doctors grafted the digit back into place, but Kate was in sharp pain for months. However, she refused to abandon the *Coco* tour.)

❋   ❋   ❋

Some months before Garson Kanin's revealing *Tracy and Hepburn: An Intimate Memoir* was published in November 1971, Hepburn's longtime friend insisted, "Kate won't mind. The book is a tribute to one of the greatest love affairs of our time." Au contraire. Hepburn did mind, feeling the biography invaded not only her privacy but also that of others. She turned icy toward Kanin and his wife, Ruth Gordon, who were currently Kate's New York City neighbors. This led to the Kanins eventually selling their adjacent brownstone and moving to new lodgings downtown.

What was ironic about Hepburn's reaction to Garson's popular book was that it accomplished just what Kate (subconsciously) wanted: to solidify the growing mystique of the Hepburn-Tracy love union, which was now being rated as one of the century's great romantic affairs. Per film historian-writer David Thomson, "That book romanced the Tracy relationship and sweetened up its tough spots (including the moods and affairs of Tracy, and her dogged independence) enough to be a best-seller." One of the results of this book and Kate's continued harping in years to come on her marvelous, liberating liaison with Tracy was that it distracted from recurrent rumors of her bisexual lifestyle.

In the course of being Hepburn's unwanted diarist Garson detailed in a 1971 magazine article a conversation he and his wife Ruth had with Spencer and Kate while relaxing at a Paris sidewalk café. The discussion revolved around Tracy attempting to explain to Hepburn the logistics involved in male-to-male sex. According to Kanin, her stony response was, "I don't believe there is any such thing as male homosexuality."

Later, writer Arthur Laurents, who had an on-again, off-again acquaintanceship with Kate, was meeting with Hepburn at her Manhattan place. He was curious enough about her remarkably narrow-minded reply to Tracy's description of gay sex to inquire if she had answered Spencer as Garson reported. (Laurents was perplexed as to how she could make such a statement given the fact of her longtime closeness to George Cukor as well as her friendship with other gays and lesbians.) Each time Arthur asked anew if Kate had made such a startling declaration she deliberately changed the subject. "Finally," said Laurents, "she simply picked up her gear and out she went."

＊　＊　＊

In 1972, MGM hired George Cukor to direct *Travels With My Aunt,* based on a Graham Greene novel. It was soon agreed that Hepburn would be appropriate as Aunt Augusta, an elderly oddball who drags her prim nephew on a somewhat shady adventure across Europe. Once involved in the screen project Kate volunteered a steady stream of ideas to improve the film and in particular to reshape the existing screenplay. She even began script rewrites herself, which upset the studio

On her usual creative roll, Hepburn also had casting ideas. She began auditioning potentials for the role of Tooley, a hippie. One such candidate was Joy Bang, a twenty-something talent who had begun her acting career in New York–shot experimental films. Later Joy went mainstream and had appeared in such pictures as *Pretty Maids All in a Row* (1971) and *Play It Again, Sam* (1972). Bang was ordered to Kate's Turtle Bay brownstone for her tryout and in short order made a terrific impression on Hepburn.

As the blond actress detailed with enthusiasm, "I blew my mind.... Here was a real great.... It was one of those magic things. We liked each other. She said, 'I don't want to hear anybody else.' She got George Cukor on the phone. I had to take a plane out that night. A big dispute came up over the plane ticket.... Kate insisted that the agency pay for my ticket, unprecedented!... I read for George Cukor. Very nervous." Time passed. Then, said Bang, "I began hearing that Kate and Cukor wanted me but that somebody else didn't. That there was a power play between Jim Aubrey, the president of MGM, and Kate, with Kate asking for changes in the script that were very, very difficult.... Then I heard that Kate had left the picture. I was so relieved that I went skiing though I don't ski."

By summer 1972, Kate had exited *Travels With My Aunt* and Maggie Smith—twenty-seven years Hepburn's junior—had replaced her. Cukor threatened to quit the project, but Hepburn insisted he remain. As for the not-so-pivotal role of the hippie girl, that eventually went to Cindy Williams (later of *Laverne & Shirley* TV fame). Regarding Ms. Bang, after a few more film and television appearances she vanished from show business and dropped off of Kate's radar.

* * *

In the early 1970s, Ely Landau, who had produced Kate's *Long Day's Journey into Night* and *The Madwoman of Chaillot*, was packaging a series of art house–type films to be based on celebrated stage offerings. He asked Kate to headline *A Delicate Balance*, derived from Edward Albee's talky, often oblique 1966 drama. Hepburn's immediate response was to say no. (This was her usual habit, as she liked to be coaxed and make it seem she was not over-anxious for work.) She told Landau of the script: "What's all this about? I'm a simple, nice person. I like to make Christmas wreaths, sweep floors, I don't understand all this complicated stuff. I'm rather like my sister [Peggy] who's a farmer and says that the most difficult thing she likes to attempt is carrying two pails of milk over a fence."

Even after agreeing to the project Kate acknowledged, "My God, that's a depressing play! I played it in order to be able to understand what it was all about." Later she admitted that once she understood the text, "I identified with these people who resented the intruders into their privacy, and I think that's what made me, after not wanting to do it at all finally decide to go ahead."

Although the verbose drama was set in suburban Connecticut, the movie was shot in a London film studio. Kate's onetime *Philadelphia Story* stage colead, Joseph Cotten, was part of the cast, as was Paul Scofield (as her husband), Lee Remick (as the couple's much-married daughter), and Betsy Drake (as Cotten's terror-stricken spouse). Originally Broadway's Kim Stanley was to portray Kate's alcoholic, spinster sister. However, Stanley, who had more than her share of emotional problems, did not get along with no-nonsense, dogmatic Hepburn. It came to the point that Kate told director Tony Richardson and the others that if Stanley did not leave the shoot, Hepburn would. Kim was replaced by Kate Reid. Released as part of the American Film Theater subscription series, the movie had limited theatrical exposure. Hepburn was chic, articulate, and dignified in the wordy proceedings, but as John Simon (*New York* magazine) carped, "Katharine Hepburn and Paul Scofield seemed about as convincing a pair of mates as a mule and a tiglon." Others commented that Kate's body shaking, trembling voice, and teary-eyed look often distracted from her characterization.

※   ※   ※

As a product of old-guard Hollywood, Kate had not been a fan of the competing television medium. (It was many years before she even allowed a TV set into her New York brownstone.) In 1970, to promote *Coco* and because she and others in the show were up for Tony Awards, she performed a song number from the musical for the spring 1970 prize program. However, she refused to do it live, instead taping the "Always Mademoiselle" production routine.

Over the years many late-night talk-show hosts had requested repeatedly that Kate appear on their showcases. She always declined. That is, until she agreed to doing Dick Cavett's ABC-TV evening gab fest in 1973. Up to the last minute neither host nor interviewee was sure that the event would actually take place. When Kate arrived at the Manhattan TV studio to rehearse, she reorganized the set, gave special instructions to the technicians, and then choose to do the interview then and there. To ease her nervousness she insisted there be no studio audience. Before the Q&A session concluded, Cavett had over four hours of tape, which was edited down to two ninety-minute programs that aired in early October 1973. *Variety*'s Addison Verrill reported, "She came quite determined to be 'fascinating' and the result was that and more. Lanky, casual, endowed with what could only be termed an exhausting vitality, Hepburn happily lacks the simpering guile which seems to afflict most actresses of certain age, and her frankness managed the Herculean task of knocking the Midwest gee-whiz right out of Cavett."

After decades of pruning her public image Kate emerged that night with her reputation even more polished. Home viewers agreed when the unique lady said on air—and then snorted in amusement—"Stone-cold sober, I find myself absolutely fascinating."

※   ※   ※

Having successfully navigated her talk-show bow, Hepburn starred in a small-screen version of *The Glass Menagerie* (1973). She was encouraged to do the telefeature by her pal Anthony Harvey,who directed the new version. She reasoned, "I thought I should do it. One should alter one's policy. We change every five years or so, and I think I've changed. My relationship to life, the press and everyone is different. I know I've changed, and maybe they've changed for the better, too. It's more comfortable now."

With Sam Waterston (as her dream-filled son), Joanna Miles (the crippled, fragile daughter), and Michael Moriarty (as the gentleman caller), Kate interpreted Amanda Wingfield, a role first played on Broadway by Hepburn's idol Laurette Taylor. The 100-minute offering was shot in London. Hepburn and Phyllis Wilbourn appeared on the set daily with homemade soup for everyone. Sam Waterston described of working with the show business notable, "Once she gave me a piece of observation that I've thought about ever since. She said, 'Oh, thank God your inner clock was ticking, because when it's ticking you're interesting to watch, and when it's not ticking, it's a disaster!" I think it means, she just wanted everybody wide awake." Director Harvey recalled, "I think it was particularly difficult for her to play a very southern woman. She's very Yankee. She was insistent on finding that funny old worn-out dress that she'd worn in *The Philadelphia Story*. She brought it to London, and it worked so wonderfully because it gave her character a sort of desperation."

For her performance Kate was Emmy-nominated but lost to Cicely Tyson (*The Autobiography of Miss Jane Pittman*).

＊　＊　＊

When not working Hepburn divided her time between Los Angeles (where she occupied Spencer Tracy's former abode on George Cukor's estate), her New York brownstone, and weekend trips to Fenwick in Connecticut. In Manhattan she distracted herself from her rather narrow personal life by keeping very busy with her early to-rise, early to-bed routine. She claimed she loved nothing better than to sit in front of a warm fire (no matter how high the temperature outside) or doing household chores. Keeping occupied with repetitive routine physical chores and a daily exercise regimen kept her trim, alert, and distracted from turning too self-reflective.

One of her pals, besides faithful Laura Harding in New Jersey or trusty Phyllis Wilbourn (who kept an apartment on East Seventy-second Street) was voice coach Sue Seton. The latter had a place behind Carnegie Hall and Hepburn often dropped by to chat. One day writer-producer Steven Whitney had an appointment with Seton to discuss a performer he was considering for a project. Whitney rang Seton's doorbell, and to his surprise, Hepburn opened the door. Whitney described, "I was a deer in the headlights. I mean, completely nonplussed. Perhaps a photo of the moment would reveal that my jaw had actually dropped. Hepburn smiled, said: 'It's all right, I don't bite. Sue's expecting you.' And she ushered me in."

❋　❋　❋

When Kate had starred on Dick Cavett's TV forum he said it was a shame that she and Sir Laurence Olivier (1907–1989) had never worked together. To which Hepburn shot back, "We're not dead yet!" This set the wheels into motion for Hepburn teaming with Olivier for the telefeature *Love Among the Ruins* (1975). Making the collaboration even more gilt-edged, George Cukor was hired to direct. Set in Edwardian times (which allowed Kate a wonderful wardrobe), it revolved around an aging stage notable being sued for breach of promise by a young gigolo. She hires a distinguished barrister who eventually reminds her that decades ago they had a brief affair. Among the crew on the set at Pinewood Studios was Spencer Tracy's daughter Susie, whom Cukor hired as the production's still photographer. Susie and Kate had not met in years but got along well, starting a long friendship.

For her performance as Jessica Medlicott Hepburn received an Emmy award (as did Olivier and Cukor).

❋　❋　❋

When Kate had made *The Rainmaker* in the mid 1950s she had informed producer Hal B. Wallis she would adore making a Western, especially one that teamed her with John Wayne (1907_1979). Twenty years later that wish came true with *Rooster Cogburn* (1975). Based on a high concept of *The African*

Queen meets *True Grit* (1969), it allowed Wayne to revive his Oscar-winning role of the one-eyed, cantankerous Old West marshal. In this wild adventure he encounters a hard-bitten New Englander whose missionary father was murdered by outlaws—the same killers the lawman is gunning after for reward money.

While Kate and the Duke could not have been further apart in their politics, they both were enduring superstar legends that advancing age and changing public tastes had not dimmed. Also, both had been good friends of filmmaker John Ford. For this feature, to be shot on location in Oregon in the fall of 1974, Wayne was paid $750,000 and Kate $400,000. When producer Wallis met with Kate at Universal Pictures' back lot for wardrobe tests he knew that she had recently undergone replacement surgery on her right hip, which had been ravaged by severe arthritis. He advised Hepburn that a double would undertake her horse-riding stunts. She disagreed: "'I'm not used to having doubles." To prove her point she climbed on a horse for the first time in years and demonstrated her fitness.

Once filming was under way in the Pacific Northwest it proved to be a mutual admiration society between the two cinema warhorses.

Said Wayne: : "I love her…she's tough, Christ! She wants to do everything. She can't ride worth a damn and I gotta keep reining my horse in so she can keep up. But I'd hate to think of what this godd**n picture would be without her…. She's so feminine—she's a man's woman. Imagine how she must have been at age 25 or 30…how lucky a man would have been to have found her."

Not to be outdone, Hepburn enthused of her burly leading man who had lost a lung to cancer: "From head to toe he is all of a piece. Big head. Wide blue eyes. Sandy hair. Rugged skin—lined by living and fun and character. Not by just rotting away. A nose not too big, not too small. Good teeth. A face alive with humor. Good humor. I should say, and a sharp wit. Dangerous when roused. His shoulders are broad—very. His chest massive—very. When I leaned against him (which I did as often as possible, I must confess—I am reduced to such innocent pleasures), thrilling. It was like leaning against a great tree. His hands are so big. Mine, which are big, too, seemed to disappear. Good legs. No seat. A man's body. Rare in these gay times…. He's sweet, gentle, and he's a monster."

Because the *Rooster Cogburn* team was away on location for eight weeks,

Kate chose not to keep strictly to her typical regimen of all work on the set and then rushing off to her privacy at night. She was more open to mingling with cast and crew. Often she showed up on the outdoors set on days when she was not in a particular scene. The studio provided her with a deluxe star motor home, but she preferred a makeshift dressing room set out under a shade tree upriver.

Sometimes in her off time Hepburn gathered wildflowers. If she happened to pass a waterfall, she would stop for a swim. When the production moved to Oregon's Rogue River she became insistent on white-water kayaking down the dangerous waterway. She reasoned at age sixty-seven, "I feel time is running out on me. I want to see and do everything."

Kate was thrilled by the idea of braving the dangerous water currents. When Wallis suggested such activity was far too dangerous, she answered, "Hal, I'm going to do it. I just know I'm going to do it." Hepburn described, "So I got me a [twenty-one foot] kayak—a cheap one since I didn't think I'd use it more than two or three times—and I was heavy enough almost to sink it. But I kept it upright—through Hell's Gate, an absolutely delirious experience."

Released in fall 1975, *Rooster Cogburn* appealed especially to older viewers. David Sterritt (*Christian Science Monitor*) weighed in by saying, "Kate and Duke gurgling down-river on a raft are not exactly the same as she and Bogart steaming into adventure in the enduring movie classic, *The African Queen*. But in its own rugged way, *Rooster Cogburn* feels quite a bit like the real Hollywood thing." *Rooster Cogburn* grossed a highly respectable $8.022 million in revenue.

Unwilling to chance vegetating, Hepburn next launched her Broadway return.

Chapter Thirty
THE SUMMING UP

"I'm not Katharine Hepburn. People think she's a saint, but she's not. She's this monster I've created, and I'm her private secretary. But I'm turning on her. I'm so damn sick of Katharine Hepburn, I'd like to kill her. On second thought, people have been so nice to me lately because they think I'm going to die. Think I'll just stick around awhile and make the most of it."

—*Katharine Hepburn, 1988*

When Kate Hepburn was in London making 1975's *Love Among the Ruins* she was shown a copy of octogenarian Enid Bagnold's new stage comedy, *A Matter of Gravity*. Said the veteran performer, "I read it and I just couldn't get it out of my mind." Hepburn explained why the British playwright's comedy struck such a chord with her. "Enid has a wonderful line about how the heart has to beat for something and it really doesn't matter for what or whom. You could say that pretty much sums up the way I feel about the subject. She also has another witty line that says, 'Such relationships must have God's blessings because you can't have children.' I'm all for that. I think there are too many of us here already."

In opting to star in this Broadway-bound production, Hepburn reasoned, "It's such an odd play and quite a departure for me. It's very interesting the steps one takes in one's life. The departures are generally the ones that are the good steps. When I did *Coco*, I thought I'd surely drown. I felt that if I could do a musical, anyone could do anything. And sitting for three hours talking about myself on the Dick Cavett [TV] show was an amazing feat to me."

In *A Matter of Gravity*, Hepburn took on the persona of Mrs. Basil, a tart yet adorable English matriarch who resides in a moldering country mansion.

The elderly lady has her eccentricities (e.g., dying her hair moss-green) and an unusual staff, including a lesbian cook with the power of levitation. During the show's New Haven tryout fledgling actor Christopher Reeve (cast as Mrs. Basil's grandson, who weds a black lesbian) fainted from opening-night jitters. Stepping out of character, Hepburn demanded the curtain be rung down until things could be put right again. (When Reeve had auditioned for his part he told the star, "Before I begin, Miss Hepburn, I'm sure that my grandmother Beatrice Lamb, who was your classmate at Bryn Mawr, would like to be remembered to you." Kate, seated out front in the darkened theater, replied, "Oh, Bea. I never could stand her.")

A Matter of Gravity bowed at the Broadhurst Theater on February 3, 1976. Even the often churlish Clive Barnes (*New York Times*) was impressed. "I have rarely seen Miss Hepburn better even in the movies.... Even her stylizations have become style in the certainty of their execution." *Time* magazine concluded, "Without Katharine Hepburn's high-voltage presence, this play would have flickered out on opening night."

During the New York run, Kate's typical daily routine was to arise at ten A.M., have a hearty breakfast, take a brisk walk or a bike ride in Central Park (where she did her best to avoid autograph seekers). By 2:30 P.M. she was back home to attend to personal business. At approximately 5:15 P.M. she dined on steak, grilled tomato, two vegetables, and a butterscotch sundae. (Hepburn had a lifelong craving for sweets and was renowned for her special recipe for brownies.) Then it was off to the theater. The limited engagement closed on April 10, 1976, so Hepburn could shoot a new film, *Olly, Olly, Oxen Free.* What appealed to the nearly seventy-year-old Kate about this haphazard project was that it called for her unconventional character to join two young boys in a hot-air balloon ride from San Francisco to Los Angeles. There they land in the Hollywood Bowl amid a concert performance. Thrilled at the idea of undertaking her own stunts, Kate was unmindful of the film's lackluster script. The mediocre movie received scant release. Most picturegoers, even devout Hepburn fans, were unaware of its existence.

Her latest film venture completed, Kate embarked on a six-month tour of *A Matter of Gravity,* which included stopovers in Colorado, Canada, California, and Arizona. While in Los Angeles, Hepburn fractured her ankle when she tripped in her garden at her cottage at George Cukor's estate.

Undaunted, she insisted on going on with the show and played Mrs. Basil from a wheelchair. According to Miller Lide, a member of the tour cast, even after Kate's ankle healed she continued performing from her special chair. Hepburn relished the special audience attention created by her assumed impairment. Once her injury had healed, she loved to surprise theatergoers by springing to her feet at the curtain call and bowing graciously to the amazed, applauding audience.

As *A Matter of Gravity* traveled about North America, Kate thrived on directing and living vicariously through the offstage activities of her stage flock. Immediately upon arriving in a new city she always posted backstage a list of doctors, restaurants, museums, and so forth that the cast and crew should rely on. She was forever arranging excursions to art galleries and to other fascinating local sights and would be disappointed if any of her followers did not follow through. When the show had completed its schedule, Hepburn was having such fun—and earning such tidy sums from her sold-out engagements—that she wanted to extend the tour. However, the logistics involved proved insurmountable.

Instead, Hepburn flew to England to visit with Enid Bagnold, her *Matter of Gravity* playwright. It was the aged Bagnold who convinced Kate that she should have a (modest) face-lift. The star journeyed to Glasgow, where a Scottish plastic surgeon performed nips and tucks on her face to positive results.

Also in 1977, Hepburn almost costarred with Bette Davis in *Whitewater,* a project conceived by producer Hal B. Wallis. The vehicle was based on a Paul Horgan novel of 1940s Texas and focused on two forceful women who change a small town there. Wallis had already set Hungarian-born Jan Kadar to direct the picture with Richard Thomas (of TV's *The Waltons* series) to be a key player. Despite the hype for this showcase of two veteran stars of Hollywood's golden age, *Whitewater* never came to be.

* * *

By 1978, George Cukor, whose filmmaking income was not what it once had been, sold the cottages on his property. Hepburn was reluctant to leave her long-term rental on the Beverly Hills estate but did not want to buy the guesthouse she took over after Spencer Tracy's death. (In the 1990s the property's new owner was Los Angeles interior designer Ron Collier, who completely renovated the former Tracy-Hepburn homestead. He doubled the interior's size and turned it into a fashionable showcase. He recalls that when he acquired the house Kate's old convertible was still parked in the driveway.)

Packing up her years of possessions, Kate returned east. One more tie to Los Angeles was gone. Now into her seventies, Hepburn was experiencing the loss of many contemporaries. Already Leland Hayward had died in 1971, with the producer insisting at the end that Hepburn had been the favorite of all the many women in his life. John Ford passed away in 1973. Producer Lawrence Weingarten (for whom Kate made her one and only appearance at an Academy Awards show, to present him with a humanitarian award) died in 1975, as did that year her director friend George Stevens. Howard Hughes expired the next year. By 1978, Hepburn's ex-husband, Luddy, was suffering from terminal cancer. His second wife had died in 1973, and his two children were now grown. He lived on Greenley Road in New Canaan, Connecticut. Frequently on weekend trips to Fenwick, Kate visited him, hoping to make amends for the way she had treated him in the past. He passed away on July 13, 1978, never having discussed publicly the realities of his long-ago marriage of convenience with Hepburn. (In later years Kate would say of her bisexual spouse: "Looking back, you have sense enough to know all the horrible things you've done to get where you're gone. Luddy was an angel. He did everything he could to make my dreams come true and I didn't even acknowledge his existence when I first arrived in Hollywood.")

With fewer and fewer close friends remaining to share adventures, Hepburn was all the more anxious to fill her free time with acting assignments. She relished working again (for what proved to be last time) with George Cukor in the made-for-TV movie of *The Corn Is Green* (1979). On location in the north of Wales for the five-and-one-half-week shoot, Kate— more so than Cukor—was in charge of artistic decision-making.

One situation during the filming badly threw the aged star. The establishing opening shots of the telefeature were geared to introduce her character (Lilly C. Moffat) to viewers. She was to be first seen riding a vintage bicycle up and down the steep hills. Cukor, always very protective of dear Kate, suggested that they use a stunt double to handle this physical chore. Hepburn bridled and insisted on doing the bicycling herself. After several efforts, she realized she just could not muster the necessary leg power to navigate the bike up the hill without doing so in a wobbly manner. She fought to control her tears as she accepted the fact that finally the mighty Kate Hepburn had to give in to the limitations of her failing body. A stuntperson was used instead (although later the sequence was deleted from the footage).

When *The Corn Is Green* aired on CBS-TV in January 1979, Kate received a rash of renewed attention, even if reviews of the project harped on how old-fashioned and lumbering the presentation was. A born survivor, Kate had not only outlasted most of her Hollywood peers but continued to work in lead assignments in generally high-profile projects. This accomplishment made her all the more special to her appreciative public.

When Rex Reed asked the much-revered Hepburn in 1979 what her professional future held, she told the journalist: "I wouldn't play hatchet murderesses or alcoholic mothers or loonies when I was young, and I won't play them now. So naturally when you eliminate the amorous parts, when you get to the age group that cannot play those parts, then out of necessity three quarters of the materials that I used to be offered is gone isn't it?"

One project that did appeal to Hepburn was *On Golden Pond* (1981), based on a stage play. She had seen and liked this drama of an elderly couple coming to terms with the husband's failing health and their divorcée daughter's efforts to reunite with her often indifferent dad. Kate thought the role of Ethel Thayer was just right for her. So did Jane Fonda who had acquired the screen rights to Ernest Thompson's work. Arranging for Universal Pictures to release the feature film, Jane envisioned that the movie would provide a cathartic experience for her and her dad, who had long been at odds with one another. Although Henry Fonda (1905–1982) was in fragile health he agreed to act in the film.

When Jane first met Hepburn at her New York brownstone (where composer-lyricist Stephen Sondheim was the show business legend's next-door neighbor), Fonda admitted she "was absolutely terrified.... I walked in, totally in awe of her, and Kate greeted me with a pointed finger, saying, 'I don't like you.' Well, it's like God condemning you. We had a rocky few hours there but then I realized she was testing the waters.... She saw me as some arrogant whippersnapper who expected to get top billing." Before long the two came to an understanding and Kate signed on to the picture. By the time filming was to get under way—with much of the movie to be shot on location in New Hampshire—Hepburn had injured her shoulder playing tennis. Her ailment required surgery. However within weeks and against her doctors' advice, she was on the set raring to go.

In all their many years in Hollywood, Hepburn and Henry Fonda had never worked together. While she appreciated his talent, she well remembered that Henry's first of four marriages had been to Kate's hated rival Margaret Sullavan, who had gone on to wed Hepburn's close friend Leland Hayward. That and the fact that both Kate and Henry were both so entrenched in their ways made for an awkward beginning to their belated screen teaming. During the initial days of rehearsals Hepburn kept telling anecdotes about Spencer Tracy. As Kate and Henry worked through their joint scenes, Hepburn constantly remarked, "But SPEN-suh did it this way." Director Mark Rydell observed what was happening. "I sensed after some days' rehearsal that Henry was withdrawing a bit. I took her [Kate] aside and told her she should make some gesture to transfer her affections to Fonda. And the following day she brought in and gave to Henry in front of everybody Spencer's fishing hat, which he wore throughout the picture. He wept. He was very touched by that."

On the ten-week New Hampshire shoot at Squam Lake, one sequence called for feisty, sympathetic Ethel and frail Norman to carry a 100-pound canoe to the dock. Despite her recent surgery, Kate insisted, "'I can carry it myself." With that, according to Rydell, "She walked over and lifted it over her head with pins in her shoulder and I shot her carrying this canoe a distance of 25 yards. As happens often in editing, you look and you see you don't need this. I don't think she ever forgave me [for cutting the scene]."

Released in late 1981, *On Golden Pond* touched a chord with filmgoers. The sentimental film received superlative reviews. Vincent Canby (*New York Times*) noted of Kate: "One of the most appealing things about her as an actress is the way she responds to—and is invigorated by—a strong co-star. When she has a vehicle to herself, she seems to lose her discipline, if not her way." Made for $7.5 million, the entry grossed a mighty $119.3 million. At the March 29, 1982, Academy Awards, *On Golden Pond* won three Oscars, with

Hepburn in absentia claiming her fourth Academy Award—an industry record still unbroken.

✳ ✳ ✳

While making *On Golden Pond,* Ernest Thompson (who had his share of artistic problems with the demanding Hepburn) talked to the star about his new play, *The West Side Waltz.* The idea of returning yet again to the stage appealed to Kate because "since the beginning of my career, I've always gone back to theater. That's where you find out if you've become fancy or artificial or plain dull." She approved of Thompson's writing because "he can present a serious topic [old age] in a comedic way, which is just great because I think life is just hilariously, awfully funny. You just have to say it is—hilarious awful."

Much of the same production crew (including director Noel Willman) who had worked with her on *A Matter of Gravity* joined with Kate for this latest theater, venture which went on an extended and highly successful pre-Broadway tour. The play debuted in New York on November 19, 1981, at the Ethel Barrymore Theater. With a cast that included Dorothy Loudon, the show ran for 126 performance before heading out on another trek about the country. Both critics and audiences rated the grand dame of show business a national treasure. As a result, despite her latest showcase being noticeably thin, she won reviewers' endorsement and sold-out houses.

Late in 1982, while driving along a Connecticut road with faithful Phyllis, Kate became distracted from watching the road and slammed into a telephone pole. Wilbourn had broken ribs and other injuries and was hospitalized for several weeks. Hepburn almost lost her foot, which had been nearly severed in the severe impact. Kate underwent several surgeries. Although she forced herself to walk without a limp when in public, the pain from the injury never really left her.

✳ ✳ ✳

When Hepburn had been staying at George Cukor's enclave in the mid 1970s, a film script addressed to her was tossed over the garden wall. She was sufficiently intrigued by A. Martin Zweiback's dark comedy to spend the next several years seeking funding to make the film. Finally in 1983, with Nick Nolte cast as the hit man who helps her arrange the killing of elderly friends facing painful, lonely ends, the picture was made. Longtime pal Anthony Harvey directed the project then known as *The Ultimate Solution of Grace Quigley.* Shown at the 1984 Cannes Film Festival, it was later shorn (Hepburn said "butchered") of several minutes and tossed out into the marketplace in 1985. Retitled *Grace Quigley,* it received scathing reviews—especially for the story's "ultimate solution"—and passed quickly from circulation.

✳ ✳ ✳

In January 1983, George Cukor passed away. (In retrospect Hepburn would say of her longtime friend, "He was not a happy person. He couldn't possibly be. His life was too complicated. Complicated to such an extent, so many layers, that he did not really know himself.") George's death severed yet one more link to Hepburn's Hollywood past. By now, another Tinseltown friend, Irene Mayer Selznick, had retired from play producing and was about to publish her intriguing memoir. Titled *A Private View,* it left many questions open about her intricate life and complex friendships—including that with Hepburn. Although both currently resided in New York City, the two women rarely saw each other anymore, often learning news of the other through a mutual friend, A. Scott Berg. The latter, a well-regarded biographer, had become friendly with Kate when he interviewed her for a potential magazine piece. He was invited to stay at Hepburn's brownstone whenever he came from Los Angeles to the East Coast for his writing projects.

There were other young people whom Hepburn welcomed into her life. On a visit to the Pittsburgh Players to see her niece, Katharine Houghton, perform on stage, Kate met Sally Lapiduss, who was working with the theater group. Hepburn responded to the young woman's enthusiasm and offered to help her with her career. When Kate toured with *The West Side Waltz,* Sally was hired to be the star's assistant stage manager. Thereafter, she became Hepburn's personal assistant, and in 1983 was unit publicist on the *Grace Quigley* film shoot in Manhattan. (Thereafter, Sally went to Los Angeles where, she and her sister became successful TV writers and/or producers involved with such sitcoms as *Mad About You, Roseanne, Ellen, The Nanny,*

Titus, and *The Tracy Morgan Show.* Both siblings are openly gay. Sally remained in touch with her onetime mentor right up to Hepburn's death and attended the star's private funeral service in Connecticut.)

Another integral member of Kate's group in the early 1980s was Cynthia McFadden, who was born in 1956 in Lewiston, Maine. During McFadden's years at Bowdoin College in Brunswick, Maine, she met Hepburn when visiting the Connecticut shore. The two women of disparate ages developed a friendship and a bond. After graduating from college with high honors, Cynthia relocated to Manhattan. She frequently was based at Hepburn's brownstone and sometimes accompanied the celebrated star on vacations. McFadden enrolled at Columbia University School of Law in 1981 and also took journalism courses. While at law school she became involved with media seminars being aired over PBS-TV. This experience led to her joining Court TV in 1990 (as an anchor, legal analyst, and producer) and thereafter switching to ABC in similar capacities.

During McFadden's increasingly high-profile years she remained a constant participant in Hepburn's life as well as becoming a close part of the inner circle of Manhattan-based gossip columnist Liz Smith. (In her memoir, 2000's *Natural Blonde,* and in an issue of *The Advocate* late that same year, the twice-wed Smith acknowledged that over the years she had had romantic relationships with women.) When Cynthia married a Connecticut newspaper publisher in 1989 the wedding reception was hosted by Kate at Fenwick. Later, after McFadden divorced her first husband she remarried. As a result of this second union, which also ended in divorce, she gave birth in July 1998 to a baby boy. The child was named Spencer in honor of Spencer Tracy. Kate thought so highly of go-getting Cynthia that Hepburn named McFadden an executor of her multimillion-dollar estate.

It was during these years that Kate and Irene Mayer Selznick's lengthy friendship disintegrated. Some observers said it was because, as with so many people, Hepburn had tired of the association and wanted to move on with her life. Other onlookers felt that Selznick had a long-standing, growing envy of Hepburn's fame. It was theorized that Irene was frustrated that her one-time friend's career and public regard continued to flourish in a major way while she had retreated into self-imposed seclusion. Also, as suggested in A. Scott Berg's *Kate Remembered* (2003), there was the possibility that Irene was envious that Kate still attracted a circle of (younger) women friends who were now her new confidants.

Selznick's brewing animosity may have inspired Irene to tell Berg, as recorded in *Kate Remembered,* after visiting Hepburn's brownstone and finding her host intrigued with a young woman guest: "Now, everything makes sense. [Film director] Dorothy Arzner, [actor-songwriter-producer] Nancy Hamilton—all those women. Laura Harding. Now it all makes sense. A double-gater. I never believed that relationship with Spence was about sex." (Some onlookers regarded this remark by Irene as both impromptu spitefulness or a deflection—for the record—of her own reputed bisexual lifestyle.)

Robert Gottlieb, a distinguished book editor who knew professionally Hepburn, Selznick, and Berg—and who was a Manhattan neighbor of Kate's— had his own take on the disintegrating Hepburn-Selznick situation. In his *New York Times* review of *Kate Remembered,* Gottlieb wrote of Irene's strong disapproval of Kate catering to the media by discussing publicly her (version of her) relationship with Tracy. "Irene's word for this abandonment of privacy and flaunting of intimate matters was 'disgusting.' And she felt betrayed—as if, through the years, she had been deliberately misled about Kate's character.... She determined to withdraw, assuring me that she would do it so gradually that Kate would have no grounds for demanding explanations."

In the same newspaper piece Gottlieb discussed an occasion in the early 1980s when pop singer Michael Jackson was asked to dinner at 244 West Forty-ninth Street. Regarding that bizarre event to which Selznick was initially invited, Gottlieb recounted, "I vividly remember the morning Irene called me, exploding with fury: 'Can you believe what she's done now? She's dared to invite me to dinner with Michael Jackson! Is she insane?' To her, Michael Jackson was just another symptom of Kate's vulgar and pathetic desperation to stay up to date and in the limelight."

❋   ❋   ❋

Once Spencer Tracy's widow, Louise, died in 1983, Kate was more inclined—to a compulsive degree—to discuss with the media her own rendition of the Tracy years. She became obsessed on indelibly fixing in the public's mind the wondrousness of their alleged heterosexual love relationship regardless of its actuality. It led her, with the cooperation of Tracy's daughter, Susie, to prepare a laudatory, carefully constructed TV documentary, *The Spencer Tracy Legacy* (1986).

On another front, Hepburn wrote a script about her enduring close friendship and lengthy working relationship with Phyllis Wilbourn. Titled *Me and Phyllis,* the anecdotal narrative was to have costarred Kate and a to-be-selected performer. When the financing failed to materialize for the project, Hepburn asked a friend to read the screenplay and tell her why the concept had not sold ultimately. His response: "Too much 'me,' too little 'Phyllis.'"

Also in 1986 Hepburn returned to acting by starring in the telefeature, *Mrs. Delafield Wants to Marry.* The well-received entry led to four additional made-for-TV films over the next six years. Many of these lightweight properties were shot in Vancouver, Canada, and several were written by James Prideaux. He had first met Hepburn in the late 1960s when she was considering directing a feature film (based on Margery Sharp novels) before being diverted by starring in *Coco.* Over the years Prideaux became a beacon of companionship for the demanding star and wrote amusingly—and in minute details—of their long friendship in *Knowing Hepburn and Other Curious Experiences* (1996). Another intimate of Kate's was affable John Philip Dayton who produced Kate's final three TV movies.

❋   ❋   ❋

Occasionally, Kate broke away from the mechanical busy work of her daily routine by permitting a stranger to tear through her strong walls of reserve. New York–based James-Daniel Radiches, a young photographer, was preparing a book on playwright Edward Albee's works. He was photographing and interviewing individuals involved in key productions of this artist. Since Kate had starred in the film version of Albee's *A Delicate Balance,* Radiches hoped to include the famed star within his project. After writing to her, she eventually granted him a brief audience at her east side brownstone. In true Hepburn fashion she set precise ground rules for the mini photo shoot: day and exact time of appointment, brief length of the session, and so forth.

On June 23, 1988, a very warm Manhattan day, Radiches arrived at 244 East Forty-ninth Street for the scheduled meeting. To the photographer's surprise, it was not the legendary tough lady he encountered but a shy and apprehensive woman. On hand were Kate's makeup artist (who had prepared her for an earlier shoot that afternoon with her "official" photographer, John Bryson) as well as ever-present companion-secretary Phyllis Wilbourn. Radiches began extensive photographing to meet her time frame. Because Kate was so thoroughly enjoying the activity she allowed the shoot to continue beyond its original time limit. In the process James-Daniel witnessed a vulnerable side to the surprisingly polite icon.

A week later when Radiches delivered the photo proofs, she told him, "You're what I call an artist." Kate invited him to stay for lunch prepared by Norah Moore. It took another two months before Hepburn finally talked to him about her work in *A Delicate Balance*. She grew comfortable with Radiches and agreed to his offer to come by and repair a tear in the canvas to her long-ago painting of Spencer Tracy reading a newspaper. The next February, when Radiches was hoping to join the International Photographers of the Motion Picture & Television Industries—something Hepburn suggested—Kate volunteered to help his admission to the union by writing a letter of endorsement on his behalf.

Over the coming months the two stayed in touch with occasional letters. calls, and a few subsequent visits to her home in 1990 (one for a chat and homemade ice cream and another to deliver prints of his shots of Kate for possible use in the upcoming televised Kennedy Center Honors, in which she was a recipient).

❋　❋　❋

After declining requests for years, Kate finally accepted participation in the televised Kennedy Center Honors in late 1990. The next year, prompted by her literary agent and friend Freya Manston, Hepburn published her second book, *Me: Stories of My Life*. (Her editor Robert Gottlieb said of the manuscript: "It was a mess of a book—strident, evasive, patchy, willful—but it had its virtues. It was direct, unfiltered; clearly in its subject's own voice.") Written in Hepburn's eclectic, abrupt style, the volume was a major best seller. It made Kate even more in demand as the subject of admiring articles in major publications—in all of which she perpetuated a self-edited version of her life and special friendships and avoided any serious introspection. The book's success led to Hepburn's 1993 TV documentary, *Katharine Hepburn: All About Me.*

Although increasingly poor health kept Hepburn from exerting herself professionally beyond the occasional TV movie, Hollywood superstar Warren Beatty was fixated on Kate playing his aunt in the major theatrical release *Love Affair* (1994). Beatty turned to Kit Kramer (Hepburn's goddaughter and the offspring of Stanley Kramer and his actress wife, Karen Sharpe) and others to help him convince Hepburn to take the role. Flattered by Beatty's persistence, Kate flew to Los Angeles to perform her cameo. While on the West Coast she revisited locales that had been significant during her Hollywood years. When the banal *Love Affair* was released, Hepburn received the film's best notices for her brief and final big-screen turn.

✻   ✻   ✻

In her final years Laura Harding was quite ill and eventually confined to a nursing home. Kate continued to visit her darling friend, who passed away on August 8, 1994. Months later, in May 1995, Phyllis Wilbourn, who had grown very senile toward the end, died. At Kate's request, her companion's ashes were buried in the Hepburn family plot at the Cedar Hill Cemetery in Hartford.

The combination of Phyllis's passing and a serious respiratory infection (for which Hepburn was hospitalized and nearly died) made Kate's family decide that she should move to Fenwick on a full-time basis. There she spent her remaining seven years. Becoming progressively more frail, with her mind sometimes wandering, the once very independent woman sat for hours starring out at the rolling waters of Long Island Sound where she used to swim and sail. Family and close friends were in close attendance, looking forward to those days when the once-vital celebrity was alert and able to converse.

Kate's sister Marion had passed away in 1986, and in October 2000 brother Dick died. Hepburn seemed largely oblivious to the passing events or the fact that so many around the world continued to wish her well. (For example, she seemed unaware that the Turtle Bay Association in her former New York neighborhood had arranged that the garden of the Dag Hammarskjold

Plaza—located to the north of the United Nations building—be named in her honor. Kate was also ignorant of the fact that *Tea at Five,* a one-woman show written by Matthew Lombardo and starring Kate Mulgrew as Hepburn (at age thirty-one and at age seventy-six), had bowed at the Hartford Stage theater in February 2002 before going on to a New York City engagement and a road tour.) Instead the frail celebrity was content with satisfying her still-healthy appetite and taking great pleasure in sitting in front of a roaring fireplace at Fenwick.

After many false alarms that the end had finally come for one of the world's most famous and enduring stars, Katharine Houghton Hepburn, age ninety-six, passed away on Sunday afternoon, June 29, 2003. To many people, it seemed unbelievable that this once-vital force was no more. Her ashes were laid to rest at the family plot at Cedar Hill Cemetery in Hartford. At the star's request, there was no public memorial service.

Subsequently, Kate's two homes were put up for sale, with the New York City brownstone selling for $3.9 million and Fenwick being sold for under $7 million. In June 2004, Sotheby's Auction House in New York sold for over $6 million a wide array of Katharine Hepburn's possessions, ranging from her 1928 wedding dress to her RKO studio lot pass to an autographed copy of photographer John Bryson's 1990 book, *The Private World of Katharine Hepburn.* (Much of the remainder of Kate's show business memorabilia and correspondence was donated to the library at the Academy of Motion Picture Arts and Sciences.)

When asked why so many of the late star's personal items were being disposed of, Cynthia McFadden, a frequent spokeswoman for all things Hepburn, said the sale was the end result of Kate having said once, "Sell it all—nobody I know needs things, they all need money." Cynthia added that Hepburn "was full of sentiment, but she wasn't sentimental."

EPILOGUE

"No. I don't regret anything. I don't believe in regretting things. But you can say that I'm sad about a lot of things. I'm sad that I wasn't a great painter or a great writer, didn't have a marvelous political career, didn't follow in my family's tradition and turn out to be a great reformer. There are a million things that I would like to have done. But you can't do everything. You should try to do what you do, well. And I'm very realistic, very Scotch. I know and have known all along what my position was. I know what my values are to other people; I also know what my values are to myself. It's fine to be admired, but it's much more important to know that you're worth admiring in certain departments."
—Katharine Hepburn, 1967

If Katharine Hepburn had an unsentimental nature, she was certainly ambiguous, oblique, and often diversionary regarding the actuality of her extraordinary life. Although held up as a great icon of feminism and women's liberation, she, unlike her mother, Kit, was not interested in being a standard-bearer for causes (except for her 1980s efforts on behalf of Planned Parenthood). Many of Kate's statements that seemed as straightforward as she wanted the world—and herself—to think she was, have residues of hidden meanings:

"I always liked bad eggs, always, always—and always attracted them. I had a lot of energy and looked as if I was (and I was) hard to get—wasn't mad about the male sex—perfectly independent, never had any intention of getting married, wanted to paddle my own canoe, didn't want anyone to pay my way."

"When I think of the things I could have done! I could have done fifty million times as much. I have a super amount of energy. If I were starting again, I would concentrate harder. I wouldn't waste as much time. Yeah, yeah. I sound smart, but I don't think I'm too bright. It takes me rather a long time to get an impression and unfetter my brain and form a conclusion. But no, I probably wouldn't have changed any of the decisions I've made."

"I've never been much interested in money. I don't give a damn about clothes and I don't care about possessions. I've gotten tremendous fees when the material was boring, and the only time I've ever really kicked myself is when I've done something I didn't want to do just because of the money involved."

"In some ways I've lived my life as a man, made my own decisions. I've been as terrified as the next person, but you've got to keep a-going; you've got to dream…. I have no fear of death. Must be wonderful, like a long sleep. But let's face it: It's how you live that really counts."

This was the same singular Hepburn who once said coyly, "I've had a fascinating life. I don't think I'm the least bit peculiar, but people tell me I am." She also admitted, "I only want to go on being a star. It's all I know how to be." According to this extraordinarily success-oriented talent, "I don't regret anything I've ever done as long as I enjoyed it at the time."

And, finally, Hepburn was the celebrated individualist who repeatedly advised the press, "You can say or write anything about me you like…. Just don't, for any reason, ever tell the truth."

❋   ❋   ❋

Only future generations will have the necessary perspective to best determine Hepburn's lasting contributions to the world of show business and her position in the chronicle of popular and social culture.

Meanwhile we are left to hypothesize answers to the many contradictions within Hepburn's paradoxical nature. Such fascinating incongruities led her to thirst for—and achieve—global fame, yet shrink with ferocity from public scrutiny of her private life. Beyond built-in New England reticence and old-fashioned modest values, was her abhorrence of being in the limelight off-camera actually based on a tremendous fear that her untraditional domestic and sexual lifestyle would be exposed for all to judge? On the one hand, there was, among others, Kate's convenient attachment to undemanding (ex) husband Ludlow Ogden Smith, her career-helping romance with dashing talent agent Leland Hayward, her flight of amorous fancy and perpetual flight from married film director John Ford, a man with repressed bisexual (or homosexual) tendencies, and her high-profile association with eccentric megamillionaire Howard Hughes. (Like Kate the eccentric entrepreneur was extremely uncomfortable with traditional personal and sexual relationships and also lacked the healthy ability to share inner feelings with others.) Obviously, as noted earlier, regardless of Kate's bisexual nature, she never hesitated to go to bed with men who appealed to her, either to promote her career or just for sexual satisfaction.

On the other hand, what propelled her close offcamera association with film director George Cukor over the years? Was it that he directed her in so many key films over the years and/or that she felt so relaxed mingling with this cultured homosexual man and his glittering, sophisticated gay crowd?

And what of the special women in Hepburn's life which began in earnest with socialite Laura Harding, actor-coach Suzanne Steele, and behind-the-film-camera talent Jane Loring? Will the full dimensions of these strong woman-to-woman bonds ever be fully defined? Or what of Hepburn's intricate attachment to film industry princess–stage producer Irene Selznick, actor-coach Constance Collier, longtime companion-secretary Phyllis Wilbourn, and Kate's brief but powerful desire in the 1970s to help professionally young talent Joy Bang? Then too, what range of motives led Hepburn to reach out to mentor and constantly befriend such latter-day show business intimates as TV scripter-producer Sally Lapiduss and lawyer–TV news commentator Cynthia McFadden?

Equally fascinatingly to contemplate is what truly lay at the core of Hepburn's lengthy friendship with married movie star Spencer Tracy. Here was a deep relationship—whatever the truth of its dimensions—that the couple took great pains to hide from the world for twenty-six years, a subterfuge that in turn created diversion from its actual substance. The couple's great ties—beyond their popular onscreen teamings—revolved around self-sufficient Kate's driving need to be subservient to self-involved Spencer who, like John Ford, hid his life's pains behind indulgence in alcohol. One can hypothesize that Hepburn's often juvenile servitude to Tracy satisfied displaced aspects of her abiding love for her emotionally remote, demanding father. Kate's compulsive devotion to Spencer, a recurrent drunk and womanizer with reputed homosexual leanings, also seemed to satisfy her lifelong yearning to make amends for having "let down" her adored brother Tom, a teenage suicide.

In retrospect, one has to be fascinated with the tremendous energy Hepburn expended over many years to mold and maintain her highly successful acting career. One stands agog at her full-throttle commitment to providing the public with a most original image that would forever set her apart from her peers: first as a divine oddity who dressed, acted, and spoke so unusually, and then later in life as a self-perpetuated cherished institution who claimed to be highly sensible and made it appear she was always being straightforward. Yet nowhere did Kate's ongoing crusade to provide the world with the "real" her go further into fiction than in her deep bonds to her special women friends and with morose Spencer Tracy.

During Spencer's life Kate constantly praised his acting style for being what hers never was—natural and unadorned. After Tracy's death in 1967 she began publicly extolling and perpetuating the myth of her three-decade "romance" with the late star. It became her great topic of conversation with the media, and she discussed it endlessly until she died in 2003. The more Hepburn embroidered the majesty of her codependent attachment with Tracy, the more she came to believe in its wonders. In the process it provided a means to divert herself from examining the unhealthy aspects of her links to Spencer. It also allowed her to ignore discussing or analyzing her special rapport with the several key women in her life.

No wonder that when evaluating Katharine Hepburn's astonishing life, one must tread with an open mind. We must be wary, for she constantly throws us off kilter with remarks that seemed full of candor but instead had perplexing layers of subtext—as when she said in 1991, "I love to paint—anything you can do alone. That's the trouble with acting; it requires other people and other places." This from an iron-willed woman who fought so hard to endure as a mighty film and stage star.

Hepburn's Broadway Appearances, Feature Films, and Made-for-TV Movies

Broadway

- *These Days* (November 12, 1928, Court Theater) as Veronica Sims.
- *Holiday* (November 26, 1928, Plymouth Theater) as understudy to Hope Williams (as Linda Seton).
- *A Month in the Country* (March 17, 1930, Guild Theater) as understudy to Eunice Stoddard (as Viera Aleksandrovna) and, later, also as Katia, the maid.
- *Art and Mrs. Bottle (or The Return of the Puritan)* (November 18, 1930, Maxine Elliott Theater) as Judy Bottle.
- *The Warrior's Husband* (March 11, 1932, Morosco Theater) as Antiope.
- *The Lake* (December 23, 1933, Martin Beck Theater) as Stella Sturrege.
- *The Philadelphia Story* (March 28, 1939, Shubert Theater) as Tracy Lord.
- *Without Love* (November 10, 1942, St. James Theater) as Jamie Coe Rowan.
- *As You Like It* (January 26, 1950, Cort Theater) as Rosalind.
- *The Millionairess* (October 17, 1952, Shubert Theater) as Epifania, the Lady.
- *Coco* (December 18, 1969, Mark Hellinger Theater) as Coco Chanel.
- *A Matter of Gravity* (February 3, 1976, Broadhurst Theater) as Mrs. Basil.
- *The West Side Waltz* (November 19, 1981, Ethel Barrymore Theater) as Margaret Mary Elderdice.

Feature Films

- *A Bill of Divorcement* (RKO, 1932) 75 minutes. Director: George Cukor. Cast: John Barrymore, Billie Burke, Katharine Hepburn (Sydney Fairfield), David Manners, and Henry Stephenson.

- *Christopher Strong* (RKO, 1933) 77 minutes. Director: Dorothy Arzner. Cast: Katharine Hepburn (Lady Cynthia Darrington) Colin Clive, Billie Burke, Helen Chandler, and Ralph Forbes.
- *Morning Glory* (RKO, 1933) 74 minutes. Director: Lowell Sherman. Cast: Katharine Hepburn (Eva Lovelace), Douglas Fairbanks Jr., Adolphe Menjou, Mary Duncan, and C. Aubrey Smith.
- *Little Women* (RKO, 1933) 115 minutes. Director: George Cukor. Cast: Katharine Hepburn (Jo), Joan Bennett, Paul Lukas, Edna May Oliver, Jean Parker, Frances Dee, and Spring Byington.
- *Spitfire* (RKO, 1934). Director: John Cromwell. Cast: Katharine Hepburn (Trigger Hicks), Robert Young, Ralph Bellamy, Martha Sleeper, and Louis Mason.
- *The Little Minister* (RKO, 1934) 110 minutes. Director: Richard Wallace. Cast: Katharine Hepburn (Babbie), John Beal, Alan Hale, Donald Crisp, and Lumsden Hare.
- *Break of Hearts* (RKO, 1935) 80 minutes. Director: Philip Moeller. Cast: Katharine Hepburn (Constance Dane Roberti), Charles Boyer, John Beal, Jean Hersholt, and Sam Hardy.
- *Alice Adams* (RKO, 1935) 99 minutes. Director: George Stevens. Cast: Katharine Hepburn (Alice Adams), Fred MacMurray, Fred Stone, Evelyn Venable, and Frank Albertson.
- *Sylvia Scarlett* (RKO, 1936) 97 minutes. Director: George Cukor. Cast: Katharine Hepburn (Sylvia Scarlett), Cary Grant, Brian Aherne, Edmund Gwenn, and Natalie Paley.
- *Mary of Scotland* (RKO, 1936) 123 minutes. Director: John Ford. Cast: Katharine Hepburn (Mary Stuart), Fredric March, Florence Eldridge, Douglas Watson, and John Carradine.
- *A Woman Rebels* (RKO, 1936) 88 minutes. Director: Mark Sandrich. Cast: Katharine Hepburn (Pamela Thistlewaite), Herbert Marshall, Elizabeth Allan, Donald Crisp, and David Manners.
- *Quality Street* (RKO, 1937) 84 minutes. Director: George Stevens. Cast: Katharine Hepburn (Phoebe Throssel), Franchot Tone, Fay Bainter, Eric Blore, and Cora Witherspoon.

- *Stage Door* (RKO, 1937) 92 minutes. Director: Gregory La Cava. Cast: Katharine Hepburn (Terry Randall), Ginger Rogers, Adolphe Menjou, Gail Patrick, and Constance Collier.
- *Bringing Up Baby* (RKO, 1938) 102 minutes. Director: Howard Hawks. Cast: Katharine Hepburn (Susan Vance), Cary Grant, Charles Ruggles, May Robson, and Walter Catlett.
- *Holiday* (Columbia, 1938) 93 minutes. Director: George Cukor. Cast: Katharine Hepburn (Linda Seton), Cary Grant, Doris Nolan, Lew Ayres, and Edward Everett Horton.
- *The Philadelphia Story* (MGM, 1940) 112 minutes. Director George Cukor. Cast: Cary Grant, Katharine Hepburn (Tracy Lord), James Stewart, Ruth Hussey, and John Howard.
- *Woman of the Year* (MGM, 1942) 112 minutes. Director: George Stevens. Cast: Spencer Tracy, Katharine Hepburn (Tess Harding), Fay Bainter, Reginald Owen, and Minor Watson.
- *Keeper of the Flame* (MGM, 1942) 100 minutes. Director: George Cukor. Cast: Spencer Tracy, Katharine Hepburn (Christine Forrest), Richard Whorf, Margaret Wycherly, and Donald Meek.
- *Stage Door Canteen* (United Artists, 1942) 132 minutes. Director: Frank Borzage. Cast: Cheryl Walker, William Terry, Marjorie Riordan, Lon McCallister, and Katharine Hepburn (herself).
- *Dragon Seed* (MGM, 1944) 148 minutes. Directors: Jack Conway and Harold S. Bucquet. Cast: Katharine Hepburn (Jade), Walter Huston, Aline MacMahon, Akim Tamiroff, and Turhan Bey.
- *Without Love* (MGM, 1945) 111 minutes. Director: Harold S. Bucquet. Cast: Spencer Tracy, Katharine Hepburn (Jamie Rowan), Lucille Ball, Keenan Wynn, Carl Esmond, and Patricia Morison.
- *Undercurrent* (MGM, 1946) 116 minutes. Director: Vincente Minnelli. Cast: Katharine Hepburn (Ann Hamilton), Robert Taylor, Robert Mitchum, Edmund Gwenn, and Marjorie Main.
- *The Sea of Grass* (MGM, 1947) 131 minutes. Director: Elia Kazan. Cast: Spencer Tracy, Katharine Hepburn (Lutie Cameron), Robert Walker, Melvyn Douglas, and Phyllis Thaxter.

- *Song of Love* (MGM, 1947) 119 minutes. Director: Clarence Brown. Cast: Katharine Hepburn (Clara Wieck Schumann), Paul Henreid, Robert Walker, Henry Daniell, and Leo G. Carroll.
- *State of the Union* (MGM, 1948) 124 minutes. Director: Frank Capra. Cast: Spencer Tracy, Katharine Hepburn (Mary Matthews), Van Johnson, Angela Lansbury, and Adolphe Menjou.
- *Adam's Rib* (MGM, 1949) 101 minutes. Director. George Cukor. Cast: Spencer Tracy, Katharine Hepburn (Amanda Bonner), Judy Holliday, Tom Ewell, and David Wayne.
- *The African Queen* (United Artists, 1951) Color, 105 minutes. Director: John Huston. Cast: Humphrey Bogart, Katharine Hepburn (Rose Sayer), Robert Morley, Peter Bull, and Theodore Bikel.
- *Pat and Mike* (MGM, 1952) 95 minutes. Director: George Cukor. Cast: Spencer Tracy, Katharine Hepburn (Pat Pemberton) Aldo Ray, William Ching, and Sammy White.
- *Summertime* (United Artists, 1955) Color, 99 minutes. Director: David Lean. Cast: Katharine Hepburn (Jane Hudson), Rossano Brazzi, Isa Miranda, Darren McGavin, and Mari Aldon.
- *The Rainmaker* (Paramount, 1956) Color, 121 minutes. Director: Joseph Anthony. Cast: Burt Lancaster, Katharine Hepburn (Lizzie Curry), Wendell Corey, Lloyd Bridges, and Earl Holliman.
- *The Iron Petticoat* (MGM, 1956) Color, 87 minutes. Director: Ralph Thomas. Cast: Bob Hope, Katharine Hepburn (Vinka Kovelenko), James Robertson Justice, Robert Helpmann, and David Kossoff.
- *Desk Set* (Twentieth Century-Fox, 1957) Color, 103 minutes. Director: Walter Lang. Cast: Spencer Tracy, Katharine Hepburn (Bunny Watson), Gig Young, Joan Blondell, and Dina Merrill.
- *Suddenly, Last Summer* (Columbia, 1959) 114 minutes. Director: Joseph L. Mankiewicz. Cast: Elizabeth Taylor, Katharine Hepburn (Mrs. Venable), Montgomery Clift, Albert Dekker, and Mercedes McCambridge.
- *Long Day's Journey Into Night* (Embassy, 1962) 108 minutes. Director: Sidney Lumet. Cast: Katharine Hepburn (Mary Tyrone), Ralph Richardson, Jason Robards Jr., Dean Stockwell, and Jeanne Barr.

- *Guess Who's Coming to Dinner* (Columbia, 1967) Color, 108 minutes. Director: Stanley Kramer. Cast: Spencer Tracy, Sidney Poitier, Katharine Hepburn (Christina Drayton), Katharine Houghton, and Cecil Kellaway.
- *The Lion in Winter* (Avco-Embassy, 1968) Color, 134 minutes. Director: Anthony Harvey. Cast: Peter O'Toole, Katharine Hepburn (Eleanor of Aquitaine), Jane Merrow, Timothy Dalton, and Anthony Hopkins.
- *The Madwoman of Chaillot* (Warner Bros.–7 Arts, 1969) Color, 142 minutes. Director: Bryan Forbes. Cast: Katharine Hepburn (Aurelia, the Madwoman of Chaillot), Charles Boyer, Yul Brynner, Richard Chamberlain, Edith Evans, and Danny Kaye.
- *The Trojan Women* (Cinerama, 1971) Color, 111 minutes. Director: Michael Cacoyannis. Cast: Katharine Hepburn (Hecuba), Vanessa Redgrave, Genevieve Bujold, Irene Papas, and Patrick Magee.
- *A Delicate Balance* (American Film Theater, 1973) Color, 132 minutes. Director: Tony Richardson. Cast: Katharine Hepburn (Agnes), Paul Scofield, Lee Remick, Kate Reid, Joseph Cotten, and Betsy Blair.
- *Rooster Cogburn* (Universal, 1975) Color, 108 minutes. Director: Stuart Millar. Cast: John Wayne, Katharine Hepburn (Eula Goodnight), Anthony Zerbe, Richard Jordan, and John McIntire.
- *Olly, Olly, Oxen Free* (Sanrio Communications, 1978) Color, 84 minutes. Director: Richard A. Colla. Cast: Katharine Hepburn (Miss Pudd), Kevin McKenzie, Dennis Dimster, Peter Kilman, and Jayne Marie Mansfield.
- *On Golden Pond* (Universal, 1981) Color, 109 minutes. Director: Mark Rydell. Cast: Katharine Hepburn (Ethel Thayer), Henry Fonda, Jane Fonda, Doug McKeon, and Dabney Coleman.
- (*The Ultimate Solution of*) *Grace Quigley* (Cannon Films, 1985), Color, 87 minutes. Director: Anthony Harvey. Cast: Katharine Hepburn (Grace Quigley), Nick Nolte, Elizabeth Wilson, Chip Zien, and William Duell.
- *Love Affair* (Warner Bros., 1994) Color, 108 minutes. Director: Glenn Gordon Caron. Cast: Warren Beatty, Annette Bening, Katharine Hepburn (Ginny), Garry Shandling, and Pierce Brosnan.

Made-for-TV Movies

- *The Glass Menagerie* (ABC, December 16, 1973) Color, 100 minutes. Director: Anthony Harvey. Cast: Katharine Hepburn (Amanda Wingfield), Joanna Miles, Sam Waterston, and Michael Moriarty.
- *Love Among the Ruins* (ABC, March 6, 1975) Color, 100 minutes. Director: George Cukor. Cast: Katharine Hepburn (Jessica Medlicott), Laurence Olivier, Colin Blakely, Richard Pearson, and Joan Sims.
- *The Corn Is Green* (CBS, January 29, 1989) Color, 93 minutes. Director: George Cukor. Cast: Katharine Hepburn (Miss Lilly C. Moffat), Ian Saynor, Bill Fraser, Patricia Hayes, and Anna Massey.
- *Mrs. Delafield Wants to Marry* (CBS, March 30, 1986) Color, 100 minutes. Director: George Schaefer. Cast: Katharine Hepburn (Margaret Delafield), Harold Gould, Denholm Elliott, Brenda Forbes, and David Ogden Stiers.
- *Laura Lansing Slept Here* (NBC, March 7, 1988) Color, 100 minutes. Director: George Schaefer. Cast: Katharine Hepburn (Laura Lansing), Lee Richardson, Joel Higgins, Karen Austin, and Schuyler Grant.
- *The Man Upstairs* (CBS, December 6, 1992) Color, 92 minutes. Director: George Schaefer. Cast: Katharine Hepburn (Victoria Brown), Ryan O'Neal, Henry Beckman, Helena Carroll, and Brenda Forbes.
- *This Can't Be Love* (CBS, March 13, 1994) Color, 95 minutes. Director: Anthony Harvey. Cast: Katharine Hepburn (Marion Bennett), Anthony Quinn, Jason Bateman, Jami Gertz, and Maxine Miller.
- *One Christmas* (NBC, December 19, 1994) Color, 86 minutes. Director: Tony Bill. Cast: Katharine Hepburn (Cornelia Beaumont), Henry Winkler, Swoosie Kurtz, T. J. Lowther, and Tonea Stewart.

BIBLIOGRAPHY

Books

Acosta, Mercedes de. *Here Lies the Heart* (reprint ed.). New York: Arno, 1975.

Andersen, Christopher. *An Affair to Remember: The Remarkable Love Story of Katharine Hepburn and Spencer Tracy.* New York: William Morrow, 1997.

_____. *Young Kate.* New York: Henry Holt, 1988.

Balio, Tino. *Grand Design: Hollywood as a Modern Business Enterprise, 1930–1939 (History of the American Cinema, Vol. 5).* Berkeley, Calif.: University of California Press, 1995.

Barrios, Richard. *Screened Out: Playing Gay in Hollywood from Edison to Stonewall.* New York: Routledge, 2003.

Barrymore, Ethel. *Memories.* New York: Harper & Brothers, 1955.

Bartlett, Donald L. and James B. Steele. *Empire: The Life, Legend, and Madness of Howard Hughes.* New York: W. W. Norton, 1979.

Basinger, Jeanine. *A Woman's View: How Hollywood Spoke to Women: 1930–1960.* Hanover, N.H.: Wesleyan University Press, 1993.

Beaton, Cecil. *The Unexpurgated Beaton.* New York: Alfred A. Knopf, 2003.

Behlmer, Rudy (ed.). *Memo from David O. Selznick.* New York: Viking, 1972.

Bell-Metereau, Rebecca. *Hollywood Androgyny* (2nd ed.). New York: Columbia University Press, 1993.

Berg, A. Scott. *Kate Remembered.* New York: Putnam, 2003.

_____. *Max Perkins, Editor of Genius.* New York: E. P. Dutton, 1978.

Bergen, Ronald. *Katharine Hepburn: An Independent Woman.* New York: Arcade, 1996.

Bogart, Stephen Humphrey. *Bogart: In Search of My Father.* New York: E. P. Dutton, 1995.

Bosworth, Patricia. *Montgomery Clift* (reprint ed.). New York: Limelight, 1990.

Braun, Eric. *Frightening the Horses: Gay Icons of the Cinema.* London, England: Reynolds & Hearn, 2002.

Britton, Andrew. *Katharine Hepburn: Star as Feminist.* New York: Continuum, 1995.

Brown, Peter Harry, and Pat. H. Broeske. *Howard Hughes: The Untold Story.* New York: E. P. Dutton, 1996.

Brownlow, Kevin. *David Lean.* New York: Wyatt/St. Martin's, 1996.

Bryson, John. *The Private World of Katharine Hepburn.* Boston: Little, Brown, 1990.

Buford, Kate. *Burt Lancaster: An American Life.* New York: Alfred A. Knopf, 2000.

Buhle, Paul, and Dave Wagner. *Hide in Plain Sight: The Hollywood Blacklistees in Film and Television, 1950–2002.* New York: Palgrave Macmillan, 2003.

Capra, Frank. *The Name Above the Title.* New York: Macmillan, 1971.

Carey, Gary. *All the Stars in Heaven: Louis B. Mayer's MGM.* New York: E. P. Dutton, 1981.

_____. *Anita Loos.* New York: Alfred A. Knopf, 1988.

_____. *Judy Holliday: An Intimate Life Story.* New York: Seaview, 1982.

_____. *Katharine Hepburn: A Hollywood Yankee* (revised ed.). New York: Dell, 1983.

Carr, Larry. *More Fabulous Faces.* Garden City, N.Y.: Doubleday, 1979.

Cavett, Dick, and Christopher Porterfield. *Cavett.* New York: Bantam, 1974.

Chamberlain, Richard. *Shattered Love.* New York: Regan/HarperCollins, 2003.

Citron, Stephen. *Noel & Cole: The Sophisticates.* New York: Oxford University, 1993.

Cronyn, Hume. *A Terrible Liar.* New York: William Morrow, 1991.

Cunningham, Ernest W. *The Ultimate Bogart.* Los Angeles, Calif.: Renaissance, 1999.

Curtis, James. *Between Flops: A Biography of Preston Sturges* (reprint ed.). New York: Limelight, 1991.

Danielson, Sarah Parker. *Katharine Hepburn: A Hollywood Portrait.* New York: Smithmark, 1993.

Davidson, Bill. *Jane Fonda: An Intimate Biography.* New York: Signet, 1991.

_____. *Spencer Tracy: Tragic Idol.* New York: E. P. Dutton, 1987.

Deschner, Donald. *The Complete Films of Spencer Tracy.* New York: Citadel/Carol, 1993.

DiBattista, Maria. *Fast-Talking Dames.* New Haven, Conn.: Yale University Press, 2001.

Dickens, Homer. *The Films of Ginger Rogers.* Secaucus, N.J.: Citadel/Carol, 1975.

Dickens, Homer, and Lawrence J. Quirk. *The Films of Katharine Hepburn* (updated ed.). New York: Citadel/Carol, 1990.

Dmytryk, Edward. *Hollywood's Golden Age as Told by One Who Lived It All.* Boalsburg, Pa.: BearManor Media, 2003.

Dody, Sandford. *Give Up the Ghost: A Writer's Life Among the Stars.* New York: M. Evans, 1980.

Doty, Alexander. *Flaming Classics: Queering the Film Canon.* New York: Routledge, 2000.

Dunlap, Richard. *Stars of a Summer Night.* Stockbridge, Mass.: Cottage Press, 2001.

Eds. *Katharine Hepburn: In the Spotlight.* New York: Galley Press, 1980.

Eds. of *Life* magazine. *Katharine Hepburn: 1907–2003.* New York: Life Books, 2003.

Edwards, Anne. *Katharine Hepburn: A Remarkable Woman* (updated ed.). New York: St. Martin's/Griffin, 2000.

_____. *Vivien Leigh.* New York: Simon & Schuster, 1977.

Eels, George. *Hedda and Louella.* New York: Warner Paperback, 1972.

Ehrenstein, David. *Open Secret: Gay Hollywood, 1928–2000* (updated ed.). New York: HarperCollins Perennial, 2000.

Eyman, Scott. *Print the Legend: The Life and Times of John Ford.* New York: Simon & Schuster, 1999.

Faderman, Lillian. *Odd Girls and Twilight Lovers.* New York: Penguin, 1992.

Fairbanks, Douglas, Jr. *The Salad Days.* New York: Doubleday, 1988.

Faith, William Robert. *Bob Hope: A Life in Comedy* (revised ed.). New York: Da Capo, 2003.

Fisher, James. *Spencer Tracy: A Bio-Bibliography.* Westport, Conn.: Greenwood, 1994.

Flamini, Roland. *Scarlett, Rhett, and a Cast of Thousands.* New York: Macmillan, 1975.

Fleming, E.J. *Hollywood Death and Scandals Sites.* Jefferson, N.C.: McFarland, 2000.

Fonda, Henry, as told to Howard Teichmann. *Fonda: My Life.* New York: New American Library, 1981.

Fontaine, Joan. *No Bed of Roses.* New York: William Morrow, 1978.

Ford, Dan. *Pappy: The Life of John Ford* (reprint ed.) New York: Da Capo, 1998.

Fraser-Cavassoni, Natasha. *Sam Spiegel.* New York: Simon & Schuster, 2003.

Freeland, Michael. *Katharine Hepburn.* London: W. H. Allen, 1984.

Freeland, Michael. *Peter O'Toole.* London: Comet, 1984.

Garber, Marjorie. *Bisexuality and the Eroticism of Everyday Life.* New York: Routledge, 2000.

Gilbert, Julie. *Opposite Attraction: The Lives of Erich Maria Remarque and Paulette Goddard.* New York: Pantheon, 1995.

Gordon, Ruth. *An Open Book.* Garden City, N.Y.: Doubleday, 1980.

Gottfried, Martin. *Jed Harris: The Curse of Genius.* Boston: Little, Brown, 1984.

Goudsouzian, Aram. *Sidney Poitier: Man, Actor, Icon.* Chapel Hill, N.C.: University of North Carolina Press, 2004.

Grant, Marion Hepburn, and Katharine Houghton Grant (ed.). *Marion Hepburn Grant.* West Hartford, Conn.: Fenwick Productions, 1989.

Grobel, Lawrence. *The Hustons.* New York: Charles Scribner's Sons, 1989.

Guilaroff, Sydney, as told to Cathy Griffin. *Crowning Glory.* Santa Monica, Calif.: General Publishing, 1996.

Guiles, Fred Lawrence. *Jane Fonda: The Actress in Her Time.* New York: Pinnacle, 1983.

Hack, Richard. *Hughes: The Private Diaries, Memos and Letters.* Beverly Hills, Calif.: New Millennium, 2001.

Hadleigh, Boze. *Celluloid Gaze* (updated ed.). New York: Limelight, 2002.

_____. *Hollywood and Whine.* New York: Citadel/Kensington, 2001.

_____. *Hollywood Lesbians.* New York: Barricade, 1994.

_____. *The Lavender Screen* (revised ed.). New York: Citadel/Kensington, 2001.

Hamann, G. D. (ed.). *George Cukor in the 30's.* Hollywood, Calif.: Filming Today, 2003.

_____. *Elissa Landi in the 30's.* Hollywood, Calif.: Filming Today, 2003.

_____. *Katharine Hepburn in the 30's.* Hollywood, Calif.: Filming Today, 2003.

_____. *On the Films Sets in the 30's.* Hollywood, Calif.: Filming Today, 2003.

_____. *Spencer Tracy in the 30's.* Hollywood, Calif.: Filming Today, 2003.

Harvey, Diana Karanikas, and Jackson Harvey. *Katharine Hepburn: A Life in Pictures.* New York: Metro, 1998.

Haver, Ronald. *David O. Selznick's Hollywood* (reprint ed.). New York: Bonanza, 1985.

Hayward, Brooke. *Haywire.* New York: Bantam, 1977.

Helburn, Theresa. *A Wayward Quest.* Boston: Little, Brown, 1960.

Hepburn, Katharine. *The Making of the African Queen or How I Went to Africa With Bogart, Bacall and Huston and Almost Lost My Mind.* New York: Alfred A. Knopf, 1987.

_____ . *Me: Stories of My Life.* New York: Alfred A. Knopf, 1991.

Higham, Charles. *Howard Hughes: The Secret Life.* New York: G.P. Putnam's, 1993.

_____. *Kate: The Life of Katharine Hepburn* (reprint ed.). New York: W.W. Norton, 2004.

_____. *Merchant of Dreams: Louis B. Mayer, M.G.M. and the Secret Hollywood.* New York: Laurel/Dell, 1993.

Higham, Charles, and Roy Moseley. *Cary Grant: The Lonely Heart.* New York: Harcourt Brace Jovanovich, 1989.

Hoare, Philip. *Noël Coward.* New York: Simon & Schuster, 1995.

Hodge, Jessica. *Katharine Hepburn.* Avenel, N.J.: Crescent/Outlet, 1992.

Hogan, Steve, and Lee Hudson. *Completely Queer: The Gay and Lesbian Encyclopedia.* New York: Owl Book/Henry Holt, 1998.

Holland, Barbara. *Katharine Hepburn.* New York: Park Lane, 1998.

Holley, Val. *Mike Connolly and the Manly Art of Hollywood Gossip.* Jefferson, N.C.: McFarland, 2003.

Horowitz, Helen Lefkowitz. *The Power and Passion of M. Carey Thomas.* New York: Alfred A. Knopf, 1994.

Huston, John. *An Open Book.* New York: Alfred A. Knopf, 1990.

Jablonski, Edward. *Alan Jay Lerner.* New York: Henry Holt, 1996.

Jewell, Richard. B., with Vernon Harbin. *The RKO Story.* New York: Arlington House/Crown, 1982.

Johns, Howard. *Palm Springs Confidential: Playground of the Stars.* Fort Lee, N.J.: Barricade, 2004.

Kalfatovic, Mary C. *Montgomery Clift: A Bio-Bibliography.* Westport, Conn.: Greenwood, 1994.

Kanfer, Stefan. *Ball of Fire: The Tumultuous Life and Comic Art of Lucille Ball.* New York: Alfred A. Knopf, 2003.

Kanin, Garson. *Hollywood.* New York: Viking, 1974.

_____. *Tracy and Hepburn: An Intimate Memoir.* New York: Bantam, 1972.

Kobler, John. *Damned in Paradise: The Life of John Barrymore.* New York: Atheneum, 1977.

Kramer, Stanley, with Thomas M. Coffey. *A Mad Mad Mad Mad World: A Life in Hollywood*. Orlando, Fla.: Harcourt Brace, 1997.

LaGuardia, Robert. *Monty: A Biography of Montgomery Clift*. New York: Avon, 1977.

Lambert, Gavin. *The Making of Gone With the Wind*. Boston: Atlantic Press/Little, Brown, 1973.

Lambert, Gavin, with Robert Trachtenberg (ed.). *On Cukor* (revised ed.). New York: Rizzoli, 2000.

Langner, Lawrence. *The Magic Curtain*. New York: E. P. Dutton, 1951.

Lardner, Ring, Jr. *I'd Hate Myself in the Morning*. New York: Thunder's Mouth/Nation, 2000.

Lasky, Betty. *RKO: The Biggest Little Major of Them All*. Santa Monica, Calif.: Roundtable, 1989.

Latham, Caroline. *Katharine Hepburn: Her Film & Stage Career*. New York: Proteus, 1982.

Laurents, Arthur. *Original Story By*. New York: Applause, 2000.

Leaming, Barbara. *Katharine Hepburn* (reprint ed.). New York: Limelight, 2000.

Lerner, Alan Jay. *The Street Where I Live* (reprint ed.). New York: Da Capo, 1994.

Levy, Bill. *John Ford: A Bio-Bibliography*. Westport, Conn.: Greenwood, 1998.

Levy, Emanuel. *George Cukor: Master of Elegance*. New York: William Morrow, 1994.

Long, Robert Emmet (ed.). *George Cukor Interviews*. Jackson, Miss.: University Press of Mississippi, 2001.

MacAdams, William. *Ben Hecht*. New York: Barricade, 1990.

Madsen, Axel. *The Sewing Circle: Sappho's Leading Ladies* (updated ed.). New York: Kensington, 2002.

Mangan, Richard. (ed.). *Sir John Gielgud: A Life in Letters*. New York: Arcade 2004.

Mann, William J. *Behind the Screen: How Gays and Lesbians Shaped Hollywood: 1910–1969*. New York: Viking, 2001.

_____. *Wisecracker: The Life and Times of William Haines, Hollywood's First Openly Gay Star*. New York: Penguin, 1999.

Martin, Mart. *Did She or Didn't She?* New York: Citadel/Carol, 1996.

Mayne, Judith. *Directed by Dorothy Arzner*. Bloomington, Ind.: Indiana University Press, 1994.

McBride, Joseph. *Frank Capra: The Catastrophe of Success* (updated ed.). New York: St. Martin's/Griffin, 2000.

McBride, Joseph. *Searching for John Ford: A Life.* New York: St. Martin's, 1999.

McCann, Graham. *Cary Grant: A Class Apart.* New York: Columbia University Press, 1996.

McCarthy, John. *The Complete Films of John Huston.* Secaucus, N.J.: Citadel, 1987.

McCarthy, Todd. *Howard Hawks: The Grey Fox of Hollywood.* New York: Grove, 1997.

McGilligan, Patrick. *Clint: The Life and Legend.* New York: St. Martin's, 1999.

_____. *George Cukor: A Double Life.* Boston: Faber and Faber, 1991.

McGilligan, Patrick (ed.). *Backstory 2: Interview with Screenwriters of the 1940s and 1950s.* Berkeley, Calif.: University of California Press, 1991.

McGilligan, Patrick, and Paul Buhle. *Tender Comrades.* New York: St. Martin's/Griffin, 1997.

McLellan, Diana. *The Girls: Sappho Goes to Hollywood.* New York: L.A. Weekly/St. Martin's, 2000.

Meyers, Jeffrey. *Bogart: A Life in Hollywood.* New York: Fromm International, 1999.

Morella, Joseph, and George Mazzei. *Genius & Lust: The Creative and Sexual Lives of Cole Porter and Noël Coward.* New York: Carroll & Graf, 1995.

Morley, Sheridan. *Katharine Hepburn.* Boston: Little, Brown, 1984.

Moss, Marilyn Ann. *Giant: George Stevens, A Life on Film.* Madison, Wis.: University of Wisconsin Press, 2004.

Nadel, Norman. *A Pictorial History of the Theatre Guild.* New York: Crown, 1969.

Nelson, Nancy (ed.). *Evenings With Cary Grant.* New York: William Morrow, 1991.

Nugent, Elliot. *Events Leading Up to the Comedy.* New York: Pocket, 1966.

O'Hara, Maureen, with John Nicholetti. *'Tis Herself.* New York: Simon & Schuster, 2004.

Olivier, Laurence. *Confessions of an Actor.* New York: Simon & Schuster, 1982.

Paris, Barry. *Garbo.* Minneapolis: University of Minnesota Press, 2002.

Parish, James Robert. *The Hollywood Bad Boys.* Chicago: Contemporary, 2002.

_____. *The Hollywood Book of Death.* Chicago: Contemporary, 2001.

_____. *The Hollywood Book of Scandals.* New York: McGraw-Hill, 2004.

_____. *The Hollywood Divas.* Chicago: Contemporary, 2002.

_____. *Hollywood's Great Love Teams.* New Rochelle, N.Y.: Arlington House, 1974.

_____. *The RKO Gals.* New Rochelle, N.Y.: Arlington House, 1974.

Parish, James Robert, and Allan Taylor (eds.). *The Encyclopedia of Ethnic Groups in Hollywood.* New York: Facts on File, 2003.

Parish, James Robert, with Gregory W. Mank. *The Hollywood Reliables.* Westport, Conn.: Arlington House, 1980.

Parish, James Robert, and Ronald L. Bowers. *The MGM Stock Company.* New Rochelle, N.Y.: Arlington House, 1973.

Payn, Graham, and Sheridan Morley (eds.). *The Noël Coward Diaries.* Boston: Little, Brown, 1982.

Peters, Margot. *Design for Living: Alfred Lunt and Lynn Fontanne.* New York: Alfred A. Knopf, 2003.

Phillips, Gene D. *George Cukor.* Boston: Twayne, 1982.

Porter, Darwin. *Katharine the Great.* New York: Blood Moon, 2004.

_____. *The Secret Life of Humphrey Bogart: The Early Years.* Staten Island, N.Y.: Georgia Literary Association, 2003.

Pratt, William. *Scarlett Fever.* New York: Collier, 1977.

Prideaux, James. *Knowing Hepburn and Other Curious Experiences.* Boston: Faber and Faber, 1996.

Quirk, Lawrence J. *Bob Hope: The Road Well-Traveled.* New York: Applause, 2000.

_____. *The Kennedys in Hollywood.* Dallas: Taylor, 1996.

_____. *Margaret Sullavan: Child of Fate.* New York: St. Martin's, 1986.

Reagan, Nancy, with William Novak. *My Turn: The Memoirs of Nancy Reagan.* New York: Random House, 1989.

Robbins, Phyllis. *Maude Adams: An Intimate Portrait.* New York: G. P. Putnam's, 1956.

Robinson, Jay, as told to Jim Hardiman. *The Comeback.* Lincoln, Va.: Chosen, 1979.

Rodriguez, Suzanne. *Wild Heart—A Life: Natalie Clifford Barney's Journey from Victorian America to the Literary Salons of Paris.* New York: CCC/HarperCollins, 2002.

Rogers, Ginger. *Ginger: My Story.* New York: HarperCollins, 1991.

Roppolo, Joseph Patrick. *Philip Barry.* New York: Twayne, 1965.

Russell, Rosalind, and Chris Chase. *Life Is a Banquet.* New York: Ace, 1979.

Russo, Vito. *The Celluloid Closet: Homosexuality in the Movies* (revised ed.). New York: Harper & Row, 1987.

Ryan, Joal. *Katharine Hepburn: A Stylish Life.* New York: St. Martin's, 1999.

Schanke, Robert A. *That Furious Lesbian: The Story of Mercedes de Acosta.* Carbondale, Ill.: Southern Illinois University Press, 2003.

Schickel, Richard. *D.W. Griffith: An American Life.* New York: Touchstone/Simon & Schuster, 1984.

_____. *The Men Who Made the Movies.* Chicago: Ivan R. Dee, 1975.

Selznick, Irene Mayer. *A Private View.* New York: Alfred A. Knopf, 1983.

Sheehy, Helen. *Eva Le Gallienne.* New York: Alfred A. Knopf, 1996.

Shipman, David. *The Great Movie Stars: The Golden Years* (revised ed.). New York: Hill and Wang, 1979.

Signoret, Simone. *Nostalgia Isn't What It Used to Be.* New York: Harper & Row, 1978.

Silverman, Stephen M. *David Lean.* New York: Harry N. Abrams, 1999.

Smith, Liz. *Natural Blonde.* New York: Hyperion, 2000.

Soares, André. *Beyond Paradise: The Life of Ramon Novarro.* New York: St. Martin's, 2002.

Spada, James. *Hepburn: Her Life in Pictures.* Garden City, N.Y.: Dolphin/Doubleday, 1984.

Sperber, A.M., and Eric Lax. *Bogart.* New York: William Morrow, 1997.

Spoto, Donald. *Laurence Olivier.* New York: HarperCollins, 1992.

_____. *Stanley Kramer Filmmaker* (reprint ed.). Hollywood, Calif.: Samuel French, 1990.

Stewart, Donald Ogden. *By a Stroke of Luck!* New York: Paddington, 1975

Swindell, Larry. *Spencer Tracy.* New York: Signet, 1971.

Tarshis, Lauren, *Kate: The Katharine Hepburn Album.* New York: Perigee, 1993.

Thomas, Bob. *Selznick.* Garden City, N.Y.: Doubleday, 1970.

Thomson, David. *Showman: The Life of David O. Selznick.* New York: Alfred A. Knopf, 1992.

Vickers, Hugo. *Vivien Leigh.* Boston: Little, Brown, 1988.

Vidal, Gore. *Palimpsest: A Memoir.* New York: Random House, 1995.

Waldau, Roy S. *Vintage Years of the Theatre Guild: 1928–1939.* Cleveland: The Press of Case Western Reserve University, 1972.

Walker, Alexander. *Vivien: The Life of Vivien Leigh.* New York: Weidenfeld & Nicolson, 1987.

Wallis, Hal, and Charles Higham. *Star Maker: The Autobiography of Hal Wallis.* New York: Berkley, 1981.

Wallis, Martha Hyer. *Finding My Way: A Hollywood Memoir.* San Francisco: HarperSanFrancisco, 1990.

Wansell, Geoffrey. *Cary Grant: Dark Angel.* New York: Arcade, 1996.

Wapshott, Nicholas. *Peter O'Toole.* London: New English Library, 1983.

Wayne, Jane Ellen. *The Golden Girls of MGM.* New York: Carroll & Graf, 2002.

_____. *The Golden Guys of MGM.* London: Robson, 2004.

White, Patricia. *Uninvited: Classical Hollywood Cinema and Lesbian Representability.* Bloomington, Ind.: Indiana University Press, 1999.

Wieder, Judy. *Celebrity: The Advocate Interviews.* Los Angeles: Advocate, 2001.

Young, Jeff. *Kazan: The Master Director Discusses His Films.* New York: Newmarket, 1999.

Publications

Among the publications utilized are:

Atlanta Journal, Biography, Chicago Sun-Times, Chicago Tribune, Classic Film Collector, Classic Image, Current Biography, Daily Variety, Empire, Entertainment Weekly, Family Circle, Film Threat, Films in Review, Films of the Golden Age, Gay & Lesbian Review, Globe, Hartford Courant, Hollywood Reporter, In Style, L.A. Weekly, Ladies' Home Journal, Life, Look, Los Angeles Daily News, Los Angeles Herald Examiner, Los Angeles Times, McCall's, Milwaukee Journal, Modern Screen, Motion Picture, Movie Collectors World, Movieline, National Enquirer, New Times–Los Angeles, New York Daily News, New York Herald Tribune, New York Observer, New York Post, New York Times, New York World-Telegram, Newsday, Newsweek, Parade, People, Photoplay, Playbill, Playboy, Premiere, St. Louis Post-Dispatch, San Diego Union, Saturday Evening Post, Scarlett Street, Screenland, Sight & Sound, Stage, Star, Time, Total Film, TV Guide, Us Weekly, USA Today, Vanity Fair, Washington Post, Woman's Home Companion, and *Women's Wear Daily.*

Web Sites

Among the Web sites used were:

All Movie Guide: www.allmovie.com; E! Entertainment TV Online: www.eonline.com; Internet Movie Database: www. pro.imdb.com; People Daily Online: www.people.aol.com/people/daily/edaily/index.html; The Smoking Gun: www.thesmokinggun.com

Television

Among the television biographies, documentaries, and news programs utilized were:

ABC: *Barbara Walters, Primetime;* A&E: *Biography;* CBS: *60 Minutes;* E! TV: *Mysteries & Scandals;* Lifetime: *Intimate Portrait;* NBC: Today; PBS, *The Dick Cavett Show, The Spencer Tracy Legacy: A Tribute by Katharine Hepburn;* Syndicated: *Access Hollywood, Entertainment Tonight, Extra: The Entertainment Magazine, Starring Katharine Hepburn, They Call Me Kathy;* TCM: *Katharine Hepburn: All About Me.*

About the Author

JAMES ROBERT PARISH, a former entertainment reporter, publicist, and book series editor, is the author of many published major biographies and reference books on the entertainment industry, including *The Hollywood Book of Scandals, Whitney Houston, The Hollywood Book of Love, Hollywood Divas, Hollywood Bad Boys, The Encyclopedia of Ethnic Groups in Hollywood, Jet Li, The Hollywood Book of Death, Gus Van Sant, Jason Biggs, Whoopi Goldberg, Rosie, The Unofficial "Murder, She Wrote" Casebook, Let's Talk! America's Favorite TV Talk Show Hosts, Gays and Lesbians in Mainstream Cinema, The Great Cop Pictures, Ghosts and Angels in Hollywood Films, Prison Pictures from Hollywood, The Hollywood Reliables, The RKO Gals,* and *Hollywood's Great Love Teams.*

Mr. Parish is a frequent oncamera interviewee on cable and network TV for documentaries on the performing arts both in the United States and in the United Kingdom. He resides in Los Angeles.

INDEX